NATIVE BIAS

PRINCETON STUDIES IN
Political Behavior

Tali Mendelberg, Series Editor

Native Bias: Overcoming Discrimination against Immigrants, Donghyun Danny Choi, Mathias Poertner, and Nicholas Sambanis

Nationalisms in International Politics, Kathleen Powers

Winners and Losers: The Psychology of Foreign Trade, Diana C. Mutz

The Autocratic Middle Class: How State Dependency Reduces the Demand for Democracy, Bryn Rosenfeld

The Loud Minority: Why Protests Matter in American Democracy, Daniel Q. Gillion

Steadfast Democrats: How Social Forces Shape Black Political Behavior, Ismail K. White and Chryl N. Laird

The Cash Ceiling: Why Only the Rich Run for Office-And What We Can Do about It, Nicholas Carnes

Deep Roots: How Slavery Still Shapes Southern Politics, Avidit Acharya, Matthew Blackwell & Maya Sen

Envy in Politics, Gwyneth H. McClendon

Communism's Shadow: Historical Legacies and Contemporary Political Attitudes, Grigore Pop-Eleches & Joshua A. Tucker

Democracy for Realists: Why Elections Do Not Produce Responsive Government, Christopher H. Achen and Larry M. Bartels

Resolve in International Politics, Joshua D. Kertzer

Native Bias

OVERCOMING DISCRIMINATION
AGAINST IMMIGRANTS

DONGHYUN DANNY CHOI

MATHIAS POERTNER

NICHOLAS SAMBANIS

PRINCETON UNIVERSITY PRESS
PRINCETON & OXFORD

Published by Princeton University Press
41 William Street, Princeton, New Jersey 08540
99 Banbury Road, Oxford OX2 6JX

press.princeton.edu

All Rights Reserved

Library of Congress Cataloging-in-Publication Data

Names: Choi, Donghyun Danny, 1983– author. | Poertner, Mathias, 1986– author. | Sambanis, Nicholas, 1967– author.
Title: Native bias : overcoming discrimination against immigrants / Donghyun Danny Choi, Mathias Poertner, and Nicholas Sambanis.
Description: Princeton : Princeton University Press, [2022] | Series: Princeton studies in political behavior | Includes bibliographical references.
Identifiers: LCCN 2022006682 (print) | LCCN 2022006683 (ebook) | ISBN 9780691222301 (paperback ; alk. paper) | ISBN 9780691222318 (hardback ; alk. paper) | ISBN 9780691222325 (ebook)
Subjects: LCSH: Immigrants—Germany—Public opinion. | Discrimination—Germany. | Xenophobia—Germany. | Group identity—Germany. | Multiculturalism—Germany. | Germany—Emigration and immigration—Social aspects. | BISAC: POLITICAL SCIENCE / Public Policy / Immigration | HISTORY / Europe / Germany
Classification: LCC JV8025 .C49 2022 (print) | LCC JV8025 (ebook) | DDC 325.43–dc23/eng/20220427
LC record available at https://lccn.loc.gov/2022006682
LC ebook record available at https://lccn.loc.gov/2022006683

British Library Cataloging-in-Publication Data is available

Editorial: Bridget Flannery-McCoy and Alena Chekanov
Production Editorial: Mark Bellis
Cover Design: Karl Spurzem
Production: Lauren Reese
Publicity: Kate Hensley and Charlotte Coyne

Cover Credit: © Irisland / Shutterstock

This book has been composed in Arno

10 9 8 7 6 5 4 3 2 1

CONTENTS

List of Figures   vii

List of Tables   xi

Preface   xv

1	Introduction	1
	The Argument in a Nutshell	8
	The Evidence	15
	Why Study Germany?	19
	Broader Impacts	25
	Plan of the Book	28
2	Reducing Social Distance, Reducing Bias	31
	Confronting Parochialism	31
	Dilemmas of Inclusion	36
	Concepts	39
	Overcoming the Native-Immigrant Divide	42
	Norms and Intergroup Conflict	47
	Hypotheses & Mechanisms	51
3	Measuring Bias and Discrimination	56
	Attitudes	58
	Measuring Anti-immigrant Attitudes in Germany	61
	Capturing Anti-immigrant Behavior in the Field	73
	Discussion	88
4	Linguistic Assimilation	91
	Native Preference for Linguistic Assimilation	91
	The Importance of Language in German Identity	95
	Experimental Intervention	102

	Main Findings	105
	Discussion	109
5	Shared Civic Norms	112
	Cleanliness	115
	Experimental Design	122
	Results	126
	Discussion	129
6	Gender Equality	133
	Women at the Core of Value Conflict with Islam	135
	Group-derived Norms	142
	Experimental Evidence from the Field	146
	Results	154
	Attitudinal Differences between Men and Women	160
	What Does the Hijab Signify?	162
	Discussion	165
7	Viewing "Them" as One of "Us"	170
	Research Design	172
	Main Findings	179
	Discussion	194
8	Overcoming Discrimination	196
	Contributions to the Literature	197
	Contributions to Methods	198
	Contributions to Theory	199
	Contributions to Policy Design	202
	Next Steps	206

Appendix 211

Bibliography 253

Index 275

FIGURES

1.1 Trends in attitudes toward immigration in Germany   22

1.2 Trends in attitudes toward immigration in Germany   23

3.1 Respondents claiming their country doesn't feel like home   59

3.2 Perception of immigrants among German natives   60

3.3 Probability that German natives prefer a person as a neighbor   65

3.4 Probability that German natives prefer a person as a friend   67

3.5 Probability that German natives prefer a person as a
son/daughter-in-law   68

3.6 Example IAT screen   72

3.7 Experiment in action   79

3.8 Varying religiosity and ethnicity of confederate   80

3.9 Experimental sites—Thirty cities in North Rhine-Westphalia,
Brandenburg, Saxony, and Lower Saxony   81

3.10 Discrimination against immigrants   84

3.11 Discrimination against immigrants by East vs. West Germany   86

4.1 Language effects: Merged (Experiment 1 & 2)   107

5.1 Screen capture of survey item on attitudes toward littering   117

5.2 Actions respondents would take when they see someone who
litters   118

5.3 Word cloud of open-ended justifications for why respondents
believe immigrants litter more than Germans   121

5.4 Experiment in progress   123

5.5 Parochialism in the level of assistance offered to strangers   127

5.6 Offsetting effects of norm enforcement on bias   129

6.1   Trends in gender attitudes in Germany   139

6.2   Perceptions of the hijab among native Germans   141

6.3   Experimental intervention in action   148

6.4   Native German women with regressive attitudes about career
      gender equality   151

6.5   Study sites—Twenty-six train stations in three German states   153

6.6   Parochialism in the level of assistance offered to strangers   154

6.7   Offsetting effects of progressive gender attitudes on
      discrimination   155

6.8   Trends in attitudes toward women's role in society   161

6.9   Evaluations of video of experiment: "Why do native women not
      help hijab-wearing women?"   164

6.10 Word cloud of open-ended responses on the meaning of
      the hijab   165

7.1   Screen capture of treatment video   173

7.2   Outcome measurement: Generalized affect   176

7.3   Outcome measurement: Decategorization and recategorization   177

7.4   Norm enforcement effects on generalized affect   180

7.5   Categorization effects   181

7.6   Heterogeneous effects: Norm importance 1   187

7.7   Heterogeneous effects: Norm importance 2   188

7.8   Text analysis: Positive/negative adjectives   192

7.9   Text analysis: Adjective topics   193

A.1   Screen captures of "manipulation check" task   214

A.2   Discrimination against immigrants by experiment   216

A.3   Discrimination against immigrants by state   217

A.4   Discrimination against immigrants: Merged (Experiment 1 & 2)   219

A.5   Language effects: Former West Germany   220

A.6   Language effects: Former East Germany   221

A.7   Equivalence testing: Two one-sided test of proportions   225

A.8   Experimental setup   227

A.9 Norm treatment dimensions 228

A.10 Heterogeneous effects: Norm enforcement effects on
generalized affect 250

A.11 Heterogeneous effects: Norm importance 3 251

A.12 Perceptions on the likelihood that Muslim will intervence
to stop norm violation 252

TABLES

3.1   Conjoint Attribute–Attribute Level List   63

3.2   Example of Profile Pairs   64

4.1   Treatment Matrix for Language Experiment   104

4.2   Treatment Effects for Linguistic Differences (Pooled Experiments 1 & 2)   108

5.1   Germans versus Immigrants/Refugees Litter More   119

5.2   Treatment Assignment Matrix   124

6.1   Treatment Conditions for Phone Call Experiment   149

6.2   Effects of Ideas on Bias by Gender   158

6.3   Effect of the Progressive Gender Attitudes, Disaggregated by Bystander Religion: Post-intervention Survey Sample   159

7.1   Treatment Matrix   174

7.2   Descriptive Statistics   178

7.3   Descriptive Statistics on Text Outcomes   191

A1   Proportion of Respondents Identifying Confederate as a German Native   215

A2   Balance Across Experimental Conditions   216

A3   Analysis with Team Fixed Effects   218

A4   Descriptive Statistics on Scene Characteristics   219

A5   Effects by Foreign Language Used   222

A6   Equivalence Tests for Linguistic Assimilation Effects   224

A7   Bystander Composition and Scene Characteristics   227

A8   Covariate Balance for Comparisons in Figure 3   229

A9   Covariate Balance for Comparisons in Figure 4   230

A10 Immigrant (Hijab + Control) versus Native Comparisons   231

A11 Hijab versus Native Comparisons   232

A12 Hijab versus Native Comparison, by Region, Clustered
     Standard Errors   233

A13 Hijab versus Native Comparison, by State   234

A14 Norm Enforcement Effects by Region   235

A15 Partial Replications with Manipulation Checks   236

A16 Effects of Ideas on Bias by Gender, Perceived Native German
     Bystanders   237

A17 Progressive versus Regressive Attitude Comparison by
     Confederate Type, Disaggregated by Gender: Individual-Level
     Analysis   238

A18 Effect of the Progressive Gender Attitudes, Disaggregated by
     Bystander Religion: Post-intervention Survey Sample   239

A19 Effect of the Progressive Gender Attitudes, Disaggregated by
     Bystander Religion: Post-intervention Survey Sample,
     Weighted by Proportion of Helpers and Non-helpers in the
     Experimental Sample   239

A20 Effect of the Progressive Gender Attitudes, Disaggregated by
     Bystander Religion: Post-intervention Survey Sample   240

A21 Effect of the Progressive Gender Attitudes, Disaggregated by
     Bystander Religion: Post-intervention Survey Sample,
     Weighted by Proportion of Helpers and Non-helpers in the
     Experimental Sample   241

A22 Effect of the Progressive Gender Attitudes, Disaggregated by
     Bystander Education: Post-intervention Survey Sample   242

A23 Effect of the Progressive Gender Attitudes, Disaggregated by
     Bystander Education: Post-intervention Survey Sample,
     Weighted by Proportion of Helpers and Non-helpers in the
     Experimental Sample   243

A24 Lack of Evidence on Differential Response/Attrition in the
     Post-treatment Survey   244

A25 Discrimination Against Hijab Immigrants, Former West/East
Germany 245

A26 Progressive vs. Regressive Message Effects, Former West/East
Germany 246

A27 Help Rates by Bystander Gender Composition 248

A28 Gender Spillovers (Iteration Level) 249

ON THE OLIVE groves of the Peloponnese, harvest season always brought migrant workers. They usually came from other parts of Greece, from poor areas of Thessaly or Epirus, entire families transplanted for a few weeks or months of hard work, living in squalor to offer the labor that native communities could not provide. After the fall of the Berlin Wall, the native Greek migrant laborers were replaced with cheaper labor from Poland, Bulgaria, and Albania, and as this first wave of immigrants either left Greece or became more economically integrated, the hills of the Peloponnese became host to Afghans, Indians, and Pakistanis in search of new opportunities. These waves of immigration changed local societies by infusing them with cultural difference. As ethnic, religious, or racial differences between native and immigrant populations grew, it was easy to notice social tensions and anxieties emerging. In everyday settings, at the coffee shop or the market, discussions of crime and break-ins became commonplace as was the recounting of news stories about muggings and gang violence in Athens. Such evidence of worsening living conditions was frequently attributed to immigrants, whose values, norms, and ideas the native population assumed were different from their own. The threat to the national identity was symbolized not only by darker-skinned laborers toiling in the fields or in construction sites, but also by immigrant children attending Greek schools, and by their customs, which threatened to change the way things were.

This book is motivated by these observations of social change that we have witnessed in our countries of origin and which have made it clear to us that a conflict over norms and values is what underlies anti-immigrant attitudes. This is apparent not only in Greece, but also in other immigrant-receiving countries. Thousands of miles away on the busy streets of Korea's megacity Seoul, encountering people of diverse ethnic and national origin has become a part of everyday life. Once considered a society hostile to foreigners, Korea's rising economic prosperity and growth has attracted an increasing inflow of migrants from China, South East Asia, and the Middle East, who seek out a place in the workforce of industries no longer favored by locals. Yet even as they fill this critical void in the economy, Koreans increasingly view immigrant presence with suspicion—weary that cultural differences between native and immigrant society are too stark, and skeptical of the willingness of immigrants to accept and integrate into what they see as the "Korean way-of-life." Indeed, Korean social media is inundated with posts criticizing the use of Chinese-language street signs in Chinese enclaves, and protests abound in opposition to the construction of mosques and halal-friendly stores in areas with a concentration of Muslim immigrants.

These reactions to immigration in Greece, Korea, and—as the book shows in detail—also in Germany, do not constitute an exception. In virtually every immigrant-receiving country where public opinion polls have measured native attitudes we have seen opposition arising from the realization that natives are forced to come to terms with the inter-connected nature of the global economy, which requires them to face different cultural practices in their daily lives. Such intergroup contact among culturally distant groups can cause conflict if contact takes place in competitive settings shaped by political messages that emphasize the threat posed by immigrants to natives' identities. Natives' fears are captured by the most visible differences—differences in skin color, language, or religion, that distinguish the majority native from the minority immigrant community. But such ascriptive differences often symbolize a deeper threat, created by the perception of a conflict between norms and values. The perception of identity threat posed by immigration will lead to bias and discrimination, which is what this book aims to understand and address.

We view native-immigrant conflict as an example of intergroup conflict that likely shares a common set of mechanisms with other forms of identity conflict, both violent and non-violent. These mechanisms can be affective/psychological or materialistic, driven by resource competition. We focus in particular on psychological mechanisms that shape individual conflict behavior and we explore the power of norms and ideas to shape that behavior. Although our analysis is necessarily limited to one type of conflict (discrimination) in one specific context (everyday life in Germany), we view our study as part of a broader research agenda designed to understand how identities shape conflict and, in turn, how conflict shapes identities.

This book began with observations of social change in our countries of origin—Greece, Korea, Germany—many years ago, but it started taking specific form during a long conversation between Nicholas and Danny on Locust Walk at the University of Pennsylvania. An experimental design originally conceived for application to the Greek context was radically adapted to explore native-immigrant relations in Germany when Danny shared with Nicholas an innovative article by Loukas Balafoutas, Nikos Nikiforakis, and Bettina Rockenbach observing reactions to norms violations in the field. That paper sparked conversations and new ideas on how to study normative conflict between natives and immigrants and formed the basis of our first experiment, which is included in chapter 5 of this book. Mathias joined the team to share his expertise with the country context and the project unfolded in steps as we grappled with the results of each successive study and designed new experiments and new surveys to understand the mechanisms underlying the behavior that we observed in our first experiment in the summer of 2018. During dinner at a Portuguese restaurant in Berlin, we reflected on why European women discriminate against veiled Muslim women. From the perspective of social identity theory, which formed the theoretical backbone of our study, this pattern was not intuitive, as one might expect less discrimination among women due to their shared gender attributes. LaShawn Jefferson gave us the idea for the follow-up experiment by suggesting that this pattern of discrimination was probably driven by fears that the hijab signified regressive attitudes toward women's rights. The experimental design was developed at yet another restaurant when the team met in Philly (a tapas bar—why was food always involved?) and LaShawn and Vivian (Mathias's better half) vetted our ideas about different experimental treatments. At a subsequent trip to Berlin (eating Middle Eastern food this time), Nicholas and Mathias piloted the design of the new experiment and finalized the theoretical framework of the book which includes an extension and elaboration of the very influential Common Ingroup Identity Model from social psychology.

The Penn Identity & Conflict (PIC) Lab provided a crucial intellectual home for the project. The School of Arts and Sciences of the University of Pennsylvania helped materialize our ideas by providing funding for the Lab, which Nicholas founded in 2016. The PIC Lab provided resources to make these experiments possible, offering a two-year postdoctoral fellowship to Danny and covering the costs of our fieldwork and surveys since the project's inception. The PIC Lab also provided a home where we could discuss and test our ideas with colleagues. Nicholas is grateful to Dean Fluharty, Provost Pritchett, and President Gutmann of the University of Pennsylvania for making the PIC Lab possible, and to colleagues at the department of

Political Science for sharing their substantive and methodological expertise, which helped make this book better. Mathias also thanks the Scowcroft Institute at Texas A&M University for providing financial support for this project through a Dean's Excellence Faculty Research Grant. The three of us have worked closely as a team and have learned a lot from each other.

In writing this book, we have benefited from the advice and support of many individuals. In particular, we would like to thank Loukas Balafoutas, Jasper Bauer, Vivian Bronsoler Nurko, William Callison, Jonathan Chu, Rafaela Dancygier, Carsten De Dreu, Eugen Dimant, Peter Dinesen, Iza Ding, Thad Dunning, Matthias Ecker-Ehrhardt, Florian Foos, Max Goplerud, Jessica Gottlieb, Don Green, Guy Grossman, Dan Hopkins, Yue Hou, Macartan Humphreys, Amaney Jamal, LaShawn Jefferson, Eunji Kim, Dorothy Kronick, Marika Landau-Wells, Benjamin Laughlin, Sunkee Lee, Taeku Lee, Matt Levendusky, Ron Linden, Michele Margolis, Georgia Mavrodi, Marc Meredith, Cecilia Mo, Scott Morgenstern, Becky Morton, Diana Mutz, Nikos Nikiforakis, Anne Norton, Brendan O'Leary, Melissa Sands, Shanker Satyanath, Anna Schultz, Stephanie Schwartz, Paul Sniderman, Jae-Jae Spoon, Libby Wood, and Nan Zhang. We thank them all for their constructive engagement with our manuscript.

Seminar participants at the Penn Identity and Conflict Lab Working Group, Workshop for Norms and Behavioral Change (NoBec) 2018, and the Cultural Transmission and Social Norms (CTSN 3) workshop, University of Pittsburgh, Texas A&M University, Carnegie Mellon University, Korea University, King's College London, NYU Abu Dhabi, Seoul National University, Ohio State University, George Washington University, London School of Economics and Political Science, University of California, Berkeley, University of Essex, Bogazici University, the Immigration Policy Lab (Zurich), Princeton University Hellenic Studies Program, Yale University, and the annual meetings of the American Political Science Association and European Political Science Association gave important feedback as well. Perry World House at the University of Pennsylvania provided resources for a Conference on Immigration in October 2019 where some of the ideas and results from this book were presented.

This project would not have been possible without the dedicated work of our enumerators and research assistants who were involved in the fieldwork for our experiments in 2018, 2019, and 2020. They endured record high temperatures, navigated frequent train delays, and picked up an extraordinary number of haphazardly rolling oranges and lemons to see our project through.

Although we cannot thank them enough, we acknowledge their names here as a sign of our immense gratitude: Sham Alkanj Abseh, Vatan Akyüz, Raneem Alasass, Nicole Aretz, Rabia Bacaksiz, Franz Beensen, Louise Brenner, Carla Cingil, Mirko Dallendörfer, Hêlîn Demirkol, Zeynep Dişbudak, Christina Dobbehaus, Bahar Dosky, Fulden Eskidelvan, Mirna Gomaa, Hamsa Abo Hassoun, Nilay Hayirli, Judith Huber, Emel Inal, Astrid Daiana Jessen, Rebecca Joest, Koray Karaoglan, Damla Keşkekci, Emine Kir, Juliane Klöden, Stefanie Knapp, Jamie Köstner, Molka Ksouri, Yasmin Künze, Charlotte Leidiger, Paula Lochau, Tassilo Malinowsky, Gesika Malko, Rudolph Matete, Martina Meier, Lilli Meissner, Clara Meiswinkel, Sascha Müller, Eric Nissen, Timon Ostermeier, Elise Okon, Florence Peschke, Dario Pösse, Regina Prade, Moritz Roemer, Merlyn Schapka, Tobias Schmitt, Sarah Schüürmann, Mariia Semushkina, Katrin Sonay, Helena Steinkamp, Luzie Sturhahn, Esma Wieacker, and David Witkowski.

We are also very thankful to Maurice Schumann for his assistance in compiling the data from the numerous existing surveys. In this context, we also thank the GESIS Data Archive for providing us access to countless datasets and the Bertelsmann Stiftung for sharing with us their data from their study *Willkommenskultur zwischen Skepsis und Pragmatik: Deutschland nach der "Fluchtkrise"* (*Welcome Culture between Skepticism and Pragmatism: Germany after the "Refugee Crisis"*). We also thank Max Spohn for his help collecting historical information for the role of language in German nationalism.

At Princeton University Press, we are indebted to four anonymous reviewers, who read the full draft of the book and provided incisive feedback that improved the quality of our manuscript. It was a pleasure to work with editors Bridget Flannery-McCoy and Alena Chekanov who were enthusiastic and supportive of the promise in our project, and shepherded this book through the publication process. We also thank Tali Mendelberg, the editor of the Princeton Studies in Political Behavior, for engaging with our work during our initial submission and accepting our book in the series.

Portions of the book draw on materials previously published or forthcoming as "Parochialism, Social Norms, and Discrimination Against Immigrants," *Proceedings of the National Academy of Sciences* 116 (33): 16274–16279 (2019); "Linguistic Assimilation Does Not Reduce Discrimination Against Immigrants: Evidence from Germany," *Journal of Experimental Political Science* 8(3): 235–246 (2021); and "The *Hijab* Penalty: Feminist Backlash to Muslim Immigrants," *American Journal of Political Science* (forthcoming). We thank the peer reviewers for these pieces for helping us refine our ideas and empirical analyses, and the journal editors for providing an engaging forum to showcase our work.

Finally we would like to thank our partners and family for their steadfast support. Danny thanks Charan Min and Yangsik Choi for being amazing parents but also letting him talk their ears off about why this project was so cool (they agreed), and Suhyeon Kim for patiently enduring his 45-minute schematic overview of the field experiments during their first date and sticking with him in spite of it. Mathias thanks his parents, Elisabeth and Helmut Pörtner, for their encouragement and for their inspiring work with refugees in their hometown, and Vivan Bronsoler Nurko for her loving support and help throughout the whole project (at countless train stations and beyond). Nicholas dedicates this book to LaShawn with all his love. Και στο Ναομάκι!

NATIVE BIAS

1

Introduction

ON JULY 3, 2018, the *New York Times* reported that in Denmark, "starting at the age of 1, 'ghetto children' [children of immigrant parents who live in neighborhoods with high concentrations of immigrant populations] must be separated from their families for at least 25 hours a week, not including nap time, for mandatory instruction in 'Danish values,' including the traditions of Christmas and Easter, and Danish language." While this public policy might have been motivated by a commitment to providing access to publicly funded education in Denmark, the undertone of the reportage suggests that any such initiative could also be perceived as a strategy of forced assimilation of immigrant populations. Indeed, policies of coercive assimilation are becoming increasingly common in Europe. In France, wearing a face covering (which is common among some Muslim women) is now illegal in public spaces; and in England, David Cameron's first speech as prime minister in 2011 declared "state multiculturalism" as having failed, calling instead for "muscular liberalism",[1] which promotes national unity by providing a "shared vision of the society to which [immigrants] feel they want to belong."[2] This viewpoint, which was endorsed by French president Nicolas Sarcozy, was also reflected in later statements by London mayor Boris Johnson in the run-up to the elections from which he emerged as the country's new prime minister.

Integration policies that amount to forced assimilation are increasingly seen as a tool in the state's arsenal of strategies to "de-radicalize" Muslim minorities in Europe. Even though available evidence suggests that these communities are actually not radicalized, fears that a "Muslim invasion" will

---

1. https://www.bbc.com/news/uk-politics-12371994 (accessed April 18, 2020).

2. "Muslims must embrace our British values, David Cameron says," *Daily Telegraph*, February 5, 2011.

threaten Europeans' national identities are prevalent and multiculturalism is perceived as a threat to liberalism. Many perceive assimilationist policies as the only way to reduce intergroup conflict between natives and immigrants by minimizing the social and cultural distance that divides them.

Underlying the growing backlash against immigration from predominantly Muslim countries is a perception that deep ideological and normative differences divide Christians and Muslims—that there is a clash of civilizations (Huntington, 1996). At the same time, in the context of Europe's liberal democratic regimes, cultural differences must be respected and accommodated as immigrant populations have the same freedoms as others to retain their group values and cultural norms. Yet, this accommodation of difference can generate anxiety among the native population, which fears that immigration from Muslim majority cultures will slowly change European culture (Caldwell, 2009). Large segments of European societies feel aggrieved; they believe that immigrants resist assimilation and establish a "parallel society" (Caldwell, 2009) that threatens to change European identity. This *identity threat* is fueled by liberal policies of accommodating cultural differences among migrant communities whose norms and ideas are perceived to clash with those of the native population. The challenge seems greater in countries where citizenship is imbued with the ideology of ethnic nationalism, where the population has been taught that there is continuity between its present makeup and an ethnic past that excluded the groups that are now trying to move in. Negative stereotypes and antipathy toward immigrants derive partly from "tribal impulses" and have perpetuated primordial identities that are challenged by the processes of globalization (Ahmed, 2018). These challenges create anxiety, further fueled by far-right voices, which result in many Europeans viewing the scale of Muslim immigration as a real threat to the very survival of "European" identity. Some go as far as to fear that Europe will soon become "part of the Arabic west, of the Maghreb."[3]

This sentiment takes various guises and is broadly shared in European countries, leading to antipathy and discrimination toward immigrants from any country that is perceived to be culturally "distant" (Hagendoorn and Sniderman, 2001). The result is growing opposition to multiculturalist policies and support for assimilationist policies designed to erase cultural differences

---

3. Interview with Princeton Islamic religion scholar Bernard Lewis in *Die Welt*, 28 July 2004; https://www.welt.de/print-welt/article211310/Europa-wird-islamisch.html (accessed 4/16/2020).

between immigrants and natives. Paradoxically, multiculturalist policies that are now seen as evidence of yielding to and accepting of cultural difference, were initially conceived as a way to ensure that migrant workers would not integrate and would eventually have to return to their countries of origin. "Guest" workers were considered as a temporary solution to support economic growth in postwar Europe, and it was assumed that cultural differences dividing them from natives could not be overcome; allowing migrants to retain their norms and practices meant that their connections to their homelands would be kept alive, making it more likely that they would go back (Vollebergh, Veenman, and Hagendoorn, 2017; Triadafilopoulos and Schönwälder, 2006). However, attitudes toward multiculturalism have changed along with the realization that migrants are here to stay and there is now a backlash against policies that encourage cultural pluralism, which is seen as a threat to European countries' national identities. Whereas multiculturalist policies were expected to build consensus, they may have inadvertently sown divisions (Sniderman and Hagendoorn, 2007, p. 5).

The term multiculturalism often has different meanings in public debates in different countries and in the scholarly literature on immigration. In this book, we do not use the term to refer to support for specific policies of immigrant integration such as affirmative action for immigrants, constitutional affirmations of respect of cultural diversity, accommodation of foreign religious practices, and so on. Rather, we use the term multiculturalism to refer to coexistence between native and immigrant populations and we study attitudinal and behavioral effects of exposure to cultural diversity in everyday settings. Specifically, we share normative theorists' orientation toward the term multiculturalism as suggesting respect for diversity; such respect should translate to recognition of the rights of immigrants to retain their culture (Kymlicka, 1995; Taylor, 1994; Miller, 2006) and it should manifest as equal treatment of immigrants in the public sphere. As such, our analysis is consistent with the colloquial use of the term multiculturalism as expressed in a well-known speech by German chancellor Angela Merkel who once described "Multikulti" as an effort "to live happily side by side" with immigrants—an effort which she claimed has "failed utterly" in Europe (cited in Koopmans (2013, p. 148)).

This negative sentiment toward immigration is reflected in cross-country research which shows that the adoption of state policies that are supportive of multiculturalism has stalled in the past two decades (Koopmans, 2013). The primary reason for this reversal of state support for multiculturalism is likely the fact that religious claims—and claims from Muslim groups in particular—now constitute the lion's share of all immigrant groups' claims for cultural accommodation in Europe (Koopmans et al., 2005). According to Koopmans (2013, pp. 150–151), religious claims are harder to accommodate than cultural claims by ethno-linguistic groups because religious claims often challenge core values of the host society. Others have explored the correlates of countries' immigration and integration policies, and such analysis is beyond the scope of this book. Yet public support for individual or group rights for immigrants, as reflected in cross-country indices of multiculturalism, should correlate with underlying public attitudes toward immigrants, albeit imperfectly. Our book is concerned with exploring such attitudes rather than citizens' support for the extension of specific rights or privileges to immigrant groups. Our empirical measures of individual-level dispositions and behavior toward Muslim immigrants are reflective of a "common sense" understanding of the term "multiculturalism," which essentially captures how one feels about "living side by side" with immigrants.

This book explores the limits of multiculturalism by considering whether conflict over ideas, norms, and values underlies discrimination against immigrants, and by analyzing whether native bias against immigrants can be overcome when natives come to believe that immigrants share valued norms that define the idea of good citizenship in native society. While most integration policies—especially increasingly common assimilationist policies—focus exclusively on immigrants and their behavior, this book focuses on natives' beliefs and stereotypes. If perceived ideational differences are what shapes bias and discrimination against immigrants, then that behavior should change when the perceived cultural threat is removed by establishing that natives and immigrants adhere to shared civic norms. The book explores this idea by focusing on recent immigration to Europe from predominantly Muslim countries and asks whether anti-immigrant attitudes and behavior are motivated by ethnic, racial, linguistic, or religious differences between natives and immigrants; and whether the social distance that is created by such differences in ascriptive traits can be overcome by forging a shared *civic identity*.

If multiculturalism creates divisions by encouraging immigrant and native communities to maintain different norms and potentially conflicting identities, how can intergroup conflict be mitigated? Complying with a society's laws is not enough to reduce conflict if bias is fueled by perceived cultural and ideological differences. Could natives and immigrants identify a set of fundamental social norms regarding civic life that they share as the foundation to overcome the perception of social distance that divides them? Could immigrants retain key markers of their distinct cultural identity and still be accepted as equal members of their adopted European societies by demonstrating their respect for the host country? How do you demonstrate such respect? Despite a surge of research on immigration and ethnic politics, these questions remain largely unaddressed.

The idea that negative attitudes and biased behavior toward immigrants are grounded in perceptions of intergroup differences has gained support in empirical investigations across disciplinary boundaries, from social psychology (Stephan, Ybarra, and Bachman, 1999) to sociology (Schneider, 2008) and political science (Brader, Valentino, and Suhay, 2008). Often grounded in seminal theories of social identity and categorization (Tajfel, 1981; Turner et al., 1987), prejudice (Allport, 1979; Paluck and Green, 2009), and ethnocentrism (LeVine and Campbell, 1972; Kinder and Kam, 2010), many of these studies trace the sources of anti-immigrant sentiment to the perceptions of threat experienced by host populations, as they come into contact with immigrants who deviate from prototypical conceptions of what members of their ingroup should be (Mummendey and Wenzel, 1999; Kauff et al., 2015).

Ethnicity and religion are at the core of what defines perceptions of the national ingroup identity in most countries. Ethnic and religious differences between native and immigrant populations can generate both "realistic" and "symbolic" identity threats (Stephan and Stephan, 2000) that cause anxiety among natives, encouraging the formation of negative stereotypes that lead to a backlash against immigration.[4] This book uses an experimental approach to identify which *types* of cultural differences between immigrants and natives generate perceptions of threat and anti-immigrant bias. Based on the analysis of the causes of bias, the book then considers possible solutions to mitigate native-immigrant conflict, focusing on whether shared social norms can be effective in reducing the perception of social distance that explains the feeling of identity threat by native populations.

Prior literature has already established that stereotypes and prejudice driven by differences in ascriptive characteristics that define race, ethnicity, and religion can cause discrimination (Adida, Laitin, and Valfort, 2010;

---

4. See Sniderman, Hagendoorn, and Prior (2004) for one of the first analyses that distinguishes between "realistic" fears (e.g., crime and unemployment associated with large waves of immigration from poorer countries) and fears generated by an abstract sense that immigration threatens the national identity.

Hainmueller and Hangartner, 2013). It is a short step from identifying such differences as the cause of discrimination to proposing strategies of bias-reduction that are premised on eliminating intergroup differences via assimilation (Adida, Laitin, and Valfort, 2010). It might be true that if immigrants change their names and their religion, this will eliminate sources of friction with the native population. That might be a step too far, however. Furthermore, many strategies of assimilation are likely to be perceived as coercive by immigrants and they might backfire. Coercive assimilation policies can take many forms: requiring cultural assimilation as a precondition for access to rights; refusing to accommodate foreign religious practices and organizations; enforcing native tongue–only rules in schools and other public institutions; or making classes on national culture and history and loyalty oaths a precondition for citizenship. While in theory coercive assimilation could work by eliminating cultural differences, in practice it could make these differences seem bigger and more important than they really are.[5] While coercive assimilation policies do not constitute the standard approach to integration across European countries, they are widely used and they have become more prevalent as support for state multiculturalism has weakened in the past two decades (Koopmans, 2013).

We do not yet know the extent to which assimilation is really necessary to reduce native-immigrant conflict. Is it really necessary to ban the use of the veil in public? Do African or Muslim immigrants really need to adopt European/Christian-sounding names so as to avoid job-market discrimination? Should it be mandatory to use the host country's language in public spaces to induce immigrants to learn it? Do Muslim immigrants have to take classes that teach them about Christmas or about the value of a firm handshake in business dealings? Or is it possible to achieve ideational convergence that reduces native hostility in other ways which immigrants might perceive as less repressive? What if immigrants signaled that they share the respect of norms that are deeply valued in the host society, while retaining their own distinctive cultural markers? Could this help reduce discrimination against them by natives? We posit this hypothesis in this book, and suggest a way to test it empirically. The key implication to be tested is that assimilation does not need to take the form of shedding the veil or hiding one's ethnic identity as long as

---

5. For an empirical example of such backfiring due to the banning of the veil in France, see Abdelgadir and Fouka, 2020. For a conceptual critique of coercive assimilationist solutions to anti-immigrant discrimination, see Norton, 2018.

ideational conflict over valued social norms is resolved. Perhaps the need to demonstrate that immigrants share natives' norms and ideas will also be perceived as repressive by some advocates of multiculturalism; but it is surely less interventionist than other ways to reduce social distance and it concerns behavior in the realm of civic—not private or family—life.

Previous work on immigrant integration focuses on much more visible signals of assimilation, defined as a one-way process of immigrants adapting to native society. Such signals include de-prioritizing religion (e.g., banning veils in France), adopting the country's language (e.g., foreign language prohibition laws in the United States after World War I), or changing dietary habits (e.g., eating pork in Denmark). Our argument is that there are subtler ways of overcoming difference by signaling appreciation and belonging. Natives' anxieties about immigrants are revealed in public discussions of their ascriptive traits, but they are not necessarily *caused* by those traits, but rather by what those traits signify according to prevailing beliefs in native society. The main fear is that immigrants reject the norms and values of that society and that they do not "fit in." Immigrants can overcome bias not necessarily by shedding the distinctive cultural features that they value, but by showing that they do not reject valued local norms and habits. Demonstrating that immigrants share natives' values and norms is a much lower bar to clear compared to outright assimilation. Although this point is subtle, the contrast with previous approaches to the study of native-immigrant conflict is sharp.

To address these important questions, we need new research that uncovers the sources of bias and discrimination in social interactions between natives and immigrants. Most of what we know about anti-immigrant attitudes comes from public opinion polls, survey experiments, audit studies, or lab experiments that are focused on the labor market or other economic domains (Hainmueller and Hangartner, 2013, p. 2). What is wanting is an investigation of how typical social encounters with immigrants in everyday settings structure the real-world behavior of natives.[6] In this book we provide such a perspective from the ground up; we design, implement, and analyze a series of large-scale field experiments that present a unique view of the forces that shape natives' behavior toward Muslims and test the power of shared norms and ideas to reduce discrimination.

---

6. An example of such a study is Enos (2014), which examines the effect of sustained exposure to foreign language–speaking nonnatives during a morning commute on exclusionary attitudes toward immigrants.

Another difference from previous studies of integration is that we focus on everyday social interactions that capture part of the "lived experiences" of immigrants. The importance of exploring the everyday content of our social lives cannot be overstated. Much of political science analyzes "big events"— elections, regime changes, wars, independence campaigns. Such events are important because they "move the needle" and can change reality seemingly overnight. But most of life is occupied by an accumulation of much smaller events, routine actions, habits, and seemingly mundane interactions. Our book focuses on those types of everyday interactions which make up the bulk of our lives because they can add up to something important. The social encounters that natives and immigrants have on the street, at the train station, in the shopping mall, or at the soccer field can play an immensely important role in shaping their perceptions of each other, their biases, and behavior. If native-immigrant interactions are characterized by several, repeated small acts of mutual disappointment, hostility, and discrimination, these daily experiences will resemble "death by a thousand cuts" and result in pervasive, lasting barriers to intergroup cooperation.

The Argument in a Nutshell

This book argues that intergroup conflict between natives and immigrants can be decreased through shared social norms that define a common ingroup identity—the identity of *citizen*. Anti-immigrant bias is reduced or eliminated if natives view that immigrants share norms and ideas that define salient social identities among the native population or among large segments of native society. It is not necessary for immigrants to change their appearance or their religion in an attempt to "pass" as members of the majority. It might not even be necessary to become fluent in the local language for them to be treated with the same respect that any other citizen is afforded. However, natives will make assumptions about immigrants' values and ideas based on their appearance; they have priors that may be based on incomplete information or prejudices that will lead them to discriminate against immigrants on the assumption that differences in appearance (in ascriptive traits) translate into differences in interests and value systems. Thus, social distance between natives and immigrants can cause discrimination, but it is not necessarily the ascriptive characteristics per se that explain that distance; rather, social distance is created by the *assumptions* that natives make about normative and ideational baggage that are implied by these ascriptive differences. Once this distinction between "appearance" and "behavior" is made clear, social distance between people who *look* different can be overcome as long as they are not perceived to *be* different. If natives believe that immigrants share key social norms that define native identity, they should feel less anxious about integrating immigrants and accommodating ascriptive differences. In that regard, norms and ideas can help define a common ingroup identity—a shared civic identity—that can overcome the native-immigrant divide.

The key here is that norms must be *shared*—the burden is not necessarily on immigrants to adopt to local norms that they find repressive; but they must behave in a way that indicates respect for their adopted country and its rules. Certainly, many immigrant populations have found that the path of least resistance is to adapt to local norms and habits, so the gradual assimilation of minority populations into the majority is one pathway through which social norms come to be shared over time. But the argument in this book is not dependent on such a pattern since it is possible for immigrants to *already* share many of the norms and ideas that define the native population. Moreover, even if norms come to be shared via a gradual process of acculturation into native society, this is a far less coercive way to reduce social distance between natives and immigrants compared to assimilation that is based on the principle of erasing (or hiding) subgroup differences, such as changing immigrants' names or forbidding the wearing of some religious symbols.

In some cases, native-immigrant conflict is based on the *misperception* of intergroup differences. Such differences might exist when one compares people across countries, but they might be less pronounced when we compare natives and immigrants, since immigrants are a self-selected group and might not fully share cultural beliefs and norms that are prevalent in their countries of origin. Thus, the expectation of cultural conflict might be exaggerated. Opening one's eyes to the full range of shared experiences in civic life will make evident that there is more common ground among natives and immigrants than is often believed. Over time, a gradual and mutual process of acculturation is likely to lead to a convergence in the norms and ideas shared by groups that live together in close proximity. In the short term, however, bias and discrimination will persist and could be driven by assumptions about the depth of ideational differences that divide the two groups. Taking this constraint of native opposition to multiculturalism seriously, this book considers whether bias and intergroup conflict can be reduced without repressing or erasing subgroup identities.

Observing behavior that suggests that natives and immigrants share common norms and ideas helps de-emphasize the native-immigrant divide by bringing to the foreground ideas about citizenship. Such observations make ethno-racial or religious differences less cognitively salient and help forge a common ingroup identity without erasing the differences that delineate group boundaries. This effect (forging a shared ingroup identity) can be achieved either by de-emphasizing the group-level attributes that accentuate social distance between natives and immigrants or by recategorizing immigrants as part of another ingroup—fellow citizens—rather than think of them primarily as outsiders. Natives might be conditioned to think that immigrants do not share their values and interests, so when they observe immigrants adhere to valued social norms or when they see them *enforce* those norms in public spaces, this will lead them to change the way they think about immigrants and it could reduce the social distance between them. When immigrants signal that they share ideas that define the social identities that are salient among the native population, the native-immigrant divide becomes secondary and immigrants can be treated as individuals or as members of a common ingroup rather than as members of an outgroup.

We substantiate this argument with evidence from a series of experiments and surveys related to the treatment of Muslims in Germany. Our analysis suggests that some—though by no means all—differences in ascriptive traits can indeed cause bias and discrimination in everyday interactions between native Germans and Muslim immigrants. However, that behavior is often driven by the normative-symbolic content of those ascriptive differences and much of the bias can be overcome. When natives acquire better information about immigrants' degree of commitment to social norms that are valued in the host society (or at least by some groups in that society), their behavior toward immigrants changes and differences in ascriptive characteristics become less important. Thus, a conclusion supported by the analysis in this book is that multiculturalism is possible, but that it also has its limits. While discrimination against immigrants based on ascriptive differences can be decreased, this requires shared norms and ideas and natives must be willing to reassess deeply held stereotypes about immigrants. Intergroup conflict between immigrants and natives can be reduced through a process of education, mutual adaptation, and understanding that highlights their shared identities.

Theoretical Advances

Our approach to studying the sources of anti-immigrant behavior is grounded on the foundational insights of social identity theory (SIT) and self-categorization theory (SCT) in psychology. These theories argue that group membership shapes the process through which individuals perceive their own identity. Human beings derive their self-worth and self-esteem in large part from their membership in social groups (Tajfel, 1981; Turner et al., 1987). As members in these social groupings, individuals venture through the process of social categorization, through which they "parse the world into manageable sets of social categories," and ultimately develop a sense of who *they* are and who *others* are (Kinder and Kam, 2010, p. 20). Once these boundaries are clearly delineated and the perception of belonging transforms into group identities, individuals tend to accentuate or reify the differences, real or imagined, between their own groups and outgroups (Tajfel, 1981, p. 276). And these distinctions become the basis upon which individuals come to treat "us" and "them" differently.

These insights are echoed in theories of conflict and cooperation in world politics and specifically in the constructivist tradition that explains inter-state conflict not as the inevitable consequence of structural conditions (anarchy) in the world system, but rather as the result of context-specific histories of conflictual or cooperative relations between states (Wendt, 1999; Hopf, 2002). Over time, and through repeated interactions with others, states (like people, if one is willing to reason by analogy) learn who their neighbors are and come to define their own interests and identities in relation to their neighbors. Thus, the fears and anxieties that are ever-present in an anarchic international system need not be so prevalent as to produce conflict as long as states can forge common expectations of cooperation over time. In world politics as in other realms, norms of cooperation are built based on shared experiences and common interests that come to define the limits of appropriate behavior (Finnemore and Sikkink, 1998; Finnemore, 1996; Darden, 2009).

Building and expanding on theories about the power of identities to shape behavior, the Common Ingroup Identity Model (CIIM) has argued that an effective way to reduce inter-group conflict is to induce a cognitive shift away from attributes that divide groups and toward a *common* identity that unites them (Gaertner and Dovidio, 2000). That paradigm is central to the argument put forward in this book, but we develop the CIIM further by showing the role of *ideational* similarity or difference in forging a common ingroup identity. Most prior empirical work on the CIIM in social psychology is focused on experimentally demonstrating that a cognitive shift that achieves the recategorization of an individual from a subordinate (e.g., ethnic) toward a superordinate (e.g., national) identity is effective in managing and reducing intergroup conflict. We share this general orientation while focusing on natives' and immigrants' ability to *forge* a new, common ingroup identity as citizens who are defined by shared ideas, norms, and interests.

Overcoming Identity Threat

From the perspective of the CIIM, discrimination and hostility toward an outgroup by an ingroup is symptomatic of ascriptive, cultural, or other differences that divide social groups. Bias against minorities held by majority groups would result from negative stereotypes and a sense of identity threat perceived by the majority, which considers itself superior (higher status) than minority groups and therefore lays claim to more resources and power. Conflict between immigrants and natives is an example of such majority-minority competition where the lack of a common ingroup identity induces conflict, as natives, who consider themselves as the prototypical and superior members of the nation perceive immigrants as threatening their influence over the nation's trajectory. The larger the ethnic and cultural differences between natives and immigrants, the more intense the conflict, as the perceived identity threat grows.

Could a simple cognitive shift that emphasizes an alternative, shared identity be sufficient to reduce bias and conflict as the CIIM would suggest? And how could the CIIM apply to native-immigrant conflict given that these groups do not possess a common national, superordinate identity that they can shift to? Setting aside how lasting the effect of such a cognitive shift is likely to be, for the CIIM to be applicable as a framework for conflict-resolution, a shared identity must already exist. The focus of any conflict-reducing intervention would consist of increasing the salience of the shared identity relative to other parochial attachments. The hard part is to create such a common identity if it does not already exist.

In political science, a vast literature on nationalism echoes this insight as it emphasizes the role of national identification in reducing the salience of subordinate ethnic, religious, regional, or other parochial attachments and inducing loyalty to the idea of the nation (Ricke et al., 2010; Charnysh, Lucas, and Singh, 2015; Levendusky, 2018; Wimmer, 2018; Mylonas, 2013). However, a common national identity does not unite natives and immigrants since their national origins are different. Indeed, perceived threat to national identity is precisely what causes conflict along the native-immigrant divide. Our book explores whether such conflict can be reduced by cultivating other shared identities based on the realization that natives and immigrants can share norms and ideas about public behavior and civic life that are either shared by most people in a society (*civic norms*) or by large segments of society (*group-derived norms*). Could shared respect for a common set of norms and ideas about group rights and responsibilities serve as the basis for the reduction of bias? Or do ascriptive differences between native and immigrant groups dominate any conflict-mitigating effect arising from shared norms?

Expanding the Common Ingroup Identity Model

We make two advances to the literature on identity politics, including previous applications of the CIIM to study majority-minority group conflicts. First, we understand common identities as implying common interests and shared ideas; it is the *shared content* of social identities that gives them power to shape behavior. Simply sharing attributes such as skin color, language, or religion is not enough to forge shared identities. We design experimental interventions during which publicly observable behavior reveals individuals' social *identification*: the extent to which individuals adhere to a set of norms that define specific social identities. Behavior that reveals that individuals have internalized those norms and ideas suggests that they identify with the group.[7] In turn, this behavior helps form the basis for natives and immigrants to realize that they share a common ingroup identity. This approach speaks to a large literature on integration, acculturation, and assimilation as we argue that strategies to reduce intergroup conflict between natives and immigrants should not be premised on erasing differences in group attributes in hopes of creating a more ethnically homogeneous population. Rather, alternative forms of similarity can be relied upon to forge a shared idea of *citizenship*.

Second, we explore the consequences of the intersectionality of social identities for the CIIM and argue that common superordinate identities can be identified on the basis of shared ideas and interests between immigrants and *specific subgroups* of the native population. Since social identities often crosscut, any number of group identities could be considered superordinate for a subset of the population and could be relied upon to reduce the salience of the native-immigrant divide. Gender, for example, could be considered as a

---

7. Identification with a group implies that individuals will take actions that are consistent with advancing the interests of the group, such as enforce group norms. Other types of behavior are also consistent with a revealed preferences approach to social identification, such as fighting for the group or pursuing strategies to increase group status and power.

superordinate identity for native and immigrant women. We focus on gender identity in chapter 6 and argue that the potential for a shared gender identity to reduce conflict between native and immigrant women will not depend on sharing superficial attributes (gender traits) that qualify one for membership in a gender group; rather it will depend on sharing the same ideas and norms that define that gender identity. Thus, if gender identity implies different types of behavior for natives and immigrants, this could actually increase conflict between them rather than decrease it; the overall effect of shared ideas about gender identity will be large or small depending on how salient gender identity is relative to other social identities. If native women and immigrant women have different concepts of what female identity means and if they espouse different ideas about gender roles, then the more salient gender identity becomes relative to other identities, and the more conflict we should expect to see. Conversely, if natives and immigrants share the same ideas about gender norms, then making gender identity salient could have a conflict-reducing effect by reducing the salience of the native-immigrant divide. This theoretical argument is developed further in chapter 2, where we elaborate on the conceptual foundations for the empirical analysis in the book. At the core of our theory is the notion that both widely held civic norms (general norms) and group-derived norms are central in defining shared interests based on common group identities that reduce the perceived distance between natives and immigrants and these commonalities can help reduce native-immigrant conflict.

The kinds of *norms* that we consider in this book include both group-derived norms that are defined with reference to specific groups, and general norms that apply to society as a whole and might well apply to different societies and countries.[8] Both are types of social norms—internalized habits or customs that suggest a set of expectations regarding civic behavior. These norms pertain to behavior that demonstrates whether one cares about society's rules, whether one respects others and wants to contribute to the common good. Many types of behaviors could satisfy those conditions; and although we analyze only one example of each type of norm, our discussion

---

8. This typology does not imply a hierarchy of norms; rather, our intent is to describe how widely the norm is likely to be internalized/adhered to by the population and whether the norm is more directly relevant to the core identity of a particular social group. Whereas "general" norms are norms that are expected to be widely adhered to in the whole society, "group-derived" norms might be felt more strongly among members of a particular social group—people whose group identities are more directly impacted by this norm.

should apply more broadly to different norms and civic behaviors. We an-alyze one example of a general norm (anti-littering) and one example of a group-derived norm (gender equality). Both of these are important in our specific country context (Germany), but they resonate in other European country contexts as they speak directly to debates regarding the integration of immigrant populations from Muslim countries.

The Evidence

In this book we present new evidence on the multiple influences on anti-immigrant bias and explore ways to reduce anti-immigrant discrimination. We rely on a series of randomized experiments that are conducted in the field in the context of day-to-day interactions that reveal immigrants' attitudes toward valued social norms in Germany. We complement these studies in the field with data from numerous survey experiments as well as observational survey data. The experiments manipulate different sources of perceived social distance between natives and immigrants and are complemented by survey experiments designed to uncover the mechanisms underlying natives' anti-immigrant bias. These studies allow us to assess the degree to which the native population's attitudes are driven by the perception that immigrants' internal-ized values and ideas are different from their own. This, in turn, allows us to observe whether eliminating the perception of normative or ideological differences reduces discrimination by natives toward immigrants.

We chose this particular approach for a number of reasons. First, the rhetoric of anti-immigration advocates in Western Europe often centers around concerns that immigrant populations are unwilling to integrate or as-similate, resisting the adoption of important socio-cultural norms that are widely accepted in host societies. Lack of respect for the native culture and di-vergent ideas about which public behaviors are appropriate are at the core of native populations' justifications for their animosity toward immigrants and their explanations for why immigrants pose an identity threat. This makes the study of native attitudes toward immigrants in settings where the acceptance or violation of valued social norms is at stake especially relevant. Second, an individual's adherence to or violation of social norms can elicit behavioral responses—often in the form of direct or indirect sanctions and rewards—from onlookers who often tend to be strangers.[9] Our experiments allow us

9. See, for example, Balafoutas, Nikiforakis, and Rockenbach, 2014 or Keuschnigg and Wolbring, 2015.

to observe these responses in settings designed to abstract from other behavioral influences. In the micro-environments that we create, individuals cannot expect a direct reward or other material benefit from enforcing civic norms. This provides a rare opportunity wherein to induce the latent immigration attitudes of native individuals to manifest into real behavior spontaneously without alerting individuals that they are being observed.

The first goal of these experiments is to identify the causes of discrimination against immigrants; the second goal is to explore whether adhering to general or group-derived norms has a bias-reducing effect. We draw evidence from experiments fielded in thirty cities with more than ten thousand subjects to show that Germans discriminate against Muslims in every-day interactions. However, we also show that when Muslims signal that they share social norms with the native majority society or with specific groups within it, discrimination against them decreases. Via targeted experimental interventions we are able to elucidate the reasons that a large segment of German society adopts a negative position vis-à-vis Muslim immigrants.

We find that natives' perceptions that Muslim immigrants do not conform to valued social norms is a key driver behind anti-Muslim discrimination. Other fears and concerns, as well as unconscious biases, are also likely to exert some influence. We identify many of those additional factors in a series of survey experiments that provide rich context to explain the behavior we observe in the field experiments. While we show evidence that discrimination declines when Muslims behave identically to natives in the context of experiments designed to reveal their preferences over social issues, or when they signal that they share common norms with natives, we also find that immigrants are held to a higher standard by the native population. Our analysis suggests that immigrants have to work harder than natives to be treated the same as everyone else.

Religion is the main axis along which discrimination is observed in the field in our experiments in Germany. We find no evidence that foreign language use or ethno-racial differences alone cause discrimination in the context of everyday interactions. This result stands in sharp contrast to prior literature in other countries, where the lack of linguistic assimilation has been identified as a primary cause of fears that immigration can threaten the national culture (Hopkins, 2014b; Citrin et al., 2007; Dowling, Ellison, and Leal, 2012; Schildkraut, 2010; Schildkraut, 2005; Newman, Hartman, and Taber, 2012). In the United States, even brief exposure to uses of Spanish by strangers in public settings has been shown to generate hostility among natives

(Hopkins, 2014b; Newman, Hartman, and Taber, 2012; Paxton, 2006; Enos, 2014). Moreover, multiple studies have presented evidence of significant bias against ethno-racial minorities across countries. Thus, the evidence we present from Germany offers a useful point of comparison from a country with a recent history of multiculturalist policies that suggests that it is possible to overcome barriers to cultural integration and that ethno-linguistic or racial differences need not result in discrimination in ordinary, everyday forms of human interaction. Although individuals may be prejudiced, their public behavior need not reflect that prejudice and discrimination is likely to manifest in settings that respond to the *politicization* of social cleavages. The Christian-Muslim cleavage in Germany, as in other European countries, remains politically salient due to the ongoing wars in the Middle East and large-scale immigration from predominately Muslim countries. Those immigration flows have been politicized by far-right political groups; in the absence of these political pressures, the salience of religious markers can decline and so could bias and discrimination. The future of multiculturalism in Western democracies might not be as bleak as is often thought.

Having identified religious differences as the key factor motivating anti-immigrant bias in Germany, we explore the mechanisms underlying that result. Our focus is on how native Germans perceive Muslim religious symbols and on whether bias is driven at least in part by inferences natives make about Muslims' social norms and values. Our approach allows us to consider why ascriptive differences generate social distance and sets the stage for an analysis of the power of general and group-derived norms to erase the salience of religious markers and reduce discrimination.

Our results suggest that adherence to general civic norms reduces bias, but it is not enough to completely offset other sources of discrimination toward Muslims. Consistent with previous studies that point to group-specific causes of anti-immigrant bias (such as sectoral economic interests), we find that adherence to group-derived norms that are very important to specific subgroups of the native population is more effective in reducing bias. While this is encouraging from the perspective of multiculturalist democracy, this also means that the scope of any intervention to align immigrants' and natives' norms is likely defined by the size of the group whose norms are being invoked, and its impact will therefore be limited to that group.

As we show later in this book, part of the reason that discrimination persists even when immigrants adhere to widely held civic norms is that natives view immigrants from the perspective of their own narrow self-interest or from the prism of the social group with which they identify. Natives have priors about immigrants' beliefs and value systems and they consider how their own interests—defined by their social identities—are likely to be affected by immigration. Thus, even when Muslims signal that they adhere to generally valued civic norms in Germany, pockets of suspicion and resistance to immigration will remain as long as natives believe that immigrants pose a threat to specific social identities shared by a subgroup of the native population. In situations where those subgroup identities are salient, adherence to general norms may not be about to eliminate anti-immigrant bias; but adherence to group-derived norms might have such a stronger effect. In that regard, our analysis differs from much of the previous literature, which has considered group threat at the aggregate level (i.e., natives vs. immigrants). In the experimental micro-environments that we create, the native/immigrant cleavage is not always the most salient identity dimension. By activating different social identities that subgroups of natives might share, we can explore the effect of group-derived norms that are central to the identity of specific groups of natives. Focusing on such parochial attachments allows us to uncover and experimentally manipulate specific forms of symbolic threat posed by Muslim immigration to subgroups of German society.

One could explore any number of group-specific identities and analyze how they shape attitudes toward immigrants. Prior literature in political economy has focused on class identity or profession as influences on immigration attitudes, with the emphasis being on the effect of economic competition for blue-collar jobs (Scheve and Slaughter, 2001; Hainmueller and Hiscox, 2010). Partisanship has also been considered as another social identity that could shape perceptions of the risks associated with immigration (Levendusky, 2018; Hopkins, 2014b). Much less attention has been paid to other social identities, such as gender. A review of empirical studies on immigration does not reveal a major focus on the impact of gender and most studies implicitly assume that men are more likely to discriminate against foreigners than women, which is an expectation that may be inspired by socio-biological theories of ingroup bias. Yet systematic analyses of gender-based differences in discrimination are in short supply and our book opens the way for an analysis of how the politics of gender intersect with the politics of immigration.

An insight that emerges from the realization that social identities are multiple and partially overlapping is that there is no reason to expect any single intervention that highlights commonalities in norms and ideas between any two groups to be fully effective in reducing intergroup bias and conflict. At best, such interventions can hope to resonate among a few subgroups of the native population. The intersectionality of social identities implies that any such intervention to establish common norms can gain allies among some groups while polarizing others and leaving the rest indifferent. This insight applies broadly to any consideration of how the crosscuttingness of social identities can be used to reduce intergroup conflict. We address this question explicitly when we consider how gender identity might intersect with the native-immigrant divide in an experiment that primes both gender and immigrant identities and manipulates the information provided to native German experimental subjects about immigrants' views concerning gender equality norms.

Our results highlight that a key mechanism underlying the anti-Muslim discrimination identified in our experiments is the perception—held more strongly among women—that Muslims are regressive with respect to ideas about gender equality. That perception is of course not the only cause of discrimination, but it is a powerful one, particularly among women. More importantly, when we experimentally manipulate natives' exposure to Muslims who appear to hold either regressive or progressive ideas about gender equality, we find that progressive ideas reduce discrimination overall and completely eliminate it among women.

These results are consistent with the expectation that the integration of large groups of immigrants in liberal, multicultural democracies threatens the interests and identities of different groups of citizens differently. Secular, progressive women are particularly impacted by the political accommodation of regressive attitudes toward gender equality and might therefore be expected to be opposed to Muslim immigration as long as immigrants are perceived to be regressive. By the same token, they should be very receptive to signals that many Muslims are actually as progressive as they are and, when confronted with such information, their behavior toward Muslims should be decidedly less discriminatory. This is precisely what we find: shared group-derived (particularist) norms can eliminate anti-immigrant discrimination.

Why Study Germany?

An ideal context for our study is a country with a high level of anti-immigrant bias due to the perception of cultural differences separating natives from immigrants; and also one where rules and norms regarding civic behavior are clearly defined and broadly shared among the native population. This would allow us to test whether sharing those norms with immigrants can reduce native-immigrant conflict. Germany is an ideal case for such an analysis. Since 2015, Germany has experienced one of the largest waves of immigration in modern European history; with more than 1.8 million individuals having applied for asylum, Germany is the largest recipient of refugees in the European Union (Bundesamt, 2018). Immigration has emerged as a salient issue in public debates and party politics, and Germans of immigrant background are affected by a backlash to the refugee crisis, which has sparked debates about the future of multiculturalism in Germany and other European countries.

As in any other country built on the foundation of ethnic nationalism, immigrants are seen as outsiders in Germany, and many natives assume that immigrants are unable or unwilling to adhere to prevalent social norms that define their national identity. We show evidence of these beliefs in our own surveys and in reviews of previous public opinion polls. Inevitably, such perceptions create significant challenges for social or political inclusion of minorities and nonnative populations. In ethnic nationalist countries such as Germany the problem is magnified since immigrant inclusion often requires challenging the notion that the concept of the nation is based on racial or ethnic homogeneity. Looking back at the history of Germany, affinities among German peoples is what enabled the unification of German states under Prussian leadership after the Franco-Prussian War, which is how the modern German nation-state emerged. Even though Germany began receiving a large number of immigrants in the aftermath of the atrocities committed by Nazi Germany in the name of ethnic purity and World War II, it was not until decades later that it would start developing coherent immigrant and integration policies. A long history of immigration from Mediterranean and near-Eastern countries was seen as necessary to fuel the growth of the (Western) German economy in the 1950s and 1960s, but it was followed by a period of both violent and nonviolent conflict with immigrants in the 1980s and 1990s. Thus, Germany satisfies the first condition for case selection: a clear divide and a politically salient conflict between natives and immigrants.

At the same time, Germany also satisfies the second condition: there is broad-based respect for rules and for norm adherence and individuals have a well-developed sense of civic duty. In that sense, Germany is a case in which we are likely to observe positive effects of norm adherence by immigrants, while controlling for other determinants of social distance between natives and immigrants.

Putting Germany in a Broader Context

Compared to immigrant nations such the United States or Canada, as well as other European countries such as France, the Netherlands, or the United Kingdom that have had a long history of large-scale immigration from their colonies, Germany began to grapple with questions of immigrant integration relatively recently. Even though Germany was on the receiving end of large migrant inflows in the postwar period, it was not until decades later that it started developing coherent immigration and integration policies.

Severe labor shortages during the so-called *Wirtschaftswunder* (economic miracle)—the economic boom in West Germany during the 1950s and 1960s—prompted the Federal Republic of Germany (FDR) to implement policies to meet soaring demand by aggressively courting foreign workers. In this context, the FDR signed a series of bilateral recruitment agreements with Italy (1955), Spain (1960), Greece (1960), Turkey (1961), Morocco (1963), South Korea (1963), Portugal (1964), Tunisia (1965), and Yugoslavia (1968) for the purpose of creating a *Gastarbeiter* (guest worker) program. However, as the term *Gastarbeiter* already implies, this initiative was never intended to be permanent, with the expectation that workers hired through the program would ultimately return to their originating countries. Yet many of the guest workers never left Germany even after the program had exhausted its purpose. It is the long-lasting demographic changes that the program brought about that set the scene for the questions we address in this book.

Although Germany has received the lion's share of asylum applications in Europe, this has not turned the population "off" immigration.[10] Looking at polling data since 1980, we see clear evidence of increasingly positive views about immigrants as well as more contact with immigrants over time.[11] Over the last four decades, opposition to immigrant participation in the workforce and in political life has decreased continuously (see panels (a) and (b) in

10. Data from the nationally representative ALLBUS surveys show that in 2016, when asked if they would support stopping the inflows of workers from non-EU countries, about 90% of Germans state that they would support at least limited inflows; and a similar level of support is extended toward limited inflows of refugees; compared to about just 60–70% during the 1990s (GESIS, 2018).

11. According to Gallup data, about 68% of Germans report knowing an immigrant; this is lower than the rate in Sweden (89%), Spain (89%), or Greece (81%) and in light of the large size of the immigrant population this could suggest that the degree of intergroup contact is still not very high relative to other countries in Europe.

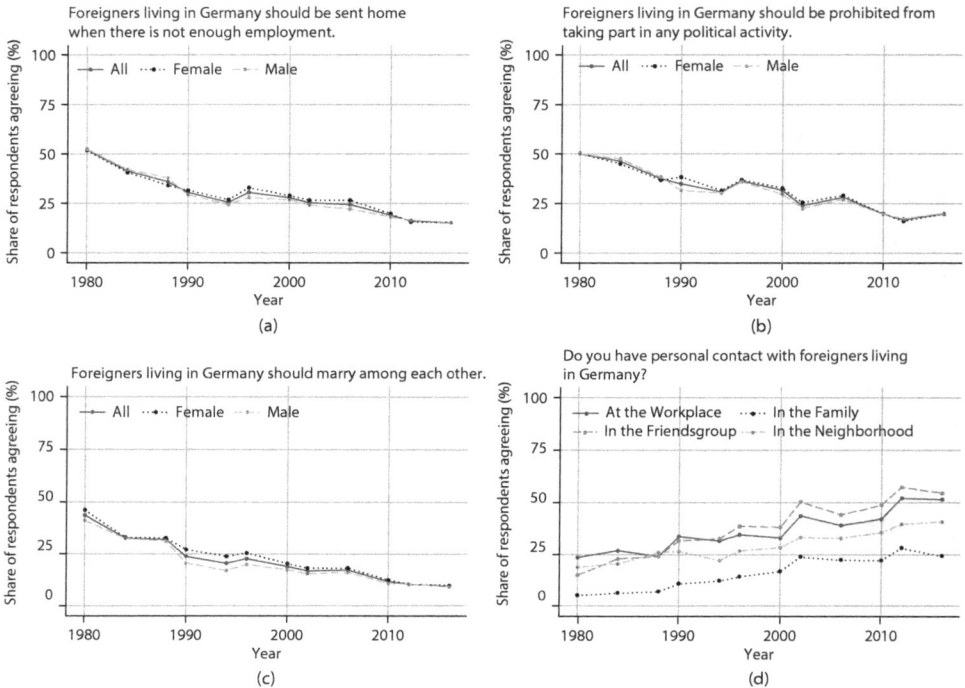

FIGURE 1.1. Trends in attitudes toward immigration in Germany
Notes: Survey responses of German citizens in the ALLBUS surveys (GESIS, 2018).

figure 1.1). Similarly, opposition to intermarriage with immigrants has decreased to very low levels and personal contact with immigrants has increased across different areas of social interaction (see panels (c) and (d), respectively, in figure 1.1).

Although German attitudes toward immigrants have been improving over time, survey data also reveal a fairly stable degree of antipathy toward Muslims. Fewer than half of survey respondents would support a statement that Turks living in Germany should have the same rights as Germans and more than half admit that they would be uncomfortable if a member of their family married a Turk (see figure 1.2). By contrast, Italians and native Germans from Eastern Europe appear to be viewed as "less objectionable."

The vast majority (75%) of native Germans believe that migration creates conflict between natives and immigrants and these conflicts appear to be cultural since more than 65% of respondents also believe that migration

Would you be uncomfortable with a member of a foreign community marrying into your family?

Would it be uncomfortable for you to have members of foreign communities as neighbours?

(a)

(b)

Turks living in Germany should have the same rights as Germans in all areas.

(c)

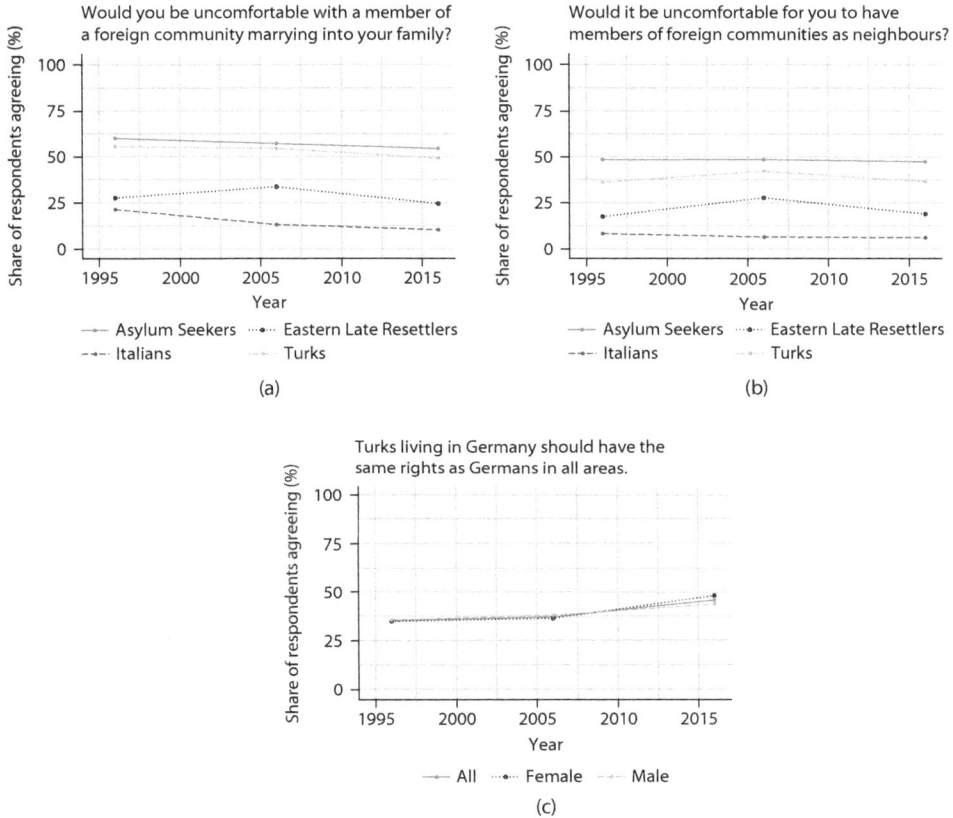

FIGURE 1.2. Trends in attitudes toward immigration in Germany
Notes: Survey responses of German citizens in the ALLBUS surveys (GESIS, 2018).

has an overall positive effect on the economy, according to a 2019 survey (Kober and Kösemen, 2019).[12] Only a small percentage (around 9%) are willing to state that it would be better if no Muslims lived in Germany (Heitmeyer et al., 2013b) and only 20% see Islam as culturally "backwards" with 11% arguing that "equality is not compatible with Islam" (Heitmeyer et al., 2013a). These views, though extreme, are held by a relatively small part of the population and more than half of respondents in the above-mentioned 2019

12. These survey data were part of a study by the Bertelsmann Stiftung about the *Willkommenskultur* (welcoming culture) in Germany after the so-called "refugee crisis." Our analysis of the survey data focuses on German-speaking respondents without migration background.

survey indicated that they would support legislation to prevent discrimination in the housing market, the job market, and education (Kober and Kösemen, 2019).

One hypothesis is that negative attitudes toward Muslims are in fact due to a culture clash with Turkish immigrants dating back to the 1960s and 1970s. Turks represented the main group of immigrants from the Middle East at the time and there was a clear education gap vis-à-vis the German population as the average Turkish immigrant during the 1970s, for example, had no more than six years of education (Marplan, 1982.). As we show later, this gap is now closing as new arrivals from Syria and other predominantly Muslim countries are more educated and their views are much closer to those of the typical German. But those early encounters may have created prejudices and stereotypes that have lasted through generations.

At the same time, survey data suggest that government policies supporting multiculturalism have not backfired to the degree that is often reported in the media. As shown earlier (see figure 1.1), anti-immigration attitudes are declining overall and immigrants themselves are less likely to perceive xenophobia as a real concern.[13] Indeed, while Germany is not the most welcoming country, it does better than many other European countries with respect to the "migrant acceptance index" constructed using Gallup data (Fleming et al., 2018, p. 12) and Germany is not an outlier with respect to attitudes toward immigrants using other metrics of inclusivity.[14] The share of German natives who view

13. Whereas about 70% of Turkish immigrants pointed to xenophobia as their main concern in the late 1980s and early 1990s, this figure dropped to below 15% by 2004, according to the Migrants in Germany survey that was conducted by GESIS regularly until 2004 (Marplan, 1988; Marplan, 1989; Marplan, 1992; Marplan, 1994; Marplan, 1996a; Marplan, 1996b; Marplan, 1996c; Marplan, 2012a; Marplan, 2012b; Marplan, 2012c; Marplan, 2012d; Marplan, 2012e; Marplan, 2012f; Marplan, 2012g; Marplan, 2012h; Marplan, 2012i; Marplan, 2012j; Marplan, 2006a; Marplan, 2006b).

14. According to the "multiculturalism policy index" compiled by researchers at Queen's University, the degree of openness of Germany's policies has been improving since the 1960s and in recent years it has been similar to that in France, Spain, Austria, and the United States, though it lags behind some Scandinavian countries, Australia, and New Zealand. See https://www.queensu.ca/mcp/home (accessed 10/2/20). According to a different index of multiculturalism—the ICRI (Indicators of Citizenship Rights for Immigrants)—which places heavier emphasis in religious rights (Koopmans, 2013, p. 154), Germany seems to lag a bit further behind than several other migrant-receiving countries in the West, but it is by no means an outlier. It is possible, however, to identify aspects of immigration policy according to which Germany (as well as Switzerland and some other European countries) appears to be relatively restrictive. Koopmans et al., 2005 draw such a distinction in discussing mechanisms

immigration as improving life in their country has also been increasing and is now roughly similar to that in other Western European countries (ESS, 2002; ESS, 2004; ESS, 2006; ESS, 2008; ESS, 2010; ESS, 2012; ESS, 2014; ESS, 2016; ESS, 2018).[15] Similarly, Germany is not an outlier with respect to the prevalence of perceptions among the native population that immigration creates a cultural threat; the share of German natives who perceive such a threat has been fairly constant, hovering around 25% over the past twenty years (ESS, 2002; ESS, 2004; ESS, 2006; ESS, 2008; ESS, 2010; ESS, 2012; ESS, 2014; ESS, 2016; ESS, 2018), and preferences for cultural homogeneity are fairly consistent with other Western European countries (ESS, 2002; ESS, 2004; ESS, 2006; ESS, 2008; ESS, 2010; ESS, 2012; ESS, 2014; ESS, 2016; ESS, 2018).

Overall, evidence from public opinion polls going back decades shows a clear picture of bias against Muslims that has persisted over time, albeit within an environment of improving attitudes toward diversity and somewhat more positive views regarding immigration. In that regard, Germany is not different from other Western European countries and therefore there is every reason to expect that our analysis can help us think about the challenges of immigration in the broader Western European context.

Broader Impacts

This book addresses core questions for ongoing debates on immigration in Europe, and it does so by placing the analysis of anti-immigrant bias within the scope of a broader study of identity politics. The book's conclusions and methods can inform a number of social science literatures and analytical approaches.

First, the theoretical framework developed in this book expands the common ingroup identity model (CIIM) (Gaertner and Dovidio, 2000) by exploring how commonalities in norms and ideas form the foundation of common identities and by testing the implications of the intersectionality of social identities for CIIM-based approaches to conflict reduction. The CIIM was

---

of mobilizing immigrants politically and consider differences in that dimension of immigration policy as relevant for the depth of immigrants' political integration. Although Germany appears more restrictive than other countries with respect to this index, it has better socioeconomic outcomes—such as labor market participation and lower housing segregation—for immigrants, than most European countries (Koopmans, 2013, pp. 162–163).

15. Absent better indicators with good coverage to identify "natives," our analysis of the ESS survey data focuses on respondents born in the country.

developed in psychology to explore how social experiences can lead individuals to recategorize outgroup members as ingroup members by highlighting a shared identity; or treat them as individuals by de-emphasizing attributes that define the outgroup. This model is increasingly used in political science as a framework to think about minority/majority group interactions across different contexts. However, empirical applications of the CIIM usually *presuppose* an established superordinate identity (e.g., national identity) that could be made salient so as to reduce the strength of subordinate, parochial attachments and unify individuals from majority and minority groups. In doing so, these studies overlook the fact that individuals have multiple social identities (e.g., gender, religion, professional occupation) and these identities often intersect. Thus it is not always obvious which identities can be selected to serve as the vehicle to unify ingroup and outgroup members without creating new ingroup/outgroup divisions. This book provides the first analysis we are aware of that considers whether the native/immigrant divide can be made less salient by activating crosscutting social identities via emphasizing shared norms and ideas that define those identities. Norms are the "constitutive grammar" that defines social identities (Bicchieri, 2006) and makes it possible for different individuals to have a shared concept of what these identities mean. This book shows that it is possible to appeal to shared norms and ideas to reduce conflict along the native-immigrant divide.

Second, we contribute to a large and growing literature on the "contact hypothesis" (Allport, 1979) by suggesting that only *meaningful interactions* that highlight shared norms and ideas can lead to changes in perceptions and behavior toward others and can overcome bias. It is a common misinterpretation of Allport's original research to suggest that more contact between culturally different groups will inevitably reduce bias and increase cooperation. There are now hundreds of studies testing the contact hypothesis and a key lesson from a meta-analysis of those studies is that the *type* of contact determines whether it reduces conflict (Paluck, Green, and Green, 2019). Although our study does not directly test the contact hypothesis, our findings are consistent with this important lesson since we show that simply making salient a shared attribute (such as gender) that establishes that natives and immigrants share membership in the same social group will be insufficient to reduce discrimination.[16] Bias reduction is reduced only if natives and immigrants

---

16. One might argue that we do not study "contact" as that has been defined in the social psychology literature and that our experiments set up encounters that amount to brief "exposures"

who share a common attribute also share the same understanding of the norms and ideas that define their shared group identity.

Third, our empirical approach provides a new model for the design and implementation of coordinated experimental interventions across different contexts. Recently, scholars have taken steps to coordinate on the design and implementation of experimental projects on common research topics across different contexts with the aim of producing generalizable findings that contribute to the accumulation of knowledge (Dunning et al., 2019). The goal of accumulating knowledge via closely coordinated, systematic analyses of data drawn from different contexts is of course not a new preoccupation; earlier initiatives have used multi-method research designs to the same effect. Our book expands that approach by drawing on multiple, closely coordinated experiments conducted over a multi-year period that aim to partially replicate and expand on each other. Thereby, it shares in the spirit of such initiatives to uncover new insights regarding discrimination against immigrants. Our approach has distinct advantages over some of the existing initiatives for cumulative learning using experimental research. By virtue of being implemented by a single research team, our experimental design has the coherence that is difficult to achieve in cross-team coordinated impact evaluations of different programs that might have been designed differently across different contexts. Furthermore, each executed phase of the project has informed how we build on and modify the research design in subsequent phases. Having completed multiple experiments over three years of research both in the field and in surveys, we are able to explore key mechanisms underlying causal effects more richly than individual experimental studies might be able to.

Fourth, the ideas and approaches that we explore in this book with reference to Germany are readily applicable to other countries in Europe. While different societies have different sets of valued norms that can form the basis of shared identities, the effect of shared norms should be observable beyond Germany. Our study opens a path forward for a novel exploration of

---

to an outgroup. Albeit brief, these encounters impart valuable information to natives and might lead them to update their beliefs about immigrants or their behavior toward them much like sustained contact with an outgroup might over time. The types of encounters that we stage in our field experiments provide content that is comparable to a meaningful conversation and could expose aspects of an individual's identity even though contact is not lengthy and does not involve sustained interaction between natives and immigrants. This justifies drawing parallels with some of the conclusions of studies of the "contact hypothesis."

identity politics across countries as the experimental framework that we have developed is readily adaptable to different country contexts.

Finally, our findings have broad implications for policy design in the management of discrimination against immigrants. Policy interventions need to reflect an understanding of what causes anti-immigrant attitudes: is discriminatory behavior driven primarily by ascriptive differences or by beliefs that immigrants do not share the same values? Initiatives designed to educate host populations to reduce negative stereotypes should be effective in the latter case. Our research provides examples of messages that are likely to resonate with different subsets of host populations. It also suggests that policy interventions to reduce native-immigrant conflict should not simply target immigrants; they should also be developed with an eye toward messages that can shift natives' perceptions and prejudices.

Plan of the Book

Chapter 2 presents our theoretical approach to understanding the origins of anti-immigrant animus, and discusses ways in which such hostility and discrimination can be overcome.

Chapter 3 builds on the argument made in the introduction about persistent anti-Muslim bias in Germany and begins to explore the nature of that bias. We draw on data from existing surveys of anti-immigrant attitudes as well as data from original surveys, experiments, and psychological tests that we implemented in the immediate aftermath of the European refugee crisis. These data show that German native populations hold strong negative attitudes and bias toward immigrant minority groups. This chapter suggests that cultural differences—religious differences in particular—play a pivotal role in structuring these attitudes. We build on these insights to further show that these attitudes translate into discriminatory behavior in the field. In so doing, we introduce a novel experimental intervention that we explicitly designed to unobtrusively observe discriminatory behavior against immigrants in everyday social interactions between natives and immigrants. Our findings from these interventions, conducted in twenty-eight cities across four states in Germany, show that native Germans are significantly less inclined to offer assistance to immigrant minorities (and religious Muslim immigrants in particular) in need of help vis-à-vis their fellow natives in need of help. These insights set the stage for our empirical investigation of the ways through which such bias and discrimination against immigrants can be overcome.

Chapter 4 tackles the question of whether the bias and discrimination documented in chapter 4 are driven by perceptions of linguistic differences between the host population and immigrant minorities. While popular discourse suggests that natives consider linguistic assimilation (i.e., the adoption of the host society's language) to be a critical condition for the acceptance of immigrants into German society, our findings in this chapter show otherwise; we find no evidence that immigrants who adopt the host society's language (in our case German) in everyday conversations are discriminated against less than immigrants who continue using the language of their originating country (i.e., a foreign language). Our precisely estimated null effects suggest that perceptions of difference generated by ascriptive identity markers such as religion are unlikely to be offset by the linguistic assimilation of immigrant minorities. At the same time, although our experiments in chapter 3 show that native attitudes are more negative toward immigrants who do not speak the native language, we find no evidence that immigrants who speak in a foreign language in everyday social interactions are discriminated against more than those who speak in German.

In chapter 5, we put the first of our main empirical predictions of our theoretical framework to the test. We show that shared civic norms between native and immigrant populations reduce native discrimination against immigrant minorities. We do so by leveraging data from the first of our field interventions (conducted in the summer of 2018), in which we experimentally manipulated whether our confederates enforced a generally held social norm against littering in public spaces. The act of norm enforcement was intended to correct German stereotypes regarding the extent to which immigrant communities adhere to standards of "cleanliness" that shows "respect for the host country." We find that immigrant confederates who enforced the anti-littering norm were significantly less likely to face discrimination from native Germans than those who did not enforce the norm. However, we also find that this reduction is limited in its magnitude; even after norm enforcement, immigrant confederates are treated significantly worse than native German confederates who demonstrate the same civic-mindedness.

Chapter 6 turns our empirical investigation to whether group-derived norms can provide the necessary foundation to reduce discrimination against immigrants among subgroups of the native population who should care deeply about those norms by virtue of their social identities. To do so, we exploit the fact that there is a gap—or at least the perception of a gap—between native Germans, and the predominantly Muslim immigration populations with respect to ideas about the "right" role for women in the job market or the household. We implemented an experimental intervention that exposed native Germans to information that countered stereotypes of regressivity with respect to gender equality-related attitudes among immigrant minorities. Our analysis finds that immigrant confederates who signal that they share progressive gender equality norms with natives are discriminated against significantly less than those that do not. Yet we also find that the reduction in discrimination is driven by members of the native population who share gender equality norms most deeply—women and non-religious individuals. No such reduction is observed among men or religious Germans.

With the centrality of shared norms as a determinant of behavior having been established in previous empirical chapters, chapter 7 brings evidence to bear on the psychological processes that lead to the reduction in anti-immigrant prejudice and discrimination. Using a series of lab experiments embedded in a nationally representative survey of German citizens, we identify the mechanism through which discrimination is reduced in the "civic norm" experiment. Specifically, we consider whether observing pro-social, norm-adhering behavior by immigrants changes natives' attitudes toward immigrants as a group or whether it pushes them to consider the immigrant confederate as an individual, differentiating her from the rest of her group and considering her as another German citizen. This speaks directly to the mechanisms of *recategorization, decategorization,* and mutual differentiation that are so central in theories of bias reduction.

Chapter 8 takes stock of the empirical results presented throughout this book and closes our discussion by summarizing the book's contributions and returning to the question that framed this study at the outset—the promise and limits of multiculturalism.

2

Reducing Social Distance, Reducing Bias

BEFORE THE COVID-19 pandemic resulted in globally mandated social isolation in the spring of 2020 and "social distancing" was needed to reduce the spread of infectious disease, the term "social distance" had a less ambiguous meaning as a metaphor for the perceived cultural differences that divide different social groups. In this book, we frequently talk about *social distance* as a cause of bias and prejudice. We use the concept to refer to the cognitive, ideological, and affective space that divides native populations from immigrants and we explore factors that make that space larger or smaller. This book is concerned with finding ways to overcome social distance in multicultural societies and, by doing so, to reduce intergroup conflict. A core idea underpinning our analysis is that reducing the perceived cultural distance that divides social groups is a vital part of conflict-reduction strategies. This chapter presents our thinking on how social distance between natives and immigrants can be overcome and sets the stage for the empirical chapters that follow. We begin from the simple premise that conflict can be reduced if groups feel "closer" to one another. We focus on whether and how a common set of norms and ideas about civic identity can overcome social distance between natives and immigrants.

Confronting Parochialism

Parochialism—the tendency to favor ingroup members at the expense of an outgroup—has been identified by observational and experimental research in the social and evolutionary sciences as a fundamental tenet of human behavior (Bowles, 2009; Bornstein, 2003; Bernhard, Fischbacher, and Fehr, 2006;

Tajfel et al., 1971). Across cultures, ingroup bias and outgroup prejudice—two components of parochialism—have been tied to various forms of conflict, ranging from discrimination in the labor market (Bertrand and Mullainathan, 2004; Adida, Laitin, and Valfort, 2010), racial profiling in criminal justice (Antonovics and Knight, 2009), to suicide bombings (Atran and Ginges, 2012), and mass atrocities such as genocide (Everett, Faber, and Crockett, 2015).

The human tendency to prefer one's own ingroup and be suspicious, distant, or even hostile to outgroups has been shown to coevolve with conditions that favor intergroup conflict (Bowles and Choi, 2007; Bowles, 2009; Bowles, 2012). Cultural group formation can be explained as a mechanism for a population of heterogeneous individuals to resolve coordination problems (Efferson, Lalive, and Fehr, 2008) so that they can compete more effectively for resources and survival. That process strengthens bonds within members of a group and can result in altruistic behavior; but it also increases the risk of conflict with outgroups. Among early humans, war promoted altruism toward members of one's ingroup (Bowles and Choi, 2007; Bowles, 2006).[1]

The innate tendency toward group solidarity exists even among artificial groups as evidenced by research on the Minimal Group Paradigm.[2] Categorizing an individual as a member of a group highlights common traits that define an ingroup and creates a contrast with outgroups. This induces individuals who share those traits to feel more similar to other ingroup members than to the outgroup. That perception of greater social distance between ingroup and outgroup, even when it is based on seemingly insignificant traits, can induce biased behavior in favor of ingroup members.[3] When group divisions are real, corresponding to deeply politicized group traits as is usually the case with ethnic or religious differences, the distance that divides groups appears larger,

---

1. Although related to theories of parochial altruism, our book is not about altruism per se; we base our analysis on the more limited claim that group membership induces ingroup bias. For a review of challenges to theories of parochial altruism, see Rusch (2014). Two dimensions of these challenges include the potential direct benefits of altruistic behavior and high relatedness between group members motivating altruistic behavior.

2. Minimal Group Paradigm (Tajfel et al., 1971) experiments consist of assigning subjects to artificial groups usually in a lab setting and asking them to make anonymous allocation decisions between an ingroup and an outgroup member. The key finding is that simple categorization of an individual as a member of a group induces them to be biased in favor of the group, even if the group is entirely artificial.

3. See Brewer (1979) and Bourhis and Gagnon (2001) for reviews.

and group attachments become stronger and harder to overcome, resulting in deep polarization.

The study of parochialism bears similarity to the study of kinship groups in anthropology, though the focus shifts from individuals and small groups to larger communities such as ethnicities or nations. Any physical-geographical or notional-ideational boundary can forge communities that, over time, develop a distinct group identity and behave like kinship groups. Ethnicities or nations share with kinship groups the idea that identity is formed on the basis of heritable attributes that are "sticky" and hard to change (Chandra, 2006). Such "markers" that define group boundaries provide security in group membership and clarity over who is "in" and who is "out." But they also induce suspicion and fear of outsiders.

In a lab setting, the behavioral implications of sharing a group identity have usually been explored via behavioral games such as the intergroup prisoner's dilemma or public goods games in which individuals with low levels of solidarity to others are "defectors"—they do not contribute to the common good—whereas those with a high degree of group solidarity are "cooperators" and end up paying the cost of advancing the group's welfare. Both deliberative and intuitive decision-making can be involved in these behaviors. Experimental evidence showing that pro-social behavior toward the group (cooperation) is intuitive and connected to neuro-biological mechanisms (De Dreu et al., 2010; De Dreu, Dussel, and Ten Velden, 2015) constitutes especially strong support for theories of parochialism as an innate human tendency.[4]

Part of the scholarly debate on parochialism has focused on the precise mechanisms that behavioral models such as the intergroup prisoner's dilemma can support and on whether the evidence based on these models suggests that individuals, who are generally much more pro-social than one might expect based on standard economic theories of utility-maximizing behavior, are *more negative* or simply *less positive* toward outgroups (Böhm, 2016). The emerging consensus is that behavior toward outgroups is *less positive* rather than outright hostile (Saucier, Miller, and Doucet, 2005). Bias and

---

4. Other research has explored how the behavioral immune system regulates sentiments toward immigrants and has posited that "individuals who experience more pathogen disgust harbor more negative attitudes toward foreigners" (Karinen et al., 2019). For such an approach to exploring socio-biological determinants of anti-immigration attitudes, see Aarøe, Petersen, and Arceneaux (2017) and Green et al. (2010).

discrimination usually manifest as a preference for the ingroup (increased positive behavior) rather than a more negative behavior toward the outgroup (Brewer, 1999).[5]

The core intuition that emerges from this large literature in social psychology, anthropology, and behavioral economics is that individuals want to identify with social groups they belong to, and that group identification promotes behaviors designed to further the group's welfare often at the expense of other groups. Ingroup bias—parochialism—induced by perceptions of social distance that derive from differences in group-based attributes is an empirical regularity across a wide range of contexts. Native-immigrant conflict is a specific manifestation of that phenomenon.

Parochialism in Native-Immigrant Interactions

Although ingroup bias has been shown to follow even arbitrary assignments to groups in behavioral games played in the lab (Chen and Li, 2009), such interactions are often too abstract and they take place in a vacuum, which serves to highlight the salience of group membership even if these groups are artificial. In the real world, multiple issues compete for individuals' attention and membership in a social group does not necessarily imply that the individual *identifies* with that group. Individuals have multiple group memberships and attachments that are not equally salient all the time. Biased behavior is more likely to occur among individuals who identify strongly with their group and under conditions that make specific identities more salient. For example, in their study of giving to victims of hurricane Katrina in the United States, Fong and Luttmer (2009) find no evidence of overall racial bias in giving. However, racial bias in giving was observed among individuals who reported "feeling close" to their racial group. Thus, to understand parochialism, it is important to understand the context that makes group attributes more or less cognitively salient, since social identification is contingent on context.[6]

---

5. However, some studies that are focused on biological determinants of intergroup conflict have shown that under conditions of physical stress negative behavior toward the outgroup increases. See Choi, Poertner, and Sambanis (forthcoming a).

6. This is a key insight that has emerged from the political science literature on identity politics and ethnic conflict. Previous studies have shown that ethnic violence makes ethnic identities more salient, which in turn induces more bias and ethnic polarization. For a model of the relationship between violent conflict and social identification, see Sambanis and Shayo (2013). For a review of the case-based literature, see Fearon and Laitin (2000) and for a natural

Any group-level competition over economic resources or power could result in heightened attention to the attributes that define membership in a group since individual members of those groups can be affected by virtue of their group membership. Ethnicity, religion, or national origin are core attributes that define group identities that are often invoked to structure political conflict, including conflict between natives and immigrants. Large-scale cross-border immigration generates conflict by presenting a multi-dimensional threat to national identity. Although immigration can be beneficial by addressing labor market needs and forging new networks across societies, it can also challenge native social norms, force societies to adapt to rapid population change, and create fears of competition over scarce resources. Such competition can incite political conflict and mobilization into such conflict is easier when ethnic or religious differences divide natives and immigrants. Wars in Syria, Iraq, Libya, and Afghanistan have caused the largest refugee crisis since World War II, leading to a sharp rise in immigration from majority Muslim countries to Europe. These events are generating socio-demographic changes that play in the hands of populist politicians and many of the media discourses across Europe are increasingly emphasizing ethnic, religious, and cultural differences between immigrants and the majority population in host countries so as to mobilize public opinion against immigration.

A survey-based literature in political science has traditionally identified competition over resources (Hainmueller and Hopkins, 2014; Bansak, Hainmueller, and Hangartner, 2016) as one of the most important contextual factors driving native-immigrant conflict (Scheve and Slaughter, 2001; Mayda, 2006; Dancygier and Donnelly, 2013; Olzak, 1992; Hanson, Scheve, and Slaughter, 2007). However, the perception of cultural threats (Sniderman and Hagendoorn, 2007) emanating from the fear of a multicultural future (Sides and Citrin, 2007; Sniderman et al., 2002) is another, perhaps more important, dimension. Indeed, an emerging consensus in the literature on economic causes of anti-immigrant sentiment is that sociotropic factors influence natives' attitudes much more strongly than perceptions of how immigration is likely to affect individuals' own economic prospects (Alrababa'h et al., 2021). While early studies posited that individual self-interest drove attitudes

---

experiment from the Israeli-Palestinian conflict, see Shayo and Zussman (2011). Violence is not the only mechanism that can reify ethnic divisions. Even nonviolent forms of political competition can make group identities salient; see Michelitch (2015) and Eifert, Miguel, and Posner (2010).

(Mayda, 2006; Scheve and Slaughter, 2001; Dancygier and Donnelly, 2013; Malhotra, Margalit, and Mo, 2013), most recent research shows that concerns about the broader economic impact of immigration on a community exerts a stronger influence on anti-immigration attitudes than individual self-interest (Bansak, Hainmueller, and Hangartner, 2016; Hainmueller and Hopkins, 2014; Hainmueller and Hiscox, 2010; Adida, Lo, and Platas, 2019). This new thinking does not diminish the importance of economic considerations— such as concerns over the impact of immigration on the welfare system—but it is also consistent with the group-level, cultural factors as primary influences of anti-immigrant attitudes.

The idea that discrimination against immigrant populations is by and large a "cultural" phenomenon is no longer contested (Hainmueller and Hopkins, 2014, p. 231). The perceived "otherness" of immigrant groups can induce natives to develop prejudices and stereotypes that ultimately culminate in negative attitudes and predispositions toward immigrants, whom they consider to pose a physical threat (Wang, 2012; Nunziata, 2015) or sociotropic threat to their own group (Hainmueller and Hopkins, 2014, p. 232). Both recent immigrant groups and other minority populations of immigrant background are vulnerable to the consequences of this "othering" process.

This discussion highlights the fact that native-immigrant conflict is in large part due to the perception of identity threats arising from the social distance that separates natives from immigrants. To reduce parochialism in native-immigrant interactions, it is necessary to reduce the distance separating those groups, something that we argue can be achieved by demonstrating that natives and immigrants share a common set of norms and ideas that define appropriate civic behavior.

Dilemmas of Inclusion

Reducing distance between natives and immigrants involves politics; it involves granting immigrants rights and freedoms and providing them with opportunities to integrate in their new "host" societies. Paradoxically, it is precisely because of this process of democratic integration of immigrant groups in native societies that conflict arises. Although integration and polarization are in many ways opposite outcomes, they are the result of parallel processes that can feed off each other. The specific challenge facing liberal democratic societies is how to integrate minority populations, including immigrant "others" without, on the one hand, repressing their individuality and cultural heritage while, on the other hand, overcoming natives' tendencies toward parochialism. However, the more rights and opportunities are afforded to immigrant minorities, and the larger and more culturally distinct those groups are, the greater the identity threat felt by the native population and the more likely it is that polarization will occur.

The principle of equal representation of all sows the seeds of cultural conflict between majority and minority populations in democratic societies; but it also provides solutions. The risk of conflict lies in what economists sometimes call "heterogeneity costs" (Alesina and Spolaore, 2005; Spolaore, 2008; Esteban and Ray, 2011)—the material or psychic costs that arise when one has to share the state and its resources with individuals or groups whose beliefs and values are different from one's own. The solution, identified by democratic theorists is, on the one hand, to design political institutions that recognize differences while treating citizens as equals and, on the other hand, educate and encourage individuals to identify as citizens rather than as co-ethnics, co-religionists, or ingroup members of any subordinate social identity that weakens their attachment to the nation.[7]

However, in countries where the national identity is inextricably tied to the identity of a core group (Hechter, 2001; Mylonas, 2012), nationality is not inclusive and cannot serve as the foundation of reducing intergroup conflict as ethnic or other parochial identities will be stronger than the national identity for some groups, especially minorities. How to achieve pluralism is contested both in everyday politics and in scholarly debates. The difficulty consists of forging a system that recognizes the diversity of minority cultures without generating insurmountable obstacles for the majority or weakening individual self-identification with the state (Habermas, 1994, pp. 137–138).

The questions addressed in this book are connected to normative debates concerning the limits of political recognition of different cultures in democratic societies. These debates will go on forever and we cannot resolve them. Rather, we take as given that in the context of Europe's liberal democracies, some degree of accommodation of cultural difference must be assumed. Such

---

7. The word "nation" here is used to refer to the set of all people who share the same citizenship. National identification is often interpreted as synonymous to identification with a particular ethnic group. This reflects the reality that national identities in multiethnic countries are often thought to reflect the characteristics of the ethnic majority; and, consequently, ethnic majorities are more likely to identify nationally than ethnic minorities. Experimental evidence from the United States consistent with this pattern is provided by Devos and Banaji (2005).

accommodation will, over time, change the concept and the identity of the nation. Immigrant integration in liberal democracies sets in motion a process of acculturation—the mutual adaptation and cultural convergence of diverse groups—the pace of which is context-specific and will differ across countries. This process is never a one-way street; over time minority cultures will exert some degree of influence on the ideas, norms, and value systems of the majority. National identity, like *human* identity, is "dialogically" created as individuals interact with one another and redefine themselves in the process (Taylor, 1994). At any given point in time, this realization can generate anxiety for individuals whose group identities might be threatened by such a process of change.

Reflecting on this insight, Rafaela Dancygier's book *Dilemmas of Inclusion* opens by recounting the controversy surrounding the decision to use separate seating arrangements for men and women during a Labour Party campaign event in Birmingham leading up to the 2015 general elections in the United Kingdom. The gender-segregated seating plan was meant to induce support from Muslim voters. In this instance, the Labour Party had to face charges that its efforts to attract the Muslim vote challenged the party's commitment to gender equality (Dancygier, 2017, p. 1). Ideological differences with respect to gender roles and women's rights are one example of a broad range of concepts that define group identities and that will constitute key dimensions of social conflict between native and immigrant groups, or majority and minority cultures. Finding common ground—sharing norms and ideas about how these concepts are reflected in civic life—is centrally important in reducing native-immigrant conflict as immigrants are integrated in democratic societies.

A commitment to democratic egalitarianism in the dominant model of multiculturalism in Europe threatens to create a mosaic of identities and shared allegiances based on the principle of the preservation of cultural autonomy of migrant and other minority groups (Kymlicka, 1995). At the same time, the parallel processes of integration and globalization continually shift the boundaries of cultural identities (Benhabib, 2002). Accommodation of cultural differences in the context of large-scale immigration in democratic societies has the potential to impact deeply held local norms, forcing natives to come to terms with ideas and practices that might be antithetical to how they define their own social identities. This is particularly true in countries where there are efforts to reshape the preconditions for political legitimacy beyond the nation-state, where multiculturalism implies an effort to forge a type of "constitutional patriotism" whereby political legitimacy is based on a shared set of norms and values of citizenship rather than national, ethnic, or racial similarities (Mueller, 2007; Habermas, 1993). Cultural integration in this context implies the gradual fusion of ideas and practices of different cultural groups that comprise the (evolving) nation, which in turn leads to a re-conceptualization of national identity away from specific ethnic attachments and toward shared civic values and norms. The process of generating those shared norms, however, is likely to generate perceptions of cultural threat for social groups who believe that their core identities and interests come under attack by such change (Helbling and Traunmüller, 2018).[8]

These anxieties could well be connected to the underlying psychological mechanisms that explain natives' responses to large-scale immigration. Recent experimental studies have shown that people can have visceral reactions to exposure to foreign norms, which some have even likened to a foreign "pathogen" that can elicit disgust.[9] Yet, the consequences of cultural change are unlikely to be uniform across all social groups; cultural threats emanating from accommodating the value systems of newly arrived immigrant groups will affect specific subgroups of the native population differently. This suggests that opposition to immigration is likely to be felt more strongly in some segments of society than others. Therefore, to understand native-immigrant conflict, we must move away from the simplistic representation of natives as an "ingroup" that is opposed to an immigrant "outgroup" and consider how preexisting ideational differences and interest-based social cleavages within the native population will shape attitudes toward immigrants. Different types of threat are likely to be perceived by different groups of natives and the strategy to reducing native-immigrant conflict will have to target the group-specific sources of opposition to immigration.

Concepts

Before moving further in articulating our theory, we should clarify key concepts that are used throughout the book. Concepts such as "norms," "bias,"

8. This is because, in the words of Jürgen Habermas (1994, p. 140), "a change in the composition of the active citizenry changes the context to which the ethical-political self-understanding of the nation as a whole refers."

9. Karinen et al. (2019) explore the emotional response to exposure to unassimilated immigrants and present experimental evidence suggesting that "disgust sensitivity" is related to anti-immigrant sentiments when natives are exposed to immigrants who have not assimilated to local norms.

"discrimination," "integration," "assimilation," and "acculturation" do not have the same meaning for all readers, so we briefly define them here to help readers understand how our analysis and our findings fit with the broader literature.

We started this chapter by discussing parochialism and bias in human behavior. We see parochialism as deriving from the perception of social distance between groups. By "social distance" we mean the subjective perception of difference between any two individuals that is formed by objective differences in attributes, such as religion, race, nationality, or ethnicity that are used to classify individuals into groups. The concept of social distance has been codified in a psychological testing scale created by Emory S. Bogardus to empirically measure how willing people are to engage in social contacts of different form with different individuals, while varying the degree of closeness with members of different social groups (Bogardus, 1933). We use this concept in the next chapter to empirically measure social distance between German natives and immigrants.

Our main objective is to is consider ways to overcome social distance as a way to reduce intergroup conflict between natives and immigrants. Integration, acculturation, and assimilation are different processes that can narrow perceptions of social distance between immigrants and natives. Although these terms are sometimes used interchangeably in the literature, they mean different things.

We define acculturation as an individual or group-level process of mutual adaptation resulting from intergroup contact (Herskovits, 1958; Teske and Nelson, 1974). Although most authors treat this as a unidirectional process, it could take different forms depending on the power relations between groups that come into contact (Teske and Nelson, 1974, p. 355). Acculturation could refer to a two-way process of cultural adaptation and change, though it usually takes place in the direction of the dominant group and it involves a subordinate group acquiring one or more attributes that allow it to "fit in."

Change in value systems is not necessary during acculturation processes (Teske and Nelson, 1974, p. 356). Such change characterizes a process of assimilation, which should be seen as distinct from and not necessarily as the natural end-point of a process of acculturation. A classic definition of assimilation is that of a process that requires the "inter-penetration and fusion in which persons and groups acquire the memories, sentiments, and attitudes or other persons or groups; and, by sharing their experience and history, are incorporated with them in a common cultural life" (Park and Burgess, 1924, p. 735). Assimilation implies a change in an individual's or group's outward orientation; it requires outgroup acceptance (Teske and Nelson, 1974, p. 359) and shared identification with the outgroup. In other words, it requires "unity of thought" (Park and Burgess, 1924), and implies movement from one cultural group to another—it is a unidirectional process designed to approximate another culture (Teske and Nelson, 1974, p. 363).

By contrast, integration does not require the elimination of cultural differences that is implied in assimilative processes (Kymlicka, 1995). It is a shallower form of embeddedness that amounts to the provision of rights and opportunities to immigrants to participate in social and political life in exchange for their adherence to the principles of the "host" society's constitutional order.

Our discussion of social identification on the basis of shared norms and ideas is closer to classic definitions of the concept of assimilation—a form of identification that penetrates well beyond what integration requires.[10] However, the norms and ideas that we identify as crucial in shaping the sort of common identities that can overcome bias and discrimination do not require the complete (or repressive) cultural homogenization of minority groups and immigrants. In other words, what is required of immigrants is to demonstrate their willingness to become part of the political culture of their new homeland, which could be a principle of the sort of immigration policy that has traditionally been followed in the United States or Canada (Walzer, 2004). In fact, democratic inclusion is achievable without requiring the "compulsive assimilation" of immigrants (Habermas, 1994, p. 138). Shared cultural norms might come about in a number of ways: it could be the result of a two-way process of acculturation after long periods of contact and co-existence; it could reflect the assimilation of minority cultures to the dominant culture in their new home country; or it could be the result of identifying preexisting areas of agreement and overlap in the normative content of native and immigrant identities with respect to issues of common interest (in other words, the social distance separating these populations could be the result of misperceptions about normative differences).

Finally, we clarify that we use the concept of "norms" to refer to "standards of appropriate behavior for actors with a given identity" (Finnemore and Sikkink, 1998, p. 891), where the identity is that of *citizen*. In other words,

---

10. This concept of social identification rests on the emergence of a subjective sense of "we-ness or belongingness" that characterizes a "psychological group" rather than simply a "formal-institutional" concept of the group (Turner, 1982, p. 16).

we understand norms as behavioral rules that are shared within a society. The literature on norms is large and growing. Useful distinctions have been made between social and descriptive norms (Bicchieri, 2006), descriptive and injunctive norms (Cialdini, Reno, and Kallgren, 1990), regulative and constitutive norms (Finnemore and Sikkink, 1998) and other typologies have also been proposed. The norms that we focus on in this book have elements of both descriptive and injunctive norms;[11] they have power because they provide information on prevalent behavior in a given society and violations of the norm are likely to be met with disapproval. We refer to these as *social* or *civic* norms because they refer to behavior in the public sphere. The norms that we consider in this book could be characterized as *evaluative* or *prescriptive* as they define an inter-subjective understanding of which behaviors should be followed by others. They are evaluative because any deviation from the prescribed behavior is expected to generate sanctioning or disapproval by others, and that disapproval stems from the fact that the prescribed behavior is viewed as broadly consistent with prevalent values in society. In our empirical analysis, we consider norms that reflect an expectation that the majority will follow the prescribed behavior. Some of these norms can be general in the sense that one can reasonably expect everyone in a given society to care about these norms and to abide by them; but they can also be norms that are felt more strongly among members of a specific social group (we call these norms "group-derived") and these norms prescribe behavior that is considered appropriate by most members of that group.

Overcoming the Native-Immigrant Divide

The dominant picture that emerges from a large literature on social identity (Tajfel, 1981), prejudice (Allport, 1954; Paluck and Green, 2009), and ethnocentrism (Kinder and Kam, 2010) is that natives' sentiments toward immigrants will be a manifestation of natives' ingroup identity, and of the extent to which immigrant groups are perceived to be "distant" and threatening to that

---

11. Descriptive norms are usually understood as norms that describe what most people would do in a given situation; they suggest what is typical behavior in that situation. Injunctive norms describe conduct that is morally approved (or not); so they are useful because they dictate what should be done in a given situation so as to avoid social sanctioning or disapproval (Cialdini, Reno, and Kallgren, 1990). In other influential works in this literature (Bicchieri, 2006, p. 63), injunctive norms are called "social" norms.

identity (Schildkraut, 2010; Hainmueller and Hopkins, 2015; Maxwell, 2017). Sources of anti-immigrant discrimination are often traced to the perceptions of threat experienced by native populations as they come into contact with immigrants who deviate from prototypical conceptions of what members of their ingroup should be (Mummendey and Wenzel, 1999; Kauff et al., 2015; Stephan and Stephan, 2000).

What types of cultural differences shape natives' perceptions of social distance from immigrants, and how can that distance be overcome? It is now established that ethno-linguistic, racial, and religious differences can all contribute to ethnocentrism, prejudice, and discrimination under some conditions (Adida, Laitin, and Valfort, 2010; Choi, Poertner, and Sambanis, 2019; Gluszek and Dovidio, 2010).

Much less is known about the power of norms and ideas to shape perceptions of social distance. After all, what do we mean when we say that we share an identity if not that we share the same understanding of what that identity implies and what behaviors are consistent with it? Beyond phenotypical and other "classificatory" ascriptive differences that place natives and immigrants in different groups, it is ideas and norms that will inform natives' perceptions of the type of cultural threat generated by immigrants. There is often an assumption—implicit or explicit—that immigrants *are* different in ways that fundamentally challenge natives' core values and identities. These perceptions shape the social distance that separates natives and immigrants and our book explores whether that distance can be reduced if it is established that natives and immigrants share a common set of ideas and norms about civic behavior.

When previous studies have considered within-group differences in the native population with regard to their attitudes toward immigration, the focus has usually been on economic differences (such as sectoral differences or employment status) or partisanship (Scheve and Slaughter, 2001; Mayda, 2006). Differences emanating from conflicting ideas and non-material interests tied to social identities have not been systematically explored as a source of bias. Our use of the concept of "interest" is broader than the standard view of interest limited to monetary or other material rewards that could motivate individual action. Rather, we use this term to refer to individual preferences over outcomes that would benefit a group's welfare and relative social standing. In other words, while "interests" could certainly take material factors into account, they also include concerns over others' welfare and about the status of one's own group. We assume that individual interests are partly defined by group identities, as in the constructivist literature in international relations (Wendt, 1999; Finnemore and Sikkink, 1998) and comparative politics (Horowitz, 1985; Chandra and Wilkinson, 2008). Any ideas that are important in shaping the content of social identities can therefore also shape interests as individuals understand their own self-interest partly via the lens of the groups to which they belong.

Forging a New Common Ingroup Identity

As outlined in the introductory chapter, our theory draws on the insights of social identity theory (SIT) and self-categorization theory (SCT), which have argued that human beings derive part of their worth and self-esteem from the groups they belong to (Tajfel, 1981; Turner et al., 1987). Group boundaries are often arbitrary or formed as a result of processes that individuals do not control or understand, yet they are often used to help people develop a sense of who *they* are and who *others* are (Kinder and Kam, 2010, p. 20). The more distant individuals perceive outgroups to themselves, the less likely they are to identify with them and the more biased they will be against them. Similarly, individuals will want to minimize the distance between themselves and a group with which they identify. These insights reflect the fact that distance is socially constructed and it can be redefined to induce conflict or cooperation between groups. This simple but powerful idea has been developed into the influential theory of the Common Ingroup Identity Model (CIIM) by Gaertner and Dovidio (2000).

The core idea behind CIIM is deceptively simple: to reduce intergroup conflict, individuals must shift their attention away from the attributes that divide them into competing groups and focus instead on attributes that unite them into a superordinate identity group. This essentially involves a cognitive shift akin to a reclassification exercise whereby an individual starts seeing outgroup members as ingroup members. Building on Allport's research, Gaertner et al. (1996) posited that intergroup contact can produce such a cognitive shift if it is structured in a way that it "transforms" an individual's representation of the aggregate from two separate groups (us and them) into one inclusive superordinate group (Hornsey and Hogg, 2000).

How feasible is it that such a cognitive shift that emphasizes a shared superordinate identity can occur as a result of spontaneous intergroup interactions in the real world; and could this cognitive shift be sufficient to produce even transient benefits in terms of reduced outgroup discrimination? This is a question that we explore empirically later in the book. There is ample empirical evidence in support of CIIM in previous studies and all of those studies draw on an unstated premise of CIIM, which is that the behavioral effects of cognitive recategorization are a function of the prior strength of the common, superordinate identity that can potentially unify ingroup and outgroup members. Without a *strong* preexisting common identity to fall back on, any shift in social identification will be shallow. This insight is often implicit in studies of nation-building as a strategy to reduce conflict among ethnic, religious, regional, or other subordinate groups by inducing loyalty to the idea of the nation (Ricke et al., 2010; Charnysh, Lucas, and Singh, 2015; Levendusky, 2018; Wimmer, 2018; Mylonas, 2013). While it is often not discussed explicitly, most successful nation-building interventions rely on a reservoir of preexisting affinity among individuals who can be unified into a nation.[12] If a precondition for CIIM is that a shared identity already exists, and that it is "available" to all and readily accessible, then how could the logic of the CIIM be used to reduce native-immigrant conflict? Indeed, native-immigrant conflict might appear hard to overcome precisely because these groups believe that they do not share a common superordinate identity that they can fall back on.

The idea that affective interpersonal ties are the foundation of common identities brings to mind an earlier debate between social identity theorists and proponents of the "social cohesion model," according to which group togetherness rests on preexisting affective ties among group members (Turner, 1982, p. 16). Social identity theory was developed in conversation with the social cohesion model and moved away from emphasizing affective processes so as to highlight cognitive processes as the foundation of group identification. A wave of research in the 1970s and 1980s aimed to show that affective ties were not necessary for group identification and that "categorization [is] more important than similarity in determining group formation" (Turner, 1982, p. 23). In several experiments, psychologists found that perceived interpersonal similarity between group members is not a necessary condition for group

---

12. An example of such a historical process that is viewed from the lens of a formal model of nation-building informed by the logic of the CIIM is Sambanis, Skaperdas, and Wolforth (2015) who analyze the process of German unification after the Franco-Prussian War; and Paci, Sambanis, and Wolforth (2020) who provide a similar analysis of the process of Italian unification. In both cases, leaders were able to strategically manipulate political developments to induce nationalism by tapping into preexisting identities among the population. By contrast, attempts to induce nation-building in countries emerging from civil war where national identities were either non-existent or exclusionary are bound to fail (see Russell and Sambanis () for a model with application to ethnic conflicts in Iraq, Libya, and Afghanistan).

identification nor is it the case that group similarity is a stronger predictor of intergroup discrimination than is social categorization.[13]

Social cohesion theory was essentially interpreted as suggesting that *interpersonal* rather than *intergroup* attraction was required for social identification and such attraction was determined by perceived similarity to ingroup vs. outgroup members (Lott and Lott, 1965). A key hypothesis in social identity theory is that "awareness of common category membership is the necessary and sufficient condition for individuals to understand how social groups are formed" (Turner, 1982, p. 27) and a hypothesis to emerge from that theory is that perceived similarity to other ingroup members is in fact a consequence of categorization.[14] That said, early experimental research showed that individuals do tend to favor others who are similar to themselves more than dissimilar others when the more similar others are perceived as ingroup members (Turner, 1982) and similarity in beliefs or opinions increases identification with an ingroup and discrimination toward outgroups (Allen and Wilder, 1975; Sole, Marton, and Hornstein, 1975).

Our theoretical advance over CIIM echoes earlier arguments about the importance of *belief similarity* for social cohesion (Rokeach and Mezei, 1966). However, unlike previous literature, in our theory, those beliefs are not defined at the interpersonal level; rather, they reflect the internalization of norms and ideas that define specific group identities. Choosing the appropriate action in a given social situation depends on a system of cognitive self-schemata that process information to forge representations of those social situations. These schemata are shaped by individuals' social and personal identities. Social identities help individuals decide how they should behave in a given social situation in light of their group membership, whereas individual traits and preferences also affect behavior (i.e., personal identities interact with social identities). In contexts where group identities are made salient (as in the experiments that we present in the empirical section of this book), group identities might exert a stronger influence on behavior than personal identities. We argue that a strategy to overcome native-immigrant bias can be based on

13. See Turner (1982, p. 23); see also Billig and Tajfel (1973) and Brewer and Silver (1973).

14. According to Turner (p. 26), social identification can create social cohesion as a result of categorizing others as members of the same group because, when group membership is made salient, individuals stereotype themselves and others in terms of core "evaluative or normative attributes" of each group's attributes. It is therefore implied that the individuals who are categorized as members of the same group must share the same evaluative or normative attributes, which makes ingroup members more similar to each other than outgroup members.

forging a new common ingroup identity—*the identity of citizen*—based on a shared understanding of norms and ideas that define appropriate civic behavior. Echoing results from social cohesion theory, we believe that sharing attributes such as skin color, language, or religion is not enough to forge interpersonal closeness or to recategorize outgroup members as ingroup members. Such recategorization must also be based on sharing the norms and ideas that define the group. In other words, it is the *shared content* of social identities that gives them the power to shape individual behavior.

This last point speaks to a large literature on the differences between "passing" and "becoming," or acculturation and assimilation. Within studies of immigration, one often sees marked attitudinal differences between those who believe that one is *born with* the native identity compared to those who believe that one *becomes* native, echoing the debate between primordialists and constructivists in the literature on ethnicity and identity. What is not up for debate is that the meaning of native identity is shared among all those who can claim it. At issue is whether one needs an innate understanding of the norms, ideas, and values that define native (or other ingroup) identities, or whether such an understanding can be acquired. The empirical analysis presented later in this book is designed to allow for a direct test of the idea that ascriptive differences that most view as defining a cleavage between natives and immigrants can be overcome if it can be established that natives and immigrants share norms and ideas that define good citizenship in a given social context. Those norms reduce bias and increase cooperation by reducing social distance. By contrast, much of the literature on identity has focused on how bias and discrimination can change as group boundaries change via intermarriage, assimilation, or "passing." We instead explore the idea that bias can be overcome without changing boundaries defined by ascriptive characteristics; we test whether native-immigrant conflict can be mitigated without pursuing assimilationist strategies that are designed to eliminate cultural difference and homogenize the population. In other words, we argue that conflict reduction need not be premised on the repression of ascriptive differences and it could instead be based on the idea of *shared citizenship*.

Norms and Intergroup Conflict

What kinds of norms and ideas can be used to define a common identity among natives and immigrants? The answer partly depends on which identities are made salient in the context of specific intergroup interactions. When national identities are salient, then adherence to *general* norms that define the identity of citizen could help reduce social distance between natives and immigrants. When subgroup identities are salient, then *group-derived* norms that define subgroup identities can help forge a new common identity among those natives and immigrants who share the qualifying attributes of that identity group. The overall effect of the norm on behavior will depend on how deeply shared the norm is in the population and how central it is for the corresponding identity that it helps define.[15]

Both general and group-derived norms are *descriptive social norms*, which are defined as "collective behaviors that depend on expectations about what others do or expect one to do in a similar situation" (Bicchieri, 2017, p. 18). Beyond adhering to such norms, an individual's decision of whether or not to become a norm enforcer can itself be seen as a social norm that reflects how strongly internalized the descriptive norm is in a given society as a habit, a custom, or a moral injunction. We are concerned mainly with what behavioral theorists call *social norms*—behaviors that reveal individuals' social preferences and are conditioned by expectations of how others behave in similar situations (Bicchieri, 2017, pp. 7–8). Adhering to a social norm reveals information about an individual's *reference network*—the group of people whose opinion the individual cares about.[16] Thus, enforcing a social norm that is deeply valued by an identity group serves as a signal of an individual's degree of similarity with (or assimilation to) the group.

We build on this conceptual foundation in the empirical section of the book, where we set up experimental microenvironments that are designed to manipulate the impression that immigrants and natives share valued social norms and we analyze how this affects natives' behavior toward immigrants. We focus on two social norms—a general civic norm against littering in public spaces and a group-derived norm of supporting gender equality (which we assume is internalized more strongly by women). By definition, general norms are less contested than group-derived norms, but also more diffuse and they do not speak to the core of natives' own parochial identities and attachments. Our prior expectation is that group-derived norms would be

15. It follows that uncertainty about the extent to which a norm is shared among the majority, or multiple hierarchies of norms with conflicting behavioral prescriptions, will complicate any effort to promote intergroup cooperation.

16. Bicchieri (2017, p. 35) writes that "a social norm is a rule of behavior such that individuals prefer to conform to it on condition that they believe that (a) most people in their reference network conform to it (empirical expectation), and (b) that most people in their reference network believe they ought to conform to it (normative expectation)."

more strongly shared by the group whose core interests and identity are directly affected by norm adherence—so in the case of norms regarding gender equality, women would be more likely to feel strongly about norms regarding gender equality. In separate field experiments, we manipulate injunctive norms against littering in public spaces and normative beliefs about gender roles and we orchestrate mini-performances in public during which immigrants appear as norm enforcers, thereby signaling their shared identity with the intended audience of native bystanders. We then observe whether bystanders who observe immigrants' adherence to valued social norms change their behavior toward those immigrants.

Norm Adherence as a Moderator of Intergroup Difference

Immigrants' ascriptive attributes (race, ethnicity, religion) are often visible and readily accessible cues that native populations use to quickly establish an individual immigrant to be a member of an outgroup. These attributes can generate bias in line with the predictions of social categorization theory. When they categorize an individual as a member of an outgroup, natives project onto that individual what they perceive to be the defining characteristics of that group—in other words, they think in stereotypes. Doing so tends to minimize intragroup differences while maximizing intergroup differences.

However, perceptions of differences between natives and immigrants can be *moderated* (Joffe and Staerklé, 2007) by stereotype-*defying* behavior if native bias derives from beliefs that immigrants do not share the same norms and ideas that define native identity. An array of civic norms (such as paying your taxes; sending children to school; not littering in public) define the boundaries of appropriate social behavior. This book analyzes how anti-immigrant bias changes as natives observe immigrants' adherence to those valued social norms.

A large literature in social and cognitive psychology has pointed out the strong effects of receiving information that is inconsistent with existing stereotypes (Hastie and Kumar, 1979; Srull, 1981; Srull, Lichtenstein, and Rothbart, 1985; Rojahn and Pettigrew, 1992). Stereotype-conforming (SC) behavior exhibited by immigrants has little informational value and is hence unlikely to change the course of how natives treat immigrants. On the other hand, stereotype-defying (SD) behavior that counters expectations of how a typical minority group member should behave is likely to be clearly noticeable and salient, possibly leading to updating of beliefs and changing behavior toward immigrants. These dynamics create fertile ground for natives to re-evaluate whether they should withhold the typical stereotypes or prejudices that they would otherwise apply to immigrant group members.

If anti-immigrant bias derives from natives' beliefs that immigrants are culturally different and, therefore, threatening to their identity, then natives will ascribe to immigrants stereotypes that violate prevalent social norms. If immigrants demonstrate that they actually share these norms and behave in a way that upholds them, this will constitute an example of stereotype-defying behavior that can moderate bias. Many different signals of cultural integration could be a potent form of stereotype-defying behavior that shape host population attitudes toward immigrants (Faist, 1994; Hopkins, 2014a). Yet the strongest effects should be observed when an individual immigrant's behavior runs counter to outgroup stereotypes vis-à-vis *core dimensions* of native identity.[17]

Drawing on a large literature on native-immigrant conflict, we identify several types of assimilative and integrative behaviors that can challenge native stereotypes about immigrants:

- *Linguistic assimilation.* Language has long been considered integral to how ethno-national identity is created and defined across the world (Gumperz, 1982; Faist, 1994; Phinney et al., 2001; Deutsch, 1953; Gellner, 1983). The willingness of the immigrant to abandon what is one of the defining characteristics of their own identity and instead communicate using the natives' language signals their resolve to integrate into the host society.[18] Natives understand that the adoption of their language is a conscious and deliberate choice on the part of the immigrant, one that requires significant investments of time and effort to acquire, but also benefits in the form of improved economic prospects and opportunities. Thus, language acquisition may help natives evaluate immigrants who speak their language to be "less different" from them than a "typical" member of the immigrant group.

17. One question that we consider closely in chapter 7 is whether stereotype-defying behavior leads natives to withhold the application of the stereotype to their evaluation of the individual immigrant only, or whether they discredit or discard the group stereotype itself (Hilton and Von Hippel, 1996).

18. Learning the native language has been singled out as a central mechanism of assimilation (Hopkins, 2014a). In the United States, studies report negative attitudes toward people using Spanish, and Gluszek and Dovidio (2010) review evidence from decades of research showing that natives perceive people who speak with non-native accents negatively.

- *Religious assimilation.* Much of the backlash against immigration in Europe is directed against Muslims, who are perceived as culturally different from the majority Christian population. Several ideological positions in interpretations of Islam, such as positions with respect to marriage, family life, or gender roles, are perceived to be antithetical to values held by the majority of the native population in Western liberal democracies. Any visible symbol of Muslim faith is likely to make these ideological differences cognitively salient, thereby increasing social distance. By contrast, suppressing such symbols makes it less likely that natives who interact with immigrants ascribe to those immigrants the negative stereotypes that they hold vis-à-vis the religious outgroup.
- *Norm-sharing.* Expectations of appropriate behavior are based on shared ideas about individual and group rights and responsibilities that reflect value systems of the native population or large segments of that population. Sharing those norms should reduce the perception of identity threat among natives, leading to lower discrimination toward immigrants. Shared norms forge a common identity among natives and immigrants who share other attributes in common and are therefore nominally members of the same ingroup. Those attributes can be used to define multiple social groups (e.g., gender; class; professional occupation) each of which could have its own valued set of norms. Abiding by those norms or actively enforcing them should be emblematic of identification with the group and should reduce intragroup social distance.

Hypotheses & Mechanisms

The preceding discussion motivates several hypotheses concerning the determinants of discrimination against immigrants and ways to reduce discrimination. The unifying theme in the individual hypotheses that we present below is that we expect discrimination to increase as social distance between natives and immigrants increases; and discrimination should decrease as distance decreases. Any intergroup differences on the basis of ascriptive traits such as race, ethnicity, or religion can create social distance leading to discrimination toward immigrants. Yet discrimination can be offset and social distance minimized when immigrants signal that they share norms and ideas that are deeply valued among natives. The core hypotheses that we test empirically in chapters 3–7 are outlined below, followed by a discussion of causal mechanisms.

Hypotheses

OUTGROUP DISCRIMINATION

Native are more likely to discriminate against immigrants whom they perceive as socially distant due to ethnic, racial, linguistic, or religious differences.

DIFFERENTIAL DISCRIMINATION

Natives are likely to discriminate relatively more against immigrants whom they perceive to be more socially distant than immigrants whom they perceive to be less distant from natives.

MODERATING EFFECTS OF SHARED NORMS

Natives are likely to discriminate less toward immigrants whose behavior suggests that they share the natives' social norms.

MODERATING EFFECTS OF SHARED IDEAS

Natives who share with immigrants the attributes of a common ingroup will discriminate less toward those immigrants only if immigrants' behavior suggests that they also share the core ideas and interests that define the common ingroup's identity.

Mechanisms

Out of the four main hypotheses articulated above, the last two are hypotheses about mechanisms of conflict reduction: sharing norms and ideas is *how* native discrimination toward immigrants can be offset. We can go further to explore the implications of norm-adhering behavior by immigrants and analyze how such behavior is perceived among natives. Specifically, how should we interpret the "boost" in helping behavior that we expect to observe when immigrants adhere to valued local norms? Does this reduction in discrimination suggest a reduction in prejudice toward the immigrant outgroup? Or is increased help a reward to an individual whose behavior is drawing attention away from the fact that she may be an immigrant (i.e., does norm-adhering behavior make observers see that person as an individual rather than as a member of her group)? Drawing directly on a typology of mechanisms introduced in the CIIM (Dovidio et al., 2010), we can distinguish between three distinct mechanisms that could explain behavioral change toward norm-abiding immigrants:

Decategorization requires de-emphasizing the group-level attributes of an individual: outgroup members are seen as unique individuals or exceptions whose personal qualities need not apply to the rest of the outgroup.

Recategorization occurs as a result of a cognitive shift whereby an outgroup member is seen as part of a common ingroup: the boundaries between ingroup and outgroup are redefined or expanded.

Mutual differentiation implies a re-weighting of the importance one attaches to the attributes that define the outgroup and that differentiate it from the ingroup: differences persist, but they become less salient and do not influence behavior toward the outgroup.

All three mechanisms could lead to a reduction in discrimination, so there is observational equivalence among them with respect to *behavior,* though there are differences with respect to the durability of *attitudes* toward the outgroup.

An important point worth re-emphasizing is that group boundaries are *preserved* in the CIIM; contact merely makes them less salient relative to the superordinate identity. It is precisely because subordinate identities are preserved that positive attitudes due to intergroup interaction can be extended to the outgroup as a whole rather than only to specific individuals who are directly involved in these interactions (Hornsey and Hogg, 2000, p. 244). This insight explains why the mechanism of recategorization is consistent with the concept of multiculturalism, which is a principle designed to respect group boundaries unlike assimilationist policies which are designed to erase those boundaries.[19] An implication of CIIM is that, if group boundaries between natives and immigrants were to be erased, then positive effects could only be extended to others on an *interpersonal* rather than *intergroup* basis.

The focus on the psychology of group attachments is pertinent to any discussion of immigration because attitudes toward immigration are "group-centric" (Nelson and Kinder, 1996). Attitudes and behavior toward individual immigrants typically follow from attitudes held about immigrants as a group.

---

19. More accurately, assimilation preserves the boundary, but induces the minority to become one with the majority, thereby practical manifestations of the boundary cannot be observed.

This implies that the mechanism of *decategorization* is likely to have relatively shallow impact on natives and group-level *attitudes* might be hard to change on the basis of observing individual immigrants behaving in a way that is consistent with native norms. Hewstone and Brown (1986) have shown that group salience does not change due to increased positive contact with an outgroup unless the interaction partners are seen as fairly typical representatives of their outgroup. Thus, if norm-abiding immigrants are seen as exceptions, this should not affect native attitudes toward immigrants even if discrimination toward *specific* immigrants is reduced.

By contrast, *mutual differentiation* should have larger effects in reducing hostile attitudes toward immigrants as a group if norm adherence is no longer seen as a behavior that is typical *only* among natives. While adhering to valued social norms does not erase intergroup differences in ascriptive traits, the symbolic meaning with which these traits are imbued changes and ascriptive differences can cease to be threatening for natives. When immigrants' behavior with respect to valued norms and ideas that define native identity is uncorrelated with the expression of traits that separate them from the native community, those ascriptive traits will seem superficial and need not influence how immigrants are perceived by natives.[20] This mechanism has been explored in previous literature as part of the Mutual Ingroup Differentiation Model (MIDM) (Hewstone, 1996; Hewstone and Brown, 1986), which generates somewhat different empirical predictions than the CIIM.[21] For our purposes, the key difference between these theories is the emphasis they place on the relative salience of subordinate (immigrant, native) vs. superordinate identities (nationality, citizenship). Our focus is to explore whether immigrants' adherence to valued social norms induces natives to think that there is *interpersonal* or *intergroup* belief similarity between them and immigrants.

A key idea we want to explore by highlighting these three mechanisms is whether norm-sharing can serve as a way to forge a common superordinate identity—that of citizen—while retaining the subordinate (ethnic, religious, regional) identities that are so important for the cultural preservation of group identities, consistent with the concept of multiculturalism. We thus seek to establish whether observing *belief similarity* between natives and immigrants in

---

20. However, if natives place intrinsic value in the ascriptive traits themselves (as some groups such as white supremacists are known to do), then norm adherence and shared ideas will have small or no effect on native attitudes toward immigrants.

21. For an empirical comparison of CIIM and MIDM, see Hornsey and Hogg (2000).

everyday interactions serves to de-emphasize differences in group attributes in ways that could reduce intergroup bias. At the same time, we acknowledge that the way to forge this new, common ingroup identity is to share norms and ideas that define core native values, which may be seen as imposing a constraint on multiculturalism.

Having identified these distinct mechanisms of conflict reduction, we can now turn to our empirical analysis, which consists of identifying causes of bias and discrimination among natives toward Muslim immigrants and testing the effectiveness of different interventions designed to reduce the perceived social distance dividing those groups. We explore several experiments designed to test whether adherence to valued social norms and *belief similarity* between natives and immigrants can overcome the social distance created by differences in their ascriptive characteristics. We analyze examples of both general and group-derived norms and test their power to overcome bias in everyday interactions between natives and immigrants, concluding our analysis with an explicit test of the mechanisms discussed above.

3

Measuring Bias and Discrimination

WESTERN LIBERAL DEMOCRACIES are seeing a surge of anti-immigrant bias. In several European countries, popular resistance to immigration and other consequences of globalization have benefited right-wing extremist parties whose electoral support has surged as migration from the Middle East, South Asia, and Sub-Saharan Africa into Europe has risen. Yet anti-immigrant sentiment is not restricted to supporters of extremist parties. What are the causes of opposition to immigration? In this chapter, we document the extent of anti-immigrant bias in Germany and explore whether negative attitudes translate into discriminatory behavior. This sets the stage for an analysis of how to overcome anti-immigrant bias among the native population in later chapters.

Throughout this book we explore sources of anti-immigrant bias among natives and the words "natives" and "immigrants" need to be defined before we proceed further. "Natives" are defined as people of Germanic heritage rather than simply those born in Germany. This is consistent with the popular notion of "*bio-Deutsch*" (biologically German) that is prevalent in Germany and also reflects the ethnic basis of German national identity. In surveys of natives' attitudes that we present later in this chapter, we drew on samples of pre-screened adult Germans whose parents were also born in Germany, thus excluding second-generation immigrants from other countries to get at the ethnic basis of native identity.

"Immigrants," for the purpose of our analysis, refers to persons with national origin other than Germany and those whose parents are not ethnic Germans. We focus on first- and second-generation immigrants from Muslim-majority countries from the Middle East and North Africa, which is the source of most immigration to Germany in recent years. Our use of the term immigrant also captures persons of immigrant background, including second-generation immigrant minorities. Although defining immigrants this way might seem ambiguous in some country contexts, such as the United States, where most of the population is of immigrant origin, the distinction is not controversial for the majority of the German population. This becomes evident later in the chapter when we show evidence that the majority of respondents to our surveys use small differences in physical traits to correctly identify natives and immigrant confederates who participated in our research. Phenotypical differences among the confederates and deviations from characteristics that are considered "typical" in Germany are sufficient for survey respondents to accurately categorize confederates as immigrant confederates as compared to natives.[1]

In some ways, the distinction between natives and immigrants is one about cultural difference. Thus, citizens of immigrant background who have assimilated to the cultural identity of the majority should be indistinguishable from natives—indeed, they have *become* native. For now, however, the distinction we draw between these two populations is centered simply on observable differences in ethnic or religious attributes that signal differences in national origin. These visible differences provide cues that could create the perception of social distance separating *typical* members of each group. Using visible attributes to signify group membership is consistent with how ethnicity has been defined and measured in previous literature (Chandra, 2006). Differences in ethnic attributes serve as cognitive shortcuts that inform experimental subjects of the group membership of our confederates and we use these shortcuts to make group identities cognitively salient so we can test whether (and which) differences in ethnic attributes motivate bias and discrimination. Later in the book, we compare the effects of differences in ascriptive characteristics to the behavioral effects of norm adherence.

Finally, "bias" and "discrimination" are two outcomes that we discuss extensively in this book. Bias is broadly defined as prejudice against or preference in favor of a person or group. Discrimination is a behavioral consequence of bias—it is the prejudicial treatment of different categories of individuals or groups, especially on the grounds of race, ethnicity, religion, or gender.

---

1. The term "confederates" is also used extensively throughout the book. It refers to research assistants who participated in various capacities in our research. We hired and trained fifty-two students from German universities to participate in our experiments. They were all undergraduate or graduate students from diverse ethnic and religious backgrounds.

Attitudes

Anti-immigrant bias is a common finding in studies of immigration. Public opinion surveys across European countries have repeatedly documented that there is broad-based opposition to immigration, reflected in negative stereotypes about immigrants. In the Netherlands, long considered one of the most progressive societies in Europe with respect to multiculturalism, Sniderman and Hagendoorn documented prevalent negative stereotypes of immigrants from the global south as "dishonest, not law-abiding, intrusive slackers" regardless of their national origin. Negative evaluations of immigrants are also prevalent and indiscriminate with respect to nation of origin in Italy (Sniderman and Hagendoorn, 2007, pp. 54–56) reflecting widespread prejudice as a key driving force underlying opposition to immigration. Anti-immigrant sentiment goes hand-in-hand with growing opposition to globalization. In Greece, a country whose easily accessible sea borders have resulted in heavy exposure to immigration influx, immigration and globalization are seen by many as parallel processes that threaten the national identity and more than half of the population says that immigration makes them "feel like a stranger in their own country."[2] In Hungary, fears of a "Muslim invasion" have led the government to criminalize the provision of any help to undocumented migrants and refugees.[3] As we show below, these expressions of anti-immigrant bias are rooted in deep-seated identity threat felt by natives who are faced with the prospect of a rapidly changing society.

It Doesn't Feel Like Home Anymore

What multiple surveys across European countries reflect is that large-scale immigration threatens individual national identities. A recent cross-country survey of European countries conducted by the survey firm YouGov found that a large percentage of the population (up to almost 50% in some countries) admit that their country "does not feel like home anymore" due to large waves of immigration. What is striking is that a large percentage of survey

---

2. See results of a public opinion poll based on a representative sample of the Greek population: https://www.moreincommon.com/media/ltinlcnc/0535-more-in-common-greece-report_final-4_web_lr.pdf.

3. See "Hungary passes anti-immigrant 'Stop Soros' laws," *Guardian*; https://www.theguardian.com / world / 2018 / jun / 20 / hungary-passes-anti-immigrant-stop-soros-laws (accessed 4/4/2020).

The most anti–immigrant countries in Europe

There are so many foreigners living here, it doesn't feel like home anymore (% agreeing).

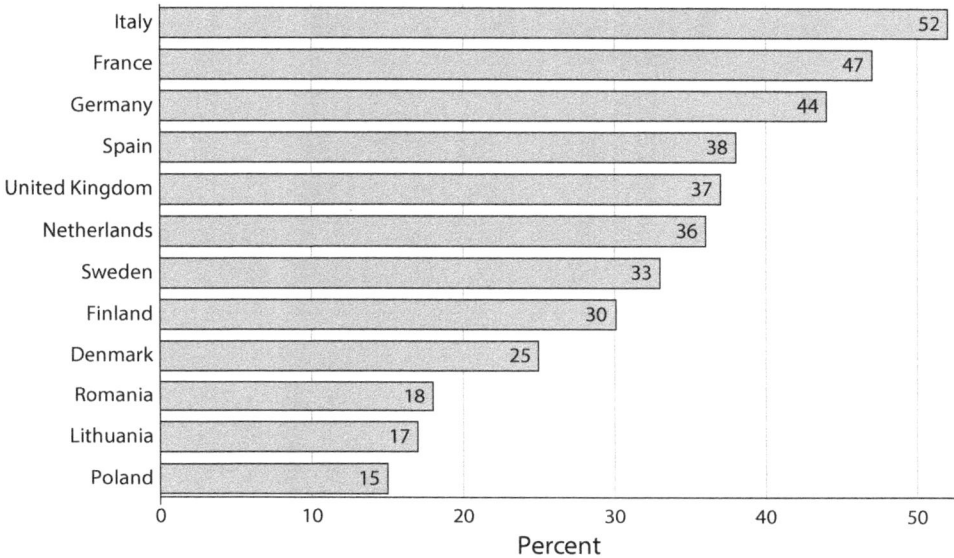

FIGURE 3.1. Respondents claiming their country doesn't feel like home
Data Source: YouGov 12-Nation Authoritarian Populism Study, 2016.

respondents, who are usually reluctant to express negative opinions freely due to fears of being labeled racist or xenophobic, openly admit their uneasiness with the consequences of immigration. The real extent of opposition to immigrantion is likely much larger.

Why do European countries not feel like home anymore to these people? Is it that ethno-racial or religious differences somehow threaten Europeans' national identity? Or are people reacting to "realistic" fears that immigration will have negative consequences for their lives? What are some of those fears? Exploring this question in a survey of 1400 adult Germans during the summer of 2019,[4] we asked respondents questions designed to reveal the extent to which they perceive immigrants as a security risk or an economic burden and

4. We implemented this survey via Qualtrics Panels, a preassembled online panel of survey respondents recruited and maintained by survey platform Qualtrics. The online panels are not nationally representative by design, but in order to move closer to the sample that is comparable to that of our field experiments, we implemented gender and state quotas calculated based

Q: Immigrants in Germany are/should...

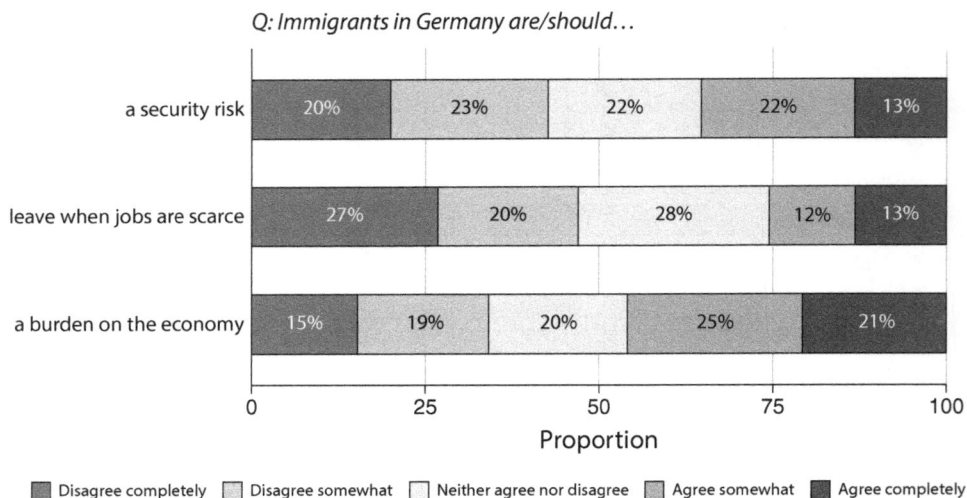

FIGURE 3.2. Perception of immigrants among German natives
Data Source: Authors' survey of German adult citizens, 2018.

found evidence for both of these explanations as drivers of anti-immigrant attitudes. We read respondents' statements such as "Foreigners should go home when jobs get scarce" and asked them how strongly they agreed or disagreed with those statements. Figure 3.2 presents the results. About 35% of respondents agree that immigrants in Germany pose a security threat and an even larger percentage (46%) see them as a burden on the economy with a quarter of all respondents stating that immigrants should leave the country when jobs are scarce.

In most survey-based studies such as this one, economic and cultural factors are treated as independent determinants of natives' attitudes toward immigrants. In reality, however, whether immigration is seen as an economic problem is likely shaped by natives' biases against immigrants from countries that natives view as culturally different from their own. That cultural distance creates anxiety that could make natives more likely to see immigrants and refugees as an economic burden.[5] It is difficult to disentangle

on census information. In addition, there is increasing evidence that the demographic profile of respondents drawn from online platforms are not significantly different from nationally representative probability samples. See Berinsky, Huber, and Lenz (2012) for a discussion.

5. The same dynamic has been observed in other countries, including the United States, where anxiety created by the economic costs of immigration is greater in public opinion

economic motives from cultural or identity-based motives in observational data analyses.

Measuring Anti-immigrant Attitudes in Germany

Next, we look closer at the underlying causes of anti-immigrant bias using data from an experiment that allows us to identify the types of attributes (e.g., nationality, religion, ethnicity) that are more strongly associated with anti-immigrant attitudes while isolating the effect of such causes from economic or other motives for anti-immigrant bias.

Discrete Choice Experiment

To document the source of anti-immigrant attitudes among German natives, we implemented a survey-based discrete choice experiment (Hainmueller, Hopkins, and Yamamoto, 2013). With a rich history in business marketing research, discrete choice experiments enable researchers to simultaneously examine the causal effects of multiple causal factors in the framework of a single experiment. This is particularly useful for our purposes, since immigrants and immigrant communities in Western Europe vary significantly in terms of their country of origin, level of education, occupation, and language proficiency, as well as their religious affiliation; factors that may structure native anti-immigrant attitudes to varying degrees. Indeed, earlier work on anti-immigrant bias has capitalized on this attractive quality, and has used conjoint experiments extensively to examine the issue of immigration (Hainmueller and Hopkins, 2015; Bansak, Hainmueller, and Hangartner, 2016).

In a typical discrete choice experimental setup, two randomly generated hypothetical profiles of individuals who vary in their characteristics or attributes are presented side-by-side in the context of the survey. After survey respondents view each profile pair, they are asked to identify which of the two profiles they prefer with regard to a particular decision task. The respondent is then invited to repeat the same evaluation task across multiple profile pairings.

A key difference between existing choice-based research on immigration and our approach is the nature of the decision (evaluation) task. Immigration scholars have traditionally presented survey respondents with profiles of two immigrants that vary on their attributes and characteristics, and asked

---

polls when native respondents are primed to think about Latino immigrants as opposed to immigrants from European counties (Brader, Valentino, and Suhay, 2008).

them to decide which of the two immigrants' applications they would approve for immigration; essentially making survey respondents play the role of a public official deciding on immigration applications. Instead, we use an alternative set of outcomes that captures an individual's willingness to engage in different social interactions of varying (increasing) intensity: to accept as a neighbor (member of the local community), as a friend, or as a family member (through marriage). These "outcomes" are drawn from seminal work by Bogardus (1933), who developed a social distance scale based on the notion that individuals will be less inclined to engage in high-intensity social interactions with individuals or groups that they are biased against.

We prefer to use these three outcomes because they address questions that matter to ordinary people and they are more likely to be more "accurate" measures of individual/personal predispositions and attitudes than the conventional measure. Asking regular citizens to effectively make a decision with regard to an immigration application might induce them to consider factors that are external to their own biases; for example, they might take into account sociotropic concerns regarding the economy or host societies as a whole rather than respond based on factors that motivate their personal animus. By contrast, asking them to reflect how immigration is likely to affect their own personal lives is more likely to elicit responses that reflect their own individual preferences.

Experimental Attributes   We generated hypothetical profile pairs from the attribute list presented in table 3.1. They include ascriptive attributes such as country of origin, language, and religion, as well as other attributes that signal an immigrant's occupational background and educational level which should ostensibly be linked to economic motivations for immigrant-regarding attitudes.[6] These attributes and attribute levels were chosen based both on the existing literature on immigration (Bansak, Hainmueller, and Hangartner, 2016; Hainmueller and Hopkins, 2015) as well as our substantive intuitions about factors that may drive host population biases against immigrants. We opt for a complete independent randomization of attribute levels, but in order to make the choice task realistic, we also made the decision to restrict certain attribute level combinations that are either impossible or highly unrealistic. A typical example of such a restriction would be a (medical) doctor without a

---

6. As mentioned earlier in this chapter, ascriptive characteristics provide shortcuts to categorize individuals as members of different social—especially ethnic—groups and are therefore a natural starting point in any attempt to measure social distance between pairs of groups.

TABLE 3.1. Conjoint Attribute–Attribute Level List

Attribute	Attribute Level
Gender	Male
	Female
Education Level	High School Diploma
	Bachelor's Degree
	Master's Degree
	Doctorate
Country of Origin (Nationality)	Germany
	Poland
	Greece
	Turkey
	Syria
	Ethiopia
	Nigeria
Current Occupation	Waiter
	Caretaker
	Computer Programmer
	Doctor
	Financial Analyst
	Nurse
	Researcher
	Taxi Driver
	Teacher
Proficiency in German	Speaks Fluent German
	Speaks Broken German
	Speaks No German
Religion	Christian
	Muslim
	No religion

college degree, which by nature of licensing practices in Germany would not be a feasible combination. While we do not enumerate the entire list here, we make sure that any ensuing analyses adjust for these restrictions.

Implementation   We implemented a survey with the choice experiment component embedded in a stratified sample of 1500 adult Germans recruited from an online panel of respondents.[7] Respondents were first instructed to

7. Respondents were recruited through clickworker.com, which is an online work platform akin to Amazon's M-Turk. As a means to overcome concerns over the problems caused by sample composition on online work platforms, we implement state and gender quotas based on

TABLE 3.2. Example of Profile Pairs

Attribute	Individual A	Individual B
Gender	Male	Female
Education Level	High School Diploma	Master's Degree
Country of Origin (Nationality)	Ethiopia	Nigeria
Current Occupation	Waiter	Computer Programmer
Proficiency in German	Speaks Fluent German	Speaks Fluent German
Religion	Christian	Muslim

answer a battery of questions that would allow us to learn about their demographic profile (age, gender, state of residence, nationality, and country of origin of their parents). We then asked them to participate in the choice task a total of four times (four profile pairs or eight individual profiles), which yielded a total of six thousand profile pairs (or twelve thousand individual profiles) evaluated. An example of a typical profile pair is presented in table 3.2.[8]

Analysis   We follow convention in the literature to estimate average marginal component effects (AMCEs), which can be interpreted as the average difference in the probability of being the preferred immigrant when comparing different attribute levels, where the average is taken over all possible combinations of the other immigrant attributes. Hainmueller, Hopkins, and Yamamoto (2013) demonstrated that the AMCE is nonparametrically identified given the conditional random assignment of attributes, and is easily estimable using regression wherein the binary outcome variable "preferred as neighbor/friend/family member" is regressed against indicator variables measuring the levels of each attribute. As noted earlier, we take into account the attribute level restrictions we imposed to eliminate non-feasible attribute level combinations in the analysis. To obtain correct variance estimates, we take note of the fact that profile evaluations are not independent within the same survey respondent, and cluster the standard errors at the respondent level.

---

census information to move closer to a sample that resembles the respondent pool for our field experiments.

8. While the profile pairs were presented to respondents in German, we present a translated version of a typical example for readers here.

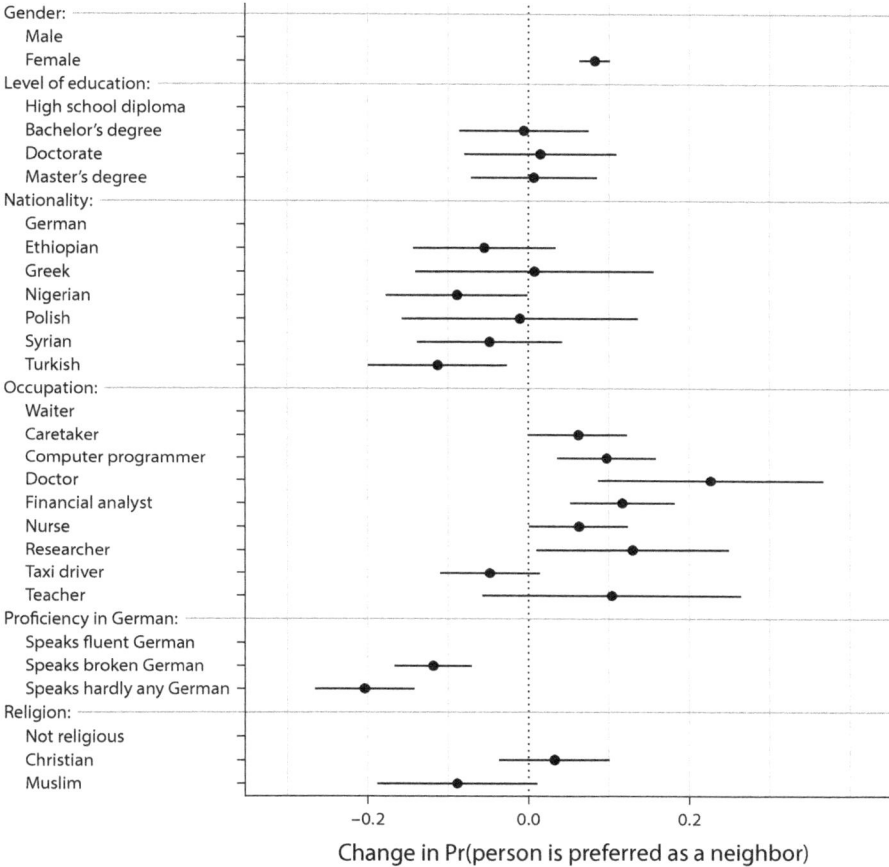

FIGURE 3.3. Probability that German natives prefer a person as a neighbor

Our analyses reveal important insights about the nature of anti-immigrant attitudes among German natives. First, and consistently across three of the social interaction outcomes, we find that female immigrants are strongly preferred over male immigrants; on average, German natives have an 8–9 percentage point preference for women immigrants, an effect that is statistically significant at conventional levels. This is perhaps in line with work that suggests male immigrants are discriminated against due to the perception that they pose a "security risk" to the host society (Ward, 2019).

We also find mixed evidence regarding the effects of educational credentials or occupational background of the immigrant on host population preferences for social interactions. With the exception of preference as a family member (even there, the effects are only marginally significant at $p < 0.1$), we observe no distinct preference for immigrants with post-secondary education over immigrants without. The results for occupational categories demonstrate some more heterogeneity; in comparison to the baseline (immigrant is a waiter), immigrants who work in high-skill fields such as computer scientists, medical doctors, nurses, and financial analysts seem to be favored by between 7–18 percentage points. These findings on the occupational background of immigrants provide partial evidence that economic motivations may underlie attitudes toward minorities. That immigrants with low-skill occupations such as waiters and taxi drivers seem to be significantly less favored than those high-skill occupations (such as computer programmers and financial analysts) is consonant with existing work that suggests labor market competition among low-skilled, blue-collar workers is at the heart of anti-immigrant sentiment.

More importantly, and largely in line with previous work, we detect some interesting patterns with regard to the effects of country of origin (or nationality) of the immigrant and our three types of social interaction. In comparison to the baseline (German), we find that German natives are predisposed to disfavor immigrants of Turkish and Nigerian origin when choosing profiles for neighbors (9–11 percentage points). Interestingly, we find no statistically significant effects for the friend outcome, which we considered as a higher intensity social interaction than being neighbors. The strongest patterns of anti-immigrant attitudes manifest in our family outcome (son/daughter-in-law), which we conceived as the *highest* intensity social interaction. In comparison to the baseline condition (German), all nonnative nationalities are likely to be disfavored. The average marginal component effects range from around 10 percentage points for Ethiopians, Greeks, and Nigerians to up to 17 percentage points for Turkish, Polish, and Syrian nationals. This finding seems to be consistent with Sniderman and Hagendoorn (2007) who argued that prejudice against one immigrant group is correlated with prejudice toward all immigrant groups—it reflects a broader antipathy and a set of predispositions that cannot be explained by the attributes of any single immigrant nationality or ethnicity.

Perhaps unsurprisingly, the largest effects in our analyses are observed for our language attribute. In comparison to the baseline (speaks German fluently), immigrants who speak either "broken (flawed) German" or "hardly any German" incur a statistically significant penalty; across all three types of social interaction, immigrants with broken German are around 10–14 percentage points disadvantaged. For immigrants who speak hardly any

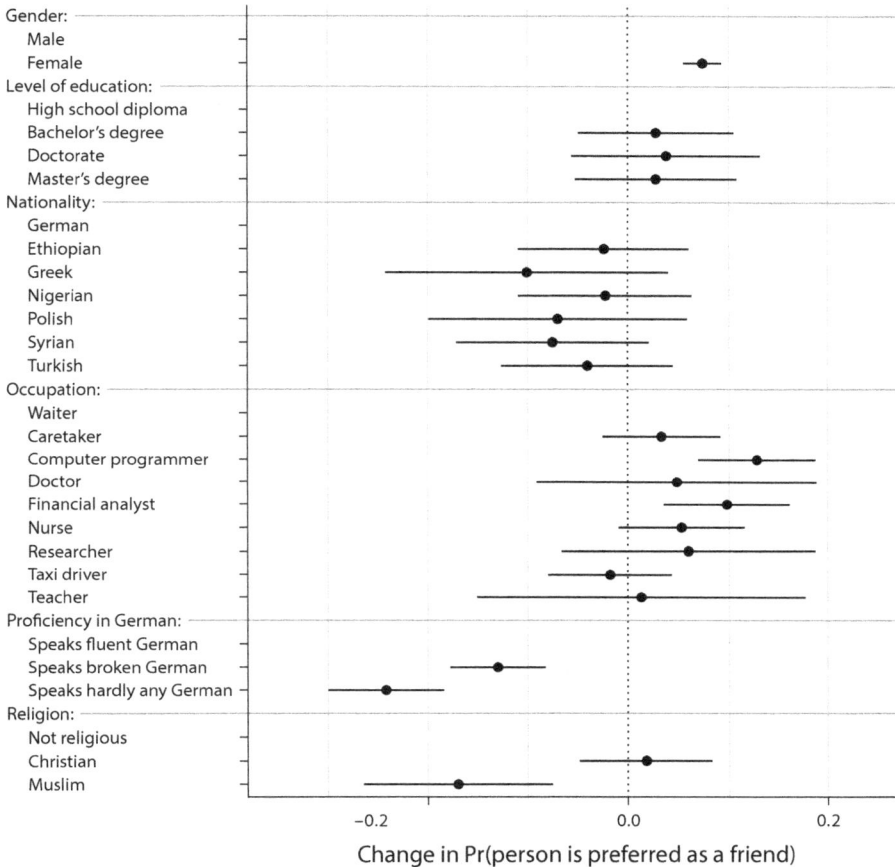

FIGURE 3.4. Probability that German natives prefer a person as a friend

German, this penalty expands to up to 25 percentage points for the friend and family evaluation tasks. These effects are large in magnitude, and commonly observed across different subsets of the host population in Germany (age, gender, and religious groups).

The findings with reference to the importance of knowledge of German require additional discussion. We turn to the importance of linguistic differences as a determinant of bias in chapter 4, but for now we point out that the fact that our experimental subjects reveal a preference for someone who speaks German when they think of whom they would want as a friend or son/daughter-in-law need not be taken as a measure of anti-immigrant bias.

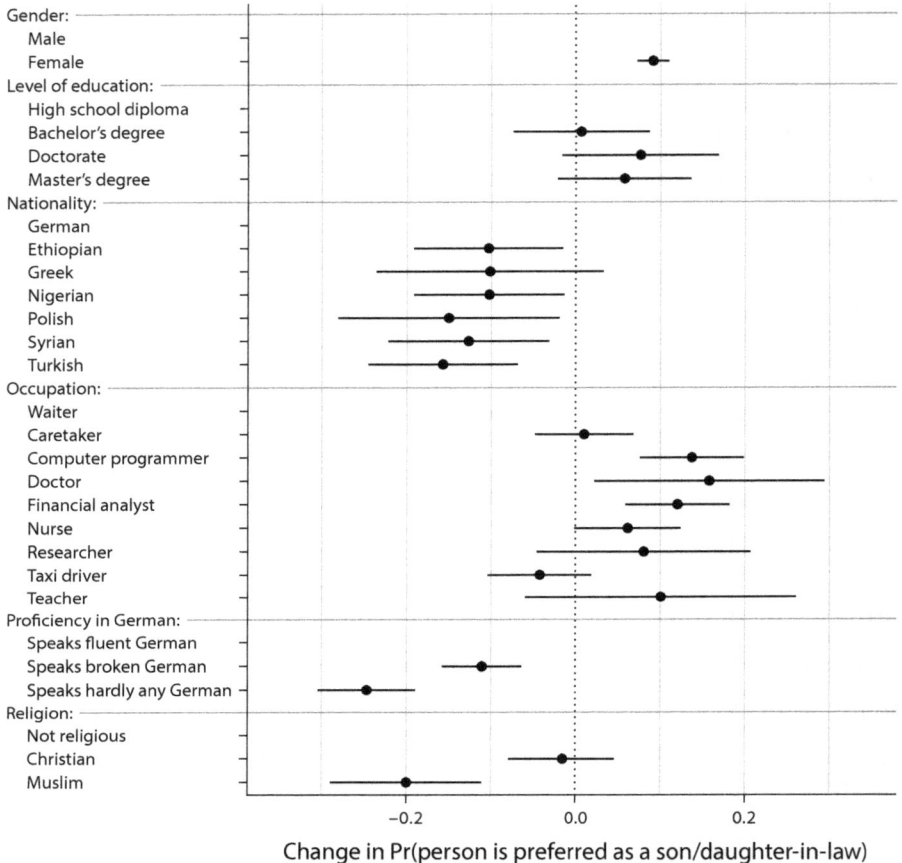

Change in Pr(person is preferred as a son/daughter-in-law)

FIGURE 3.5. Probability that German natives prefer a person as a son/daughter-in-law

Sharing the same language with a friend or family member is a reasonable expectation; hence the results with respect to preferences over different types of neighbors might be more instructive. We do observe a preference for German-speaking neighbors, which could be seen as registering a preference against living in close proximity to immigrants. In later sections we explore whether the expression of such negative attitudes translates into biased behavior in everyday interactions.

Although the magnitude of the effects are slightly smaller than the language attribute, we also observe significant penalties for our religion attribute. Consistent with earlier research that discovered the prevalence of discrimination and hostility against Muslims, we also observe that the German native population has strong reservations about engaging in high-intensity social interactions with Muslim immigrants (Creighton and Jamal, 2015; Helbling and Traunmüller, 2018). Specifically, Muslim immigrants suffer between an 18–20 percentage point penalty for our friendship and family outcomes.

Our findings from the choice experiment provide evidence that ascriptive characteristics—national origin, language, and religion—of the immigrant population are the factors that drive anti-immigrant attitudes among German native populations. In conclusion, however, a few additional points warrant note. First, it is interesting to observe that there is a "Muslim" penalty *independent* of the "country of origin" penalty. While earlier work has pointed to a penalty for immigrants originating from a predominantly Muslim country (see, for example, Hainmueller and Hopkins (2015)), our findings show that ethno-national origins and religion/religiosity might be two dimensions that motivate anti-immigrant bias in distinct ways. This invites the question of which of these dimensions is likely to drive bias to a greater degree. Second, although the magnitude of the AMCE for the language attributes is ostensibly larger than that of the religion attributes, in reality, it is hard to conclusively state with statistical precision that these are meaningful differences. This motivates us to examine how these two dimensions will underpin native behavior toward immigrants, and their relative standing.

Implicit Association Test

Evidence from public opinion polls reviewed in chapter 1 and the results from the discrete choice experiment just presented highlight the importance that religion/religiosity—specifically whether an immigrant is a Muslim—plays a pivotal role shaping perceptions of social distance in Germany. We delve deeper by exploring whether religious symbols that define Islam in the popular imagination of the native population generate bias toward Muslims. We focus on the hijab, which is an easily identifiable symbol of Islamic faith and has been the subject of extensive public debate in Western societies as a symbol of Islamic ideas regarding the role of women in society (a subject to which we return in chapter 6). To measure bias toward Muslims, specifically hijab-wearing women, we use techniques that can elicit information regarding both implicit and explicit bias. We begin with a discussion of implicit bias, which in many ways is harder to measure. Implicit bias is likely to be revealed when subjects are placed under time pressure or when cognitive overload does not allow them to fully process information and they therefore reveal their true preferences (Bertrand, Chugh, and Mullainathan, 2005). To test whether German natives have internalized biased perceptions of Muslims, we use an implicit association test, which has a long track record in the psychology literature.

Implicit association tests (IATs) measure differential association of two target concepts (e.g., Muslims vs. Christians; Blacks vs. Whites) with an attribute (e.g., "good" or "bad") (Greenwald, McGhee, and Schwartz, 1998). The basic intuition behind the IAT is that sorting (or categorizing) target concepts with an attribute is easier and can be done more quickly if the target concept and the attribute are more closely associated in an individual's memory or subconscious. They have been used extensively to measure unconscious bias across countries and contexts.

A typical IAT follows this sequence: first, the respondent is asked to use two buttons ("E" or "I" keys) on a keyboard to classify a series of pictures into the correct category. For example, in an IAT designed to measure implicit bias against Black people, the respondent would be first shown a series of pictures of a Black or White person and asked to categorize the person in the picture as either "Black" or "White." Then, they would be shown a different series of words or pictures (that are not the pictures of Black and White people) that could be sorted into the abstract categories of "good" and "bad." After a series of these relatively straightforward tasks, the IAT proceeds to mix up these categories and creates pairwise combinations of them, and instructs the respondent to categorize the same set of pictures of Black or White people, as well as the other pictures that were categorized earlier into valence categories, into "bins" that represent different combinations of these objects and valence categories (such as "Black and good" or "White and bad").[9] For example, a respondent could be instructed to press the "E" key to categorize pictures

9. At this stage, the pictures of the Black and White people as well as the pictures for the valence categories are pooled together and sorted randomly; the respondent therefore faces a slightly more challenging categorization task, wherein they will often have to alternate between categorizing a picture of a person versus a picture that falls into the valence category.

It is important to note that the respondents are never classifying the pictures of Black and White people into a valence category per se. Even in these mixed tasks, respondents are instructed to classify the picture of people into the Black versus White category. However, since the categories or "bins" have been paired (for example, "Black" with "good") the cognitive dissonance experienced by a respondent who is biased against Black people when clicking on the key that also happens to be associated with the valence term "good" will likely result in a delay in successfully completing the task.

that belong to the "Black" category or pictures that belong to the "bad" category, while instructed to press the "I" key to categorize pictures that belong to the "White" category or "good" category. In the next round, the instructions change so that the respondent would be instructed to press the "E" key to categorize pictures that belong to the "Black" category or pictures that belong to the "good" category, and the "I" key to categorize pictures that belong to the "White" category or pictures that belong to the "bad" category.

Implicit bias is measured by the difference in the average response times in these categorization tasks. For example, the respondent sees a picture of a Black person and in some cases the category "Black" will appear on the screen paired with the valence "good" (paired with a second option, matched to the other key, of "White" and "unpleasant"). The program tracks to the millisecond the time it takes for the respondent to correctly press the key that corresponds to "Black" and, if it detects a slower response time when "Black" and "good" are linked together through the same key, or when "bad" and "White" are linked together through the same key, compared to a situation when "Black" and "bad" (or "White" and "good") are linked together in the same key, then the respondent is considered to be revealing some degree of implicit bias against Black people.

Scholars in psychology and political science have used the IAT to assess the extent of implicit attitudes toward a diverse set of social categories including racial, religious, and other minority groups such as women and LGBT groups, as well as people with disabilities (Nosek et al., 2007). Although there has been a protracted debate about whether the IAT is a valid method for measuring implicit bias, large-scale meta-studies and replications have recently shown that implicit attitudes are pervasive and correlated with explicit bias, and the test successfully predicts individual behavior (Greenwald, Nosek, and Sriram, 2006; Greenwald et al., 2009).

We adapt the IAT for the purpose of measuring whether native Germans hold implicit (negative) biases against Muslims, and specifically, against Muslim women wearing a hijab. To do so, we replace the photos of Black and White people in the race IAT with pictures of women of Middle Eastern descent either wearing a hijab or not. We also replace the valence term (good versus bad) with pleasant versus unpleasant.

Implementation   Our IAT was conducted on a stratified sample of 1,317 adult Germans, recruited through the online survey platform Qualtrics Panels. Although the core architecture of the implicit association test was retained,

No Hijab or Unpleasant	Hijab or Pleasant	No Hijab or Unpleasant	Hijab or Pleasant

Press E or I to go to the next word or picture.
Correct mistakes by pressing the space bar.

Press E or I to go to the next word or picture.
Correct mistakes by pressing the space bar.

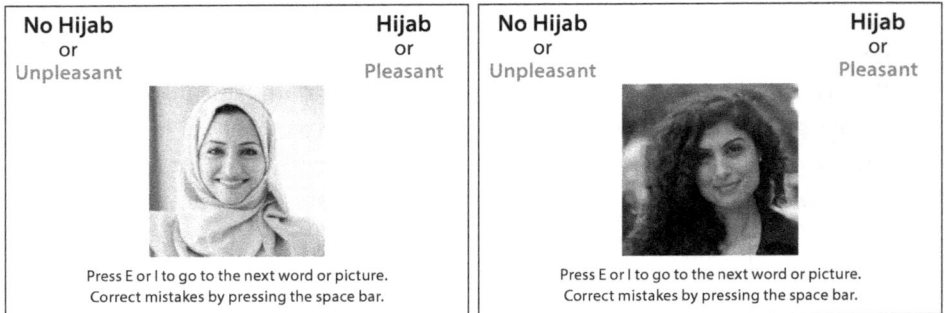

FIGURE 3.6. Example IAT screen

Notes: We deploy a graphical version of the IAT, generated by software created by Nosek et al. (2007). We chose a total of sixteen photos of Middle Eastern women with and without a hijab, that are on average of ostensibly comparable attractiveness and emotional valence. Each respondent was asked to classify one picture (only a single picture was shown per screen) into the correct category.

our IAT presented respondents with pictures (sixteen total) of Middle Eastern women with or without a hijab and then measured their associations of these two groups with the positive and negative valence terms "pleasant" and "unpleasant"; this is a close approximation of race-based IATs where the invocation of the target concepts is done by showing words or abstract graphical illustrations. Because we were conscious of the potential for measurement error induced by the pictures selected, we were careful to select a wide-ranging pool of generic photos of putatively Middle Eastern women with and without a hijab of comparable attractiveness, and whose demeanor in the photo were of similar positive emotional valence (happiness).

By keeping constant the ethno-racial background and other extraneous attributes of the individuals in the two groups, we are able to isolate the effect of the hijab *or religiosity* in triggering implicit bias. The measure of implicit bias was computed by comparing the mean response times for discordant pairings of our hijab vs. no hijab categories to valence categories (*hijab-pleasant* and *no hijab-unpleasant*) to concordant pairings (*hijab-unpleasant* and *no hijab-pleasant*).

Results Our IAT reveals that German natives hold strong implicit (negative) biases against veiled immigrant women. The mean D-score for our full sample is 0.72 (SD = 0.44), which is around double the implicit racial bias, skin tone bias, and bias against Arab Muslims (D scores of 0.37, 0.30, and

0.14, respectively) measured in IATs on large samples of the US population as reported by Nosek et al. (2007). Disaggregating the mean D scores by the self-reported gender of the respondents reveals that native German men hold somewhat stronger implicit biases than women. The mean D score for men is 0.74 (SD = 0.45). For women, it is around 0.06 smaller at 0.68 (SD = 0.43).[10]

These findings from the IAT regarding women wearing the hijab are placed into richer context later in this chapter and in chapter 6, where we explore in more depth what the hijab actually signifies for German natives. The bias revealed by the IAT is large, but it remains to be seen how well correlated they are with behavior. In the next section, we present findings from a field experiment designed to measure discriminatory behavior toward Muslim women in the field, which will help establish whether German natives' behavior is correlated with the findings from the IAT. These experiments vary situational factors that are likely to affect the intensity of bias and could help us understand how individual implicit bias could be manipulated and mitigated.[11]

Capturing Anti-immigrant Behavior in the Field

The analysis presented up to this point makes clear that a significant amount of anti-immigrant bias exists among the German native population and, indeed, across Europe. Cultural threat generated by symbols of Muslim religion *and* political Islam (such as the hijab) are among the driving factors behind anti-immigrant attitudes, though our survey also suggests that the religious symbols such as the hijab also make salient other causes of anti-Muslim bias, such as concerns over security or over the impact of large-scale immigration on the welfare state. Previous research is consistent with our findings as it has shown that cultural differences exert an important effect on anti-immigrant attitudes beyond their association with any realistic fears that are generated by immigration.[12]

---

10. We also disaggregate the IAT scores by whether the respondent reported residing in former East vs. West Germany. The IAT D scores are marginally larger in the former East (0.74) than in the West (0.70) and statistically indistinguishable from each other.

11. Bertrand, Chugh, and Mullainathan (2005) discuss the need to correlate results from IATs with economic or other behavior in the field and discuss how situational factors can aggravate or reduce the expression of implicit attitudes in behavior.

12. See, in particular, the decoupling experiments by Sniderman and Hagendoorn that distinguish identity threat from material interests as possible motives for bias.

While we have established how prevalent and ingrained the animus is, the evidence thus far does not shed light as to whether negative attitudes structure native interactions with immigrants, and in particular, whether they translate into discriminatory behavior. We believe this question is of central importance, as research in psychology and political science has shown that there is often a *disconnect* between the attitudes that individuals hold and how they behave. In fact, most research on between-group animus has focused on attitudes themselves—often with observational data or in a lab setting—and has neglected to examine their behavioral manifestations in the real world (Paluck, 2016).[13]

We turn to this question next by introducing an experimental intervention designed explicitly to observe discriminatory behavior against immigrants in the real world. Our experimental design is novel in that it examines a domain of native-immigrant interaction that has evaded the attention of earlier work: everyday social interactions.[14] Before we describe our design in detail, we discuss the definition and conceptualization of core concepts, and explain how we operationalize and measure them.

Setting the Scene

Defining Discrimination   Discrimination is defined as the unequal treatment of different categories of people on the grounds of ascriptive characteristics (ethno-racial or religious differences). A number of different measures of discrimination have been used in field experiments across countries. The key finding, synthesizing scores of studies across different disciplines, is that "members of a minority group (women, Blacks, Muslims, immigrants, etc.)

---

13. A recent literature has also pointed out this lacuna, and focused on observing discriminatory behavior using field experimental methods (Scacco and Warren, 2018). Not only is it the case that biased attitudes need not translate directly into discriminatory behavior; but also perceptions of discrimination might not correspond to the prevalence of discrimination in the real world (Pager and Shepherd, 2008).

14. A relatively large number of studies have examined group-based discrimination in the context of the labor market, and have shown that low-status minorities suffer a significant penalty in terms of labor market prospects. See, for example, Bertrand and Mullainathan (2004), Adida, Laitin, and Valfort (2010), and Pager and Shepherd (2008). While we recognize that this is an important domain in which discrimination can occur, it is uncontroversial that discrimination can occur in many other areas of social life. We elaborate on our decision to focus on everyday social interactions later on in the chapter.

are treated differentially (less favorably) than members of a majority group with otherwise identical characteristics in similar circumstances" (Bertrand and Duflo, 2016). This reflects a shared understanding of discrimination as negative treatment and unfavorable evaluations of others on the basis of their group membership.

A useful distinction introduced in the economics literature is between so-called "statistical" versus "taste-based" discrimination. The original treatments of discrimination in economics were consistent with "taste-based" explanations (Becker, 1957). Some employers may have preferences against hiring women, Blacks, or other minorities and might therefore not hire them or hire them but pay them less. Such a position, however, might end up being costly to employers if their bias leads them to pass up competitive job candidates and employees. Employers have a financial incentive not to discriminate. To explain this puzzle, studies of "statistical" discrimination (Phelps, 1972; Aigner and Cain, 1977) explained discriminatory treatment of minorities in the job market as a result of imperfect information about individual qualities. Minority attributes can be used (or interpreted) as signals of specific qualities that employers care about, thereby influencing their decisions. We will not engage with this intriguing debate on whether discrimination is "taste-based" or "statistical" because tastes can also affect how one evaluates evidence that might lead to "statistical" evaluations of minorities (which further complicates the distinction between the two types of discrimination); and because knowledge of systematic differences in group attributes and histories invariably affects the evolution of individual tastes over time. We also do not engage with normative debates on whether discrimination is warranted; we take the position that discrimination is not warranted and that it is costly to societies as a whole. The experimental designs that we utilize in our empirical analysis are more likely to measure behavior due to fundamental—if vague and undefined—*tastes* for discrimination.

Helping Behavior   We measure discrimination on the basis of observed differences in *helping behavior* toward natives versus immigrants. Specifically, we measure assistance offered to strangers who need help during everyday social interactions. These measures are obtained unobtrusively via methods that we explain in detail later in this chapter. Our focus is on measuring differences in helping behavior toward immigrant minorities of different ethno-religious background relative to native Germans.

Our choice to use *helping behavior* as a medium through which to observe discrimination is motivated by a broad set of studies in psychology that have explored the causes of variation in helping behavior in different contexts. These studies suggest that helping behavior is a good proxy of pro-sociality. Multiple studies have tested for differences in help offered to ingroup and outgroup members in different contexts, such as asking for money (Bickman and Kamzan, 1973); retrieving dropped items (Lerner and Frank, 1974; Balafoutas, Nikiforakis, and Rockenbach, 2014) or finding lost ones (Benson, Karabenick, and Lerner, 1976); calling wrong numbers (Gaertner and Bickman, 1971); needing medical assistance (Piliavin, Rodin, and Piliavin, 1969); and having car trouble (West, Whitney, and Schnedler, 1975) or escaping emergency situations (Saucier, Smith, and McManus, 2007). A review of that literature reveals different motives for providing help (Cialdini et al., 1987; Maner et al., 2002) under different conditions, such as concern over self-presentation (Dovidio et al., 2006; Gustavo et al., 1991), paternalism (Clark, 1974; Katz, Cohen, and Glass, 1975), social norms and peer pressure (Archer et al., 1981; Moss and Page, 1972); expectations of material rewards (Moss and Page, 1972) or reciprocity (Regan, 1971; Whatley et al., 1999); aversive racism (Gaertner and Dovidio, 1986); and cost-reward calculations.[15] However, a key lesson to emerge from that literature is that helping behavior can be a good proxy for pro-sociality.

How does helping behavior compare to other possible measures of discrimination? Withholding a common courtesy (such as holding a door open or picking up a stranger's dropped items) is a relatively costless act of pro-sociality and something one could do (or choose not to do) without much thought. This measure should therefore set a high bar for us to identify evidence of discrimination relative to other possible ways to measure discriminatory behavior. Other ways to uncover evidence of discrimination, such as *audit studies* (Fix and Struyk editors, 1993; Heckman and Siegelman, 1993) or *correspondence studies* (Bertrand and Mullainathan, 2004), require the processing of information across multiple dimensions to decide how to treat individuals who differ with respect to a dimension that is thought to lead to discrimination (e.g., race). Evaluations of individuals in such studies are also made with reference to some standard (Bertrand and Duflo, 2016) and therefore they are the result of conscious decision-making to a much greater degree than extending a common courtesy. Moreover, helping behavior of the

15. For a useful review, see Saucier, McManus, and Smith (2010).

sort that we measure in our experiments is a realistic and readily observable truthful proxy of individual bias.[16]

Everyday Interactions   Next, we should consider the context in which helping behavior is analyzed. Much of political science is focused on "big events"—elections, wars, treaties, protest movements, or independence campaigns. Such events are important to study because they punctuate the equilibria of our everyday lives that are typically much less eventful. However, the usually less noticed—seemingly mundane—everyday interactions between citizens occur much more frequently and are usually more personal than those remote, "big events." The importance of studying everyday interactions cannot be overstated. They can play an immensely important role in shaping our perceptions, biases, and behavior. If native-immigrant interactions are characterized by several, repeated small acts of mutual disappointment, hostility, and discrimination, these daily experiences will resemble "death by a thousand cuts" and result in pervasive, lasting barriers to integration.

Withholding help to an immigrant could be read as an act of defiance directed at a political system that pushes multiculturalism and tolerance. Discrimination in the context of seemingly trivial behaviors registers, indirectly and passively, one's true feelings toward the politics of accommodation that is advocated by a system focused on promoting integration and globalization. Discrimination in everyday interactions is therefore a form of "resistance" to integration (Certau, 1984). Indeed, observing acts of assistance or withholding of assistance to strangers of different racial and ethnic backgrounds is a natural test of political theories of "conviviality"—the idea that multicultural, multiethnic cohabitation and interaction in European urban centers is making race and ethnicity irrelevant (Gilroy, 2004a). According to that idea, racism and xenophobia are "melancholy" interpretations of European powers' imperial past that become worn over time and are replaced by transnational solidarity (Gilroy, 2004b). But are they? Observing small, spontaneous acts of inter-ethnic solidarity or neglect in public spaces places theories of conviviality under a sharp empirical lens.

---

16. In survey-based research, list experiments and endorsement experiments have also been used effectively to elicit truthful responses that capture bias and discrimination (Kuklinski, Cobb, and Gilens, 1997; Sniderman et al., 1997).

A Micro-environment to Observe Discrimination in Everyday Life

To move away from measuring *attitudes* and toward measuring *behavior,* we conducted two large field experiments in thirty cities across former West and East Germany involving thousands of subjects. The experiments were designed to create a realistic "micro-environment" (Sands, 2017) which allowed us to observe discrimination in everyday real-world social interactions between natives and immigrants. We experimentally varied the ethno-religious attributes of confederates who were part of an intervention that was designed to elicit help toward the confederates from unknowing bystanders in public places (train stations). We tested whether bystanders' helping behavior was a function of the confederates' ethno-religious differences (phenotypical differences and differences in perceived religion/religiosity). The main expectation, consistent with the theoretical discussion in chapter 2, was that bystanders (native Germans) would help ingroup members (other Germans) more than they would help immigrants; and that the greater the perceived social distance between natives and immigrants, the less help would be provided. Taking our theory to the field rather than testing it in the lab or through surveys overcomes some of the concerns regarding demand effects or social desirability bias, which is especially relevant in research on sensitive issues such as immigration and minority discrimination (Creighton and Jamal, 2015; Blair, Chou, and Imai, 2019).

Experimental Intervention

The intervention proceeded as follows: A female confederate approached a bench at a train station where other individuals (bystanders) were waiting for their train (step 1). The confederate got the bystanders' attention and then answered a call, addressing a friend regarding a personal matter (step 2). As the call ended, the confederate dropped fruit (oranges or lemons) from a paper bag that had seemingly torn at the bottom. The fruit dispersed and the confederate appeared to be in need of assistance to pick them up (step 3). We observed whether bystanders who were exposed to the intervention helped the confederate pick up the fruit (step 4). A collage of a few instances of this intervention is included in figure 3.7.

Treatment Dimensions   The key experimental dimensions that we varied were the ethnicity of the confederate (immigrant or native) and her perceived religion or religiosity (hijab-wearing Muslim; native; or immigrant with no religious symbols). As mentioned earlier, religious differences are salient in

FIGURE 3.7. Experiment in action
Notes: The experimental interventions were conducted in thirty German cities and
towns across four states in the former East and West Germany in summer of 2018 and 2019.
A total of 2,927 iterations of the intervention, involving 8,624 bystanders, were implemented.

Germany and our conjoint experiment identified significant negative attitudes toward foreigners and Muslims. Our focus here is on whether such
negative attitudes are also reflected in negative behavior in the field.

Apart from these dimensions, we maintain perceived social class constant
both across experimental conditions and across teams of confederates by
having the confederates wear similar attire indicative of a middle class background. Crucially, we use immigrant minority confederates whose ethno-
racial attributes are such as to invoke the native-immigrant distinction in the
minds of ordinary Germans. In the appendix, we present survey-based evidence that confirms that most Germans accurately categorize our confederates in the *control condition* (i.e., immigrant-no hijab) as having a non-German
nationality. We mitigate concerns regarding the possibility that differing levels of confederate attractiveness is likely to affect assistance rates by having
the same confederate play both the hijab-wearing immigrant and non-hijab-
wearing immigrant roles and by using a rather large number of confederates
(across teams). We also report in the appendix that our results hold using team
fixed effects, which analyze within-team variation in assistance rates across
iterations.[17]

17. These strategies are less effective in dealing with differences in perceived attractiveness
between native confederates and minority confederates. However, given the large number of

| Immigrant hijab | Immigrant no hijab | Native |

FIGURE 3.8. Varying religiosity and ethnicity of confederate

Choosing Women as Confederates   In designing this intervention, we were faced with both conceptual and practical challenges. We explain our choices as we introduce different components of the experimental intervention in this chapter and later chapters, but we highlight one feature here: the choice to use women in confederate roles. That choice served practical goals since using both men and women would have required double the number of iterations, but it also made it easier to signal Muslim faith in a natural, subtle manner by using women wearing hijabs in some treatment conditions. Our experiments could certainly be replicated with men in the role of enforcer and we would expect levels of discrimination to be higher toward men. Although we do not explore this question systematically, prior research suggests that helping behavior toward women is more prevalent than toward men (Balafoutas, Nikiforakis, and Rockenbach, 2016) and that there is more hostility and antipathy toward immigrant men than immigrant women (Ward, 2019; Gereke, Schaub, and Baldassarri, 2020). Concentrating anti-immigrant attitudes on men is consistent with evolutionary theory (Navarette et al., 2010) and likely to be justified by beliefs that immigrant men are more likely than women to violate social norms, commit crimes, and uphold cultural differences which natives find objectionable (Ward, 2019).

Outcome Collection   We are interested in measuring the level of assistance offered to the female confederate who drops her possessions (bag of oranges or lemons) in the intervention, as specified in our pre-analysis plan. Enumerators observing each iteration of the intervention collected the

---

both immigrant and native confederates conducting the iteration across teams, we are less concerned that on average there are systematic differences in the attractiveness of native versus immigrant confederates.

West Germany

Münster
Bielefeld
Minden
Rheine
Köln (Hbf)
Köln (Messe-Deutz)
Mönchengladbach
Neuss
Siegen
Bonn
Düsseldorf
Wuppertal
Dortmund
Duisberg
Bochum
Gelsenkirchen
Hagen
Essen
Wanne-Eickel
Osnabrück
Hannover

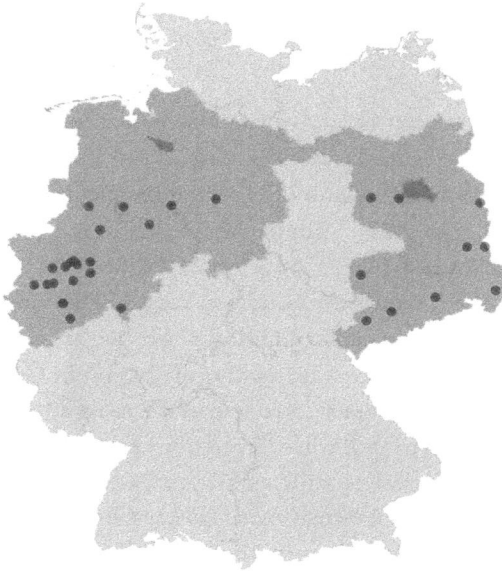

East Germany

Leipzig
Görlitz
Chemnitz
Dresden
Zwickau
Potsdam
Forst (Lausitz)
Cottbus
Frankfurt (Oder)
Brandenburg

FIGURE 3.9. Experimental sites—Thirty cities in North Rhine-Westphalia, Brandenburg, Saxony, and Lower Saxony

following information regarding the reaction of bystanders. *This information was collected at the level of the iteration, which constitutes our unit of analysis.*

1. Number of bystanders within a 3-meter radius of the confederate (count)
2. Number of female bystanders within the 3-meter radius (count)
3. Number of bystanders with headphones or earphones (count)
4. Whether any bystander offered assistance to the confederate (dichotomous)
5. Number of bystanders who offered assistance (count)

Site Selection Our field experiment was initially implemented in Germany during the summer of 2018 and replicated in a follow-up which shared common treatment arms with the first experiment. The interventions were conducted in twenty-nine train stations across North Rhine-Westphalia (NRW), Saxony, and Brandenburg in 2018; and replicated in twenty-six train stations in North Rhine-Westphalia, Saxony, and Lower Saxony in 2019. We implemented a total of 1,098 iterations of the intervention, involving 4,827 bystanders over a three-week period between July and August 2018; and an additional 1,829 iterations with a total of 3,797 bystanders over five weeks from

July to August 2019. A total of 8,624 bystanders across 2,927 iterations participated in the two experiments (for the experimental treatment arms discussed here).

These states were not chosen at random; rather, we arrived at the decision to conduct these interventions in these states after carefully weighing a combination of state- and region-level sociodemographic factors that we believed would be of interest.[18] The most obvious difference between North Rhine-Westphalia and Lower Saxony versus the two other states (Brandenburg and Saxony) is that they fell under West (FDR) and East Germany (GDR) prior to reunification. In addition, these two areas have traditionally been exposed to very different levels of immigration in Germany's postwar history. Whereas NRW is considered one of the most ethnically diverse federal states, with a high proportion of foreign-born populations, the two other states have remained relatively ethnically homogeneous.

Furthermore, the recent refugee crisis, as a result of the protracted wars in the Middle East, has had a differential impact on the three states. The Königstein quota system, which combines state-level tax revenues and population to assign asylum seekers, has naturally resulted in a high influx of refugees into NRW, which also happens to be one of the most populous and affluent states in Germany, and a low influx of refugees to Brandenburg and Saxony, which are sparsely populated and lag behind western German states in terms of tax revenue.

But perhaps most importantly, there is ample reason to suggest that the level of racial resentment might vary significantly across the west (NRW) and the east (Saxony, Brandenburg); the level of electoral support for the far-right Alternative für Deutschland (AfD), which primarily campaigned on an anti-immigration agenda, in state and federal elections has been markedly higher in the east in comparison to the west. In some parts of Saxony, the AfD managed to secure the highest party vote share.

Experimental Results

Using the data on outcomes collected, we constructed one main outcome and additional auxiliary outcomes that we used for the empirical analyses. These variables were calculated at the iteration level.

---

18. The appendix includes a list of all cities, train stations, and the number of platforms in each station. It also provides additional information on logistics of the experiments.

- *helped*: Did *any* bystander offer assistance by moving to pick up possessions that the confederate dropped? (main)
- *proportion helped*: The *proportion* of bystanders who offered assistance by moving to pick up possessions that the confederate dropped (auxiliary)

We follow our pre-registered analysis plan and employ a standard two-tailed difference-in-means test to examine assistance rates at the iteration level across our treatment conditions. When estimating covariate-adjusted average treatment effects (ATE), we use linear regression. The primary results reported here are based on data that pools observations from experiment 1 (summer 2018) and experiment 2 (summer 2019), since the design remained constant. Results disaggregated by each experiment are provided in the appendix, but they remain substantively unchanged.

Discrimination Against Immigrants   What is the extent of discrimination against immigrant minorities among German natives? Does our experimental design successfully detect the same degree of animus against immigrants that we observed with respect to attitudes? Our conceptualization of discrimination suggests that immigrants would receive less assistance than natives; and that identity markers (hijab) that increase the perception of difference (social distance) between natives and immigrants would decrease assistance.

First, our analyses provide strong evidence that there is systematic discrimination against Muslim minorities in Germany. As figure 3.10 suggests, female German confederates, who serve as our control, were assisted in retrieving their possessions in 76.65 percent of all iterations. By contrast, confederates of an immigrant background (immigrant with hijab and immigrants without religious attire) were assisted less, in 72.1 percent of iterations (this number reflects the assistance rates for the two columns with the two immigrant treatment conditions). The difference between the level of assistance offered to immigrants versus natives is therefore around 4.5 percentage points and is statistically distinguishable at conventional levels ($t = -3.03$, $p < 0.01$, two-tailed).

The discrimination against immigrants, however, is almost entirely directed at confederates who wore a hijab, which makes salient native-immigrant differences in religious identity. As shown in column (3) of figure 3.10, immigrant confederates wearing a hijab, which clearly signals that they

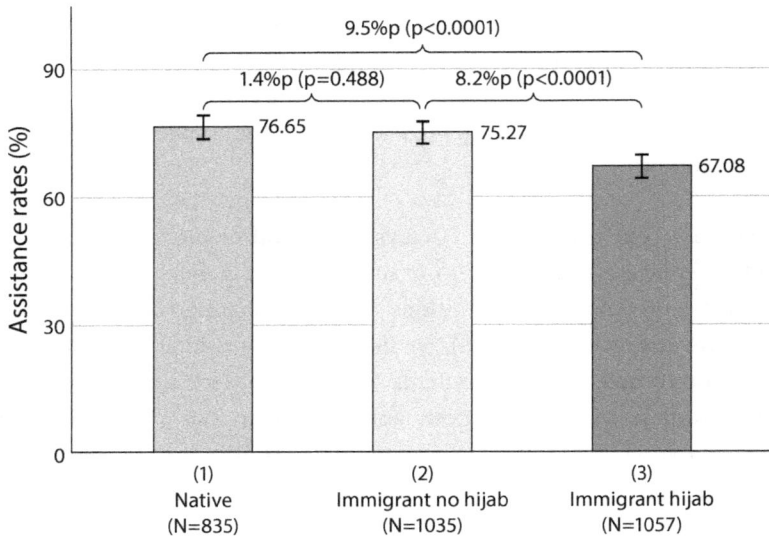

FIGURE 3.10. Discrimination against immigrants

Notes: The figure is generated based on data that pools across experiment 1 (summer 2018) and experiment 2 (summer 2019) across common treatment conditions. Bars represent the mean rates of assistance for the treatment conditions. The error bars present 95% confidence intervals for the means. The brackets and accompanying information report results of a standard two-tailed difference in means test of treatment conditions with p-values in parentheses.

are of Muslim faith, were assisted only 67.08 percent of the time.[19] This is 9.5 percentage points less than assistance offered to German confederates ($t = -4.59$, $p < 0.001$, two-tailed). No such differences in assistance rates are observed for our immigrant confederates who did not signal their religious

19. Some readers may note that even for the immigrant confederates wearing a hijab, the rate of assistance is seemingly high (67%), perhaps suggesting that discrimination against Muslim immigrants may not be pervasive. There are a few reasons why we believe this is not the correct interpretation. First, as we note below, the fruits dropped in the intervention dispersed in a manner that clearly made it challenging for our confederates to retrieve them expediently by themselves. Given strong norms in Germany, it would have been common courtesy to provide assistance. This is evident in the significantly higher levels of assistance for the native condition (76.65%). Furthermore, our main outcome—whether *any* bystander offered assistance—masks the fact that in most iterations, there were some bystanders who did not offer assistance. We reorient the readers' attention toward the *differential* levels of assistance provided across identity conditions, which is the causal quantity of interest and by design, a more compelling measure of discrimination.

identity; they were assisted 75.27 percent of the time, only 1.4 percentage points less than our German native confederates ($t = -0.694$, $p = 0.488$) and 8.2 percentage points more than our hijab-wearing confederates ($t = -4.147$, $p < 0.001$, two-tailed).[20]

The magnitude of this discrimination is especially noteworthy given the nature of the items dropped in the intervention; the oranges and lemons dispersed in a manner that made it challenging for our confederates to retrieve them expediently by themselves, which should have created strong pressures for bystanders to offer assistance regardless of the identity of the confederate.

These results strongly corroborate our findings from the attitudinal analysis that highlighted the importance of religious differences in shaping bias against immigrants. Somewhat surprisingly, however, we find no evidence to suggest that ethno-racial differences between immigrants and natives underpin discriminatory behavior (see column 2 and compare help rates to column 1). This stands in strong contrast to an expansive literature that documents the importance of visible, phenotypical markers in driving group-based animus and hostility (Adida, Laitin, and Valfort, 2016; Chandra, 2006). We return to this question in the next chapter, where we explore the effects of linguistic differences on behavior.

Overall, although we uncovered patterns of discriminatory behavior toward some immigrants, the baseline level of assistance offered to immigrants is high and the lack of significant differences in the treatment of native and immigrant confederates in the control condition provides encouraging evidence in favor of the "conviviality" hypothesis (Gilroy, 2004b) and is consistent with the main thrust of contact theory. The underlying cause of the lack of an effect for ethno-racial differences is not clear, though it is consistent with the expectation that high levels of contact between native and immigrant populations within a broader sociopolitical framework that promotes multiculturalism can reduce discrimination in everyday interactions between natives and immigrants.[21]

20. These findings are robust to alternative modes of analysis. Regression-based analyses that include scene characteristics fixed effects, location fixed effects, and team fixed effects do not change the results substantively. See this chapter's section of the appendix for details.

21. The opposite prediction would follow from the analysis of Adida, Laitin, and Valfort (2016, pp. 178–179) showing that there is more divergence between Christians and Muslims with respect to religious and cultural norms in multiculturalist as opposed to assimilationist countries in Europe.

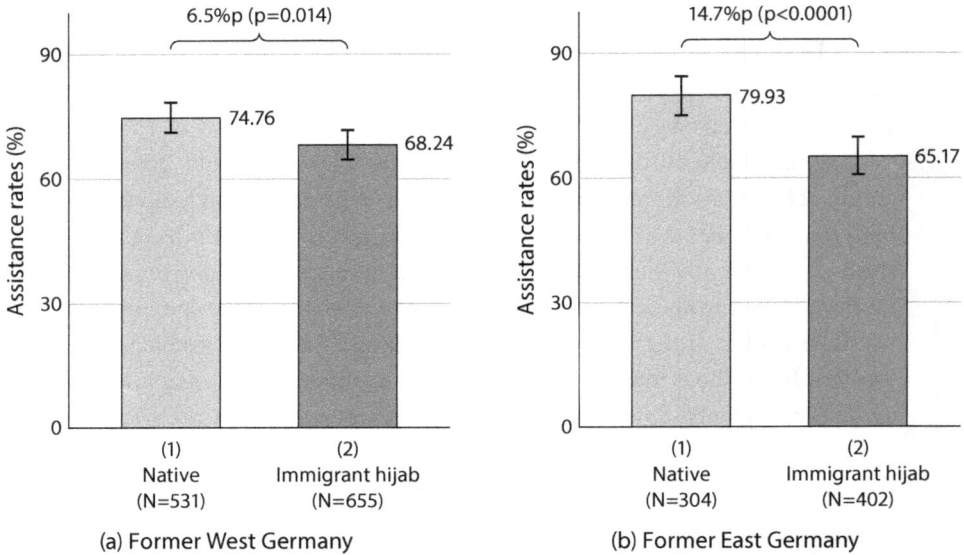

FIGURE 3.11. Discrimination against immigrants by East vs. West Germany
Notes: The figure is generated based on data that pools across the two experiments, but disaggregated by region (former West vs. East Germany). Bars represent the mean rates of assistance for the treatment conditions. The error bars present 95% confidence intervals for the means. The brackets and accompanying information report results of a standard two-tailed difference in means test of treatment conditions with p-values in parentheses.

Discrimination in Former West/East Germany   The degree of discrimination against immigrants is not constant across all regions and cities in Germany. One of the reasons we made the decision to field the experiments across multiple different German states is because we anticipated heterogeneity in the level of discrimination based on location. We expected that discrimination would be larger in areas that fell under former East Germany than the former West.[22]

We tested this expectation by comparing the level of assistance offered to native German vs. hijab-wearing confederates, disaggregated by region. The results of this subgroup analysis is presented in figure 3.11.[23] In line with our expectations, we find that the magnitude of discrimination observed is larger

22. This "subgroup analysis" and expectation of heterogeneity were specified prior to data collection in pre-analysis plans.
23. The observed difference in discrimination reflects in part greater bias against Muslims in the East, but also greater pro-sociality toward the ingroup. We also provide analysis

in former East German cities than West German cities. Panel (a) of figure 3.11 shows that in the former West, our hijab-wearing confederates were 6.5 percentage points less likely to be helped by a bystander than our native German confederates ($t = -2.469$, $p = 0.0137$, two-tailed). By contrast, the level of discrimination observed in the former East is more than double that in the West, at 14.7 percentage points ($t = -4.355$, $p < 0.001$, two-tailed). Although we are not adequately powered statistically, this 8.2 percentage point difference in the size of the discrimination effects (*difference in differences*) is statistically significant at $p < 0.1$.

This heightened level of discrimination in the former East could be due to a number of structural and social factors. First, large parts of the East (especially the vast rural areas) suffer from high unemployment, limited economic opportunities, and lower salaries and pensions, leading to heightened fears of economic deprivation and perceptions of increased competition for jobs and state resources. These structural differences between the former East and West continue to persist even three decades after German reunification, despite important advances in some areas.

Second, many areas in the former East have experienced significantly less exposure to immigrants. Historically, both the GDR and the FDR had actively pursued policies to attract foreign workers. However, the number of *Vertragsarbeiter* (contract workers) who came to East Germany (primarily from other socialist states, such as Vietnam, Cuba, and Angola) was much lower than the large group of of *Gastarbeiter* (guest workers) from Italy, Greece, Turkey, etc. who lived and worked in West Germany. Even after reunification, this pattern persisted with the more recent immigrant groups arriving to Germany during the 1990s and early 2000s.[24] Most recently, in the years following the so-called "refugee crisis" of 2015 during which Germany received over 1.5 million asylum applications, this trend further continued: the quota system used to allocate asylum seekers to different states (*Königsteiner Schlüssel*), which is based on state-level tax revenues (weighted 2/3) and population sizes (weighted 1/3), has resulted in a high influx of refugees into states in the former West, which happen to be among the most populous and affluent states in Germany, and a low influx of refugees to states in the former East,

---

that disaggregates by state rather than region. These results are provided in figure A.3 in the appendix.

24. The state of Berlin presents an important exception to this trend.

which tend to be sparsely populated and lag behind western German states in terms of tax revenue.

Third, an extensive network of local far-right and anti-immigrant groups have taken root in many towns and cities in the former East, at least since the 1990s. Already well before the well-publicized anti-immigrant protests in Chemnitz and elsewhere during the summer of 2018 (and the electoral success of the far-right AfD in many districts in the East), these groups played a crucial role in organizing assaults on refugee homes in the '90s and creating support for the far-right NPD in the late '90s and early 2000s.

Discussion

The evidence presented in this chapter suggests that both religious and linguistic differences shape Germans' negative attitudes toward immigrants; but that religion—specifically opposition to Islam—stands out as a factor that explains both negative *attitudes* and negative *behavior*. The central role of religious difference in anti-immigration attitudes is reflected in the catchy phrase "Islam is like Spanish" (Zolberg and Woon, 1999), which suggests that, just as language is the dominant cleavage generating identity threat and native-immigrant conflict in the United States, so is religion the central cleavage structuring native-immigrant conflict in many Western European countries. An implication of the central role of religious difference in shaping attitudes toward immigrants is that natives' beliefs about Islam are likely to be projected on to individual Muslim immigrants as natives will use stereotypes in making quick assessments of Muslim immigrants they encounter in everyday interactions. Thus, beliefs about value-conflict between Islam and Christianity are likely to shape how individual natives treat individual immigrants in the absence of more specific information about what these immigrants actually believe and how different they really are from natives as a whole.

The ongoing wars in the Middle East and the rise in Islamic terrorism in the West since the September 11 attacks on the United States are at least partly responsible for the rise in anti-Muslim attitudes in Germany and other European countries. This is reflected in our survey data in the relatively high percentage of respondents who cite security concerns as one of the main reasons for their anti-immigrant attitudes. However, our surveys also suggest that Islamophobia (fear of Muslims) has multiple causes and the discrete choice experiments presented in this chapter reveal a more generalized aversion to foreigners that runs deeper than what security concerns could possibly explain.

Our analysis generates important lessons for the viability of multiculturalism in European societies such as Germany's. Many have declared Germany's experiment with multiculturalism as having failed,[25] and our results could be read as providing some support to such views. However, amidst the evidence of growing anti-immigrant bias in Germany, the news is not all bad.

It is bad news for multiculturalism in Germany that our survey experiments reveal a generalized aversion to outsiders regardless of their specific nationality; immigrants are likely to face barriers to social acceptance and inclusion regardless of their country of origin or ethnicity. It is also bad news that implicit bias against Muslims is high; that many Germans feel that immigration from Muslim countries threatens their identity; that so many natives see immigrants as a drain on the economy and on public finances; and that large-scale immigration makes their homeland not feel like home any more.

But the good news is that there is no one-to-one conversion of these negative attitudes into negative behavior. Our field experiments, implemented across many cities and states in Germany over two years, reveal no significant evidence of discrimination against immigrants on the basis of their ethnicity or language. This is a big finding, to the extent that we care about how people *behave* rather than simply whether they appear to be prejudiced in surveys. Our experiments implement a novel intervention that allows us to measure discrimination in everyday interactions—the sort of encounters that, as a result of repeated experiences over time, could shape individual perceptions of how one is perceived in society. We use helping behavior as a measure of discrimination and this allows us to observe spontaneous acts of solidarity during chance encounters in public spaces that are shaped by the internalized consequences of the multiethnic, multicultural fabric of German society. These encounters provide opportunities to identify any latent evidence of "taste-based" discrimination against immigrants and, while we do find clear evidence of such discrimination against Muslims, we also find a high baseline rate of help offered to all immigrants—including those wearing symbols of Islam.

The differences between the treatment of hijab-wearing women and other immigrant women or German natives is significant and substantively large.

25. See the BBC article "Merkel says German multicultural society has failed," https://www.bbc.com/news/world-europe-11559451 (accessed 4/4/2020).

Our carefully controlled experimental design allows us to isolate the effect of symbols of Islamic faith and contrast them to the effects of other ascriptive characteristics and attributes that ordinary people use to categorize strangers into ingroups and outgroups. Seen against the backdrop of a huge interdisciplinary literature that finds evidence of ingroup bias and outgroup prejudice across multiple dimensions of social life, the fact that we only identify bias along the single dimension of religion is encouraging news for the future of multiculturalism in Europe. However, it also pushes us to look deeper into the distinction between religion and other immigrant attributes and to consider ways to reduce such discrimination. We provide a more detailed examination of the effects of ethno-linguistic difference in the next chapter, where we test whether linguistic assimilation can offset the bias against Muslims; and in chapters 5 and 6 we consider the ideational and normative content of anti-Muslim bias.

4

Linguistic Assimilation

THE PREVIOUS CHAPTER presented clear evidence of bias and discrimination toward Muslim immigrants in Germany. To what extent is this behavior driven by religious difference alone? Are perceptions of linguistic differences between the native population and immigrant minorities part of what generates discrimination? Both popular discourse and prior research suggest that natives consider linguistic assimilation—the adoption of the host society's language—to be a critical condition for the acceptance of immigrants into native society. In this chapter, we explore whether linguistic assimilation can reduce discrimination due to religious differences between natives and immigrants. We do so by measuring the impact of linguistic assimilation in an expanded version of our experiment that includes additional treatment arms to manipulate language.[1]

Native Preference for Linguistic Assimilation

Immigrants, refugees, and asylum seekers will need to be economically integrated in their host societies so they can provide for themselves and their families, and be productive members of society. An important step toward successful economic integration is the acquisition of language skills that allow immigrants to communicate effectively in the marketplace. However, learning the "host" country's language is not merely a practical consideration that improves immigrants' employment opportunities; it has implications far beyond the marketplace. Becoming part of the nation requires sharing the nation's language—a common language can be crucial for disparate groups

---

1. Material presented in this chapter draws on Choi, Poertner, and Sambanis (2021).

of people to begin imagining themselves as part of the same national unit (Anderson, 1983, p. 44). Sharing a language enables cultural understanding and is a step toward forging a common identity. "To speak [a language] . . . means above all assuming a culture and bearing the weight of a civilization . . . a man who possesses a language possesses as an indirect consequence the world expressed and implied by that language" (Fanon, 2008[1952], p. 2). The immigrant's decision to learn the host country's language, particularly in cases where immigration flows from less-developed countries to former colonial metropoles, is often understood as an assimilative strategy; natives recognize that linguistic assimilation requires effort by immigrants, and is a demonstration of their intent to "fit in." Some may even take linguistic assimilation as a signal that immigrants' "local cultural originality has been committed to the grave" as they adopt the "civilizing language: i.e., the metropolitan culture" (Fanon, 2008[1952], p. 2). To the extent that linguistic assimilation is an individual choice, persistent language differences are likely to be perceived by the native population as an unwillingness by immigrants to become part of their new country. Rejection of the native language by the immigrant could be construed as indifference or resistance to the native culture.

An extensive literature has identified the unwillingness of immigrants to linguistically assimilate as a particularly important cause of fears that immigration threatens the national culture (Hopkins, 2014b; Citrin et al., 2007; Dowling, Ellison, and Leal, 2012; Schildkraut, 2010; Schildkraut, 2005; Newman, Hartman, and Taber, 2012). Indeed, linguistic differences are the most commonly used measure of cultural fragmentation used in the political science literature, where analysts have used indices of diversity in the languages spoken within countries as the basis of quantitative indices of those countries' social or cultural "heterogeneity" or their "fractionalization" (Fearon, 2003; Posner, 2004). Those indices are then correlated with various outcomes and a common hypothesis is that higher levels of heterogeneity, measured by the degree of ethno-linguistic fractionalization, are associated with more dysfunctional societies. Fractionalization is thought to produce less trusting, less productive, and more conflictual societies.[2] In countries with a high influx of immigrants, ethno-linguistic differences are

2. Typically, researchers compute fractionalization indices as the probability that any two randomly selected individuals speak a different language. The most commonly used source of data on languages is *Atlas Narodov Mira*, a compendium by the Department of Geography and Cartography of the State Geological Committee of the USSR dated in 1964, though other

bound to be more pronounced and noticeable by ordinary citizens in everyday interactions, potentially creating fears of a growing degree of cultural heterogeneity.[3] Those fears can generate identity threat, which in turn can cause exclusionary attitudes toward outsiders among the native population (Enos, 2014).

Consistent with the theories of social identity (Tajfel, 1981), prejudice (Allport, 1979; Paluck and Green, 2009), and ethnocentrism (Kinder and Kam, 2010) that we reviewed in chapter 2, previous literature has presented extensive evidence that ethno-linguistic differences are associated with lower social trust (Alesina and LaFerra, 2002; Dinesen and Sønderskov, 2015; Dinesen and Sønderskov, 2018), economic discrimination (Habyarimana et al., 2007; Riach and Rich, 2002; Michelitch, 2015), diminished contributions to public goods (Alesina, Baqir, and Easterly, 1999; Baldwin and Huber, 2010), and violent conflict (Horowitz, 1985; Hegre and Sambanis, 2006; Montalvo and Reynal-Querol, 2005; Cederman and Girardin, 2007). In the United States, linguistic differences make ethnic and national identities salient; studies have shown that exposure to even brief uses of Spanish by strangers in public settings generates hostility among natives (Hopkins, 2014b; Newman, Hartman, and Taber, 2012; Zolberg and Woon, 1999; Paxton, 2006; Hopkins, Tran, and Williamson, 2011) and these ethnic differences have profound effects on the country's politics (Abrajano and Hajnal, 2015; Hill, Hopkins, and Huber, 2019). This effect could be due to the fact that proximity to an outgroup makes the outgroup identity cognitively salient and heightens the contrast to the ingroup (McGuire et al., 1978; McGarty and Penny, 1988). Politicians can exploit this heightened sensitivity to ingroup-outgroup distinctions to mobilize support behind a partisan agenda. Language differences reinforce the perception of "otherness" that can induce natives to develop prejudices leading to discrimination toward immigrants, whom they consider to pose a sociotropic threat to their own group (Hainmueller and Hopkins, 2014, p. 232). The

---

sources also exist. For more discussion on how to measure ethno-linguistic fractionalization and its impact on social and political outcomes, see Posner, 2004.

3. Interestingly, commonly used measures of ethno-linguistic fractionalization in the political science literature do not incorporate linguistic differences due to recent immigration. Instead, they are fairly static representations of the share of languages spoken in the country over long periods of time (decades). One study that takes immigrants partially into account to produce indices of cultural heterogeneity (Fearon, 2003) shows that doing so can have outsize effects on the overall country-level index of cultural heterogeneity.

more distant the immigrant, the greater the perceived threat (Theiss-Morse, 2009).[4]

The breadth of studies showing negative effects of linguistic differences across a wide range of contexts is growing as the size of immigration flows also grows. This is therefore an appropriate time to ask whether large-scale immigration will necessarily lead to more conflict and less desirable social outcomes due to the perception of persisting linguistic differences between natives and immigrants. The answer to that question is: "not necessarily; it depends on the context." One of the central insights to emerge from the political science literature on identity politics is that the salience of ethno-linguistic divisions varies over time and across contexts (Chandra and Wilkinson, 2008) and that conflict along ethnic lines will covary with the salience of ethnic cleavages (Tajfel, 1981; Cikara and Bavel, 2014; Sherif et al., 1961; Brewer and Kramer, 1985). Thus, models of social identity and conflict posit that the association between linguistic or other cultural differences on the one hand and discrimination or conflict on the other hand will be contingent on the sociopolitical context (Sambanis and Shayo, 2013). While linguistic differences might cause discrimination in some contexts, as studies have shown is the case in the United States (Sniderman et al., 2002; Kinzler et al., 2009; Gluszek and Dovidio, 2010), in other contexts we might observe no such relationships. It follows that while linguistic assimilation might help reduce intergroup conflict in some contexts (Hopkins, 2014b), in other contexts assimilation might not have such a beneficial effect. In countries where the population has been accustomed to a deeper level of multiculturalism, linguistic assimilation might not reduce bias due to differences in other ascriptive characteristics.

We pursue this idea further in two large field experiments conducted in thirty cities across former West and East Germany and involving thousands of subjects. The experiments build on the design we introduced in chapter 3, where we manipulated the ethno-religious attributes of confederates who were part of an "intervention." We now also manipulate the language these confederates use to conduct a conversation within earshot of unknowing bystanders who can overhear the content and language of the conversation. We observe how bystanders react to the conversation, varying the

---

4. Even small differences in accents—let alone speaking a foreign language—are sufficient to classify an individual as a member of an outgroup; and accents sometimes provide a stronger signal of categorization than physical appearance or ethno-racial traits, as evidenced in experiments conducted in Germany by Rakic, Steffens, and Mummendey, 2011.

language used by the confederates. As in chapter 3, bystanders' helping behavior is the main behavioral outcome we observe. We now analyze the effects of the language used to make the call. We test whether exposure to foreign language–speaking minorities of immigrant background generates bias among natives; and whether immigrants who appear to be linguistically assimilated are treated better than others. The results, which are presented in more detail below, suggest that exposure to foreign language use does *not* cause bias among German natives and that linguistic assimilation does *not* reduce bias toward Muslims. These precisely estimated null findings go against expectations of large effects of linguistic difference on discrimination, and *might* be encouraging news for the future of multiculturalism in Europe.

Before we proceed to describe our study and discuss our findings, we briefly consider the political context that has affected the role of language in the evolution of nationalism and national identity in Germany. Our review of the survey-based literature on immigration in chapter 1 helped put Germany in a broader context and it is now important to establish whether the role of language in relations between natives and immigrants in Germany is somehow unique or atypical in relation to the rest of Europe.

The Importance of Language in German Identity

> Has a nationality anything dearer than the speech of its father? In its speech resides its whole thought domain, its tradition, history, religion and basis of life, all its heart and soul. To deprive a people of its speech is to deprive it of its eternal good. . . . With language is created the heart of the people.
>
> —JOHANN HERDER (1793)

Ethnic nationalism is typically founded on a shared language that forms the cornerstone of national myths and traditions which can unify disparate groups via mass schooling and the inculcation of ideas of common origin and common identity (Gellner, 1983; Hobsbawm and Ranger, 1983). Germany is no exception to that rule. The German language was particularly central in the process of German identity formation since German regions were fragmented after the dissolution of the Holy Roman Empire. A shared language was the initial seed for cultivating "a spirit of loyalty to the Emperor" (Jansen, 2011). The shared feeling of "Germanness" prior to the period of German unification was based on the shared German language (Lytra, 2016; Kamusella, 2001). In the absence of a unified German state prior to the Franco-Prussian War,

German romantics interested in cultivating the idea of "Germanness" invested heavily in the value of a shared language (Dow, 1999). A shared language put the German people in contact with an idealized version of its past, cultivating *Deutschtümelei*, a nostalgic view of the German people that is subsequently reinforced with ideas regarding the superiority of the German nation (Dow, 1999; Abizadeh, 2005).

As in other countrys' contexts, so in Germany, language was used as a way of establishing a social hierarchy, an indexical approach to *purity*. German romantics advanced ideas of Germans as the "pure" descendants of the original Indo-European peoples. Common references to Tacitus have been made (see, e.g., Dow, 1999, p. 286), as Tacitus regarded the Germans as "aboriginal, and not mixed at all with other races," an idea which was readily picked up by German philosophers, poets, and linguists interested in cultivating a sense of ethnic and racial homogeneity, distinctiveness, and superiority for the German people. German baroque linguist scholars highlighted the artistic "correctness" of the German language, its large number of non-borrowed stem words, and its historical depth, arguing for a standardization of German (Mattheier, 2003).[5] They were not merely concerned with reinforcing the socio-communicative advantages of a shared language; they defended the standardization and use of the German language with a mix of patriotic and cultural arguments reflecting a belief in the superiority of the German language and German people.[6] These tendencies were reflected in the ideology that supported the national socialist movement leading up to the start of World War II.

World War II and the time of the Nationalist Socialist reign in Germany refocused the idea of German identity around the concept of a shared bloodline

---

5. Gardt, 2001 analyzed texts from the sixteenth century until the mid-1930s and found four discourses related to the purity of the German language, focused on language structure, ideology, pedagogical implications, and stylistic concerns. The ideological discourse is characterized by a praise of the German language, its purity, and its history—very often language is explicitly considered a part of individuals' self-concept. Pfalzgraf, 2009 identifies several waves of language purism in Germany in the same period—each wave was launched by concerns that "Germanness" was threatened and led to a nationalistic burst that involved movements for language purism that relied on an ideological discourse against the use of foreign words and languages. To protect their national identity, Germans have repeatedly defended their language as the core of Germanness against the corrupting influence of foreign languages that threaten to make it less pure.

6. Jacob Grimm writes in his *German Grammar* from 1819 that "no folk on earth has such a history for its language as does German" (cited in Dow, 1999, p. 288).

rather than shared language. The disastrous outcome of the war also changed how Germans felt about their country and induced a widespread feeling of shame in expressions of nationalism and in German national identity (Miller-Idriss and Rothenberg, 2012; Dresler-Hawke and Liu, 2006, pp. 142–143). For most of the postwar period, this is reflected in very low levels of national pride in Germany relative to other advanced industrial democracies (Inglehart et al. 2000; ISSP, 1998). For many Germans, expressions of national pride could be equated with Nazism and were therefore avoided. Nationalism was confined to feelings of pride in Germany's economic strength and on ideas of constitutional patriotism which allowed them to coalesce as a nation while avoiding the guilt and shame brought by the legacy of Nazism. This muted nationalism lasted through the period of Germany's ascendancy in the European Union and until a backlash to globalization and immigration led to a strengthening of support for far-right groups (Dodd, 2015; Linke, 2003).

The feeling of collective shame in the postwar period led to downplaying the role of shared language as a core component of German identity (Mattheier, 2003, p. 240) as the very idea of the German nation was contested and re-imagined. Reflective of this development was the gradual de-standardization of German and calls for linguistic purism were largely absent in Germany until the 1990s (Pfalzgraf, 2009). Stylistic and linguistic norms changed and the idea of a national language as a core social value became less prevalent as regional languages and linguistic standards gained strength (Mattheier, 2003). Since World War II, only about 20% of Germans use the standard language exclusively, and 80% speak their regional languages or switch between dialects and standard German (Mattheier, 2003). This emphasis on regionalism is also evident in Germans' high degree of attachment to their states: 76% state that they feel connected to their state—a proportion equivalent to the proportion of Germans who feel connected to Germany.[7]

Denglisch? *Nein, Bitte!*

Since the 1990s, the challenges following Germany's reunification, the deepening and broadening of the process of European integration, and growing cultural threats due to the globalization of trade and increasing labor mobility

---

7. Schaal, Gary S., Hans Vorländer and Claudia Ritzi (2009). 60 Jahre Grundgesetz. Deutsche Identität im Spannungsfeld von Europäisierung und Regionalisierung. Ergebnisse einer repräsentativen Bevölkerungsbefragung. Available online at: https://tu-dresden.de /gsw/phil/powi/poltheo/ressourcen/dateien/zvd/news/Bericht_60-Jahre-Grundgesetz.pdf (accessed: August 1, 2020). Hereafter cited in text as Schaal et al., 2009.

all combined to reignite German nationalism particularly among supporters of right-wing parties. For some communities, the threat of multiculturalism translated into a renewed focus on taking pride in speaking German as a way to resist both the growing prevalence of immigrant communities and the influence of the English language that was thought to erode German culture (Linke, 2003). One related development was the growth of organizations dedicated to resisting the use of anglicisms in the German language.[8] Combating "Denglisch" and protecting the German language from foreign influences is the purpose of such organizations.

Several of these organizations supporting linguistic purity had close connections with important figures of the political right (Pfalzgraf, 2003). The language purism they promoted was reflective of ideas shared by a small, conservative fraction of the population (Pfalzgraf, 2009). Among the many initiatives promoted by these organizations, perhaps most widely accepted was an initiative of the Verein Deutscher Sprache e.V., and its magazine *Deutsche Sprachwelt* (German language world), to petition for the German Basic Law to recognize German as the official language of Germany. The petition was first submitted in 2012 with more than 75,000 signatures, but did not receive the required two-thirds of votes in the German Bundestag (Dodd, 2015). Since then it has lost momentum. However, the idea of amending the Basic Law to specify German as the country's official language is widely supported. Eighty-five percent of citizens support the amendment, with support even higher among older citizens and citizens from former East Germany (Schaal et al., 2009). The issue seems largely symbolic,[9] as it would not change the practice of everyday life in Germany, where German is clearly the dominant language and speaking German is also a formal requirement of the naturalization process.

8. An example of such an organization is Verein Deutscher Sprache e.V. (Association of the German Language), which perceives the growing influence of international organizations and increasing Americanization of everyday life as a threat to German identity. In the organization's website, Denglisch is described derogatorily as Kauderwelsch—gibberish.

9. This is reflected well in a speech by Gitta Connemann, member of the German Bundestag for the CDU, who said, "I love the German language . . . . It is more than an instrument, it is the expression of our culture. It is the language of philosophy, the poets and the thinkers, because of its expressiveness" (Gitta Connemann, in front of the German Bundestag). The full text of her speech is available at: Hereafter cited in text as Deutscher Bundestag (2018). Deutsch als Landessprache. Retrieved on October 7, 2020. Available online at: https://www.bundestag .de/dokumente/textarchiv/2018/kw09-de-deutsch-landessprache-544508 (accessed August 1, 2020).

In this context, immigration posed another threat for the purity of the German language. As mentioned in previous chapters, Germany never saw itself as a country of immigrants, and immigrant workers in the 1960s and 1970s were thought of as "guest workers" who would eventually leave. As the intention was never to fully integrate guest workers but to encourage their repatriation to their countries eventually, these workers enjoyed cultural freedoms, including use of their language. Over time, immigrants who became fully settled in Germany developed new hybrid identities that came with a hybrid language—or *ethnolects*—such as *Kiezdeutsch*, a mixture of German with Turkish which for many natives calls to question the idea of Germany as a single nation with a single, unifying language. Popular resistance to Kiezdeutsch has been widely documented[10] and the public perception among large groups of natives is that Kiezdeutsch is an inferior language spoken by outgroup members.[11]

10. An illustration of the negative public reaction to multilingual practices was the media frenzy surrounding the revised Immigration Law. In 2005–2006, the administration of a school in Berlin decided to declare that German was "the language of the school" and that other languages were not to be used on school premises, even though 92% of the students spoke languages other than German as their first language. The new immigration legislation made "language knowledge" a key measure of "national belonging" and a criterion for acquiring German citizenship (Stevenson, 2015).

11. An interesting set of experiments by Freywald et al. (2011) provide comparisons between student perceptions of language in monoethnic vs. multiethnic schools in two different school districts of Berlin. The authors conduct a study in two schools in different districts in Berlin. One district is multiethnic, the other district monoethnic, but they don't differ in terms of socioeconomic characteristics. Students were presented with short (four-word) sentences, some of which were in standard German, some in Kiezdeutsch, and some were using false grammar. Students were asked to rate the "acceptability" of these sentences in everyday use by themselves or their friends. The results show that Kiezdeutsch is emerging as a new linguistic system among some citizen groups. Standard German was equally accepted in school districts regardless of the degree of ethnic diversity, while grammatically false sentences were equally rejected in both districts. But the districts differed with respect to their degree of acceptance of sentences in Kiezdeutsch. In the multiethnic district, Kiezdeutsch was accepted in the majority of iterations of the experiment (58%), whereas in the monoethnic district the degree of acceptance was much lower (25%). Monoethnic students described Kiezdeutsch as "prole-like," "typical for foreigners," "for stupid people," and "bad German," and relied on a "we" vs. "them" rhetoric to signal they don't use Kiezdeutsch because they are German, unlike foreigners. In the multiethnic school, students recognized that Kiezdeutsch was often incorrect, but they considered it the language of their environment.

The immigration law reform was informed by public reactions to Germany's growing multiculturalism and language acquisition was emphasized as a key part of the naturalization process. Integration courses are offered by the ministry with very high enrollments by immigrants (2.3 million since 2005). In addressing this issue, the Federal Minister of the Interior at the time, Otto Schily, defined integration as "knowledge of the German language, and acceptance of the German constitution as well as of the political culture" (Ehrkamp, 2006). The local public discourse regarding immigrant integration parallels the debate at the national level. An ethnographic study (Ehrkamp, 2006) in Duisburg-Marxloh (in North Rhine-Westphalia), a relatively poor neighborhood negatively affected by economic restructuring with a large immigrant population, offers a glimpse of natives' anxieties. German-speaking natives of the region lamented that Turkish immigrants did not put enough effort into assimilating and that their "Turkish behaviors" made them inherently different. They highlighted that many Turkish shops advertised in Turkish rather than post German signs on their windows and rejected bilingual posters by political parties. Many felt offended or excluded by the use of Turkish and concerns about religion seemed at least equally important. Debates around teachers wearing headscarves and demands to broadcast calls for Friday prayers across the neighborhood were perceived as palpable examples of cultural threat that were framed by religious difference rather than by language.

Despite these pockets of resistance to the use of foreign languages, the broader trend has been one of normalization of non-German language use across Germany. For example, in defeating a bill advanced by the AfD in 2018 to specify German as the country's official language in the Basic Law, the majority in the Bundestag (consisting of members of the SPD, FDP, The Left, and the Alliance 90/The Greens) expressed the view that the initiative was polarizing and defended language diversity. Johann Saathoff of the SPD spoke in relation to that initiative partly in Low German, arguing that Germany would "not be poorer because of other languages, but richer" and that language naturally develops and changes (Deutscher Bundestag, 2018).

Beyond such symbolic actions at the federal level, we can observe a growing willingness of regional and local governments to accommodate the use of languages other than German in everyday interactions between citizens and the state. This trend has accelerated even further in response to the so-called refugee crisis of 2015, which brought millions of people to Germany who at least initially had limited or no German language skills. Such a development would have been unthinkable twenty years ago or earlier; and even the Kiezdeutsch ethnolect is becoming increasingly acceptable to a broad range of social groups (Auer, 2003).

To sum up, while historically German language played a crucial role in the formation of German identity and in the design and propagation of exclusivist ideologies leading up to the outbreak of World War II, the legacy of the war and other macro-level changes, including immigration, have reduced the emphasis on linguistic purity and tolerance of foreign languages is more widespread in Germany today. At the same time, learning German remains important, especially for the economic integration of immigrants in Germany as it is in other European countries, and most Germans identify native language proficiency as a very important qualification for accepting immigrants.[12] As a result, German language use has become increasingly separated from a national identity in recent years and instead might be viewed more as a "practical" matter concerning immigrants' economic integration.

While the importance of language is reflected in the results of our conjoint experiment in chapter 3,[13] and echoes Habermas's view of Germans' "understanding of themselves as a nation of *Volksgenossen* or ethnic comrades centered around language and culture" (Habermas, 1994, p. 145), the decreasing emphasis put on "linguistic purity" for German identity over time and multiculturalist immigration policies may have reduced the salience of ethno-linguistic differences separating native Germans from immigrants. Indeed, in the climate of post-2015 immigration with the waves of new arrivals

12. According to data from the European Social Survey from 2014, 74.8% of Germans think it should be important for immigrants to be able to speak the country's official language in order to be able to come and live in Germany. The importance that people placed on speaking the host country language is similar to Switzerland (75.0%), Hungary (73.4%), the Netherlands (79.9%), and Ireland (79.9%). Only respondents in Belgium (82.4%), France (83.2%), Austria (83.3%), and the United Kingdom (87.6%) placed slightly more importance on the topic. People in all of these countries placed much more importance on immigrants learning the countries' official languages than respondents across Scandinavia (Norway: 53.9%, Finland: 49.9%, Denmark: 47.7%, and Sweden: 31.9%).

13. Additional evidence in support of the view that linguistic assimilation is as important in Germany as in other European countries is provided in a multicountry conjoint analysis of attitudes toward refugees by Bansak, Hainmueller, and Hangartner (2016). They present respondents with a forced choice experiment which reveals their preferences over refugees with different attributes, and language skills is one of the included attributes. The results with respect to the importance of language look similar in every European country with more negative preferences registered toward asylum seekers who have weaker native language skills.

from Middle Eastern countries, religion might have become more salient. We now turn to an empirical analysis of the effects of linguistic differences in everyday interactions between natives and immigrants across several cities in Germany.

Experimental Intervention

One could think of several different ways to collect data on natives' views of the importance of linguistic assimilation by immigrants. Most of the literature we referenced earlier in this chapter has used survey-based data to describe and analyze attitudes toward immigrants and linguistic difference. Our approach is to build on the design presented in chapter 3 to explore the consequences of linguistic difference or assimilation for everyday forms of interaction between immigrants and natives. That perspective presents a new context within which to appreciate the importance of language for identity and discrimination. Effectively we ask whether natives behave differently toward strangers who speak their own language versus those who speak a foreign language.

The experimental intervention proceeded as follows: a female confederate approached a bench at a train station where other individuals were waiting for their train (step 1). The confederate attracted the bystanders' attention by answering a phone call in either German or a foreign language (Turkish or Arabic).[14] The confederate's telephone conversation was with a friend, discussing a personal matter (step 2).[15] To ensure that the confederate got the bystanders' attention before the onset of the call, her phone rang with a loud, noticeable ringtone, while she was standing right in front of the bystanders. She remained in this location for the duration of the call. The content of the phone call revealed the confederate's putative level of linguistic assimilation as all immigrant confederates in the German language condition spoke fluent German and, implicitly, hinted at the identity of the confederate's social network since the conversation was held in German. As the call was ending,

14. As explained in chapter 3, our field experiment was initially implemented during the summer of 2018 and replicated in the summer of 2019 in a follow-up experiment which shared common treatment arms with the first experiment. In 2018, the foreign language conversation was in either Turkish or Arabic; in 2019, it was always in Turkish. Results disaggregated by foreign language are presented in the appendix.

15. In reality, she had received a call from another member of our team of confederates who was not acting in that particular iteration.

the confederate dropped fruit (oranges or lemons) from a paper bag that had seemingly torn at the bottom (this is the same as in the experiments discussed in the previous chapter). The fruit dispersed in a random manner and the confederate appeared to need help picking them up (step 3). We observed whether bystanders who were exposed to the prior steps of the intervention offered assistance to the confederate in recollecting her possessions (step 4).[16]

Treatment Dimensions

Our interventions in the two experiments varied three key experimental dimensions: the ethnicity of the confederate "performing" the intervention (immigrant or native); their perceived religion or religiosity (hijab-wearing Muslim; native; or immigrant with no religious symbols); as well as their putative level of linguistic assimilation (speaking German, Turkish, or Arabic).[17] We manipulate the putative religion of the confederate (Muslim) by making our immigrant minority confederate implement our intervention while wearing a hijab or without, as in the previous chapter. We restrict

16. In order to give bystanders a chance to offer help and to avoid unscripted communication between confederates and bystanders, confederates were instructed to continue talking while "wrapping up" the call while bystanders were helping retrieve the oranges/lemons. They were instructed to tell their friend on the phone that they just dropped something and that they would have to call them back later, allowing a period of a few seconds (around 5–10) to elapse before concluding the phone call and putting away the cell phone so bystanders could help without engaging in unscripted conversation with the confederate. Helping behavior was observed during that 5–10 second period, after which the confederate, if applicable, would thank bystanders verbally with a simple "Thank you" (in German) and pick up any remaining lemons/oranges.

17. As mentioned earlier, "natives" are defined as people of Germanic heritage rather than simply individuals who were born in Germany. This is consistent with the popular notion of "*bio-Deutsch*" (biologically German) that is prevalent in Germany and reflects the ethnic basis of German national identity. "Immigrants" are persons with national origin other than Germany, including second-generation German citizens of immigrant origin. The "manipulation checks" that we present in chapter 3's section in the appendix suggest that subjects correctly perceived the confederates' native vs. immigrant identities. This distinction was made salient by using confederates with phenotypical differences from the typical German, and those differences evoked the identity of immigrants of Middle Eastern origin. A scope condition for our study is that it refers to immigrants who are visibly "different" and our results need not apply to immigrants who resemble native Germans.

TABLE 4.1. Treatment Matrix for Language Experiment

Condition	Ethnicity	Religious Symbol	Language
1	Immigrant	Hijab	Foreign
2	Immigrant	Hijab	German
3	Immigrant	No Hijab	Foreign
4	Immigrant	No Hijab	German
5	Native	—	German

our native confederates to only speaking in German and we experimentally manipulate the perceived level of linguistic assimilation of the nonnative confederate by varying the language used by the confederate in conducting the phone conversation. Our focus is to test the widely accepted idea that foreign language–speaking non-co-ethnics (who are therefore less likely to be linguistically assimilated) will be perceived as more culturally distant, and therefore be subject to discrimination by native populations (Hainmueller and Hiscox, 2010; Gluszek and Dovidio, 2010). Our design therefore allows us to test whether the level of linguistic assimilation by immigrants affects the level of discrimination they face from native populations. The treatment and control conditions for the experiment are presented in table 4.1.

As in chapter 3, apart from these three dimensions, we maintain perceived social class constant both across experimental conditions and across teams of confederates by having the confederates wear similar attire indicative of a middle class background. We mitigate concerns regarding the possibility that differing levels of confederate attractiveness is likely to affect assistance rates by having the same confederate play both the hijab-wearing immigrant and non-hijab-wearing immigrant roles and by using a rather large number of confederates across teams. We also report in this chapter's section of the appendix that our results hold using team fixed effects, which analyze within-team variation in assistance rates across iterations.

Data Collection

The interventions were conducted in twenty-nine train stations across North Rhine-Westphalia, Saxony, and Brandenburg in 2018; and replicated in twenty-three train stations in North Rhine-Westphalia, Saxony, and Lower Saxony in 2019. We implemented a total of 588 iterations of the intervention, involving 2,560 bystanders over a three-week period between July and August 2018; and, then conducted an additional 980 iterations with a total of 2,097 bystanders in a replication over a five-week period during July and August 2019, following a pilot study in May 2019.

For each iteration, research assistants who did not participate in the intervention themselves recorded the behavior of bystanders. The main outcome of interest, which was coded at the *iteration level*, was whether *any* bystanders offered assistance to the confederate in retrieving her possessions. They also noted the total number and gender of bystanders within a pre-specified radius, as well as other characteristics of each iteration. Only bystanders within earshot (i.e., a radius of three meters around the confederate) were included. We obtained measurements of ambient noise[18] and, during a pilot study in May 2019, we collected data to confirm that bystanders could hear the conversation and recall its content[19] (see appendix for more details on the share of bystanders with earphones and other relevant variables).[20]

Main Findings

We build on the analysis from the previous chapter that established that there is significant discrimination against Muslim immigrants and we examine whether linguistic assimilation by immigrants *reduces* discrimination by natives. As specified in our pre-analysis plans, we employ a standard two-tailed difference in means test to examine assistance rates at the iteration level across our treatment conditions. When estimating covariate-adjusted average treatment effects (ATE), we use a standard linear regression. The primary results

18. The noise levels were low enough to ensure that bystanders could discern the language of the phone call and hear the conversation. The mean background noise was 62 dB; the median was 57 dB, according to noise measurements we took for a sample of the iterations at the exact locations of the interventions on the platforms. This is relatively quiet (comparable to the noise level of a fridge or air conditioning unit one hundred feet away) and should allow that bystanders were easily able to listen to a conversation right in front of them.

19. We did this by conducting a debriefing survey after the intervention was executed; 95.3% of bystanders reported noticing the call. Despite strong social desirability not to admit overhearing other people's private phone conversations, 68.2% of bystanders were *willing* and *able* to recall full details of the call.

20. The research protocol was reviewed and approved by the University of Pennsylvania's Institutional Review Board (IRB Protocols #829824 and #833206). A waiver of the consent process was obtained.

reported in the main text of the paper are based on data that pools observations from experiment 1 (summer 2018) and experiment 2 (summer 2019), since the design remained constant.

Our main objective is to examine whether linguistic assimilation by immigrants *reduces* discrimination by natives. We briefly show in figure A.4 in the appendix that our experimental setup can replicate and successfully recover discrimination effects against Muslim immigrants. Specifically, we find that natives are less likely to offer assistance to Muslim immigrant women (ATE: 9.5 percentage points, p = 0.003), but are no less likely to offer assistance to immigrant minorities whose religious beliefs are not made explicit (ATE: −2.7 percentage points, p = 0.347).[21]

Having established that our experimental design captures discrimination against Muslim immigrants, we investigate whether perceived linguistic assimilation by immigrants *reduces* discrimination. We disaggregate help rates for our two immigrant conditions (with and without hijab) by whether the immigrant confederate conversed in Arabic/Turkish or German. We present these results, as well as our native condition (German confederate who conducted an identical phone call in German), in figure 4.1.

Contrary to our expectations—which were grounded on an expansive literature that predicts linguistic difference to be a powerful driver of discrimination against immigrants (Sniderman et al., 2002; Gluszek and Dovidio, 2010; Hopkins, 2014a)—we find no evidence that linguistic assimilation reduces discrimination. Bystanders do not offer more help to linguistically assimilated immigrants. The point estimates for the assistance rates for hijab-wearing confederates speaking in German versus foreign language—reported in columns (4) and (5) of figure 4.1—are virtually identical (65.57% vs. 65.49%), and the difference is statistically indistinguishable from zero (p = 0.984). Similar results are observed in the assistance rates for our immigrant confederates who did not wear a hijab; columns (2) and (3) show that the difference between these two conditions is around 3 percentage points and fails to reach statistical significance at conventional levels (p = 0.320). In the appendix, we disaggregate results by region, showing that our conclusions hold for both former East and West Germany; German-speaking immigrant minority confederates were no more likely to be assisted by bystanders than foreign language–speaking confederates (ATE = −0.06 percentage points, p = 0.893 in the former East

---

21. Balance statistics for the main results presented in this chapter are presented in the supplementary information appendix file for Choi, Poertner, and Sambanis (2021).

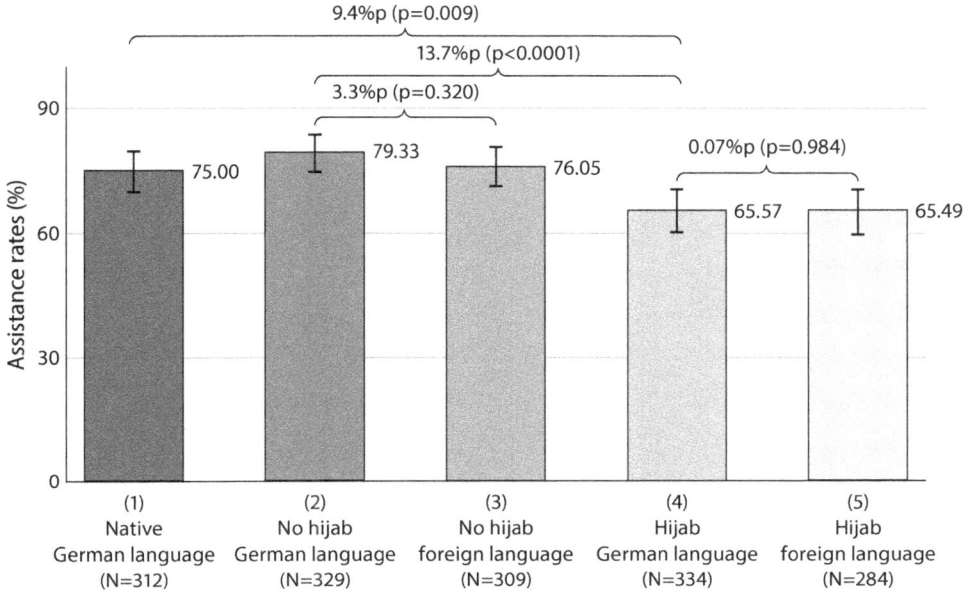

FIGURE 4.1. Language effects: Merged (Experiment 1 & 2)

Notes: The bars reflect the mean rate of assistance for each of the treatment conditions, with 95% confidence intervals. The lines that connect the bars are from a two-tailed difference in means test of the conditions, with associated p-values. The figure pools data across experiments 1 (summer 2018) and 2 (summer 2019).

and −1.4 percentage points, p = 0.828 in the former West). In table A5 of the appendix, we also disaggregate the results by foreign language used—Turkish vs. Arabic—finding no significant differences in assistance rates.

These null effects for linguistic assimilation are confirmed in our covariate-adjusted regression-based analysis, reported in table 4.2. Across specifications that include fixed effects for experiment (experiment 1 vs. 2), the number of bystanders, and team that conducted each iteration, we fail to recover significant effects in assistance rates between immigrants who conversed in a foreign vs. German language; as reported in columns (4)–(6), the point estimate for the comparison consistently remains at 1.4 percentage points, and is statistically indistinguishable from zero. In terms of magnitude, this point estimate is extremely small relative to the effect of religious discrimination, especially considering that an extensive literature reviewed earlier suggests that the effect of linguistic differences should have been very pronounced. These findings, based on insignificant results on conventional modes of significance

TABLE 4.2. Treatment Effects for Linguistic Differences (Pooled Experiments 1 & 2)

	Did Any Bystander Help? (Dichotomous)					
	(1)	(2)	(3)	(4)	(5)	(6)
Hijab	−0.117***	−0.109***	−0.112***			
	(0.030)	(0.030)	(0.030)			
Foreign Language	−0.012	−0.009	−0.019	−0.014	−0.014	−0.014
	(0.031)	(0.031)	(0.033)	(0.025)	(0.026)	(0.028)
Hijab × Foreign	0.011	0.009	0.012			
	(0.047)	(0.047)	(0.047)			
Constant	0.772***			0.724***		
	(0.018)			(0.017)		
Sample	Full	Full	Full	Immigrant	Immigrant	Immigrant
Experiment FE	No	Yes	Yes	No	Yes	Yes
Bystander FE	No	Yes	Yes	No	Yes	Yes
Team FE	No	No	Yes	No	No	Yes
Observations	1,568	1,568	1,568	1,256	1,256	1,256
R^2	0.015	0.039	0.050	0.0002	0.032	0.045

Notes: Standard errors in parentheses. *$p < 0.1$; **$p < 0.05$; ***$p < 0.01$.

testing, are not driven by a lack of statistical power. Our experiments are sufficiently well-powered to detect discrimination along a different dimension (religion) and, according to prior literature, linguistic differences should have had a *larger* effect relative to any other dimension of cultural difference. The coefficient estimates for bias due to language differences are so small as to suggest that there is no substantively important effect.[22]

A note on accents   Before turning to a discussion of the significance of these results, we briefly consider the question of accents. An accent is a non-arbitrary marker for group membership, so when proper German is spoken with an accent individuals may still be classified as nonnative. Accents may trigger unconscious bias according to affective processing theory and research in neuroscience and psychology has shown that accents can influence the perception of threat in voices. In fact, even the "distinctiveness" and "attractiveness"

22. We provide additional evidence in the appendix that null effects on linguistic assimilation should be interpreted as an *absence* of a *substantively meaningful* effect using a series of equivalence tests (Berger, Hsu, et al., 1996; Seaman and Serlin, 1998; Wellek, 2010). We set equivalence bounds based on the size of the discrimination effect due to religious difference and present results using different bounds. See figure A.6.

of voices spoken with accents is rated as different by linguists from that of voices in the "prototypical" language and recent research suggests that non-native accents can also reduce "cognitive fluency" and impair understanding (Gill, 1994). This barrier to understanding is unlikely to be a problem since the message conveyed in the phone call was of no importance.[23] There is evidence that nonstandard accents serve as a cue in the evaluation of speakers and influence their likelihood of getting a job (Aboud, Clement, and Taylor, 1974; Elwell, Brown, and Rutter, 1984). A host of studies have shown that voice cues are used to infer personality characteristics (Allport and Cantril, 1934) and the stronger the degree of a nonstandard accent, the more negative are the evaluations of targets (Ryan, Carranza, and Moffie, 1977). It has long been established that spoken language is crucial for the ethnic categorization of self and others (Giles and Johnson, 1987; Giles, Bourhis, and Taylor, 1977) and that "non-accommodation," i.e., using a nonstandard accent, (Shepard, Giles, and Le Poire, 2001) can involuntarily reveal category membership especially ethnic minority status (Bourhis, Giles, and Tajfel, 1973). The key point here is that the combination of visual and auditory stimuli are likely to be integrated by experimental subjects in ways that the slight accents used by the confederates in the immigrant control condition emphasize the perception that these confederates are in fact of immigrant background.[24] This further strengthens our confidence that the null findings presented in this chapter with respect to the effects of language on native behavior are substantively meaningful.

Discussion

Previous literature has shown that group threat can be evoked by the physical proximity of an outgroup and that foreign language exposure combined with

---

23. We return to this approach in chapter 6, where we use phone calls to convey a specific message designed to be overheard by bystanders and then test the effect of that message on bystanders' behavior toward the confederate making the phone call. The message is delivered by many of the same people using the same accents as in this chapter and the fact that we identify effects of the message even when it is delivered by immigrant women suggests that the slight accents they used did not prevent bystanders from absorbing the intended message of the experimental intervention.

24. On how visual, auditory, and other stimuli are integrated in human perception to emulate real-life conditions of encountering others, see Rakic, Steffens, and Mummendey (2011) who test how looks and accents determine ethnic categorization, both separately and in combination with each other.

visible ethnic differences can make ingroup-outgroup distinctions salient along the native-immigrant divide, inducing biased behavior against immigrants (Enos, 2014). A large literature on immigration, much of it focused on the United States, has established that linguistic assimilation reduces bias against immigrants. Building on that literature and on our earlier findings of discrimination against Muslims in Germany, we tested whether anti-immigrant bias can be mitigated by linguistic assimilation and found no evidence to support this hypothesis.

The anticipated bias-reducing effects of linguistic assimilation that are prevalent in prior literature are reasonable. The ideology of nationalism is often cultivated via a shared language, as are cultural norms and ideas that define the national identity. A shared language improves cultural understanding and forges tighter bonds within ethnic ingroups (Deutsch, 1953). A shared language filters the effects of economic modernization and facilitates social mobilization—two processes that have historically been integral to managing inter-ethnic conflict (Deutsch, 1961; Gellner, 1983). Learning the language of the ethnic majority facilitates acculturation (Maher, 1991; Cuellar et al., 1997) and often is a requirement for the successful economic integration of newly arrived groups (Goodman, 2012). It is therefore reasonable to expect that exposure to foreign language–speaking non-co-ethnics could generate unease, possibly being perceived as an identity threat, and could result in bias and exclusionary behavior among natives. It is also reasonable to expect that observing immigrants who converse fluently in the host society's language reduces feelings of unease among natives, thereby reducing discrimination.

Yet, our empirical results do not support that hypothesis. A pessimistic interpretation of our finding that linguistic assimilation does not reduce bias might be that immigrants cannot do much to counteract bias and discrimination—an argument that has been previously made by others (Vernby and Dancygier, 2019). While there may certainly be truth to that statement—and this is something we explore in detail in later chapters—we understand our findings as suggesting that the political salience of linguistic difference is moderated by social context. Linguistic assimilation in the United States has been shown to reduce bias toward immigrants because language acquisition has been such a central part of assimilationist strategies among immigrants to America. Multiple studies have shown that linguistic differences cause bias in that context. But in the German context, where the population has become accustomed to hearing foreign languages in everyday settings as a result of long-standing policies of multiculturalism, linguistic differences are not as salient for the native population.

Our results do show, however, that religious differences between Christian and Muslim populations are very salient and can result in biased behavior by natives. By disentangling the effect of language and religion, we find that in Germany, a country with successive waves of immigration and generations of successfully integrated immigrant communities, ethno-linguistic differences alone do not cause bias. The precise cause for the lack of significance of linguistic assimilation is not clear. It is possible that increased social contact combined with state policies to encourage multiculturalism have taken Germany to a point where linguistic assimilation is not perceived as necessary for immigrants to be treated respectfully and without bias by natives. Our analysis cannot definitively establish whether policies of multiculturalism are responsible for the decreased salience of linguistic difference; other mechanisms are also plausible. Furthermore, the fact that we find no significant regional differences with respect to impact of linguistic assimilation in former East and West Germany might indicate that factors such as local exposure to immigrants and fear of labor market competition—both of which vary immensely between the former East and West—matter less than the national context. The main conclusion that our experiments support is that, even if Muslim immigrants integrate or learn the language of the majority, this will not provide them with protection from discrimination as long as religious differences are cognitively and politically salient. Linguistic assimilation does not provide a strong enough signal of acculturation to offset bias due to religious differences, which are a salient reminder of symbolic cultural threat in the German context. In the next chapters, we consider this insight further and ask how this bias generated by religious differences can be overcome. For this, we turn to a focused analysis of the power of shared norms and ideas to reduce discrimination.

5

Shared Civic Norms

HAVING IDENTIFIED THE salient divide between Muslim immigrants and non-Muslim German natives in our field experiments on discrimination in chapter 3, we now turn to ways to overcome discrimination. We focus on the effect of shared social (civic) norms on reducing bias and discrimination. That outcome can arise as a result of cultural assimilation, mutual acculturation, or preexisting overlap in social norms valued by each group. As a reminder, in chapter 2 we defined assimilation as the adoption and internalization of a common value system, which aligns individual identity with the identity of the majority group. Our experiment does not distinguish between assimilation and different pathways toward norm-sharing; it does, however, make it possible to measure the effect of shared norms on discrimination and to contrast that effect to the consequences of shallower ways of reducing perceived distance between natives and immigrants, such as dressing the same way so as to "pass" as an undifferentiated member of native society. The key here is to explore behaviors that reveal how immigrants really feel about civic values that define native society and to ask what happens if immigrants' behaviors show natives that they do not differ significantly from them with respect to deeply valued social norms.[1]

Drawing on the theory developed in chapter 2, we explore whether shared norms can reduce discrimination by reducing the perceived distance between natives and immigrants. Prior literature has shown that challenging norms can threaten the foundations of social order, and individual well-being diminishes when group norms are violated (Bicchieri, 2017; Akerlof and Kranton, 2000). Considering how norms shape behavior is natural given our focus on social identities. Throughout this book, we discuss social identities as more than

---

1. This chapter draws on Choi, Poertner, and Sambanis (2019).

labels that are used to categorize individuals into groups. These identities are based on shared traits, but they imply a set of beliefs and behaviors that are consistent with advancing the group's welfare. To understand the power of those beliefs in shaping behavior, we analyze the effect of widely held *civic norms*—behaviors that reveal citizens' degree of internalization of the same logic of appropriateness with respect to their civic duty and behavior in public. Sharing the same ideas about behaviors that are deemed appropriate when confronted with a social dilemma is a key way of demonstrating a shared identity.[2] This is because the rules that establish what behaviors are appropriate in specific situations are institutionalized in observable public behavior and are learned over time. We designed an experimental setup that invokes the logic of appropriateness by placing confederates (i.e., research assistants acting out specific roles) in situations where their behavior reveals their commitment toward civic norms that are valued among natives and where norm adherence carries no direct benefit for the confederates. The behavior of immigrant confederates—the choice to enforce those norms—therefore signals whether they putatively share a common civic identity with natives despite their visible differences in ascriptive characteristics.

Observable behavior that invokes the logic of appropriateness relies on (and reveals) an individual's self-concept of his or her own identity. When one is confronted with a social dilemma or norm violation that explicitly or implicitly asks the person to consider "what would someone like me to do in a situation such as this?" the answer given is at least partly dependent on the identity of the individual making the decision and on the application of an internalized rule or heuristic that matches individual choice to established norms (Weber, Kopelman, and Messick, 2004). This is why an individual's decision to enforce civic norms reveals a lot of information about their identity, which in turn allows observers to make explicit or implicit comparisons to their own identity.

---

2. The "logic of appropriateness" provides a perspective to interpret human action. The canonical definition of the concept, provided by March and Olsen (1995, pp. 30–31) is that "Action . . . is seen as driven by rules of appropriate or exemplary behavior, organized into institutions. . . . Rules are followed because they are seen as natural, rightful, expected, and legitimate. Actors seek to fulfill the obligations encapsulated in a role, an identity, a membership in a political community or group, and the ethos, practices, and expectations of its institutions. Embedded in a social collectivity, they do what they see as appropriate for themselves in a specific type of situation."

Our first task is to identify a norm that can serve as our focal point for the discussion of norm-sharing. Adherence to such a norm by immigrants could be the result of cultural assimilation or mutual adaptation or acculturation over time; or it might be that the norm is equally salient in the immigrants' countries of origin. The source of norm similarity is not crucial in this context, though in reality most natives assume that they are culturally different from immigrants and, therefore, norm similarity might be interpreted as evidence of assimilation. While one might consider several different norms, we find the *norm against littering* in public spaces uniquely appropriate for our purposes. Littering in public spaces affects everyone negatively, but collective action problems will arise in trying to enforce this norm, just like any other behavior designed to contribute to the collective good. Adherence to the anti-littering norm is extremely strong in Germany, as we show later in this chapter, and the strength of this norm makes it more likely to evoke the logic of appropriateness in expectations of how individuals should react to violations of the norm. Moreover, there is symbolic value to the anti-littering norm—keeping the country clean is a way of publicly demonstrating one's commitment to the nation. At the same time, anti-littering norms are unlikely to come into conflict with religious convictions or other valued cultural practices among minority populations, therefore, this is an example of civic norm adherence which need not rely on repressive or coercive assimilation.

The key here is that adherence to valued civic norms reveals how strongly one identifies with the nation. The word "nation" here does not refer to the ethnic concept of the German nation as biologically determined; rather, it captures the political identity of a territorially defined community that depends on a common set of norms and values that members of that community are expected to have internalized. Shared civic norms are therefore seen as a way of forging a common ingroup identity as a *citizen*. Identities, forged by personal experiences and imbued with cultural context specific to an individual's upbringing, are likely to differ across countries or regions, generating different expected responses when an individual is confronted with a social dilemma that reveals the individual's beliefs about socially defined roles and appropriate behavior (Akerlof and Kranton, 2000; March, 1994). Thus, natives' expectations might be that immigrants, by virtue of their different cultural heritage, will not share the same civic norms. By observing norm-adhering behavior that is consistent across natives and immigrants, natives can update these priors. Our experimental setup places them in a context where they can do so, and that allows us in turn to observe whether such updating reduces the impact of ascriptive differences on natives' behavior toward immigrants.

Cleanliness

Across societies, opposition to newcomers, migrants, or minorities often manifests itself in accusations that they are *dirty*. Fears of disorder usually accompany racist or xenophobic stereotypes that shape the way members of the majority often think about minorities and the neighborhoods where minorities live. This seems to be a constant theme across many different countries. Studies have shown that white Americans' stereotypes about black neighborhoods is that they are "impoverished, crime-ridden, and dirty" (Bonam, Bergsieker, and Eberhardt, 2016). Chinese tourists to London were advised by Chinese authorities against visiting ethnic neighborhoods, which they viewed as "dangerous and dirty."[3] South Asians are routinely discriminated against in the housing market in Singapore due to the widely held perception among landlords that they are unsanitary.[4] Greeks who oppose immigration say they are afraid that immigrants will introduce new diseases.[5] Similarly, conservative news anchors in the United States openly claim that the dirtier districts of New York are those with the highest proportion of illegal aliens and that immigrants litter from the southern border all the way to the Potomac River in Washington, DC.[6]

Implicit in the perception that immigrant neighborhoods are dirtier than others is a belief that immigrants do not care about their host country; to many observers, littering reveals the fact that immigrants do not consider themselves part of society. This widely shared view was echoed in this statement by Heinz Buschkowsky, former mayor of the Neukölln borough of Berlin, an area with a high concentration of immigrant residents:

3. https://www.telegraph.co.uk/news/2016/09/07/row-as-air-china-warns-on-londons-indian-pakistani-and-black-nei (accessed 4/4/20).

4. https://qz.com/india/768706/the-racist-reality-of-house-hunting-in-singapore-sorry-your-wife-is-indian (accessed 4/4/20).

5. https://www.moreincommon.com/media/ltinlcnc/0535-more-in-common-greece-report_final-4_web_lr.pdf (accessed 4/19/2020).

6. https://nymag.com/intelligencer/2019/12/tucker-carlson-guest-suggests-immigrants-make-new-york-dirty.html (accessed 4/4/2020); https://www.washingtonpost.com/opinions/2019/12/16/tucker-carlson-theres-an-immigrant-litter-apocalypse-potomac-data-not-so-fast (accessed 11/11/2020).

An immigrant does not have to prove his willingness to integrate by wearing lederhosen, drinking beer only by the liter or eating weisswurst for breakfast. Accepting the principles of our laws and norms as elements for his life and the life of his family is enough. . . . It is enough, if he sends his children to school and if he carries his trash to the trash can instead of throwing it from the balcony.[7]

Whether it reflects reality or not, the former mayor's depiction of immigrants throwing trash from their balcony paints a picture of people who do not care for the rules and have no appreciation or love for their environment or their host country. This intuitive interpretation of littering resonates with prior experimental research in social science, according to which littering is an unobtrusive measure of social attitudes—with more littering to be expected as a result of ideological opposition or negative affect (Cialdini and Baumann, 1981).[8]

Norms against Littering in Germany

To explore how Germans think about littering, we conducted a brief survey on a stratified sample of 316 German native respondents. Online convenience samples have been used extensively in political science and in this case we used a sample stratified by state and gender. This survey provides useful information to frame the experimental analysis presented later in the chapter. We also conducted a media analysis on the topic of littering using publicly available information which, combined with our online survey, should give us a good sense of how much Germans care about the norm of non-littering.

The survey allows us to test the premise that Germans share strong norms against littering and that they believe that immigrants, especially those who are not culturally integrated in German society, would be more likely to litter than natives. The survey included a battery of questions designed to probe the

7. "Die bittere Wahrheit über unsere Schulen," *Bild*, September 19, 2012.

8. The bulk of the literature on littering focuses on other determinants of that behavior, such as lack of consideration of the public health consequences of littering; the belief that others will clean up after those who litter; or littering as the result of emulation of bad behavior by others. Littering as an indication of social identification and emotional attachment to the nation is less prevalent in the literature. The view that littering reflects the feeling of disenfranchisement and powerlessness is reflected in the work of NGOs such as Keep America Beautiful that organize "cleanup" interventions. A shared identity, from which concern over cleanliness and environmental protection arises, is often assumed implicitly by all such initiatives.

Q. How upset would you be if someone
dropped their trash on the floor in front of you?

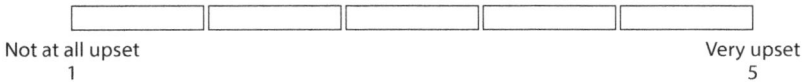

Not at all upset   Very upset
1   5

FIGURE 5.1. Screen capture of survey item on attitudes toward littering
Notes: This screen capture is a translated version of the original German language survey
screen presented to the respondents. The video screen that was presented to respondents
has been substituted with two pictures that are an accurate representation of the core content
of the video clip, which was around five seconds in length.

strength of the norms against littering amongst German host populations, as well as their perceptions regarding which demographic groups are more likely to violate the norm.

Norms against littering are strongly held   In order to test whether norms against littering are strongly held and shared by a broad majority of Germans, we presented a short three second video clip of a person throwing litter on a train platform. We followed by asking two questions to respondents regarding their reactions to the video clip. First, we asked respondents to evaluate the extent to which they would find it upsetting if they saw someone littering in a public space. Answers were given on a five-point scale, ranging from 1 ("it would not upset me at all") to 5 ("it would upset me very much"). Samples of the screen presented to respondents are shown in figure 5.1. Responses to this survey item demonstrate that norms against littering are widely held. On a five-point

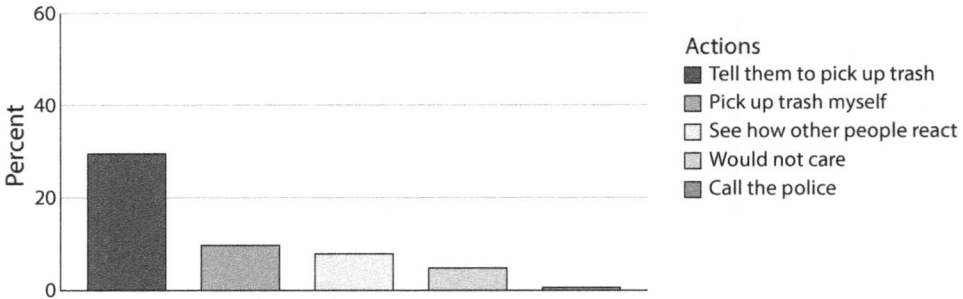

FIGURE 5.2. Actions respondents would take when they see someone who litters
Notes: Respondents were provided with the option to choose multiple response items.
The percentages reported in this figure reflect the proportion of respondents who chose the
particular response item.

Likert scale (1–5), 86% of responses were either 4 or 5, meaning that Germans find violations of the anti-littering norm to be highly upsetting. A mere 0.6% responded that they do not find littering to be upsetting at all.

Second, we asked what actions respondents would take when confronted with a situation in which they observed someone littering in a public space. The options presented included "I would tell the person to pick up the trash," "I would pick up the trash myself," "I would see how other people near me respond and would point it out to them, where appropriate," "I would call the police," and "I would not care." As presented in the fourth bar (row) in figure 5.2, only 4.8% of respondents said that they "would not care" and 95.2% replied that they would take some form of action to sanction and correct the norm violation.

Germans expect immigrants and foreigners to litter   In addition to questions designed to probe the strength of the anti-littering norm, our survey included items aimed at understanding whether German natives expect immigrant minorities to be less respectful of the norm against littering relative to native Germans. Specifically, we presented respondents with a photo of a littered street, and asked "In many German cities, people simply discard waste (such as coffee mugs, empty bottles, or packaging material) onto the street. Who do you think does this most often, Germans or immigrants and refugees?" We phrased the question item in a direct manner, fully acknowledging the possibility of social desirability bias to work against respondents choosing the "immigrants and refugees" answer.

TABLE 5.1. Germans versus Immigrants/Refugees Litter More

Immigrants Litter More	Germans Litter More	Difference	p-Value
61.99%	38.01%	23.98%p	0.0011

Responses to this item are presented in table 5.1. In calculating the means of responses, we apply the same approach that we used earlier for the manipulation checks and use weights based on the distribution of the observations in our main experimental sample (focusing on the states where the field experiments were implemented), although the results remain substantively unchanged without the weights or with weights based on national population estimates. Despite the concern that social desirability would bias against respondents choosing the "immigrants and refugees" answer, 62% of respondents said that immigrants are more likely to litter than Germans. This means that only 38% of respondents said that Germans are more likely to litter than immigrants. This difference is statistically significant at the $p < 0.01$ level. Given that social desirability bias is likely to work against observing a difference, we consider this differential as a lower bound.

The expectation that immigrants and foreigners litter more than Germans is also often expressed by politicians in public discourse. In fact, newspapers regularly cover complaints about immigrants littering in public spaces. The mayor of Duisburg Sören Link, for example, claims that the increase in immigration in recent years has led neighbors to feel "strongly bothered by piles of garbage, noise, and rat infestation."[9] In a similar vein, the controversial former Senator for Finance for Berlin, Thilo Sarrazin, claims that "the [city's] cleaning department clears up 20 tons of mutton leftovers from the Tiergarten [park] every Monday left by the Turkish community."[10] Even though Sarrazin expresses this position particularly provocatively, similar perceptions are expressed by politicians across the political spectrum: even politicians from the progressive Green Party, such as the former Berlin state assembly member Claudia Hämmerling, conclude that "this is how people behave who have never fully arrived here."[11]

While such positions are expressed by politicians from all major parties, they are particularly common on the far right. The president of the far-right

9. "Rasanter Anstieg beim Kindergeld alarmiert Städte," T-Online, August 10, 2018.
10. "Sarrazin ist nah dran und doch daneben," *Tagesspiegel*, Oct. 8, 2009.
11. "Die Affäre Hammelbein," *Zeit*, August 20, 2009.

NPD party in North Rhine-Westphalia, Claus Cremer, for example, asks, "What do you say to such cultural enrichers, [immigrants "enriching the German culture"] who first need to be taught not to poop on other people's properties and to throw garbage in trash cans and not simply on the street?"[12] The same party warns residents in Berlin (in the Rudow neighborhood) that, if asylum seeker accommodations are to be opened in their neighborhood, they will have to prepare for "being long-term neighbors with asylum seekers, with all the negative side effects, such as frequent noise, litter, and criminality."[13] The connection between littering by immigrants and lack of respect for Germany is implied in AfD politician Matthias Niebel's statement that proper handling of trash "belongs . . . to the core area of good German culture."[14]

Why Germans expect immigrants to litter more than Germans   To understand *why* native Germans expect immigrants to litter more, we asked respondents to our survey who had indicated that immigrants are more likely than Germans to litter to provide an open-ended justification for their views. Their comments are illuminating and we present a collection of these comments, translated into English, in a word cloud in figure 5.3.

Respondents most frequently said that immigrants litter because of the "lack of norms or rules regarding littering in the home country" of the immigrants. One respondent explicitly mentioned that "there are no rules on waste disposal in their homelands." Another respondent claimed that immigrants and refugees "may come from a country where the rules [against littering] are less strict." All in all, 22% of respondents invoked the differences in home country norms and rules, with some respondents invoking a "lack of culture" against littering in immigrants' home countries. Including the number of respondents who claimed that immigrants litter more than Germans because of their "habit," this number increases to 30%. A relatively substantial number of respondents attributed their expectations to what they perceived as a "lack of respect among immigrants for Germany and German traditions." The second largest category of responses invoked the term "respect." Littering

12. "Kapitulationserklärung: Polizisten aus Rumänien und Bulgarien sollen in NRW für Ordnung sorgen," NPD Bochum, October 22, 2013.

13. "Ein Asylbewerberheim in Rudow? Nicht mit uns!," NPD Neukölln, October 16, 2012.

14. "Presseerklärung Müllentsorgung tägliche PHV. Stadtrat Matthias Niebel wundert sich," Alternative-heidelburg.de, November 25, 2015.

FIGURE 5.3. Word cloud of open-ended justifications for why respondents believe immigrants litter more than Germans

Notes: The word cloud was generated based on the frequency count of the open-ended survey items. The German terms were translated into English. The size of the terms in the word cloud reflects the relative frequency with which the term appears in the entirety of the open-ended responses.

is an act that reveals not caring and not respecting host country rules and norms.[15]

The main lesson we take from the survey evidence presented thus far is that a large segment of the German public believes that immigrant norms

15. In their influential experiments on littering, Cialdini and Baumann (1981) and Cialdini, Reno, and Kallgren (1990) showed that most people would tend to litter more in situations where they experienced others littering or in dirty environments. Even though there were some people who would litter no matter what and some who would never do this, the majority was influenced by prevalent norms regarding littering and was sensitive to being sanctioned for violating this social norm. What is implied in this result is that a shared identity is the source of that sensitivity to social sanctioning, which echoes the results of our survey in that most Germans feel that immigrants' littering is driven by a lack of respect for German civic identity.

and values are different from theirs and that these normative differences—including the lack of concern with littering—are emblematic of a lack of respect for the host country. This finding presents an opportunity to use littering behavior as a way to experimentally manipulate perceptions about immigrants' adherence to norms that are highly valued in Germany. This, in turn, can help us assess whether norm adherence by immigrants would influence how natives would behave toward immigrants. We ask: what if immigrants took steps to show that they have adopted Germany as their new home by demonstrating their respect for prevalent norms against littering? What if they enforced anti-littering norms in public in plain view of others? Would such behavior reduce native bias and discrimination toward norm-abiding immigrants? Answering this question allows us to explore how important are shared civic norms in shaping natives' attitudes toward immigrants. We turn to such an analysis next.

Experimental Design

Similar to the approach taken in the previous chapter, we added a module to the experimental design presented in chapter 3, intended to observe whether the degree of assistance offered to strangers changes as a function of whether strangers appear to be respectful of norms against littering. Specifically, the added module involved a separate confederate (male, native German) violating the anti-littering norm in plain sight of bystanders waiting for a train on a train platform, followed by our female confederates either sanctioning the norm violator or not. This behavior separated confederates in two categories: those who were apparently undisturbed by the littering that took place before them and those who took it upon themselves to enforce the norm by reprimanding the violator.

The intervention proceeded as follows: a male German confederate (violator) steps onto the platform in the vicinity of our confederate and violates the widely held norm against littering by dropping an empty coffee cup on the platform. This is done in plain view of bystanders who are waiting for the train. A female confederate (punisher) immediately sanctions the violator by asking him to pick up his trash and dispose of it properly. The violator unwillingly but promptly complies with the request and leaves the scene. As the violator is walking away, the punisher receives a call in view of bystanders who have witnessed this previous interaction. While engaged in the call, she accidentally drops a bag of her possessions, the contents (oranges) of which disperse on the platform. The confederate appears to be in need of help

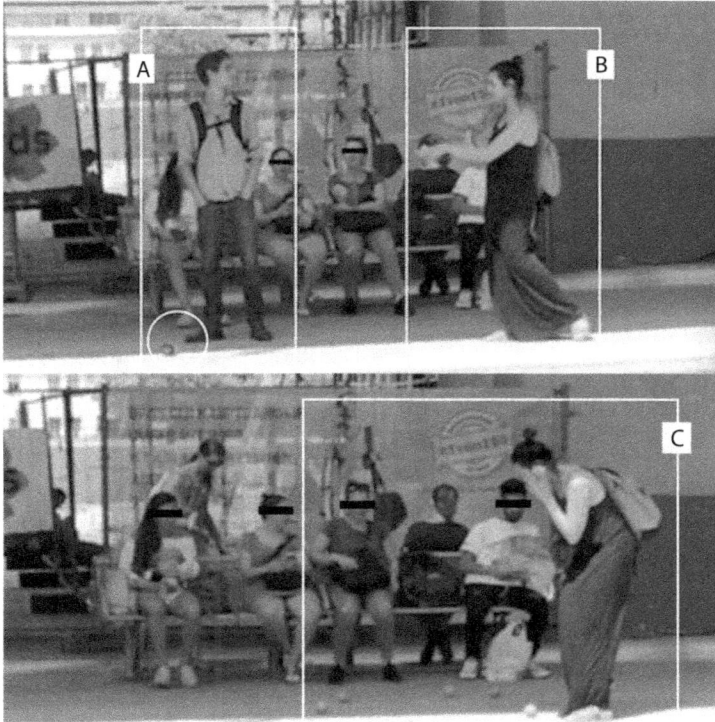

FIGURE 5.4. Experiment in progress

Notes: In the first step, the male confederate violates the norm against littering by discarding an empty coffee cup (A). The female confederate promptly sanctions the male confederate for the norm violation (B). The female confederate then drops personal possessions and is in need of assistance (C).

retrieving her possessions, and we measure whether bystanders provide that assistance. A schematic representation of the whole intervention is depicted in figure 5.4.[16]

Two key dimensions of the intervention were manipulated experimentally. First, in order to vary the female confederate's perceived membership in the ingroup (natives) or outgroup (immigrants), we randomly assigned the

16. Balafoutas et al. use a related approach to measure direct vs. indirect punishment of norm violators and whether altruistic punishment covaries with the severity of norm violations. We modify their design to address different questions pertaining to immigrant-native conflict (Balafoutas, Nikiforakis, and Rockenbach, 2014; Balafoutas, Nikiforakis, and Rockenbach, 2016).

TABLE 5.2. Treatment Assignment Matrix

Condition	Punisher Identity	Religious Markers	Norm Enforcement
1	Immigrant	Hijab	Yes
2	Immigrant	No Hijab	Yes
3	Native	-	Yes
4	Immigrant	Hijab	No
5	Immigrant	No Hijab	No
6	Native	-	No

Notes: This matrix presents the experimental treatment and control conditions corresponding to two confederate ethno-racial categories, two immigrant religious attribute categories, and two norm enforcement conditions.

ethno-religious attributes of the confederate to one of three conditions; an immigrant wearing a hijab, the *same* immigrant in plain attire without a hijab, or a native German female, who would serve as our control condition (skin tone and phenotype were the variables that would help the bystanders identify confederates as immigrants in the control condition).[17]

Second, we also manipulated *whether* the female confederate enforced the anti-littering norm. This action signaled to bystanders that she shared their norms and was a civic-minded person. In roughly half of our sample, the female confederate sanctioned the norm violator prior to requiring assistance. In the remaining half, a different confederate enforced the norm instead (third-party enforcement) (see figure 5.2 for the matrix of treatment conditions).[18] This second treatment dimension is cross-randomized on top of the other dimension.[19]

17. We also included a condition in which the immigrant confederate was wearing a large Christian cross so as to signal their Christian faith. While we omit discussion of the findings in the main text since it is not central to our overarching theoretical argument (our Christian immigrant confederates received similar levels of assistance to our immigrant confederates in plain attire), results for this treatment condition are reported in Choi, Poertner, and Sambanis (2019).

18. This was done so that we could keep norm enforcement constant throughout all iterations. Observing someone acting pro-socially might have induced bystanders to also act pro-socially when the confederate needed assistance, so we wanted them to observe an act of pro-sociality in all iterations.

19. Therefore, to the extent that bystanders punish our main confederate for her inaction in the third-party enforcement conditions, which seems unlikely given that many of the bystanders also did nothing to enforce the norm, we can hold this behavior constant when comparing across identity categories.

Apart from these two dimensions, we controlled for social class by having confederates wear similar attire across the different teams and iterations. We minimized the potential for differences in attractiveness to affect assistance rates by having the same confederate play both immigrant roles. Since it is not possible for the same actor to portray immigrant and native, we rotated the person playing the role of the German female confederate in each team. In the appendix, we also show that our results hold using team fixed effects, which capture unobserved sources of heterogeneity across teams and analyze within-team variation in assistance rates across iterations.

Some readers might be skeptical that the norm enforcement treatment signals to bystanders that our immigrant confederate has *internalized* the host society's anti-littering norm; it might be the case that norm enforcement is interpreted by bystanders as a trivial demonstration that immigrants have simply learned not to act in ways that violate local norms. We believe that our experimental design is much more consistent with internalization. The confederates go out of their way to enforce norms at potential personal cost; for all the bystanders know, these confederates risk confrontation with the norm violator, who is a German man. Such behavior indicates a strong belief in the social norm and a commitment to enforcing it; we chose this behavior deliberately to guard against the more conservative interpretation of the results that might have been plausible if the confederates were passively adhering to social norms simply by not violating them themselves.

The interventions were conducted in twenty-nine train stations across three German states (North Rhine-Westphalia, Saxony, and Brandenburg). We implemented a total of 1,614 iterations of the intervention, involving 7,142 bystanders, in major train stations of these cities over a three-week period between July and August 2018. During each iteration, confederates were tasked with recording the behavior of bystanders who observed the intervention (as in the experiments in chapter 3, coders were not blinded; see chapter 3's section of the appendix for more discussion). The main outcome of interest, which was coded at the *iteration level*, was whether *any* bystanders offered assistance to the female confederate in retrieving her possessions. Confederates also noted the total number and gender of bystanders within a pre-specified radius, as well as other characteristics of each iteration.[20]

---

20. The research protocol was reviewed and approved by University of Pennsylvania's Institutional Review Board (IRB Protocol #829824). A waiver of the consent process was obtained.

Results

Per the theoretical discussion presented in 2, we expected that immigrants would receive less assistance than natives; and that identity markers (hijabs) that increase the social distance between natives and immigrants would decrease assistance. Furthermore, since enforcement of local social norms regarding appropriate behavior signals that immigrants have internalized the logic of appropriateness that most Germans also share, we hypothesized that enforcing the anti-littering norm would offset the negative bias toward immigrants.[21]

First, as in chapter 3, we find strong evidence in support of our hypothesis of bias against immigrants and religious difference is the main marker that defines immigrants as an outgroup.[22] Female German confederates, who serve as our controls, were assisted in retrieving their possessions in 78.3 percent of all iterations. By contrast, confederates of an immigrant background (immigrants with hijab and immigrants in plain attire) were assisted less, at 71.3 percent of iterations (see appendix table A10 for further discussion of these analyses using regression with state-fixed effects and bystander-fixed effects). The difference between the level of assistance offered to immigrants versus natives is therefore around 7 percentage points, and is statistically distinguishable at conventional levels ($t = -2.11$, $p < 0.05$, two-tailed). The results shown in figure 5.5 pool across other conditions (i.e., results are pooled for norm enforcers and non-enforcers within the native and immigrant groups).

The negative bias against immigrants, however, is only due to intergroup differences in religious identity. As discussed in previous chapters,

---

The same ethical and safety considerations that were discussed with respect to the bias experiments in chapter 3 also apply in this case; see chapter 3's section of the appendix for more discussion.

21. The appendix includes results from auxiliary analyses, including regression-based analysis of treatment effects including state-fixed effects, bystander-fixed effects, and various controls. All analyses presented in the main text, unless otherwise noted, were pre-specified in an analysis plan registered with the Evidence in Governance and Politics (EGAP) network (#20180725AB) prior to commencement of data collection.

22. Recall that in chapter 3, we pooled across experiments with common treatment arms conducted over two years. In this chapter, we disaggregate that analysis to focus on the effects of a specific intervention focused on shared civic norms in experiments conducted in the summer of 2018.

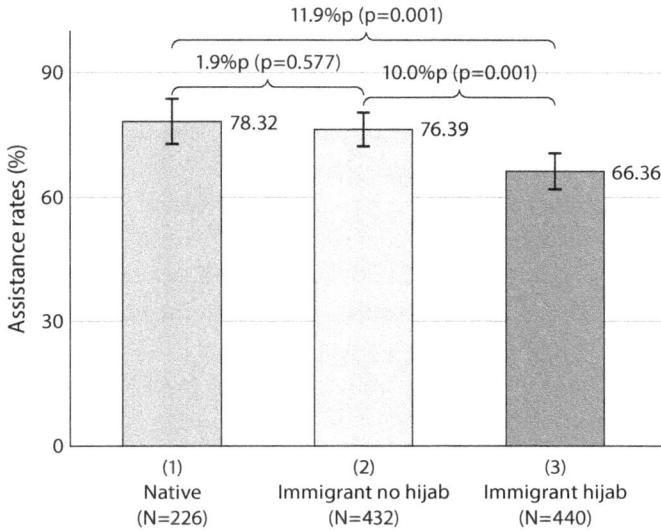

FIGURE 5.5. Parochialism in the level of assistance offered to strangers
Notes: Bars represent the mean rates of assistance for the treatment conditions.
The error bars present 95% confidence intervals for the means. The brackets and
accompanying information report results of a standard two-tailed difference in means test
of treatment conditions with p-values in parentheses. Bystanders provided significantly
more assistance to natives than to immigrants.

ethno-linguistic differences on their own are not sufficient to cause bias in everyday interactions between natives and immigrants. By contrast, as shown in column (3) of figure 5.5, immigrant confederates wearing a hijab, which clearly signals that they are of Muslim faith, were assisted only 66.3 percent of the time (these results pool across other treatment conditions, including norm enforcement). This is 12 percentage points less than assistance offered to German confederates ($t = -3.22$, p $<$ 0.001, two-tailed). In the sub-sample of interventions from the former East German state of Saxony, which was the site of violent far-right anti-immigrant protests in August 2018, this differential increases to almost 22 percentage points (see appendix, table A13).

Differences in discrimination in former East vs. West Germany are explored in appendix table A12, where we show that bias is larger in the East, though we cannot establish the cause of these differences. We also find that the rise in assistance levels due to good citizenship (i.e., pro-social behavior toward immigrants due to norm enforcement) is significantly larger in the East (appendix table A14). Economic differences between East and West, the legacy of communism, as well as differences in religiosity and in the degree of contact with immigrants could explain those results. The magnitude of this negative bias is especially noteworthy given the nature of the items dropped in the intervention; the oranges dispersed in a manner that made it seem challenging for our confederates to retrieve them expediently by themselves, which should have created strong pressures for bystanders to offer assistance regardless of the identity of the confederate.

This analysis provides corroborating evidence for the centrality of religious differences as the basis of parochialism in everyday interactions in Germany. Specifically, the average rate of assistance to immigrant confederates in the control condition is statistically indistinguishable from the assistance given to native Germans. Thus, there is no evidence of ethnically driven discrimination. This is despite the fact that bystanders recognize our immigrant confederates as non-German (evidence for this is included in the manipulation tests presented in chapter 3's section of the appendix). The fact that racial and phenotypical differences alone are not sufficient to induce discrimination in the context of minor everyday interactions might be due to the fact that immigrants in the control condition are dressed similarly to the native confederates and therefore signal some degree of cultural/economic integration. However, there is a decrease of around 10 percentage points in the assistance offered to the immigrant wearing a hijab relative to the immigrant control group ($t = 3.29$, p $<$ 0.01, two-tailed) and the only difference between how confederates in these two groups are dressed and how they behave is the hijab. Given that the level of assistance offered to immigrants in the control condition is roughly the same as the assistance offered to natives, we can conclude that religious difference is what explains the negative attitudes toward immigrants. In the appendix (table A11), we conduct analyses using alternate outcome measures and show consistent results with respect to the share of bystanders who provide assistance.

Can a shared understanding of good citizenship—demonstrated through an immigrant's enforcement of civic norms against littering—help partially counteract the bias against Muslim immigrants? Analyses presented in figure 5.6 show that it can. In the first step, we compare between treatment conditions wherein an immigrant confederate wearing a hijab enforces the anti-littering norm (column 3) and conditions in which they do not (column 4); the mean level of assistance provided to immigrant enforcers is more than 12 percentage points higher than that of immigrant non-enforcers (we only compare native Germans to immigrants with hijab in figure 5.6), and is statistically significant at conventional levels ($t = 2.772$, p $<$ 0.01, two-tailed).

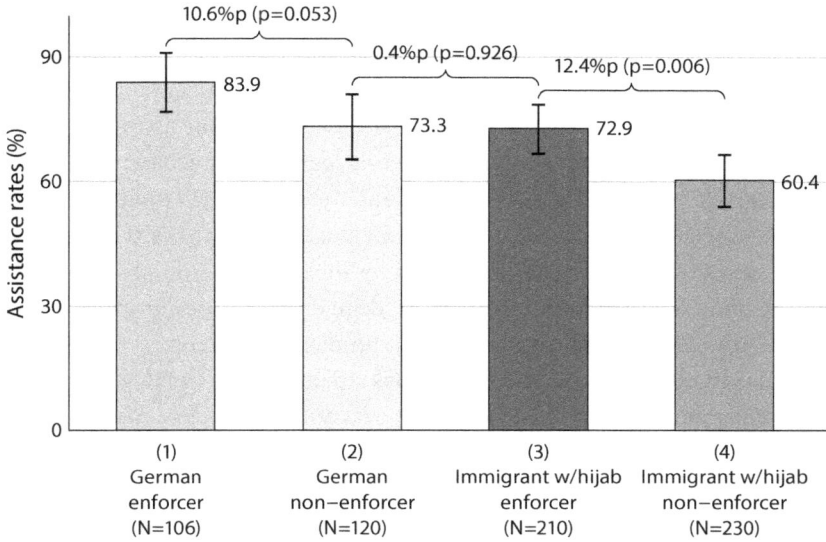

FIGURE 5.6. Offsetting effects of norm enforcement on bias

Notes: Bars represent the mean rates of assistance for the treatment conditions. The error bars present 95% confidence intervals for the means. The brackets and accompanying information report results of a standard two-tailed difference in means test of treatment conditions with p-values in parentheses.

The magnitude of the offsetting effects of norms is clearly demonstrated when we examine the difference in assistance rates for immigrant enforcers and native non-enforcers. As columns (2) and (3) from figure 5.6 demonstrate, norm enforcement brings the assistance provided to an immigrant confederate within 0.4 percentage points of a native who did not enforce the norm; the difference is statistically indistinguishable from zero ($t = 0.093$, p $= 0.926$).

While the evidence presented above highlights the capacity of shared norms to *counteract* bias against immigrants generated by ascriptive (religious) differences, it nonetheless suggests that civic norm enforcement is unable to eliminate the bias *in its entirety*; the t-test between assistance offered to native (column 1) and immigrant enforcers (column 3) reveals a substantial difference of 11 percentage points, which is statistically significant at the p $<$ 0.05 level ($t = 2.211$, p $<$ 0.05, two-tailed).

Discussion

A common identity, defined by a shared understanding of valued civic norms, can serve as the foundation of democratic citizenship. Nationalism, which is what often creates unity and a sense of common identity, cannot be relied on to unify natives and immigrants, since their national identities are different. This is especially true in countries where national identity among natives is ethnically defined so it is difficult for newcomers to *become* members of the nation. In an increasingly multicultural world, parochial attachments become important for individuals' self-concepts and the salience of ethnic, religious, or other social identities can influence individual behavior toward outgroups.

Parochial attachments are reinforced by social norms and ideas that define ingroup identity and ensure some degree of conformity in behavior. Frequently, identity threat strengthens the desire to preserve socially accepted cultural norms and values; previous studies have found that this desire is stronger among individuals with less education and a less cosmopolitan worldview—those who are increasingly threatened by economic competition in an era of globalization (Coenders and Scheepers, 2003; Hainmueller and Hiscox, 2010; Sniderman, Hagendoorn, and Prior, 2004; Wright, Citrin, and Wand, 2012). Our experiment, set against the backdrop of increasing intergroup conflict between German natives and Muslim immigrants in Germany, was designed to measure the effect of shared civic norms on discrimination against immigrants and minorities of immigrant background in a setting which abstracts from the influences of economic competition, which can motivate anti-immigrant attitudes.

Our findings clearly show that wholesale abandonment or change in immigrant identities is not the only way to meaningfully reduce prejudice and discrimination targeted at immigrant minorities. A shared understanding of civic norms can form the foundation for acceptance and integration. A demonstration of good citizenship among socially distant immigrant minorities is not discounted by the majority population.[23] Yet we also find that the effectiveness of norms in forging integration is constrained by the salience of intergroup differences. In the German context, religious difference increases social distance between native and immigrant populations and motivates discrimination, but that distance is not insurmountable. Public policies and political rhetoric have heightened the salience of religious markers so that cultural practices that are perceived foreign will increase conflict.

---

23. It would be instructive to explore sources of heterogeneity in these effects in follow-up studies. One could consider several possible sources, including partisanship, education level, income or employment status, as well as psychological attributes of different individuals, such as a proclivity to authoritarianism or religiosity.

One feature of our experimental design is that norm enforcement cannot be separated from revealed preferences against littering (i.e., sharing the norm). This is not a limitation of the design since the fact that enforcement is costly sends a signal to bystanders that the enforcer feels very strongly about this norm and, therefore, perceived social distance between that person and native society is narrowed.[24] However, one could consider design modifications and extensions to address different facets of the broader theoretical question of interest. One interesting change to consider would be to have the (immigrant) confederate pick up the cup herself rather than scold the male norm violator. Would the boost in bystanders' helping behavior due to norm adherence be larger or smaller in such a setup as a result of norm enforcement being less costly? Similarly, an intriguing design change that could provide interesting new results would be to have the norm violator be an immigrant so as to test the effects of ingroup policing as a signal of cultural assimilation.

Theories of social psychology and political science suggest that a common set of norms can unify individuals who would otherwise be divided by their ethnic or religious identities. Our evidence is consistent with those theories. However, the process through which natives and immigrants come to share a logic of appropriateness is varied; norm adherence by immigrants could be indicative of cultural assimilation; or it could be the result of a successful acculturation—the two-way convergence on a common set of norms that are shared by both communities. A third alternative could be that *actual* cultural differences separating natives and immigrants are smaller than *perceived* differences. Our results do not help clarify which underlying process leads to norm-sharing, though in principle, norms need not reflect the one-sided imposition of cultural practices that immigrant communities find foreign or threatening to their own identities. Shared norms could emerge as the result of a dialogue and mutual adaptation by host and immigrant communities. Our experiment is focused on measuring responsiveness to a norm that is both broadly shared among Germans and not inherently antithetical to cultural

24. Bystanders cannot possibly know what the confederate's personal beliefs are about littering, but they can infer her beliefs from her behavior. Because the experimental design places bystanders in a situation where intergroup differences are made salient by the hijab, individual behavior by our Muslim confederates is likely to be considered representative of the group as a whole rather than simply attributed to the individual. This is a crucial issue that we return to in chapter 8, where we focus on mechanisms underlying the observed behavioral effects of our intervention.

values or religious practices of immigrant groups. Thus, adherence to this norm by immigrants is certainly not indicative of coercive assimilation and the fact that our intervention presents immigrants as willful enforcers of the norm signals to bystanders that they care about their local environment and that they consider themselves part of their German communities.

A second question raised by these findings is whether other social norms exist that can have a larger effect by eliminating *all* bias and discrimination against immigrants? In light of the results of the Minimum Group Paradigm and related research in psychology, it is perhaps unrealistic to expect natives not to exhibit any ingroup bias during interactions with outgroups. That said, the effects of civic norms could be superseded by shared group-derived norms that could help recategorize immigrants as part of a common ingroup identity that a subset of the native population also shares. We turn to this idea in the next chapter.

6

Gender Equality

THE TREATMENT OF WOMEN is often portrayed as the core of value conflict between Western European and immigrant Muslim populations.[1] Ask a
Western person to picture a woman in the Middle East, and "probably the
first thing that comes into [their] mind will be the hijab. [They] might not
even envision a face, just the black shroud of the burqa or the niqab."[2] These
symbols of female oppression dominate Western perspectives of sexism in the
Middle East, fuel antipathy toward Muslims, and generate fear about the consequences of immigration from Muslim countries. According to a prominent
theorist of ethics, democracy, and identity, "Women's bodies have become the
site of symbolic confrontations between a re-essentialized understanding of
religious and cultural difference and the forces of state power, whether in their
civic-republican, liberal-democratic or multicultural form" (Benhabib, 2010,
p. 453).

This widely held belief that many Muslims hold non-egalitarian or regressive ideas about gender roles dates back to the period of the first mass migration to Europe from Muslim countries.[3] In Germany, as in the Netherlands
and other European countries, the majority of Muslim immigrants during the
first phase of mass immigration to Europe in the postwar period came from
Turkish Anatolia and other rural areas of Middle Eastern and Mediterranean
countries, where prevalent gender norms were quite different from those

---

1. See Sniderman and Hagendoorn (2007, p. 21).

2. https://www.theatlantic.com/international/archive/2012/04/the-real-roots-of-sexism
-in-the-middle-east-its-not-islam-race-or-hate/256362 (accessed 8/18/2020).

3. We use the term "progressive" in this book to characterize a commitment to gender equality and egalitarian gender roles. "Regressive" is used to refer to conservative, non-egalitarian
attitudes about gender roles that limit women's authority and decision-making over their own
lives.

shared by the majority population in European countries. These cultural differences helped define stereotypes that are at the heart of natives' negative attitudes toward Muslims today. Although these stereotypes reflect conflict between secularism and religiosity, the normative differences between native and immigrant populations in Europe might be less applicable today than they were decades ago. It is instructive to consider whether the "ideas gap" between Muslims and Western European Christians with respect to the role of women has closed over time and we will review some data on this question later in the chapter. The gap may be closing as a consequence of globalization, increased cultural contact across countries, and the advancement of a human rights and women's rights agenda globally by a broad range of civic society actors. Alternatively, the gap may be growing due to resurgence of Islamism in several countries in the Middle East and North Africa which suggests a growing rejection of values that are labeled "Western." At the same time, immigrants and refugees are a self-selected group and their values may differ from the values of their co-ethnics back in their countries of origin. It is difficult for Western publics to weigh these divergent influences on immigrants' values, and natives' fears are stoked by media coverage of Muslim women suffering due to forced marriages, honor killings, denied educational opportunities, or violent customs such as female genital mutilation.

Public opinion polls suggest that there is a clear gap—or at least the perception of a gap—between Muslims in Muslim-majority countries and large segments of Western European populations vis-à-vis their attitudes toward marriage (e.g., whom women can marry and at what age); ideas about the "right" role for women in the job market or the household; views on appropriate dress codes for women in public spaces; and other questions that help define norms and ideas about gender. These differences loom large in public perceptions of the social "distance" separating Muslim immigrants and native Europeans and previous studies have shown that many Europeans believe that the conflict between them and Muslims is irreconcilable because it reflects differences in *value systems* (Sniderman and Hagendoorn, 2007, p. 23). At the core of that conflict between value systems are differences in attitudes toward women.

This chapter delves into an exploration of Islamophobia using a new lens focused on norms and ideas about gender roles. Whereas security threats or economic competition with immigrants have been proposed as the main reasons for Islamophobia, we focus instead on conflict over gender roles, which is more likely to elicit conflict over value systems than are security or economic threats. We go beyond approaches that measure attitudes toward Muslims using survey data and experimentally test our hypothesis that anti-Muslim bias is at least partly driven by perceptions of a conflict over gender norms and women's rights. We test whether natives discriminate toward Muslims because they view Muslims as regressive vis-à-vis gender roles; and we test whether discrimination can be overcome if Muslims demonstrate that they respect women's rights, reflecting their alignment with the majority's core values and ideas. If we find evidence in support of our hypothesis, this would help distinguish the ascriptive differences that separate Muslims from Christians on the one hand from the ideological content of these religious identities on the other hand. These tests build on our empirical approach from previous chapters, which explore the role of civic norms in shaping native-immigrant conflict.

Unlike previous literature, we do not treat women simply as the *object* of value conflict with Islam; we also analyze women as *actors* that shape the contours of that conflict. Although in chapter 1 we showed that attitudes toward gender rights seem to be uniform across German men and women, the behavior of German men and women toward Muslim immigrants differs when we put them in an environment that makes female gender identity cognitively salient and when we manipulate perceptions of the degree to which Muslims appear to hold progressive attitudes toward women's rights. We are able to show that native women's discriminatory behavior toward Muslim women is driven by beliefs that Muslims hold regressive views on gender; and that this discrimination is overcome when Muslim immigrants are perceived to hold progressive views, which are aligned with the prevalent views of the majority population. Picking up the analytical thread from previous chapters, we explore in depth German attitudes toward the hijab, which to the popular imagination is a symbol of Islam, but also of female oppression.[4]

Women at the Core of Value Conflict with Islam

Ideas about women's role in society are a key dimension of a value conflict among people from predominantly Christian vs. majority Muslim countries and that conflict shapes public perceptions of the risks associated with integrating Muslim immigrants in Western societies. Indeed, ideas about the classification of gender roles constitute a crucial test area for any society's

---

4. Parts of this chapter draw on Choi, Poertner, and Sambanis (forthcoming b).

"self-understanding" (Habermas, 1994, p. 115). Debates about gender discrimination in the workplace and, earlier, about women's suffrage have defined American democracy in ways that echo the political effects of contemporary debates about the use of the veil (hijab) and its implications for citizenship. For some, wearing a veil is an individual right that can be affirmed by ideas of "Islamic feminism" whereas for others, the veil is a symbol of misogyny in political Islam, which is viewed as a growing threat to secularism that could threaten a reversal of hard-won advances in women's rights (Benhabib, 2010; Bourhis, 2013; Goldberg, 2005). To many Europeans, the veil is a symbol of "reverse globalization" posing a threat to secularism and Western values (Benhabib, 2002). Western perceptions of veiled Muslim women "project gender oppression onto Islam" and serve as a "mirror" of Western constructions of identity (Al-Saji, 2010).

There is at least an implicit presumption, shared by many in the West, that the Western world affords women more rights and privileges than Islam. However, the East-West divide is not strictly what defines this conflict, which is also played out in the Muslim world as part of an unfolding contrast between liberal and conservative visions of Islam. In Muslim-majority countries such as Indonesia, where Islamism and democratization are unfolding parallel to each other, political competition between rival visions of Islam aims to take control over public morality and focuses attention on the familiar refrain of controlling gender activism as a focal point of the debate (Brenner, 2011). Elsewhere, as in Turkey, debates about the hijab echo deeper divisions regarding secularism and the country's political orientation toward the West.[5]

Attitudes Toward Gender Equality Among Muslims

Cross-country evidence from surveys of public opinion suggests that there *is* a gap between the cultural values reflected in majority opinion in Middle Eastern and North African countries and the prevailing norms and shared cultural values in Western European societies (Inglehart, 2000). For example, data from the Arab Barometer show that when asked whether they agree or disagree with the statement that "husbands should have the final say" in the

---

5. Indeed, concerns about secularism vs. Islamism frame many secular Turks' attitudes toward Syrian immigrants, who many Turks perceive as a cultural threat due to their religiosity and the perception that they hold more regressive views toward women and marriage (see, for example, Terzioglu, 2017 and Safak-Ayvazoglu, Kunuroglu, and Yagmur, 2020).

family, a majority of respondents agrees with the statement across a dozen Muslim-majority countries (Thomas, Arab Barometer, 2019). There are significant cross-country differences with 70% or more of respondents agreeing with the statement in Iraq, Algeria, and Sudan compared with just around 50% in Lebanon and Jordan (and just below 50% in Morocco). But there is little evidence of a generational gap as these beliefs permeate age groups and seem relatively stable over time. There is a notable gap in the degree to which these beliefs are held by men and women, with women much more likely to support women's rights issues, such as equal inheritance shares for women or women's access to education. According to the Arab Barometer, more men now support statements about the dominant role of men in the family than was the case in surveys fielded a few years ago.

A 2013 study by the PEW Research Center (PEW Forum on Religion and Public Life) explored the role of women in society in Muslim-majority countries and the survey results reveal clear support for positions that, from the perspective of the majority of European citizens, might be considered conservative or regressive. According to the report, "in nearly all countries surveyed, a majority of Muslims say that a wife should always obey her husband" (PEW Forum on Religion & Public Life, 2013, p. 91), though there are pronounced differences with respect to other issues that are central to debates about gender rights. Large majorities support unequal inheritance laws that favor men over women in most countries from the Middle East that were included in the survey with the exception of Turkey.[6] There are significant differences in the share of Muslims who say that a wife should be able to divorce her husband. Whereas there are large majorities in favor of this right in Bosnia (94%), Albania (84%), Tunisia (81%), and Turkey (85%), support is much lower in Lebanon (56%), Palestine (33%), Egypt (22%), Jordan (22%), and Iraq (14%) (PEW Forum on Religion & Public Life, 2013, p. 94).

Such attitudes are at odds with the trend toward greater gender equality that is evident in the surveys of public opinion in Germany that we reviewed earlier in this book. Undoubtedly, these cultural differences are at the core of public perceptions of a significant distance separating native Germans from Muslim immigrants because Germans likely ascribe to immigrants the

---

6. In Tunisia, Morocco, Iraq, Jordan, Egypt, Lebanon, and the Palestinian territories the percent of Muslims who support equal inheritance rights for sons and daughters is low, ranging from 15–43% (PEW Forum on Religion & Public Life, 2013, p. 95). In Turkey it is quite high at 88%.

views of the majority in their countries of origin. These perceptions may be misguided, however. Surveys of public opinion among Muslim immigrants in Germany reveal important differences between the social attitudes of those immigrants and corresponding attitudes among the majority in their home countries. Recall our earlier discussion of whether husbands should have "the final say" in the home. We reported large majorities across Middle Eastern countries in favor of a statement that "husbands should have final say," but less than 27% of recent Syrian immigrants to Germany would support that statement.[7] Merely 21% of Syrian women and 28% of Syrian men who arrived in Germany between 2013 and 2016 share that view. Among the same group of Syrian refugees, more than 95% believe that "in a democracy women have the same rights as men" (98% among women), 84% believe that "having a job is the best way for a woman to be independent" (89% among women), and fewer than 17% (11% among women) would favor educating their sons rather than their daughters.

These figures suggest that refugees and immigrants who make their way to Europe are a self-selected group that differs from the majority in their home countries. It could also be the case that these individuals' progressive views are simply more easily expressed openly in Europe than in their home countries, where many might believe that expressing support for progressive gender norms is not acceptable.[8] A third possibility is that, over time, immigrants' views change and converge to those of the majority as their perspectives change in their new country or as a result of a conscious strategy of civic integration and assimilation. This explanation, however, is less likely to apply to newly arrived immigrants since cultural assimilation or acculturation takes time, though there is clear evidence of such convergence over time in public opinion polls in Germany, as seen in figure 6.1.

When asked if they agree or disagree with the statement that "it is better for the whole family if the woman stays home and takes care of the household

---

7. Source: data from the first wave of the IAB-BAMF-SOEP Survey (2016) conducted by the Research Center of the Federal Agency for Migration and Refugees (BAMF), the Institute for Labor Market and Employment Research (IAF), and the Socioeconomic Panel (SOEP) at the DIW Berlin.

8. This insight is supported by a path-breaking field experiment in Saudi Arabia (Bursztyn, González, and Yanagizawa-Drott, 2020), which showed that the vast majority of young married men in that country would support women working outside the home, but they are reluctant to do so because they believe that others do not share the same views and they would be chastised by others in their network for their progressive views on gender roles. When men are given new information about the fact that many others also share those progressive views, they update

It's better for the whole family if the woman stays
home and takes care of the household and the children.

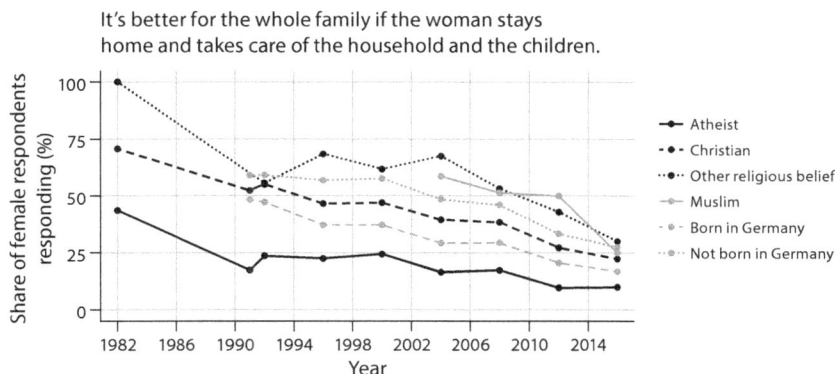

Data on categories Atheist, Christian, and Other Religious Belief collected
since 1980. From 2002 onwards respondents could further specify if
choosing "Other Religious Belief."

(a)

In a famliy, the man can also take care
of the children and the household.

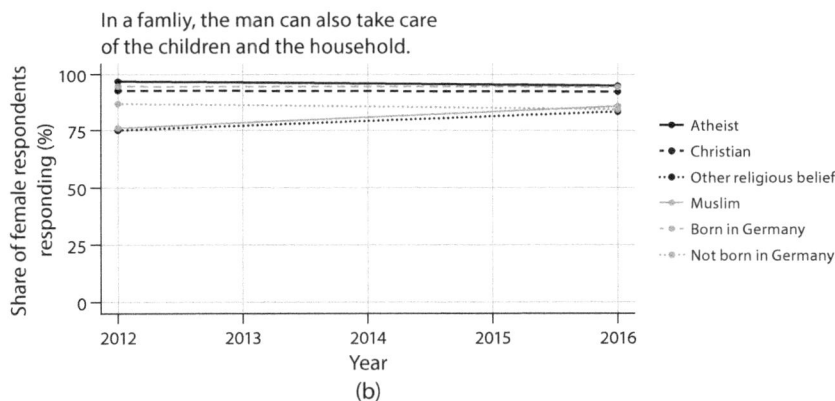

(b)

FIGURE 6.1. Trends in gender attitudes in Germany
Notes: Survey responses of German citizens in the ALLBUS surveys (GESIS, 2018).

and the children," the majority of women in Germany would disagree. This
is clearly visible in the left panel of figure 6.1, which plots responses to this
question in surveys conducted over time starting in 1982. Whereas the majority (nearly 75%) of German women who self-identify as Christian agreed
with this statement in 1982, fewer than 25% agreed with it in 2016. The majority of German women who self-identified as "atheist" would not agree with
this statement in 1982 and fewer than 15% agreed in 2016. This over-time shift

their priors about the social acceptability of women working, and they become more likely to
support their wives taking jobs outside the home.

toward more progressive positions on gender roles is also seen among Muslim women in Germany. Given the demographic characteristics of Germany's immigrant population, Muslims would have made up the vast majority of the "other religious belief" category in this survey prior to 2002, when data on Muslims was collected separately from other religions. We see a nearly 100% agreement with the regressive statement in 1982 among women from "other religions" but that share was already below 75% in 2002 and by 2016 the views of Muslim women are almost indistinguishable from the views of Christian women. Similarly, the difference between the views of respondents who were born in Germany vs. those who were born outside Germany are very small and both groups are showing a convergence to progressive views over time. Similarly, the degree of agreement with the statement that "in a family, the man can also take care of the children and the household" reveals that the difference between foreign-born and native-born women is trivial; and, although there is slight difference between Muslim women and atheist women (with atheist women more likely to agree with the statement), that difference is very small and the gap has been closing over time (see right panel of figure 6.1).

The data reviewed above make clear that public perceptions that Muslim immigrants in Germany—especially Muslim women—hold regressive views toward gender roles are largely wrong. There are likely other misconceptions that feed into negative stereotypes that, in turn, lead to anti-immigrant discrimination. Perhaps the most widely shared stereotype is that Muslim women are oppressed and there is no better symbol for that type of oppression than the hijab, which most Germans believe Muslim women are forced to wear. In a survey of 1,500 adult Germans that we fielded in 2019, we asked respondents why they believe Muslim immigrants wear the hijab and about 55% of respondents stated their belief that Muslim women are forced to wear it; fewer than 5% thought that Muslim immigrant women are *always free* to choose whether to wear the hijab or not (see panel (a) of figure 6.2).

As it turns out, this stereotype is not quite right. The PEW Research Center survey that we cited earlier addresses the question of veiling directly. It shows that Muslims' attitudes regarding veiling are not uniform across countries of origin of immigrants to Germany. When asked whether women should "decide if they wear a veil" 90% of Muslims in Turkey said that women themselves should decide. The same liberal perspective is reflected in the sample from Bosnia (92% in favor of letting women decide), Kosovo (91%), Albania (85%), and other countries, such as Tunisia (89%) and Morocco (85%). There is less support for women's freedom to choose to wear the hijab in several other

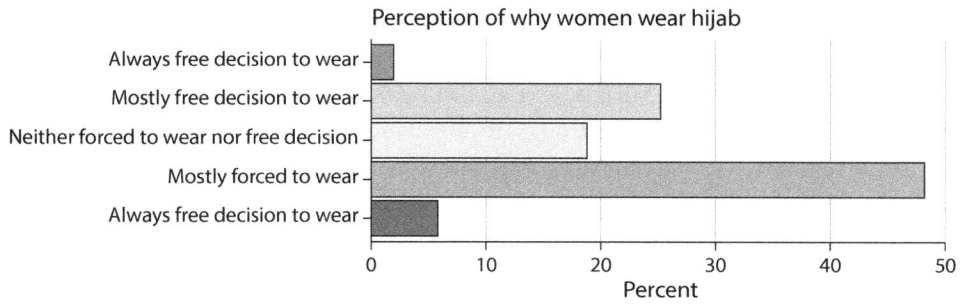

Perception of why women wear hijab

Always free decision to wear
Mostly free decision to wear
Neither forced to wear nor free decision
Mostly forced to wear
Always free decision to wear

Percent

(a)

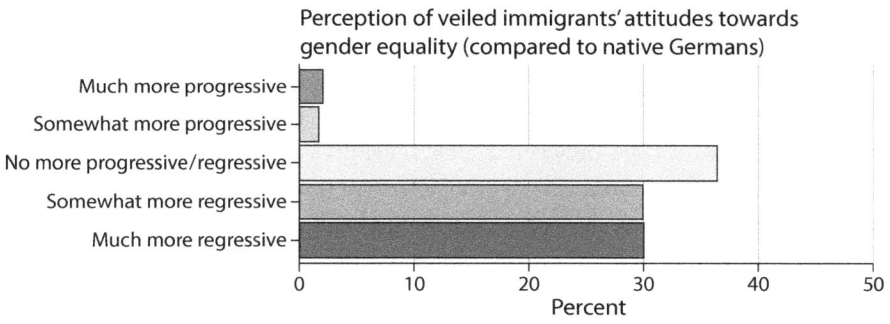

Perception of veiled immigrants' attitudes towards gender equality (compared to native Germans)

Much more progressive
Somewhat more progressive
No more progressive/regressive
Somewhat more regressive
Much more regressive

Percent

(b)

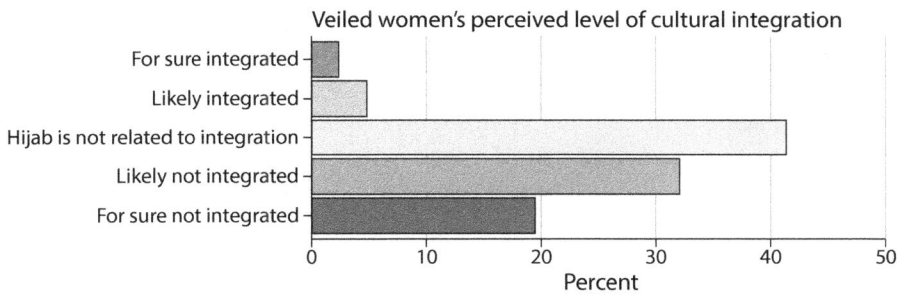

Veiled women's perceived level of cultural integration

For sure integrated
Likely integrated
Hijab is not related to integration
Likely not integrated
For sure not integrated

Percent

(c)

FIGURE 6.2. Perceptions of the hijab among native Germans

Notes: Survey responses of German adult citizens; authors' survey conducted in 2019.

Muslim-majority countries, such as Pakistan (70%), Lebanon (61%), Palestine (53%), Egypt (46%), Jordan (45%), and Iraq (45%). These percentages are even lower in sub-Saharan African countries. Thus, the picture is mixed: in some countries, there are strong norms that might translate into social pressure on women to wear the hijab in public, while in others it almost certainly is an individual choice. Moreover, as we saw earlier, the opinions of Muslim immigrants in Germany are often different from majority public opinion in their countries of origin. In 2008, the share of female Muslim immigrants in Germany who stated that they always wear a hijab was 28% whereas 63% said they never wear it.[9] Among the women who said they wear the hijab, almost all (96%) said they saw this as their "religious duty" and only a tiny fraction (5–7%) suggested that they wore it due to "expectations" to do so on the part of their family, their partner, or their social environment. Many wear it so they can be recognized as Muslims (35%) or because it "imparts security" (42%).[10]

The connections between Islamic religious symbols such as the hijab and cultural distance from the "typical" German is evident in our survey. When asked if they believe that women wearing a hijab are more progressive or more regressive than native Germans with respect to their views on gender equality, 60% of our respondents state that they believe the hijab is associated with more regressive beliefs, fewer than 5% believe that it is associated with more progressive beliefs, and less than 40% of all respondents find no clear association between the hijab and gender attitudes (panel (b) of figure 6.2). Indeed, more than 50% of respondents say that when they see a woman wearing a hijab, they assume that she is likely not integrated culturally in Germany (panel (c) of figure 6.2). Later in this chapter we tap into these beliefs among German natives as we design a new experimental intervention that allows us to test how important are beliefs that Muslims have regressive attitudes toward gender in explaining anti-Muslim discrimination.

Group-derived Norms

The survey data reviewed above suggest that there are differences with respect to women's rights and gender equality norms when we compare German

9. Source: Muslim Life in Germany survey (first- and second-generation immigrants from predominantly Muslim countries (2008)).

10. Source: Muslim Life in Germany survey (first- and second-generation immigrants from predominantly Muslim countries (2008)).

natives and citizens of Muslim majority countries. Those differences may be narrowing, and the opinions of Muslim immigrants appear to be different from those of their co-ethnics in their prior home countries. But those differences, which were reflected in a significant gap in attitudes toward social issues in the 1980s or earlier (as suggested by the survey data we reviewed above), have shaped German natives' priors and have created the impression that Muslim women, particularly those who wear the hijab, are likely to share regressive views toward gender. The hijab is therefore a symbol that can make salient the cultural distance separating natives from immigrants, and it is likely to symbolize identity threat for the native public. As such, the hijab highlights the role of ideational factors in generating opposition to immigration from Muslim countries.

In other domains of intergroup conflict (e.g., racial discrimination), prior research has identified significant differences among men and women in the types of symbolic threat they perceive when they are confronted by the same outgroup (Navarette et al., 2010; Sidanius and Veniegas, 2000). Similarly, women and men in Western societies are likely to perceive different *types* of threats emanating from Islam and its cultural symbols; specifically, widespread beliefs that Muslims hold regressive ideas about gender roles are likely to affect women and men differently.

As mentioned in chapter 2, when previous studies have considered within-group differences in the native population with regard to their attitudes toward immigration, they have usually focused on sectoral differences or party identification and they have not considered differences emanating from social identities.[11] The key idea reflected in that literature is that an individual's position in the economy dictates her attitudes toward immigrants as she considers how immigration affects her material interests primarily due to competition for jobs or other economic channels.[12] By contrast, we focus on interests that emanate from group identities; these interests are more likely tied to norms and values than to individual material payoffs.

Our concept of "interests" therefore deviates from standard use of the term in the comparative politics literature. Whereas usually the term denotes individual material welfare, we use it to reflect key insights of social identity theory which suggest that when individuals identify with social groups they belong

11. However, partisanship can be considered a type of social identity; see Schickler and Green, 1997.
12. See Peters, 2014; Goldstein and Peters, 2014; Mayda, 2006.

to, they are likely to internalize and adhere to group-prescribed behaviors and norms (Tajfel et al., 1971; Akerlof and Kranton, 2000). Their own self-interests are aligned with the group's because individuals draw part of their self-esteem from their group memberships, which pushes them to care about the group's welfare and to prefer outcomes that elevate the group's status and relative power. Individuals who identify with a group will also care to minimize their perceived social distance from the rest of the group and they are more likely to identify with groups from which they feel less distant.[13] It follows that, if the large-scale integration of immigrants to the nation increases the perceived distance between natives and the nation, this can threaten natives' identification with the nation and make their other identities—such as their parochial ethnic, regional, or religious identities—more salient. This process makes conflict between natives and immigrants more likely.

In chapter 2, we drew on these ideas to argue that intergroup conflict between natives and immigrants could be reduced if they could forge a common ingroup identity. It is possible to reduce the salience of ethnic, racial, or religious attributes that make the native-immigrant cleavage more apparent by highlighting commonalities in norms, ideas, and values between the two groups. Thus far, we have explored the effect of general norms on reducing bias by narrowing perceived social distance between natives and immigrants and we now consider norms and ideas that arise from the social identities of subgroups of the native population (group-derived norms). The key insight here is that different groups will perceive different threats from Muslim immigration due to the implications of immigration for their group identities; to reduce conflict, one strategy is to establish that immigration does not threaten the core norms and ideas that define those group identities.

The Role of Ideas in Forging a Common Identity

When group identities are made cognitively salient by intergroup contact or competition for resources, group-prescribed norms are more likely to shape individual behavior, resulting in bias and outgroup derogation toward those who do not share those norms. This is even more likely if the majority holds negative stereotypes about the minority (Kalla and Broockman, 2020). Under conditions of status or economic competition, prior literature has shown

---

13. For a general model of this process with application to ethnic politics, see Sambanis and Shayo, 2013.

that intergroup contact generates conflict due to the perception of identity threat (Allport, 1954; Pettigrew, 1998; Brewer, 1996). The key constructivist insight is that identities and interests—which jointly determine the perception of threat from outgroups—coevolve, so we hypothesize that perceptions of threat can be diminished if intergroup competition subsides or if individuals begin to see outgroup members as less of an identity threat. These effects can occur if outgroup members are recategorized as members of a common ingroup identity, or if key attributes that define group boundaries are de-emphasized (Gaertner and Dovidio, 2000).

How can recategorization of outgroup members be achieved? A cognitive shift that emphasizes a shared superordinate identity between an ingroup and outgroup has been shown to be effective in reducing some forms of intergroup conflict. Yet, in chapter 2 we argued that this will not be sufficient to reduce bias unless both ingroup and outgroup members share the same concept of their superordinate identity. Whether two individuals share the same concept of a superordinate identity may be observable by whether or not they behave in ways that are consistent with group-derived norms. In this chapter, we provide empirical evidence in support of this claim by exploring the implications of the intersectionality of gender, religion, and nationality in the formation of attitudes and behavior toward immigrants.

We revisit the results presented in chapter 3, where we found a more significant degree of discrimination against Muslims among native women. A hypothesis consistent with the argument we make above is that this native women's discrimination against Muslim women is likely driven by group-specific identity threat felt by native women; and that if Muslim women show that they do not threaten core ideas and norms that define gender identity among German natives, this could reduce or eliminate discrimination.

This logic pushes us to consider how and why immigration from predominantly Muslim countries is perceived as threatening by native German women and brings us back to the idea first introduced in chapters 2 and 3, which is that Muslims are perceived to be regressive vis-à-vis women's rights.[14] In a liberal democracy such as Germany, integrating large numbers of Muslims poses a

---

14. The term "regressive" here is used to characterize conservative, non-egalitarian attitudes about gender roles that limit women's authority and decision-making over their own lives. The term "progressive" is used to refer to a commitment to gender equality and to egalitarian gender roles.

direct threat to native women because it empowers a group that holds very different ideas about gender roles and gender identity. If this intuition is correct, then Muslim religious symbols such as the hijab should trigger group-specific identity threat felt by women; and this could underlie the discriminatory behavior that we identified in chapter 3. We explore this hypothesis further in this chapter to analyze the "feminist backlash" to Muslim immigration.[15]

Hypotheses

The preceding discussion suggests a number of testable hypotheses.[16] All hypotheses focus on the role of social identification in motivating discriminatory behavior measured by differences in helping behavior toward natives vs. immigrants.

H1: Religious discrimination   Natives are more likely to discriminate against (provide less help to) immigrants wearing religious attire (hijab) than immigrants who do not wear religious attire.

H2: Ingroup bias   Natives are more likely to help other natives than immigrants wearing religious attire (hijab).

H3: Gender attitudes   Natives are less likely to help immigrants who reveal regressive gender attitudes than immigrants who hold progressive or neutral gender attitudes.

H4: Feminist backlash   Female natives are less likely to help Muslim immigrants if they hold regressive ideas about gender roles.

H5: Gender solidarity   Female natives will not discriminate against female Muslim immigrants who hold progressive ideas about gender roles.

Experimental Evidence from the Field

We return to the experiments first presented in chapter 3 and expand the design to test our hypotheses regarding the ideational basis of discrimination

15. We use the term "feminist" to refer to a commitment to gender equality. "Feminist backlash" refers to a negative response to individuals perceived to threaten hard-won advances in women's rights and toward those who support regressive views on gender roles.

16. These hypotheses were registered in a pre-analysis plan filed with the Evidence in Governance and Politics (EGAP) network (#20190711AC) prior to commencement of data collection. There were no deviations from the pre-analysis plan.

against Muslims. Specifically, we test the idea that discrimination is driven by perceptions that Muslims hold regressive views with respect to women's rights and women's role in the family. This perception should be especially important in shaping native women's behavior toward Muslims since women are more directly affected by such views than men, consistent with the theoretical discussion in chapter 2. Our intervention places female confederates in public spaces (train stations) in situations where they need assistance from bystanders after they first publicly reveal their beliefs with respect to what they consider as appropriate roles for women in the family and the workplace. As in previous chapters, we focus on helping behavior (helping women pick up fruit they have dropped on the floor). We observe how unknowing bystanders who were exposed to this "message" about our confederates' ideas about gender react to that message—do they help these women pick up their oranges or lemons? Or do they refrain from helping as a result of what they have heard those women say?

A New Micro-environment

Our intervention was set up to observe the behavior of unknowing experimental subjects (bystanders) who are exposed to a highly realistic and carefully choreographed sequence of social encounters in public spaces.[17] Our intervention was set up in the train stations visited in previous experiments and followed four steps: first, a female confederate approached a bench at a train station where other individuals were waiting for their train and drew their attention by asking them a question ("Do you know if I can buy tickets on the train?"). Shortly thereafter, and in the presence of the bystanders, the confederate received a phone call, and audibly conversed with the caller in German (thereby indicating that she is likely economically integrated in German society) regarding a member of her family (her sister).[18] The script of the conversation was designed to reveal the confederate's position on women's right to work versus the perception that women should stay at home to take

17. As stated in previous chapters, our study is part of a vast literature on minority group discrimination in psychology (Mummendey and Wenzel, 1999; Fiske, 1998), sociology (Pager and Shepherd, 2008), and economics (Bertrand and Mullainathan, 2004; Bertrand and Duflo, 2016). The focus on norms and ideas is new, particularly as mechanisms for overcoming discrimination.

18. In reality, the call was from another member of our team who did not have an acting role for that particular iteration.

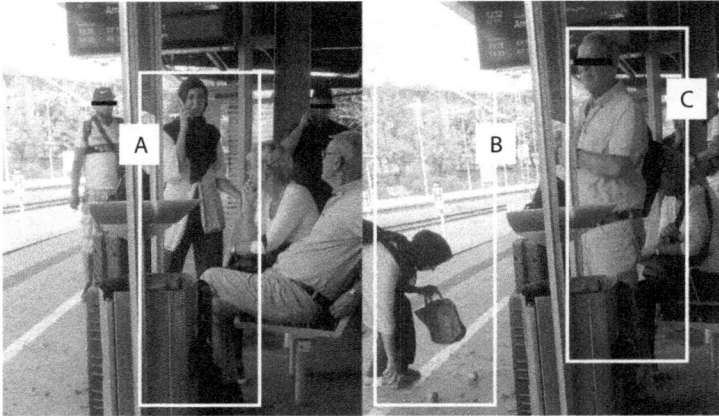

FIGURE 6.3. Experimental intervention in action

Notes: Unknowing bystanders watch and listen as the confederate takes a call and conducts a conversation with a friend (A), in the process revealing her attitudes toward the role of women in society (family and work). Following the phone call, the confederate drops her possessions (lemons), which disperse on the platform (B). We observe whether bystanders assist the confederate in collecting her possessions (C).

care of the family.[19] At the end of the phone call, a bag that the confederate was holding seemingly tore, making her drop a number of lemons, which dispersed in a haphazard manner on the train platform. The confederate appeared to be in need of assistance to pick them up.[20] In the final step, team members who were not a part of the intervention recorded whether each bystander helped the confederate retrieve her lemons. A collage of photographs that capture the key sequences of our experimental intervention is presented in figure 6.3.

Experimental Manipulations

We conducted our field experiment in twenty-five cities in Germany, by exposing 3,797 unknowing bystanders to these brief social encounters and observing their behavior. The treatment and control conditions are presented in table 6.1.

19. While confederates spoke loud enough to be heard, these conversations were not unreasonably loud and comparable to a typical cell phone call that one would hear in public spaces routinely. To ensure treatment symmetry, we trained the confederates extensively to ensure that the volume was similar for all confederates and treatment conditions.

20. She had been instructed to wait 5–10 seconds before picking up the fruit while wrapping up her phone call, which gave bystanders a chance to help if they were inclined to do so.

TABLE 6.1. Treatment Conditions for Phone Call Experiment

Condition	Ethnicity	Religious Symbol	Gender Attitudes
1	Immigrant	Hijab	Progressive
2	Immigrant	Hijab	Regressive
3	Immigrant	Hijab	Neutral
4	Immigrant	No Hijab	Progressive
5	Immigrant	No Hijab	Regressive
6	Immigrant	No Hijab	Neutral
7	Native	-	Progressive
8	Native	-	Regressive
9	Native	-	Neutral

Dimensions 1, 2: Ethnicity and religiosity of confederate   We experimentally varied the identity of the confederate who was always female. The confederate was either a member of an immigrant minority group (from the Middle East) or a native German.[21] We also manipulated her religiosity by having the *same* immigrant confederate wear a *hijab* as opposed to modern Western clothes with no religious symbols. Linguistic proficiency was held constant. All confederates spoke fluent German with a faint accent to indicate a high degree of (economic) integration. In the immigrant control condition, they were also dressed with clothes that were similar to those worn by native confederates and they appeared to be from a similar age bracket and socioeconomic background. The German confederate always wore no distinctive religious symbols.

Dimension 3: Content of the phone conversation   To reveal confederates' attitudes about gender roles, we also manipulated the content of the phone conversation. This dimension took on *three* values:

1. In the *regressive* gender attitude condition, the confederate expressed *disappointment* with her sister, who had decided to get a job rather than stay at home and take care of her husband and kids. The confederate stated that she believed her role as a woman was to stay at home and take care of her family.[22] Confederates signaled their immigrant status at the end of the phone call so as to indirectly help bystanders

---

21. As in the previous experiments, the immigrant confederates were easily identifiable as nonnative Germans and were not ethnically ambiguous.

22. The full script went as follows: "Hi! Thanks for calling back! I am really mad. . . . My sister is an absent mother [*Rabenmutter*]. She prefers to work instead of looking after her

think about the fact that these confederates were recent immigrants rather than German citizens who were second- or third-generation immigrants.

2. In the *progressive* attitude condition, the confederate expressed her strong *approval* of her sister's decision to get a job rather than stay home and take care of her husband and kids. She stated that she believed that women should not sacrifice their careers to stay at home and take care of their family. As above, confederates signal their immigrant status at the end of the phone call.[23]

3. In the neutral control condition, the confederate has a conversation of roughly equal length about an innocuous matter *unrelated* to her attitudes regarding women and also of no sociopolitical valence.[24]

Immediately after the last sentence, the confederate dropped the lemons and then ended the phone call, saying "Oh, I just dropped something. . . . I will call you back later. Bye." She took a few seconds before trying to retrieve her lemons, which gave bystanders a chance to help.[25]

The specific issue of women's career advancement was chosen because it has been a crucial concern of the women's rights movement in Germany. Although close to 75% of women in Germany agreed with the idea that women

---

children and her husband at home. [Pause] I think as a woman she should stay home and look after her family. [*only for immigrant conditions:*] I've never been so mad since we moved to Germany."

23. The full text of the progressive condition went as follows: "Hi! Thanks for calling back! I am really happy. . . I am very proud of my sister. She is pursuing her career; she decided to go to work instead of just looking after her children and her husband at home. [Pause] I think women should not sacrifice their careers just to stay home and look after their family. [*only for immigrant conditions:*] I've never been so happy since we moved to Germany."

24. Neutral condition text: "Hi! Thanks for calling back! Will you come later? [Pause] My sister and I are really looking forward to it. [*only for immigrant conditions:*] I've never been so happy since we moved to Germany."

25. Readers may note that this message treats bystanders with ideas about gender roles but also about the confederate's work ethic. However, there is no reason to expect that all bystanders would regard the decision to work at home as indicative of a diminished work ethic relative to a woman who joins the labor market. In the appendix, we explore this question further and show that our results are inconsistent with a "work ethic" interpretation of our treatment.

It's better for the whole family if the woman stays
home and takes care of the household and the children.

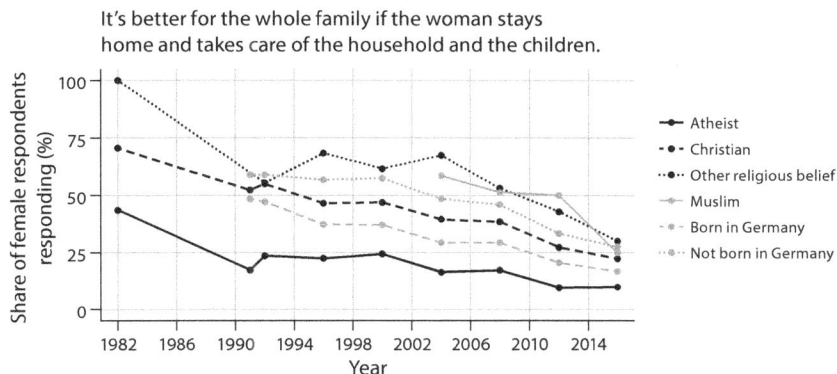

Data on categories Atheist, Christian, and Other Religious Belief collected
since 1980. From 2002 onwards respondents could further specify if
choosing "Other Religious Belief."

FIGURE 6.4. Native German women with regressive attitudes about career gender equality
Notes: Share of German women (without immigrant background) who agree completely or
rather that "it is better for everyone involved if the man is pursuing a professional career and
the woman stays at home and takes care of the household and children" in nationally
representative surveys. Source: ALLBUS surveys (GESIS, 2018).

should primarily concern themselves with handling the care-giving responsibilities at home while the man is the primary "bread earner" in the early 1980s,
there has since been a precipitous drop over time, signaling a generational
shift toward equality. By 2016, less than 20 percent of women agreed with the
same statement. See figure 6.4 for trends over time, as tracked by nationally
representative surveys of the German adult population.

The phone call conversation was held loud enough for bystanders to overhear. Noise levels were low enough to ensure that bystanders could hear a
conversation that took place right in front of them.[26] We measured noise
levels for a sample of iterations; the mean background noise was 62 dB and
the median was 57 dB at the exact locations of the interventions on the
platforms. This is relatively quiet, comparable to the noise level of a refrig-
erator or AC unit a hundred feet away. To ensure that a phone conversation would be an adequate medium for treatment delivery, we conducted

26. The analysis includes fixed effects for bystanders with earphones and other bystander
characteristics. We show in the supplemental information (online) appendix of Choi, Poertner,
and Sambanis (forthcoming b) that we have balance with respect to these characteristics across
treatment conditions.

a pilot study and partial replication of the intervention with manipulation tests. These assessments were specifically designed to evaluate whether bystanders had listened to the phone conversation being conducted by the confederate and could recall details of its content. We found that the vast majority of bystanders could overhear the conversation and could recall its contents.[27]

Data Collection

The experimental interventions were conducted in twenty-six train stations across twenty-five cities in North Rhine-Westphalia, Saxony, and Lower Saxony in five weeks during July and August 2019, following a pilot study in May 2019. These states were chosen to build on the experiments conducted during the summer of 2018.[28] We implemented a total of 1,830 iterations of the intervention, involving 3,797 bystanders. The specific locations of study sites are presented graphically in figure 6.5.

As in previous chapters, discrimination was measured unobtrusively by observing differences in helping behavior toward Muslim immigrants and German natives. For each iteration, enumerators who did not participate in the intervention themselves recorded the behavior of bystanders. The main outcome of interest, which was coded at the *iteration level*, was whether *any* bystander offered assistance to the female confederate in retrieving her

27. We did this by conducting a debriefing survey after the intervention was executed during the pilot study; 97.8% of bystanders reported noticing the call. Despite strong social desirability not to admit to overhearing other people's private phone conversations, 80.8% of bystanders were *willing* and *able* to recall full details of the call, including whether the confederate held progressive or regressive attitudes toward women's role in society, without being given any answer choices regarding the content of the phone call within the survey.

28. As mentioned earlier, these states were not chosen at random; rather, we arrived at the decision to conduct these interventions in the three states after carefully weighing a combination of state- and region-level sociodemographic factors that we believed would be of interest. The most obvious difference between North Rhine-Westphalia (NRW) and Lower Saxony versus Saxony is that they fell under West and East Germany prior to reunification. In addition, these two areas have traditionally been exposed to very different levels of immigration in Germany's postwar history. Whereas NRW and Lower Saxony are considered two of the most ethnically diverse federal states, with the highest proportion of foreign-born populations in the country, Saxony has remained relatively ethnically homogeneous. In the appendix, we discuss regional differences in outcomes in our study.

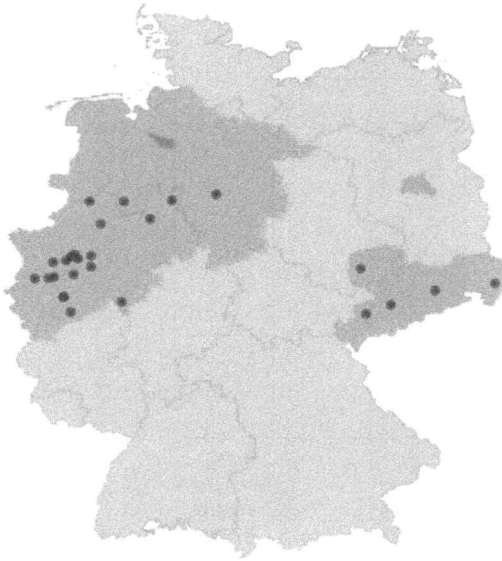

FIGURE 6.5. Study sites—Twenty-six train stations in three German states
Notes: The study sites were located across three German States (*Bundesländer*) in the former East and West. Information regarding each station, including the names of the stations, as well as other miscellaneous details are included in the appendix.

possessions. Although our unit of analysis is the *iteration*, we collected a mixture of both iteration-level and individual-level outcomes. For each iteration we coded the behavior of anywhere from one to five bystanders within earshot (i.e., a radius of three meters around the confederate).

Outcomes were also coded at the individual level. We collected the following information per each iteration: the number of bystanders within three meters of the confederate; and for each bystander: whether they offered assistance; a subjective estimate of their gender, age bracket, and immigrant minority status; and whether they were wearing earphones.

Following each iteration, two enumerators approached the bystanders and invited two of them to participate in a seemingly unrelated, incentivized survey (the sampling protocol used for the survey is discussed further in the appendix). Each respondent had a chance to win two hundred euros from a lottery that was held after the end of data collection. Using this information, we can test hypotheses about heterogeneous treatment effects, which we return to later.

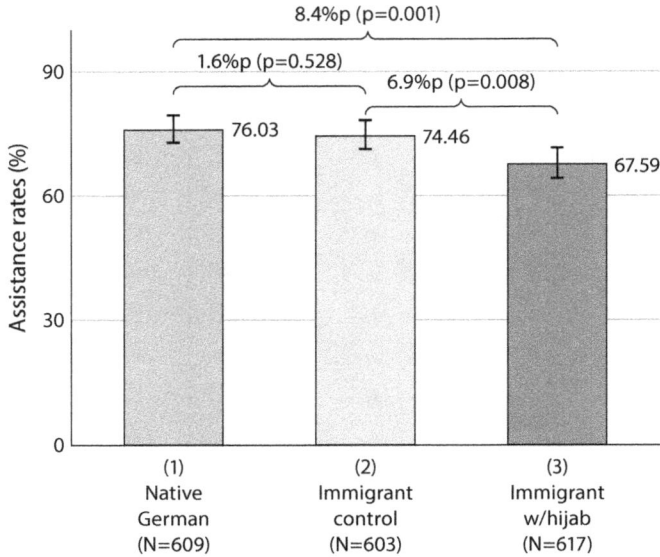

FIGURE 6.6. Parochialism in the level of assistance offered to strangers
Notes: Bars represent the mean rates of assistance for the treatment conditions. The error bars present 95% confidence intervals for the means. The brackets and accompanying information report results of a standard two-tailed difference in means test of treatment conditions with p-values in parentheses.

Results

Iteration-Level Analysis

We begin by presenting results from analyses conducted at the *iteration level,* which was pre-registered as our main empirical approach.[29] Our analyses provide strong evidence in support of hypotheses 1 and 2, which posited that native populations will discriminate against immigrant minorities. As figure 6.6 shows, discrimination is driven by religious difference; Muslim immigrants receive markedly less assistance from bystanders (column 3, 67.59%) than either native Germans (column 1, 76.03%) or immigrants who do not wear religious attire (column 2, 74.46%). The differences between the native and immigrant without religious attire condition versus the immigrant

---

29. The research protocol was reviewed and approved by the University of Pennsylvania Institutional Review Board (IRB Protocols #829824 and #833206). A waiver of the consent process was obtained.

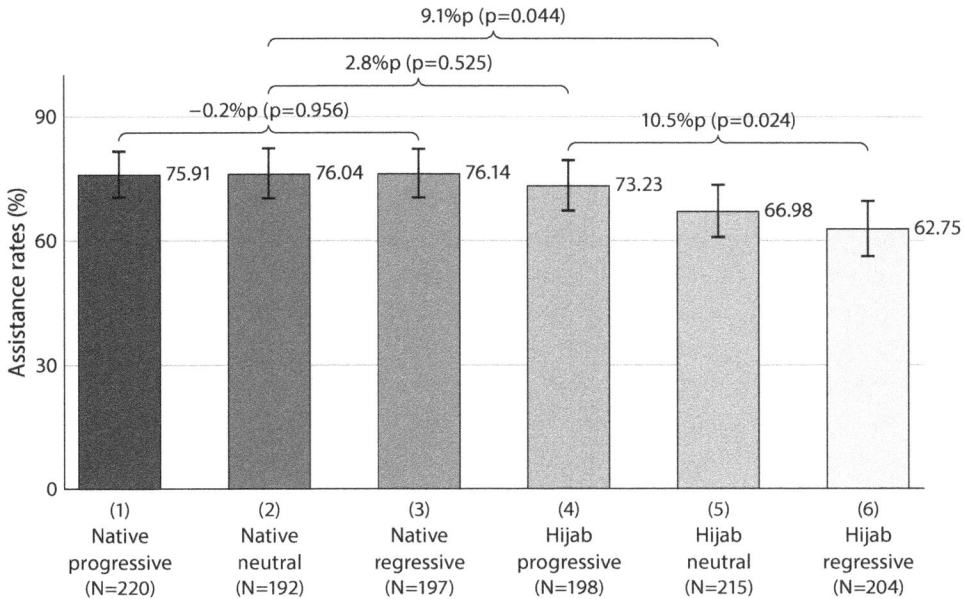

FIGURE 6.7. Offsetting effects of progressive gender attitudes on discrimination
Notes: Bars represent the mean rates of assistance for the treatment conditions. The error bars present 95% confidence intervals for the means. The brackets and accompanying information report results of a standard two-tailed difference in means test of treatment conditions with p-values in parentheses.

with hijab condition are large in magnitude and statistically significant at conventional levels (8.4 percentage points, p = 0.001, and 6.9 percentage points, p = 0.008, respectively). This experiment replicates the analysis of discriminatory behavior that we presented in chapter 5 based on data from the prior year, further increasing our confidence in those results.

Next, and perhaps more importantly, we turn to the effect of gender attitudes on discrimination. We restrict our analyses to comparisons of natives vs. hijab-wearing immigrant conditions only, since we observed no evidence of discrimination toward immigrants without a hijab. Consistent with hypothesis 3, figure 6.7 shows that bystanders are less likely to help Muslim women who reveal that they hold regressive ideas about gender roles. Muslim immigrants who hold regressive views (column 6) are significantly less likely (13 percentage points) to receive assistance than similarly regressive native German women (column 3). The regressive message of the phone call likely confirms negative stereotypes against Muslims held by bystanders (we return to this in the next section, where we further explore these mechanisms in follow-up survey experiments).

By contrast, when the phone call reveals that Muslim women hold progressive ideas with regard to gender roles (column 4, 73.2%), discrimination toward them is reduced and assistance increases roughly up to the level offered to natives (column 1, 75.9%). The positive effect of the progressive message fully offsets the discrimination generated by the hijab, which is likely seen as a symbol of regressive beliefs about gender roles. The fact that Muslim women in the neutral message condition (column 5, 66.9%) receive significantly less assistance than native women in the control condition (column 2, 76.0%) is consistent with the view that enough bystanders share negative assumptions about Muslim immigrants and that the hijab makes those assumptions cognitively salient.[30]

Interestingly, we find no evidence that the phone call message affects behavior toward natives.[31] Native German women who hold regressive beliefs (column 3) are no less likely to receive assistance than native women who hold progressive beliefs (column 1). This asymmetry in the results may suggest another, more subtle form of bias: while co-ethnics are allowed to have a diversity of beliefs regarding issues that are most salient to women, the same privilege is not recognized for Muslims, who are expected by natives to conform to dominant norms and ideas about gender to be treated the same way as native Germans are treated. In other words, native women are likely seen as individuals, whose views are allowed to deviate from the group's because they are not necessarily seen as representative of their group and bystanders may not hold strong priors about native women's ideology vis-à-vis women's rights. By contrast, hijab-wearing women are primarily viewed as stereotypical members of their group (Muslims; immigrants) and only in response to stereotype-defying cues provided in the phone call do bystanders update their beliefs about the individual. We return to this question in the next chapter

---

30. In the appendix, we show that our results are robust to dropping bystanders whom our coders perceive as potentially of immigrant origin. The sample does not include enough immigrants to explore patterns just among immigrants.

31. In order to alleviate concerns that this finding might be driven by bystanders paying more attention to veiled confederates' phone calls, we implemented manipulation checks during our pilot study and a partial replication study. Confederates across the different treatment conditions were noticed almost always and the content of their phone calls was recalled correctly at similar rates.

where, with the help of a survey experiment, we explore whether our confederates are seen as representative members of their group or as unique individuals or exceptions.

Individual-level Analysis

Having established that ideas and norms about gender roles exert an important effect on behavior toward Muslims, we now consider whether these effects are different for men and women. In order to disaggregate the effects by bystander gender, we must draw on the individual-level coding of whether an individual bystander offered assistance, and the characteristics of each bystander as coded by our enumerators.[32] The upper panel (panel A) of table 6.2 presents individual-level data analysis of the difference in help rates toward hijab-wearing immigrants versus native Germans, disaggregated by the bystanders' gender.

First, it is worth noting that both men and women discriminate against Muslim women with regressive ideas about gender roles (columns (3) and (4)); yet only women bystanders (column (1)) are responsive to a progressive message vis-à-vis gender roles and no longer discriminate against Muslim women after establishing that they are not regressive. More importantly, and consistent with our theoretical expectations, men (column (2)) are not responsive to the progressive message; assistance rates to progressive immigrant women are markedly lower than in the neutral condition. On the other hand, women respond to the progressive message and increase help toward veiled immigrants, to the extent that the difference in help rates is no longer distinguishable from zero at conventional levels (column 1).[33]

In the lower panel (panel B) of table 6.2, we present these results from the perspective of the progressive vs. regressive message effects, disaggregated by the identity of the confederate and the gender of the bystander. In line with

32. For a discussion of potential behavioral spillovers that can occur when there are multiple bystanders, see appendix. The analysis suggests that behavioral spillovers are unlikely to pose a huge threat to individual-level estimates of our experimental treatment effects, and should partially be remedied by the fixed effects approach taken in the regression analysis of individual behavior.

33. These results are obtained via OLS regressions that control for different types of team and bystander fixed effects (see this chapter's section of the appendix for more discussion and additional results).

TABLE 6.2. Effects of Ideas on Bias by Gender

Panel A

	Hijab vs. Native Comparison					
	Outcome: Did an individual bystander help?					
	(1)	(2)	(3)	(4)	(5)	(6)
Hijab vs. Native	−0.031 (0.048)	−0.156*** (0.053)	−0.145*** (0.050)	−0.134** (0.056)	−0.094* (0.050)	−0.086 (0.054)
Gender Attitude Condition	Progressive	Progressive	Regressive	Regressive	Neutral	Neutral
Bystander Gender	Female	Male	Female	Male	Female	Male
Fixed Effects	✓	✓	✓	✓	✓	✓
Observations	465	338	415	323	425	326

Panel B

	Progressive versus Regressive Phone Call Comparison					
	Outcome: Did an individual bystander help?					
	(1)	(2)	(3)	(4)	(5)	(6)
Progressive vs. Regressive Attitude	0.106** (0.045)	0.059 (0.058)	−0.028 (0.048)	0.001 (0.050)	−0.015 (0.051)	0.078 (0.053)
Confederate Identity Condition	Hijab	Hijab	No Hijab	No Hijab	Native	Native
Bystander Gender	Female	Male	Female	Male	Female	Male
Fixed Effects	✓	✓	✓	✓	✓	✓
Observations	441	323	450	339	431	338

Notes: Models are estimated with linear regression. Robust standard errors clustered at the iteration level in parentheses. * p < 0.1; ** p < 0.05; *** p < 0.01. Fixed effects included number of bystanders at the iteration level, as well as all individual-level attributes that enumerators coded; these included: perceived age bracket and whether or not the bystander was wearing earphones.

TABLE 6.3. Effect of the Progressive Gender Attitudes, Disaggregated by Bystander Religion: Post-Intervention Survey Sample

| | Progressive vs. Regressive Message | | | | | |
| | Did an individual offer help? | | | | | |
	(1)	(2)	(3)	(4)	(5)	(6)
Progressive vs. Regressive,	0.178***	0.160**	−0.004	−0.009	0.240***	0.215**
Hijab	(0.066)	(0.068)	(0.152)	(0.160)	(0.088)	(0.092)
Sample	Full	Full	Christian	Christian	Atheist	Atheist
# of Bystander FE	Yes	Yes	Yes	Yes	Yes	Yes
Bystander Attribute FE	No	Yes	No	Yes	No	Yes
Observations	230	220	53	49	109	105
R^2	0.176	0.191	0.170	0.207	0.247	0.245

Notes: Models are estimated with linear regression. Robust standard errors clustered at the iteration level in parentheses. *$p < 0.1$; **$p < 0.05$; ***$p < 0.01$. Columns (3) and (4) subset to individuals who self-identified as Christian in the post-intervention survey (Protestant and Catholic). Columns (5) and (6) subset to individuals who self-reported as having "no religion." Bystander attribute fixed effects includes all individual-level attributes that enumerators coded: perceived age bracket, perceived immigrant status, whether or not the bystander was wearing earphones.

the results presented in the upper panel, we observe that the progressive message effects are primarily driven by female bystanders assigned to overhear the phone call by the hijab-wearing Muslim immigrant (column (1)); exposure to the progressive message increases assistance rates by more than 10 percentage points, an effect that is statistically significant at the 95% level. The treatment effect for male bystanders assigned to the same confederate identity condition is around half the size that of females, and statistically indistinguishable from zero (column (2)).

In addition to these individual-level analyses, drawing on data from the post-intervention survey allows us to take a closer look at the effect of religious identity on shaping attitudes toward Muslim immigrants as a function of the gender-specific ideological message conveyed in the phone call experiment. This analysis is only exploratory, yet it is instructive and consistent with our expectations (all of which were registered in our pre-analysis plan).

Table A18 shows that the progressive message increases help to hijab-wearing Muslims (column 2, 16.0 percentage points) while controlling for the number of bystanders as well as bystander-attribute fixed effects (e.g., wearing earphones). This effect is much larger for bystanders who declare no religion (column 6, 21.5 percentage points) than for those who report that they

are religious Christians (column 4, −0.9 percentage points). Due to high attrition rates, we are limited in the analysis of conditional effects that we can
do. However, the results indicate that the progressive gender roles message
resonates with secular bystanders. While there is not necessarily a causal relationship here, these results are consistent with our theoretical expectations.
Further disaggregation of the survey data by bystander religion (see appendix,
table A20) shows that this result is driven by secular women; there is almost
a 50 percentage points difference in assistance rates separating atheist from
religious women (columns (3) and (4)).[34]

Attitudinal Differences between Men and Women

A striking finding from the results presented thus far is that men are not responsive to the progressive message about gender roles. Why? Is it because
they have different attitudes from women vis-á-vis gender roles and women's
rights? If most German men hold "traditional" views on these issues, this
could explain why the progressive treatment in our experiment only "works"
on women. As it turns out, however, there are no significant differences among
German men and women with respect to commonly used measures of attitudes toward gender. This is evident in figure 6.8, which presents survey data
on trends in attitudes toward women's role in society, disaggregated by gender.

The top left panel of figure 6.8 plots the degree of respondent agreement
with the statement that "A working mother can have the same warm and trustful relationship with her child as a mother who is not working." We plot data
since the early 1980s and we see clearly that opinions among men and women
are converging to a higher degree of agreement with that statement over time.
There are no meaningful differences in men's and women's opinions with respect to this question or in any of the other three panels of figure 6.8. The
top right panel plots the degree of agreement with the statement that "For a
woman, it is more important to help her husband with his career than pursuing a career herself." There is decreasing support for this viewpoint over
time and the views of men and women on this question are nearly identical.

---

34. These survey data also provided support for our premise that attitude-based prejudice
and discriminatory behavior often go hand in hand: our observed outcome (helping behavior) and attitudes toward immigrants are significantly correlated. For example, bystanders who
believe that immigrants are a threat to German culture (as reported in the post-intervention survey) are around 16 percentage points *less* likely to help veiled immigrants ($p = 0.025$, two-tailed
test).

Do you agree with the following statement?
A working mother can have the same warm and
trustful relationship with her child as a mother who
is not working.

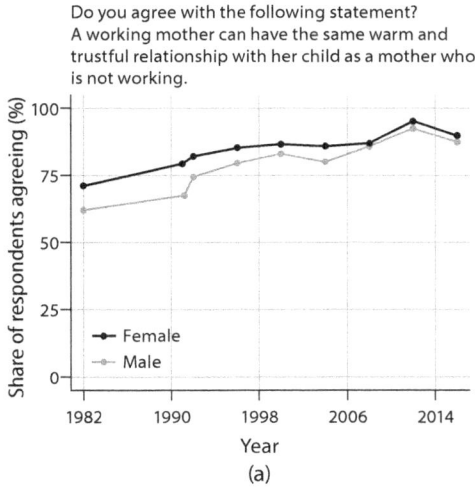

(a)

Do you agree with the following statement?
For a woman it is more important to help her
husband with his career than pursuing a career
herself.

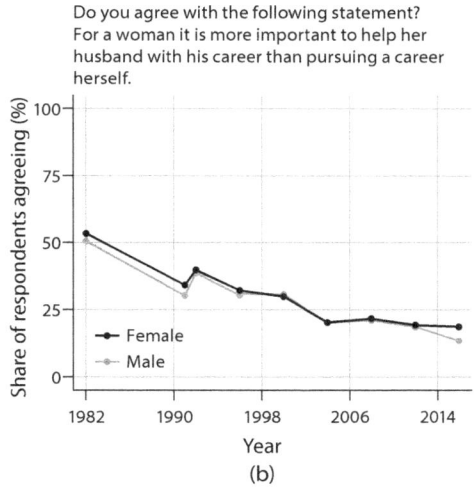

(b)

Do you agree with the following statement?
It's better for the whole family if the woman stays
home and takes care of the household and the
children.

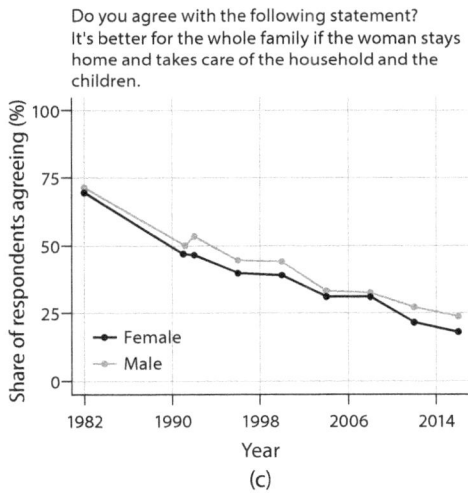

(c)

Do you agree with the following statement?
A married woman should not work if her husband
can provide for the family and there is a limited
number of jobs.

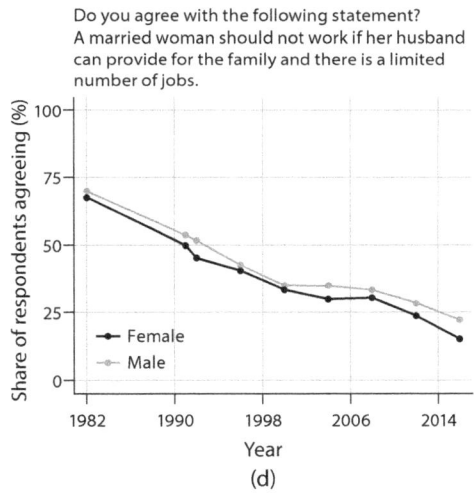

(d)

FIGURE 6.8. Trends in attitudes toward women's role in society
Notes: Share of German citizens who agree completely or rather agree with the different
statements in nationally representative surveys. *Source:* ALLBUS surveys (GESIS, 2018).

In the bottom left panel, we plot the degree of agreement with the statement
that "It is better for the whole family if the woman stays home and takes care
of the household and the children." We again see declining support for this
viewpoint over time both among men and women and no significant differences between them. Finally, in the bottom right panel, we plot the degree
of agreement with the statement that "A married woman should not work if
her husband can provide for her family and there is a limited number of jobs."

The pattern is the same as in the other plots: fewer and fewer people (less than a quarter of the sample overall) agree with this statement and there are no differences between men's and women's opinions on this issue.

This analysis makes clear that any differences in the extent to which men and women are receptive to the progressive message in our experiment are not due to prior differences in attitudes toward women's rights/gender roles. Therefore, a more plausible explanation is that our treatment (the "message" conveyed via the phone call) combined with the hijab in some cases, makes gender identity more salient for women than for men; and therefore our treatment has a more pronounced effect on women. Alternatively, it could be that the gender issues that our experiment taps into are simply more important for women than for men. The degree of agreement in attitudes of men and women in figure 6.8 does not necessarily reflect how *strongly* they feel about these issues. It is quite possible—indeed it is likely—that women feel more strongly about gender equality than men.

What Does the Hijab Signify?

Our field experiment was designed to assess the role of ideas and norms about gender as a mechanism underlying discrimination against Muslims. We have presented evidence that anti-Muslim discrimination by native women is driven in large part by the perception that Muslims are regressive with respect to women's rights. We now delve deeper to provide additional survey-based evidence to support the claim that these ideational factors are a key mechanism underlying discriminatory behavior. Specifically, we explore whether the "hijab penalty" is due to other possible mechanisms that might underlie explicit or implicit biases against Muslims; and whether different mechanisms could explain the behavior of men as compared to women. While the experimental evidence we have presented also speak to mechanisms underlying discriminatory behavior, our surveys allow us to consider alternative explanations. At the same time, they help us better understand the meaning of the hijab in German society.

Public Perceptions of the Hijab in Germany

Perhaps the most salient symbol of Islam in the imagination of Western publics is the hijab. The hijab and the closely related term *khimār* (in Arabic) were used in classical Arabic texts to denote a headscarf; the hijab denotes a partition or curtain, which complies with Islamic rules of female modesty and dress. The meaning of the hijab is contested both in the West and in the Middle East. What does it signify for native Germans? Do native Germans assume that a woman wearing a hijab is oppressed or that she is willingly subordinated to men? Or does the hijab bring other concepts to mind, perhaps symbolizing a physical/security threat posed by Islam even if the threat does not come directly from the women who wear the veil?

We fielded an online survey on a stratified sample of 1,515 German adults, recruited through Qualtrics Panels.[35] Our survey results provide further support for our experimental findings.

We tested what types of symbolic or realistic threats are made salient by the hijab for men and women by presenting respondents with video recordings of the experimental intervention in which bystanders at train stations did *not* provide assistance to female confederates wearing a hijab. These respondents were likely to be similar in many ways to the bystanders in our field experiment and we asked them why they thought the bystanders in the videos did not help the Muslim woman needing help.[36] Respondents were given a list of plausible reasons for why native women might not help women wearing a hijab and asked to choose all that applied. The answer options included that native women "are upset that Muslim immigrants are taking away jobs" (job competition mechanism), "are jealous of young Muslim women" (mating competition mechanism), "think that Muslim immigrants receive too much financial support from the state" (welfare dependence mechanism), "are afraid that migrants with a hijab could be dangerous to them" (security risk mechanism), and/or that "they think that women with a hijab have views about gender equality that are outdated" (gender equality mechanism).

While we find some support for commonly discussed sources of discrimination such as fear of job competition, mating competition, and perceptions

---

35. In order to improve representativeness of the sample, we used population-proportional stratas for the sixteen German states (*Bundesländer*), gender, and age groups.

36. One may wonder whether we should expect ordinary people to have insights into the motivations behind discrimination? It is possible that answers to this question might reflect learned "folk narratives" about the causes of discrimination. If so, however, answers to our question are still informative since these narratives would reflect shared public perceptions about Muslims, which is precisely what we want to capture here. Moreover, there is no reason to expect that survey respondents are unable to reflect on why others discriminate. Indeed, in survey-based studies on norms, it is common to ask respondents questions about what others might do in a given situation. It is also possible that respondents are not reflecting learned folk narratives, and that they are simply sharing their own beliefs/bias, which would also generate valuable insights for our analysis.

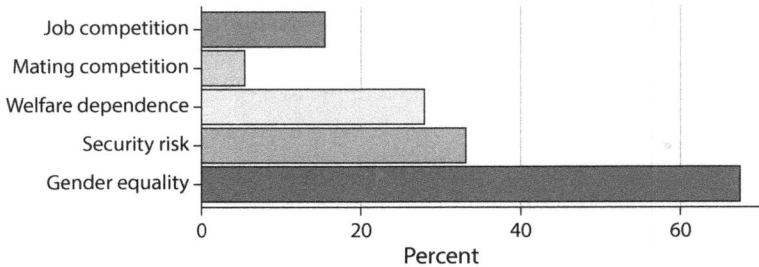

FIGURE 6.9. Evaluations of video of experiment: "Why do native
women not help hijab-wearing women?"
Data source: Authors' survey of German adult citizens, 2018.

that immigrants are welfare dependent or pose a security risk,[37] the most
chosen explanation by far is the gender equality mechanism. In fact, 67.4%
of respondents indicated that they thought that German women do not
help because hijab-wearing women have regressive attitudes about gender
equality.

This perception of the hijab as a symbol of regressive attitudes about gender equality is also evident in the survey responses to a number of other survey
items. Most natives (59.9%) believe that hijab-wearing women are more regressive than non-Muslim women in Germany; and the majority of native
respondents (54.0%) see the hijab as being forced on the wearer, with only a
minority (27.2%) stating that wearing a hijab is a free choice. When presented
with a statement by a well-known German journalist and feminist saying that
the hijab is not a religious symbol, but rather an attempt to control the female
body,[38] 51.4% of native respondents agree with the statement and only 21.0%
disagree. Moreover, women are more likely to agree with this interpretation of
the hijab as a symbol of oppression of women than men,[39] as are respondents
who were socialized after the 1960s, when gender-equality norms became

37. The perception of a security risk might in fact be a symbolic fear, given that the
confederate's demeanor arguably was non-threatening.

38. The text of the statement by Alice Schwarzer was: "The hijab is the flag of political Islam" (*Focus*, 05/09/2019); "The hijab is a not a religious commandment. Only for the Islamic
fundamentalists is the obsessive veiling of women as the prohibition of abortion for Christian
fundamentalists. It is always about the control of the female body" (*Die Zeit*, 07/25/2019).

39. Agreement of 54.4% among women vs. 48.5% among men (p = 0.035).

FIGURE 6.10. Word cloud of open-ended responses on the meaning of the hijab
Notes: Word cloud generated from answers from male (panel (a)) and female (panel (b))
respondents. For male respondents, the three most common terms were "Religion (religion),"
"religiös (religious), and "Islam (islam)." For female respondents, the three most frequently
used terms were "unterdrückt (oppressed)," "Religion (religion)," and "religiös (religious).

more prevalent in Germany.[40] Consistent with these views, only 20.9% of natives state that the hijab is "compatible with German culture," whereas 48.5%
see it as incompatible.

These negative cultural interpretations of the hijab are even more prevalent
among female respondents. In responses provided to open-ended questions
about what people think when they see a woman with a hijab, we see a clear
pattern highlighting the fact that women are more likely than men to see the
hijab as a symbol of oppression of other women. Figure 6.10 shows this pattern clearly by plotting the words that are used frequently in these open-ended
responses. The most frequently used term among female respondents is "oppressed" (*unterdrückt*) whereas this word is significantly less prevalent among
men's responses, which overall do not reveal any clear associations of the hijab
with gender norms.

Discussion

Via a large-scale field experiment in twenty-five cities in Germany and two
follow-up studies, we find evidence that natives' behavior toward Muslim immigrants is shaped by stereotypes concerning ideological differences with

---

40. For respondents who came of age after 1968, 60.4% agree with the characterization,
compared to 50.0% of those growing up earlier (p = 0.012).

regard to gender norms. German women, most of whom share progressive views about gender, discriminate against Muslim women because they assume that Muslims hold regressive views on gender. When Muslims' behavior challenges those beliefs in the context of everyday interactions with natives, German women no longer discriminate against Muslims.

The negative emotions elicited by the hijab in our baseline experiment in chapter 3 are striking in light of the fact that veiling has been common in the memory and experience of Christian Orthodox, Catholic, Mennonite, and other faiths. In recent times, the veil has become a focal point of opposition to Islam and its political implications. Some view the intolerance of the veil in public spaces as reinforcing a secularist tradition in government, while others view it as symptomatic of weakening democratic ideals in Western society (Norton, 2013). The imposition of a veiling ban in France was an example of an effort to reinforce France's secularist tradition, but it could also be perceived as an example of forced assimilation, designed to promote a narrow perspective on gender identity and a degree of cultural homogeneity that is impossible to achieve in a liberal society (Scott, 2007). Our study contributes to this ongoing debate by showing that the perception of the hijab as a symbol of regressive views on gender roles is not an elite phenomenon, as is commonly argued by proponents of multiculturalism; rather, this is a perception that is shared by ordinary people and it shapes their behavior toward Muslims. Women in particular seem sensitive to that perception. Our experiment demonstrates that when the veil's religious and political meanings are separated, it becomes a much less salient marker of cultural difference and it no longer generates discrimination among a large segment of the native population.

Our analysis in this chapter has shown that discrimination measured by differences in helping behavior is explained in large part by the ideas and norms that define shared social identities. Ideas about gender shape perceptions of cultural difference between natives and immigrants and are imbued in common perceptions of the hijab, particularly among women. Our findings are surprising from the prism of a large literature on immigration, which has not yet explored gender identity as a key determinant of anti-immigration attitudes. The gender differences we observe—whereby native women respond to the idea that Muslims hold progressive views on gender, but native men are unmoved by that treatment—cannot be explained by theories of economic competition between natives and immigrants, or by cultural conflict between immigrants and natives construed as a group with homogeneous preferences. These results point to significant subgroup differences in preferences within the native population and suggest that the way to tap into these differences to reduce discrimination is to identify the core set of norms and ideas that define subgroup identities.

Our analysis fits neatly within the psychological literature on helping behavior, which for the most part has focused on exposing causes of discrimination rather than on considering ways to overcome discrimination. A review of the literature on helping noted that most studies "do not allow for the motivations for the differences in behavioral expressions to be assessed and evaluated" (Saucier, McManus, and Smith, 2010, p. 106). Our study provides just such an analysis, focusing on mechanisms of prejudice-reduction. In that regard, our results speak directly to the Common Ingroup Identity Model (CIIM), which is one of the most prominent attempts to theorize mechanisms of prejudice-reduction and is directly applicable to our experimental framework. Grounded in the specific context of intergroup conflict over immigration, our study is directly relevant to the CIIM. We affirm the conclusions of prior studies by finding that a common ingroup identity reduces bias and discrimination. Gender constitutes the common ingroup identity in our framework—an identity that can unify natives and immigrants under specific conditions of ideational agreement about gender rights. In our framework we find evidence of gender solidarity when our experimental treatments establish that native and immigrant women have similar ideas regarding their shared identity.[41]

Bias-reduction in CIIM applications usually occurs via reducing positive behavior toward the ingroup (Brewer, 1999); in our setup establishing a common ingroup identity increases positive behavior (helping) toward the outgroup (immigrants). The intersectionality (crosscuttingness) of gender, national, and religious identities implies that any of these can serve as a unifying, common ingroup identity for segments of the population that share common group attributes. Our experiment shows that shared ideas can help forge shared identities. Gender identity, which could be used to define a common ingroup unifying native and immigrant women, is only activated in a way that reduces native-immigrant bias when there is ideational agreement among

41. This echoes the results of prior research (Brewer, 1996, 291–303), which established that members of each subgroup must have "common, superordinate goals" (Brewer 1996, 291–303). Different conceptions of the superordinate group can cause appeals to a common ingroup identity to backfire (Rutchick and Eccleston, 2010, p. 111). For another discussion of this idea, see Brown and Wade (1987).

natives and immigrants about the meaning of gender identity. We show that gender identity can serve as a crosscutting identity that eliminates discrimination by native women toward immigrant women only when they agree on what it means to be a woman. In the progressive gender norm condition, where such ideational agreement between the majority of natives and immigrants is achieved, the native/immigrant divide as well as the Christian/Muslim divide lose significance for native women and gender identity becomes more salient.

Crosscutting identities can "constrain and modify" each other (Kang and Bodenhausen, 2015, p. 550), thereby reducing the salience of any single dimension of differentiation (Urada, Stenstrom, and Miller, 2007) and, by doing so, they can also reduce the intensity of social conflict (Kang and Chasteen, 2009; Roccas et al., 2008; Coser, 1956; Lipset and Rokkan, 1967; Dahrendorf, 1959; Horowitz, 1985; Mutz, 2002). Gender could serve as a super-ordinate identity that unifies native and immigrant women; however, consistent with our theoretical discussion, this could only be so if native and immigrant women share the same concept of what it means to be a woman.[42] If natives and Muslims have salient differences with respect to their ideas about appropriate gender roles, then making gender identity salient could induce *more* conflict rather than less.

Thus, a key contribution of our study is to emphasize that shared ideas can reduce the perceived social distance that separates natives and immigrants by forming the basis for re-categorizing both as members of a common ingroup identity—that of citizen. While this shows that cultural markers such as the hijab need not always divide natives from immigrants, it is also true that the intersectionality of social identities limits the ways that such recategorization of immigrants as members of a new ingroup can be achieved via targeted policy interventions.[43] Any such intervention that establishes a commonality of

42. This insight is also reflected in a different context in a study by Klar, 2018. She explores the intersection of partisanship in gender identity and shows that lack of uniform support for female candidates in politics among women might indicate partisan divisions with respect to ideas about women's rights and what it means to be a woman.

43. Lack of uniformity in viewpoints regarding women's rights—something that is evident in survey-based work in the United States and other countries (Burns et al., 2015; Cook and Wilcox, 1991; Huddy and Terkildsen, 1993)—will make it harder to design policy interventions targeting shared gender identity as a way to overcome native-immigrant divisions. This is further complicated by evidence that there is an even greater divide with respect to men's and women's attitudes toward equality in gender roles (Burns et al., 2015).

ideas and interests among immigrants and subgroups of natives might also accentuate differences from other subgroups of natives. In our experiment, gender, religious, and national identities all become salient as we expose bystanders to nonnative (immigrant) women wearing a hijab. When the ideational threat the hijab poses to native women is eliminated, only women are responsive to this intervention and men continue to discriminate against Muslim women. Thus, the types of cultural threat that men and women perceive are likely to be different. Any intervention designed to alleviate concerns arising from a specific threat that is salient to women—specifically the perception that Muslims are regressive vis-á-vis women's rights—makes gender identities more salient than religious or national identities for women *only* and is not an effective way to reduce bias among native men. Therefore, while in theory crosscutting identities can help reduce intergroup conflict by facilitating the recategorization of individuals into a common ingroup identity, in practice, such an effect will be hard to achieve since policy interventions designed to diminish bias by specific subgroups may create new outgroups that are not affected by those interventions.

Finally, our empirical results in this chapter have direct implications for the design and implementation of policies to promote multiculturalism in the context of Europe's immigration crisis. The strong effects of shared norms and ideas suggest that multiculturalism is possible, but it also has its limits. While tolerance of ascriptive differences between native and immigrant populations is an attainable goal, success depends on the degree of cultural (rather than simply economic) integration of immigrants. Superficial differences in ethnic, racial, or linguistic traits can be overcome, but citizens will resist abandoning valued civic norms and ideas that define their identities in favor of a liberal accommodation of the values of others.

7

Viewing "Them" as One of "Us"

PREVIOUS CHAPTERS HAVE shown that anti-Muslim bias is driven at least in part by beliefs that Muslim immigrants do not care about the local society and they do not share its norms. These beliefs reflect the perception that a large gap exists between native Germans' and Muslims' values, customs, and habits. This gap is to some extent reflected in the significant cross-country differences in social attitudes toward gender that we reviewed in chapter 6; there is clear evidence that public opinion in Germany with respect to the role of women in society is different from majority public opinion in many countries in the Middle East and North Africa. Our own surveys of German natives presented in chapter 6 confirm that Germans believe that Muslims hold regressive views toward gender norms and they view the hijab as a symbol not only of religious difference, but also of Muslims' resistance to cultural integration. In chapter 5, we saw similar evidence with reference to norms regarding littering in public spaces; our surveys revealed that Germans believe that immigrants litter more than natives and that this is indicative of immigrants' lack of respect for Germany.

We have shown that when natives' beliefs about the degree of ideological or normative differences with Muslim immigrants change, anti-Muslim discrimination is reduced. This result is consistent with the idea that positive contact with outgroup members can change one's behavior or attitudes toward the outgroup member if that person is assumed to be representative of the outgroup (Hewstone and Brown, 1986). But do bystanders perceive our confederates as representative members of their group when they enforce local norms or when they reveal that they hold progressive views? Or do they view them as exceptions? Interactions that defy prior expectations could reduce discrimination against the specific stereotype-defying confederate, but they can also change attitudes toward the outgroup more generally. We now consider this question directly and ask whether positive interactions that consist of observing the immigrants enforce valued local norms lead German natives to view our immigrant confederates as less "typical" of their group and more similar to an upstanding German citizen. If norm enforcement does not fit comfortably within Germans' preconceived notions of how Muslim immigrants would act in specific situations, then they might deal with that dissonant information by viewing the immigrants as exceptions to the rule rather than update their views about Muslims in general. However, natives' negative views of Muslim immigrants as a group need not imply that they would not accept such immigrants as members of an alternative ingroup of "good citizens" which would reduce bias toward them. Even if natives view norm-adhering Muslim immigrants as exceptions, a parallel process of *recategorization* might occur and the more similar one believes Muslims are to the "typical" good citizen, the more it becomes possible to see Muslim immigrants and natives as members of a common *citizen* ingroup.

We look for evidence of these different mechanisms by returning to the context of our littering experiment from chapter 5. We now explore the psychological processes that lead natives to discriminate less toward norm-adhering immigrants. We have shown evidence that Germans have strong norms against littering and that they believe immigrants are less likely to share those norms.[1] Now we explore how seeing Muslim immigrants defy those expectations changes natives' views of the individual and the group at large. Does observing immigrants adhere to valued social norms reduce discrimination because it makes natives less prejudiced toward Muslim immigrants in general? Or does it make them view the individual confederate in a better light, perhaps assigning to that individual qualities that are not typical of her social group? Is the norm-enforcing confederate seen as unique, as an exception to the rule and therefore not a "typical" immigrant? If so, the reduction in discrimination might not result in changed perceptions of Muslims as an outgroup.

We use a large online survey experiment to answer these questions and to identify psychological mechanisms that explain the reduction of discrimination that we observed in the "littering" experiment presented in chapter 5. This brings us back to the discussion of three mechanisms of social categorization that we presented in chapter 2: *decategorization, recategorization,* and *mutual differentiation*. We summarize these below for easy reference:

---

1. See figure 5.2 and table 5.1 in chapter 5 for survey-based evidence on these points.

- *Decategorization* involves de-emphasizing the group-level attributes of an individual. Outgroup members are seen as unique individuals or exceptions whose personal qualities do not apply to the rest of the outgroup.
- *Recategorization* occurs as a result of a cognitive shift whereby an outgroup member is seen as part of a common ingroup. The boundaries between ingroup and outgroup are redefined or expanded.
- *Mutual differentiation* results in a reassessment of the importance one attaches to the attributes that define the outgroup and that differentiate it from the ingroup. While these differences persist, they become less salient and they do not influence behavior toward the outgroup or evaluations of that group.

All three mechanisms could lead to a reduction in discrimination, but which ones are likely to explain the effects we presented earlier in the book? *Recategorization* is the key mechanism underlying our theory. Is there evidence that natives are more likely to perceive norm-enforcing immigrants as members of a common ingroup—that of "citizen"? We test this idea formally using new data and also test whether there is evidence of decategorization—perceiving of that person as an exception and seeing her as an individual rather than as a Muslim immigrant—and mutual differentiation—downplaying the differences that separate natives from Muslim immigrants.

Research Design

The intervention that we presented in chapter 5—the "littering experiment"—allowed us to measure differences in individual-level behavior toward confederates who exhibited different degrees of norm-adherence while we manipulated the ascriptive characteristics of those confederates. Muslim immigrant confederates as well as German natives were placed in encounters in public spaces where they sometimes enforced anti-littering norms and sometimes not. Bystanders had an opportunity to observe this behavior and we measured outcomes in the form of changes in bystanders' helping behavior toward native and immigrant confederates. We now modify that approach in the context of an online survey experiment, which exposes respondents to short videos of the encounters between natives and confederates that took place on the train platforms. In the videos, confederates can be natives or Muslim immigrants standing on a train platform and interacting under conditions that were identical to those during our field experiments. We are mainly interested in the cognitive effects of observing how our confederates react to a violation of the norm against littering.

The intervention proceeds as follows: a male native confederate (viola-tor) violates a widely held norm against littering by dropping an empty coffee cup on a train platform in close proximity to a bystander who is waiting for the train. This bystander (enforcer) is a female confederate who observes his behavior and intervenes by asking him to pick up his trash. The violator un-willingly but promptly complies with the request and leaves the scene. The enforcer is either a German native or Muslim immigrant and she is standing on the platform as if waiting for a train.

The bystander who captures the interaction on video appears to have been filming the station and to have caught the interaction on his phone by chance. The camera seems to be scanning the station and stops momentarily on the confederate who is standing by, at which point a native male confed-erate walks into the frame, drinking a cup of coffee. The male confederate drops his empty cup on the floor and our female confederate scolds him. The video captures this exchange between them and the entire interaction takes about twenty seconds. Screen shots from the video depicting those scenes are included in figure 7.1. The scene is filmed from a short distance away, so

FIGURE 7.1. Screen capture of treatment video
Notes: Figure represents a screen capture of a treatment video. Mirroring the norms experiment, the male confederate discards an empty coffee cup in plain view of the female confederate. The female confederate enforces the anti-littering norm, telling the male confederate to pick up the trash and put it in the trash can nearby.

TABLE 7.1. Treatment Matrix

Condition	Punisher Identity	Punisher Religion	Enforcement
1	Immigrant	Hijab	Punisher
2	Immigrant	No Hijab	Punisher
3	Immigrant	Hijab	Third Party
4	Immigrant	No Hijab	Third Party
5	Native	–	Punisher
6	Native	–	Third Party

the conversation among the confederates is audible.[2] We uploaded this video clip onto YouTube and included a link to the YouTube video in a survey of about 2,500 German adults that we fielded in November 2020. The video has a similar feel to other amateur videos that are routinely uploaded on YouTube and which depict actual events and frequently have brief comments by those who captured those events on camera. The video was filmed on a telephone camera precisely to increase this "reality TV" feel. The research protocol was reviewed and approved by the University of Pennsylvania's Institutional Review Board (IRB Protocol #843964).

Treatment Conditions

In all iterations of this experiment, the anti-littering norm is enforced by a confederate, who can be (a) a native German; (b) an immigrant wearing a hijab; or (c) the same immigrant wearing no religious markers. In iterations where the norm is not enforced by the confederate who is the focus of the experimental intervention, the norm is enforced by a third party. This third-party enforcement is always done by a native who appears to come into the frame of the video to scold the violator and enforce the norm. In these iterations, we focus on the confederate who does *not* punish the violator. The experimental conditions are presented in table 7.1.

We filmed videos of equal length for each treatment condition. As in our field experiments, we use all female confederates (except for the norm violator), but manipulate the perceived immigrant identity of the specific confederate in any given video. We vary three dimensions:

Dimension 1: Ethnicity of the confederate   Respondents are presented with the video of an immigrant of Middle Eastern origin or a native German. In the

2. We added subtitles to the video clip to make sure all respondents could follow the entire conversation.

immigrant "control" condition, the confederate wears no distinctive religious symbols. The German confederate is dressed similarly to the immigrant and always wears no distinctive religious symbols.

Dimension 2: Religious identity   We also manipulate the confederate's putative religiosity by having a confederate who either wears no religious symbol (in the immigrant control condition described above) or wears a hijab to show that she is Muslim.

Dimension 3: Norm enforcement   We manipulate whether the confederate (native or immigrant) enforces the anti-littering norm. There is always norm enforcement in the videos shown to respondents; what varies is whether enforcement is done by the confederate who is the focus of our study, or by a third party (always a native German). In iterations where a third party is enforcing the norm, the non-punishing confederate remains in the picture but is effectively sidelined by the third party, which might create the impression that she is indifferent to the norm violation.

Data Collection on Outcomes

We surveyed a stratified sample of about 2,500 adult native Germans (stratified by state and gender).[3] After a battery of questions asking about socioeconomic and demographic characteristics, respondents were randomized across six different videos of the intervention corresponding to the conditions listed in the treatment matrix. We then asked a battery of questions to measure how respondents perceive the confederates in the video. We were primarily interested in testing whether norm enforcement caused respondents to feel more warmly toward the immigrant confederate; and whether they perceived norm-enforcing immigrants as more similar to German citizens and less typical of their group. We also tested whether the videos changed the way natives perceive Muslim immigrants in general.

Key outcomes in this study are measured in several ways. First, we ask respondents to rate how favorably they feel toward the women in the video.[4]

---

3. We screened out nonnative Germans (those born in other countries or with non-German parents).

4. We refer to the confederate as an immigrant in all immigrant conditions to reinforce this dimension of the treatment.

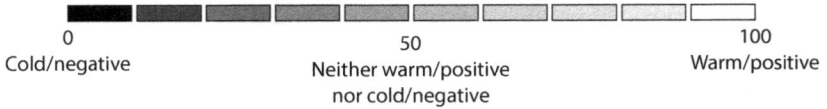

FIGURE 7.2. Outcome measurement: Generalized affect

Second, we ask them to write five adjectives that come to mind when they think about the relevant person. These words are analyzed to explore differences in perceptions of the confederates in the enforcement condition vs. control group. The act of writing down these adjectives should amplify the treatment effect as respondents have to reflect on what they watched. Third, in all immigrant conditions, we ask respondents to indicate how *typical* they think the immigrant confederate is of Muslim immigrants in Germany (survey item: *decat*); how similar or dissimilar they view the specific confederate's behavior is to the behavior of upstanding citizens in Germany (survey item: *recat*); and how similar they view Muslim immigrants to good German citizens (survey item: *gpcat*). These questions correspond to measures of our three key mechanisms—decategorization, recategorization, and mutual differentiation. We therefore collect data on perceptions of similarity between (a) the immigrant confederate and Muslim immigrants as a group; (b) the immigrant confederate in the experiment and good German citizens; and (c) Muslim immigrants as a group and good German citizens. Our design allows us to test whether these perceptions change as a result of exposure to norm enforcement by the confederate compared to third-party enforcement of the anti-littering norm. Finally, we ask everyone to assess the propensity of Germans and immigrants to enforce anti-littering norms if they are confronted with behavior similar to the littering depicted in the videos.[5] This question provides another possible test for the "mutual differentiation" hypothesis as a result of norm enforcement. The different measures are presented in more detail below.

Generalized Affect   Figure 7.2 depicts the survey item designed to collect data on respondents' feelings toward our confederates. Confederates in each treatment condition are asked how warmly they feel toward the confederate on a scale from 0 to 100, where higher scores correspond to "warmer" or more positive feelings.

5. Survey items: *intervene_n* for Germans and *intervene_m* for immigrants.

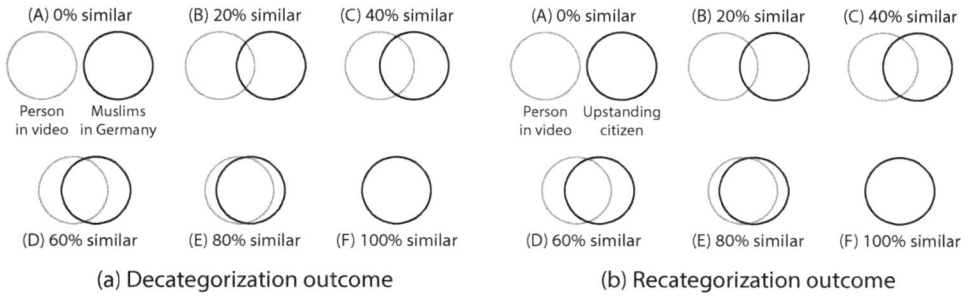

FIGURE 7.3. Outcome measurement: Decategorization and recategorization
Notes: Subfigures (a) and (b) show the instrument used to measure decategorization and recategorization. Subfigure (a) asks respondents to report the extent to which Muslim confederates portrayed in the video are typical of/similar to Muslims living in Germany. Subfigure (b) asks respondents to report the extent to which they believe Muslim confederates to be similar to outstanding citizens in Germany.

Decategorization and Recategorization   Figure 7.3 depicts the survey items corresponding to our measures of *decategorization* and *recategorization*. After viewing the video, respondents are asked to think about the confederate in the video and to rate how similar that confederate is to other Muslims living in Germany or upstanding German citizens. They could rate the degree of similarity by choosing one of several pairs of overlapping circles. The degree of overlap indicates the degree of perceived similarity (or difference). One circle represents the Muslim confederate portrayed in the video and the other represents the comparison group—either all Muslims living in Germany in panel (a) of figure 7.3 or good German citizens in panel (b). Respondents could rate the two as completely dissimilar to the confederate (choice A in both panels), completely similar (choice F), or somewhere in between (choices B–E, with the degree of similarity increasing in increments of 20%). This measure of perceived similarity allows us to test our key hypotheses regarding *decategorization* (panel (a)) or *recategorization* (panel (b)).

Descriptive Statistics

Information on the demographic characteristics of our sample, respondent religion and partisanship, as well as summary statistics for each outcome, is included in table 7.2.[6]

6. By design, the "decategorization" question cannot be asked in the two "native" treatment conditions, which is what explains the smaller number of observations for that outcome.

TABLE 7.2. Descriptive Statistics

Statistic	N	Mean	St. Dev.	Min	Pctl(25)	Pctl(75)	Max
Demographics							
Age	1,261	38.407	14.797	18	26	50	100
Female	1,261	0.495	0.500	0	0	1	1
High Education (College +)	1,259	0.199	0.399	0.000	0.000	0.000	1.000
Full Time Employed	1,260	0.531	0.499	0.000	0.000	1.000	1.000
Religion							
Protestant	1,261	0.282	0.450	0	0	1	1
Catholic	1,261	0.300	0.458	0	0	1	1
Atheist	1,261	0.388	0.487	0	0	1	1
Political Affiliation							
CDU	1,261	0.243	0.429	0	0	0	1
SPD	1,261	0.122	0.328	0	0	0	1
Greens	1,261	0.183	0.387	0	0	0	1
AfD	1,261	0.109	0.311	0	0	0	1
Dependent Variables							
Decategorization	835	3.029	1.473	1.000	2.000	4.000	6.000
Recategorization	1,260	3.859	1.577	1.000	3.000	5.000	6.000
Mutual Differentiation	1,064	3.416	1.518	1.000	2.000	5.000	6.000

Hypotheses

The main hypotheses that we test using these data are listed below. These were all pre-registered prior to data collection and in each case we specified the anticipated direction of the effects. Since the design of this study is not ideal for an exploration of differences across identity types (i.e., native vs. immigrant) due to the small number of confederates in each identity group, we focus on hypotheses that can be tested via within-actor comparisons.

Hypothesis 1. (*Recognizing good citizenship*): Confederates who enforce valued civic norms should be perceived more favorably than those who do not enforce those norms.

Hypothesis 2. (*Benefits of norm enforcement*): Norm enforcement by immigrants should make respondents perceive them more favorably.

Hypothesis 3. (*Recategorization*): Immigrants who enforce valued civic norms are more likely to be perceived as citizens rather than as immigrants.

Hypothesis 4. (**Decategorization**): *Immigrants who enforce valued local norms are more likely to be perceived as exceptions who do not resemble the typical immigrant.*

Hypothesis 5. (**Mutual differentiation**): *When immigrants are observed enforcing valued civic norms, this makes native respondents more likely to deemphasize the differences that separate natives and immigrants as a group.*

Main Findings
Recognizing Good Citizenship

The first two hypotheses refer to the anticipated effect of norm enforcement, which should be positive for both natives (hypothesis 1) and immigrants (hypothesis 2) as long as respondents recognize good citizenship. Here we are testing whether behavior that signals to respondents that confederates are good citizens generates warmer feelings toward them. The treatment effect is registered on a feeling thermometer with higher values indicating warmer feelings. Hypothesis 1 is tested with reference to the baseline condition where only native confederates are used in the intervention. The feeling thermometer data plotted in figure 7.4 make clear that respondents feel much warmer toward the native confederate when she enforces the anti-littering norm than when the *same* native confederate does not enforce the norm (the difference is nineteen points on the thermometer). A similar-size effect (twenty-one points) is observed for immigrants, for whom norm enforcement increases feelings of warmth consistent with hypothesis 2.

It is worth noting that we do not observe a difference between feelings toward the hijab-wearing and no-hijab-wearing immigrant (pooling across enforcement conditions, or looking at each condition separately). This represents a difference from the field-experimental results that we reported in previous chapters, but this difference could be explained by the fact that we are now measuring attitudes rather than behavior, so we need not expect to observe the same exact relationships that we observed in the field. Moreover, the wording of the questions in the survey instrument emphasizes the Muslim immigrant identity of the confederate in the relevant treatment conditions, including the no-hijab condition, which could attenuate the subtle effect that the hijab might have on respondents' perception of the confederates.

Feeling thermometer
On a scale from 0–100, how negative/unfriendly (0) or
positive/friendly (100) do you feel towards this woman?

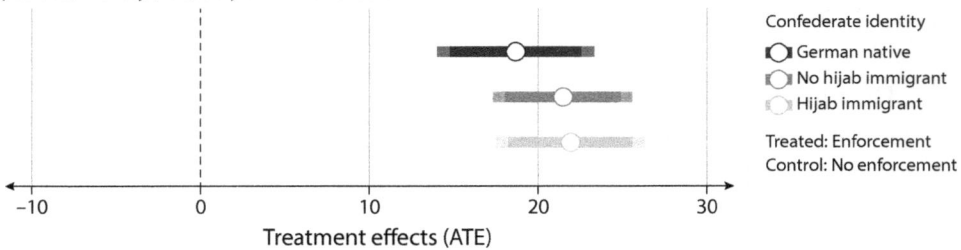

FIGURE 7.4. Norm enforcement effects on generalized affect
Notes: Dots represent the estimated average treatment effects, with the darker and lighter bars
denoting 90% and 95% confidence intervals, respectively.

Recategorization

Having established that respondents recognize good citizenship, we now turn
to hypotheses 3–5, which are at the heart of our discussion of mechanisms of
bias reduction. Our analysis, presented below, provides clear evidence in support of our key mechanism of *recategorization* and offers additional insights
into whether the treatment effect is generalized to all Muslim immigrants, or
if it is limited to the specific confederate.[7]

Our analysis reveals that respondents are more likely to recategorize Muslim immigrants as good citizens if they observe immigrants enforce the anti-
littering norm, consistent with hypothesis 3. We plot the main effects in
subfigure (a) of figure 7.5. The survey item asks respondents, "How similar
do you think the woman in the video is to upstanding citizens?" The results
strongly support our theoretical expectations regarding the recategorization
mechanism as confederates who enforce norms are seen as much more similar
to upstanding German citizens than those who do not. This is true for both
hijab-wearing immigrants and immigrants without a hijab.

---

7. We present intention-to-treat effects. We also explored complier average causal effects
(CACE) to estimate treatment effects among respondents who answer a manipulation check
question about the content of the video correctly. We employ the standard instrumental variables regression framework with the experimental treatment indicator used as an instrument
for the endogenous compliance variable (manipulation check). The analysis does not substantively change our results because the degree of non-compliance was very small; only about
1∼3% of our sample fail the manipulation check.

How similar do you think the confederate is to upstanding citizens?

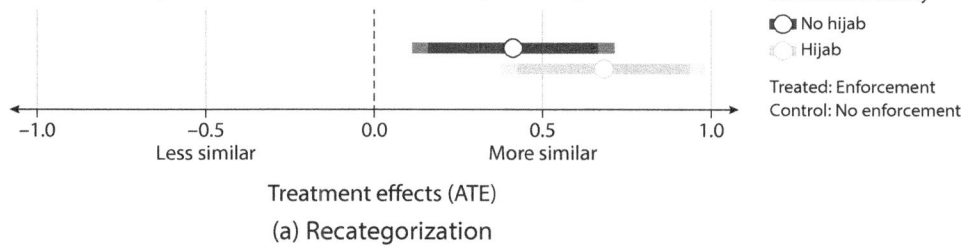

Confederate identity

○ No hijab
○ Hijab

Treated: Enforcement
Control: No enforcement

−1.0   −0.5   0.0   0.5   1.0
         Less similar   More similar

Treatment effects (ATE)

(a) Recategorization

How typical do you think the confederate is of Muslims in Germany?

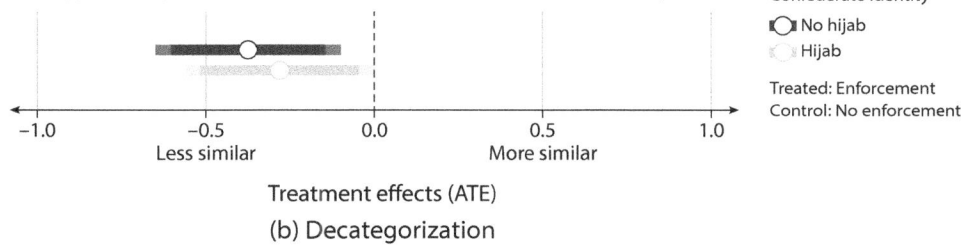

Confederate identity

○ No hijab
○ Hijab

Treated: Enforcement
Control: No enforcement

−1.0   −0.5   0.0   0.5   1.0
         Less similar   More similar

Treatment effects (ATE)

(b) Decategorization

How similar do you think Muslims in Germany are to upstanding citizens?

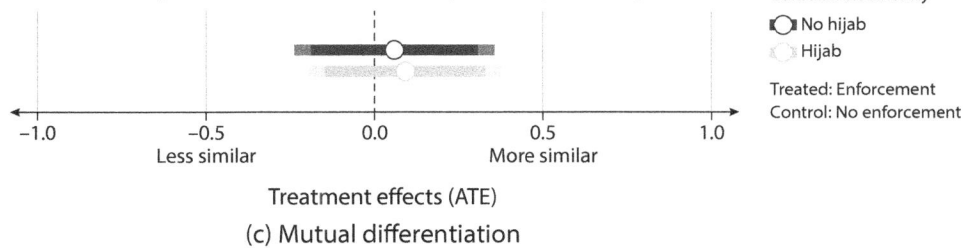

Confederate identity

○ No hijab
○ Hijab

Treated: Enforcement
Control: No enforcement

−1.0   −0.5   0.0   0.5   1.0
         Less similar   More similar

Treatment effects (ATE)

(c) Mutual differentiation

FIGURE 7.5. Categorization effects
Notes: Dots represent the estimated average treatment effects, with the darker and lighter
bars denoting 90% and 95% confidence intervals, respectively.

This result is important from the perspective of the "outgroup homogene-ity" effect—the perception that outgroup members are more similar to one another than they really are (i.e., stereotyping), which is usually accompanied by a "belief-similarity" effect with respect to ingroup members. We know from seminal contributions to social identity theory that, when identity categories are salient, individuals will exaggerate the differences between groups and downplay the differences within groups.[8] We also know from our own surveys in previous chapters that the hijab makes group identities salient and highlights the native-immigrant divide. Thus, it is to be expected that respondents (who are natives) will accentuate the differences between them and immigrants and are likely to believe that members of the outgroup (Muslims) are more similar to one another than they really are, while also being different from the ingroup (German natives).[9]

Outgroup homogeneity is a barrier to considering immigrants similar to natives, but our results suggest that watching acts of norm enforcement by immigrants breaks down this barrier and allows natives to think of immigrants as "one of them." This resonates with our findings from earlier chapters, as we showed that a big part of the reason that German natives are biased against Muslim immigrants is the perception of belief *dis-similarity* between Germans and immigrants as opposed to the expectation that there is significantly more belief *similarity* among members of the ingroup (Germans). Indeed, in chapter 6 we showed that discrimination in helping behavior is completely erased when we establish a congruence between natives' and immigrants' beliefs and values regarding gender norms.

A premise underlying the recategorization mechanism is that some type of updating occurs that changes natives' attitudes toward immigrants. In other words, to recategorize an immigrant as a member of a common citizen ingroup in the context of our experiment, it must be that natives believe that most immigrants do not care about norms against littering. We saw earlier (in chapter 5) that this is the case and it follows that any immigrant who shows that she cares about this norm might appear as an exception to the rule, hence also less "typical" of Muslim immigrants in general. We can test this hypothesis directly, which allows us to evaluate the decategorization mechanism.

In subfigure (b) of figure 7.5, we plot treatment effects for immigrant enforcers vs. non-enforcers focusing on the decategorization mechanism. The

---

8. Turner (1982, p. 28) describes this as "Tajfel's law," adding that "the accentuation of intraclass similarities and interclass differences is further enhanced by the value significance of the classification."

9. See Alabastro et al. (2013). Ingroup-outgroup status—which is a relevant dimension to consider in light of the native (high status) and immigrant (low status) divide—also shapes perceptions of within-group similarity and difference; ingroup members are perceived as being similar to oneself and outgroup members more dissimilar from the ingroup (Brewer, 1991; Abrams et al., 1990).

survey item corresponding to this plot asks respondents who have watched the videos with Muslim confederates to say how typical they think the confederate in the video is to other Muslims living in Germany. Consistent with hypothesis 4, we find that norm enforcement makes respondents view the Muslim confederate as *less typical* of her group. We view this result as providing clear support for the *decategorization* mechanism. Both the recategorization and decategorization effects may be stronger for people for whom norms matter, if only because they are the ones who are more likely to update their priors regarding the outgroup homogeneity bias as a result of observing stereotype-defying behavior by immigrants that involves norm enforcement. We consider this source of heterogeneity in the data in the next section.

It is striking that we observe such strong effects in response to a video that is just twenty seconds long. With the help of this survey, we can complement the analysis of our field experiments and say with greater certainty that the discrimination reduction that we observed in the field is due in large part to natives recategorizing immigrants as part of their common *citizen* ingroup.

Perhaps not surprisingly, there is no evidence that our very short, one-shot treatment changes respondents' attitudes toward Muslim immigrants in general. Subfigure (c) of figure 7.5 plots responses to the question "how similar or different are typical Muslim immigrants to upstanding fellow citizens?" We again focus on treatment conditions with immigrant confederates and look for any effects of norm enforcement, but find none.

Mutual differentiation is a higher bar to clear since it requires that general outgroup attributes be de-emphasized, blurring the boundary between natives and immigrants. It is conceivable that this could occur as a result of observing acts of norm enforcement by immigrants over a prolonged period, and by having multiple positive encounters with the outgroup. An isolated, brief encounter or a single video with a positive message will clearly not be enough to change attitudes about an entire group. Indeed, the strong effects with respect to the decategorization hypothesis in a sense speak against the likelihood of mutual differentiation since respondents reveal that they have strong ideas about what behaviors are typical for each group and the typical members of each group are still perceived as different from one another.[10]

10. The null effects with respect to the mutual differentiation question also indicate that responses to our survey are unlikely to reflect demand effects. If one were concerned that results with respect to the recategorization outcome were in some way due to respondents perceiving

The null effects with respect to mutual differentiation are corroborated by an analysis of responses to a different question regarding the percent of natives or immigrants who the respondents believe would intervene if they saw someone litter in public. This question reveals respondents' beliefs about immigrants' propensity to enforce valued local norms and there is no evidence that our treatment moves those beliefs in either direction significantly. Results regarding perceptions of norm pervasiveness across groups are plotted in figure A.12 in the appendix.[11] These null effects help us clarify the overall mechanism: if seeing an immigrant enforcing the norm were to lead bystanders to update their beliefs about the whole group (as the group differentiation mechanism would entail), we should see movement on these questions. The fact that we do not observe such effects amplifies the result that our intervention does not change how natives perceive Muslims as a group; and it is consistent with the decategorization and recategorization mechanisms, as discussed previously. The positive judgments resulting from norm enforcement do not extend to Muslims as a whole.

Heterogeneous Effects

The bias-reducing effect of norm enforcement in the video likely operates by establishing a personal connection between the respondent and the confederate enforcer in the video. This is analogous to the mechanism through which perspective-taking interventions work, by encouraging experimental subjects to project the Self onto another (a member of an outgroup) and by doing so they reduce the cognitive salience of the Other's group-level attributes, making it more likely that the Other will be seen as a member of an ingroup.[12] Previous experiences with norm enforcement that respondents

---

"more similarity" to the "correct" answer in this survey, they should have also displayed demand effects in a similar direction in the mutual differentiation question. With respect to the decategorization outcome, it is not a priori clear what answer might be perceived as "politically correct" across treatment conditions.

11. We plot the share of the Muslim immigrant (panels (a) and (b)) population who would intervene to enforce anti-littering norms according to our respondents. Exposure to our treatment clearly has no significant effect regardless of whether we focus on respondents for whom norms matter or not.

12. Perspective-taking involves putting a subject in another's shoes and asking them to view the world from their eyes. Such interventions have been shown to reduce outgroup bias. According to Galinsky and Moskowitz (2000, p. 711), "perspective-taking should prevent the hyperaccessibility of stereotypes because the personalized approach toward the target reduces the focus on group-level characteristics that aid in the activation of stereotypes (Brewer, 1996;

may have had could be brought to mind by the video as the respondent imagines how she/he would have reacted in a similar situation. If the respondent puts himself/herself in the shoes of the confederate enforcer in the video, this can increase the likelihood of both decategorization and recategorization of the outgroup member. This effect should be stronger for people who believe in the value of social norms and would therefore be more likely to see an alignment between themselves and the norm-enforcing confederate.

This argument leads us to expect stronger treatment effects among respondents who report caring a lot about norms and about "the common good." Indeed, our priors were that the effects of our treatment might be stronger or even only present among people who value norms and might therefore appreciate acts of norm enforcement.[13] If the bias-reducing effect of norm enforcement in the video operates by establishing a personal connection between the respondent and the confederate enforcer, this is more likely to happen among respondents for whom norms matter as the others are more likely to discount the significance of the confederate's intervention.

We are able to test this hypothesis directly by comparing treatment effects by whether "norms matter," using data that we collected before exposing respondents to the different treatments. Without making any explicit references to littering, we probed the degree to which respondents care about norms by embedding two questions about norms in a multi-item question that asked respondents to rate the importance of different ideas and activities in their lives. We asked them if they agreed with the statement that "rules, norms and customs are necessary for good social coexistence," and whether they agreed that "society can only function if everyone contributes to the common good." The other items asked them questions about the importance of seemingly unrelated items, such as a balanced lifestyle, the importance of reading the newspaper, exposing oneself to art, or exercising regularly. Respondents could indicate their degree of agreement with these statements on a scale ranging from 1 to 7, where 1 indicated complete disagreement and 7 indicated complete agreement. A score of 4 means that respondents are neutral toward norms, so we code all responses equal to 5 or above as indicative of a concern with norms and explore whether there is heterogeneity in treatment effects for respondents in that group. About

---

Brewer, 1988) while simultaneously increasing trait overlap between representations of the self and of the group represented in the photograph."

13. This prior expectation was explicitly included in our pre-analysis plan.

three quarters of our sample clear this threshold and would agree that "norms matter."[14]

What we find is consistent with our expectations. The heterogeneous effects of placing high value on norms are best seen with reference to the recategorization mechanism. In figure 7.6 we plot treatment effects for hijab-wearing and no-hijab-wearing immigrants while distinguishing between respondents for whom norms matter from those for whom norms do not matter. Subfigure (a) in figure 7.6 presents recategorization results and we present the same analysis in figure 7.7 using our second question to classify respondents in the "norms matter" or norms "do not matter" groups. Treatment effects are much stronger and statistically significant for the "norms matter" group, whereas they are not significantly different from zero in the "norms do not matter" group. This pattern is seen regardless of the question we use to code whether norms matter. Indeed, it is consistent with our theoretical expectations that respondents who value good citizenship would be more prone to downplaying the outgroup attributes of norm-enforcing confederates as they place more emphasis on the "belief similarities" between those immigrant confederates and themselves.[15]

Turning now to decategorization, we see some interesting patterns when we disaggregate responses by whether norms are particularly important to respondents. Our prior expectation is that respondents for whom norms matter are more likely to recognize good citizenship in the norm enforcement videos (there is clear evidence of this in the heterogeneous effects plot of the feeling thermometer results; see the differences in warmth toward the norm-enforcing and non-enforcing native (co-ethnic) by whether or not respondents say that "norms matter").

The treatment effect for norm enforcement by immigrants without hijab is slightly larger among respondents for whom "norms matter" than for those for whom norms are less important, even though the difference is not statistically significant; and the same pattern is observed with respect to the second survey

14. A third question aimed to identify those who would "say something if [they] saw someone jay-walking in front of children." This question measures attitudes toward a specific norm and asks respondents if they would take action against a norm violator rather than measure their attitudes toward norms and social order more broadly, so we consider this question item separately in the appendix.

15. Results are broadly consistent using data from the question regarding attitudes toward violations of the jaywalking norm. In this case, we use a higher threshold of 6 out of 7, since adherence with this particular norm is not as pervasive. Results are presented in the appendix.

How similar do you think the confederate is to upstanding citizens?

Treatment effects (ATE)

(a) Recategorization

How typical do you think the confederate is of Muslims in Germany?

Treatment effects (ATE)

(b) Decategorization

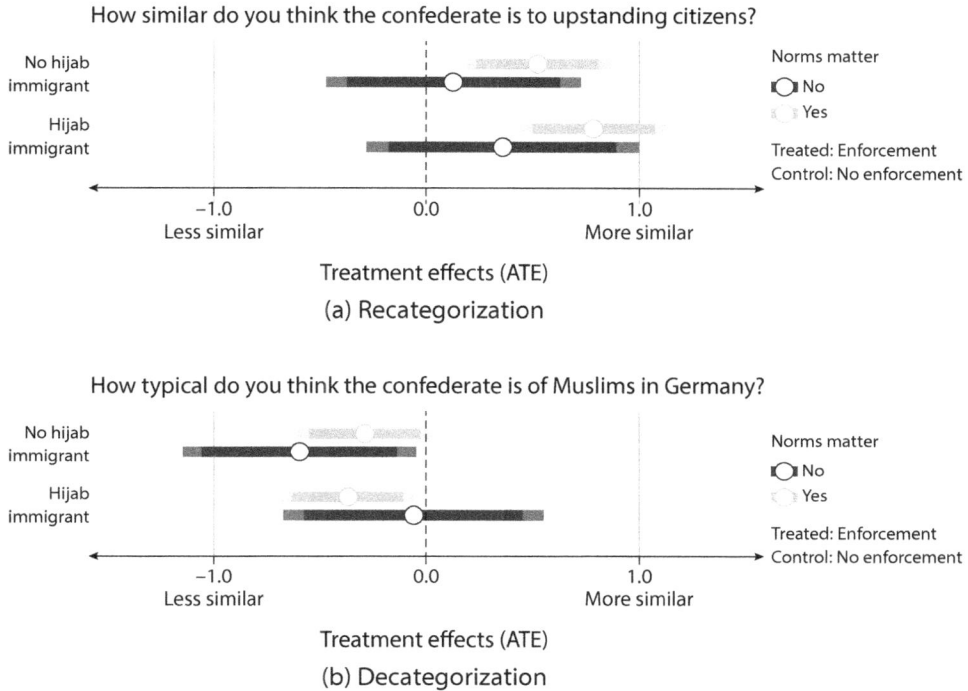

FIGURE 7.6. Heterogeneous effects: Norm importance 1

Notes: Heterogeneity in treatment effects disaggregated based on survey item that asks respondents whether they agree with the statement: "I believe rules, norms, and customs are necessary for social coexistence." Dots represent the estimated average treatment effects, with the darker and lighter bars denoting 90% and 95% confidence intervals, respectively.

question we use to code whether norms matter. In a regression of decategorization scores on norm enforcement and "norms matter," we see that these variables affect the decategorization outcome in opposite ways (negative coefficient for enforcement; positive for "norms matter"). Our explanation for this pattern is that it suggests that people for whom "norms matter" are likely more biased against Muslims in the sense of having stronger "outgroup similarity" bias, thinking that all Muslims are the same, thereby not making any significant differences between hijab-wearing and non-hijab-wearing Muslims.[16]

16. Although we do not have any pretreatment data on bias that we can use to test this explicitly, the alternative explanation for this pattern is not plausible. The alternative explanation is that "norms matter" people do not recognize norm enforcement as evidence of good citizenship, but this is the opposite of what we actually observe. For example, in the plot of

How similar do you think the confederate is to upstanding citizens?

(a) Recategorization

How typical do you think the confederate is of Muslims in Germany?

(b) Decategorization

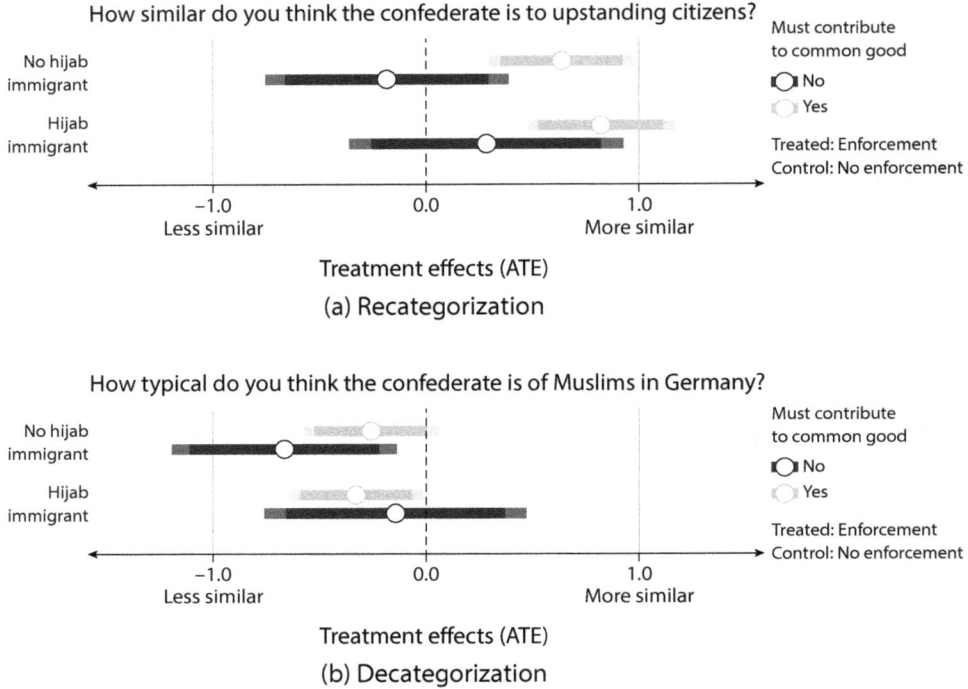

FIGURE 7.7. Heterogeneous effects: Norm importance 2
Notes: Heterogeneity in treatment effects disaggregated based on survey item that asks respondents whether they agree with the statement: "I believe society can only function if everyone contributes to the common good." Dots represent the estimated average treatment effects, with the darker and lighter bars denoting 90% and 95% confidence intervals, respectively.

The other group (respondents for whom norms do not matter as much) may have a lower bias toward Muslims and might be less likely to think that all Muslims are the same, but they are also less sensitive to "good citizenship"

heterogeneous effects with respect to the "feeling thermometer" outcome, we see that "norms matter" respondents warmly reward their co-ethnics (natives) in the enforcement condition. This strengthens the claim that "norms matter" respondents are very sensitive to good citizenship and they likely start from a baseline of stronger priors regarding homogeneity of opinion among Muslims. The more likely they are to think that all Muslims are alike, the smaller the differences we should observe for this group of respondents when we compare outcomes with respect to hijab-wearing vs no-hijab-wearing immigrants, which is the observable pattern in figures 7.6 and 7.7.

than people for whom norms matter, so they are less likely to reward norm enforcement by immigrants by updating their views regarding outgroup homogeneity. Thus, among respondents for whom norms do not matter, the "outgroup homogeneity" assumption might be stronger for the hijab-wearing immigrants than the no-hijab category, which would explain slightly stronger treatment effects in the no-hijab group, which is what we see in the data if we focus on the coefficient sizes in figures 7.6 and 7.7. For the "norms do not matter" group, recognition of good citizenship is more pronounced for the no-hijab group than the hijab-group because this good behavior is discounted in the hijab group, most likely due to larger baseline bias.

Text Analysis

In addition to the main survey-based outcomes included in table 7.2, we collect open-ended single word responses in reaction to the screening of the treatment videos; specifically, we asked respondents to suggest *five adjectives* that they would use to describe the individual portrayed in the clip. The act of writing down these adjectives should increase the salience of the treatment, as respondents reflect on what they have just seen in the video. Furthermore, the open-ended nature of these responses allows individuals to evaluate and express their opinion about the confederates in the video, relatively unconstrained by the concepts and ideas that would bind them in conventional survey measures. These additional measures should provide us with an opportunity to find further corroborating evidence for our hypotheses; they also offer glimpses into the mechanisms underlying the decategorization and recategorization processes that we have shown occur as a result of exposure to treatment.

Method   To make use of this rich data using methods of text analysis, we implement the following steps. We first extract all available textual data (five adjectives per respondent, for a total of 8,812 valid adjectives or adjective-phrases) from our open-ended responses and create a respondent-level panel data set with adjectives clustered within the individual. We recruited three German students (college graduates or graduate students in the social sciences) to independently and manually code each of these words across two key dimensions—valence (or generalized affect/sentiment) and "topic."

For the valence dimension, we instructed the coders to classify the adjective in one of two categories conveying either positive or negative sentiment/affect toward the individual portrayed in the video. To guard against the possibility that our instructions might force coders to impose a sentiment on terms that might be devoid of affective content, we also created and coded for a third "neutral" category.

Moving beyond the valence dimension, we also asked coders to classify the adjectives into various "topics," based on the intuition that if the process of decategorization and recategorization were to occur in response to treatment, we should be able to observe differences in the terms and concepts our experimental subjects would invoke to describe our confederates. We instructed our coders to specifically focus on four "topics": (a) whether the adjective invokes the notion of "religion" or "religious affiliation"; (b) nationality or migratory background; (c) common good, or citizenship; and (d) individual attributes or characteristics of the confederate, as opposed to group-level traits (such as the previous three types—religion, immigration background, or citizenship). We chose these four non-mutually exclusive topical categories based on our theoretical intuition regarding the processes of decategorization and recategorization. We expected that the process of *decategorization* would lead respondents to describe our confederates *less* in terms of concepts related to religious group membership (using terms such as "Muslim," "Islam," or "Hijab") or nationality or migratory background (using terms such as "immigrant" or "foreign-born"). We also hypothesized that the process of *recategorization* would simultaneously lead respondents to reorient the descriptors they use away from individual-focused adjectives (e.g., "courageous" or "nice") towards terms that have a connection to civic-mindedness and citizenship.[17] For both coding tasks, coders were blinded to the treatment conditions.

Using the data compiled by the coders, we constructed an aggregated dichotomous variable to denote whether any given adjective should fall into each of these categories, using majority rule—i.e., if two independent coders agreed that the word should be classified as such, we assigned a value of 1, and zero otherwise. This rather stringent threshold should shield us against the possibility that the idiosyncratic tendencies of any single coder could bias the classification process. We use these aggregated dichotomous classifications as the dependent variables in our text analysis. Descriptive statistics of the classifications are presented in table 7.3. As expected, a much larger proportion

---

17. We gave the coders instructions to classify terms as "invalid" or "unclear" if they believed that the adjectives were unrelated to the topics we selected, so they did not feel that they had to force each term into these categories.

TABLE 7.3. Descriptive Statistics on Text Outcomes

Statistic	N	Mean	St. Dev.	Min	Pctl(25)	Pctl(75)	Max
Valence Categories							
Positive	8,736	0.597	0.490	0.000	0.000	1.000	1.000
Negative	8,736	0.226	0.418	0.000	0.000	0.000	1.000
Neutral	8,736	0.150	0.357	0.000	0.000	0.000	1.000
Topic Categories							
Religion	8,812	0.023	0.151	0.000	0.000	0.000	1.000
Migratory Background	8,812	0.027	0.163	0.000	0.000	0.000	1.000
Common Good/Citizenship	8,812	0.146	0.353	0.000	0.000	0.000	1.000
Individual Focused	8,812	0.912	0.283	0.000	1.000	1.000	1.000

of the adjectives were classified as holding affect-related content than topical content; close to 60% of the adjectives written down by our respondents, for example, were classified as holding positive sentiment, as opposed to 23% for negative sentiment. The adjectives were much more infrequently placed into the topical categories; with the exception of the coding of whether a term was focused on the individual qualities or attributes of the confederate (accounting for more than 91% of all adjectives), adjectives were classified into the religion, migratory background, and citizenship categories at 2.3%, 2.7%, and 14.6%, respectively.

Analysis For the purpose of examining whether the prevalence of a specific sentiment or topic changes as a function of treatment, we conduct an *adjective level* analysis, where we take each adjective and use the classification of the adjective as the unit of analysis. We regress the sentiment or topic categories on our different treatment indicators, clustering the standard errors at the respondent level so that we can adjust for within-individual correlations in term usage. This approach provides a transparent method of analyzing the textual outcomes.[18]

Figure 7.8 reports the estimated effect of norm enforcement on positive versus negative valence adjectives, disaggregated by confederate identity conditions (hijab-wearing immigrant, no-hijab immigrant, and German native).

18. In additional analyses, we aggregate these adjective level observations to the respondent level, creating a variable that records the proportion of adjectives (out of five maximum) that fall into each of these sentiment and topical categories. While these analyses are omitted for brevity, the findings reported in this chapter remain substantively unchanged.

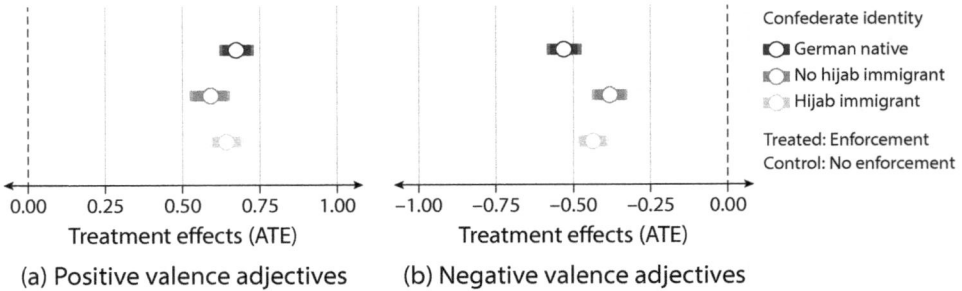

FIGURE 7.8. Text analysis: Positive/negative adjectives
Notes: Dots represent the estimated average treatment effects, with the darker and lighter bars denoting 90% and 95% confidence intervals, respectively.

Corroborating our earlier analysis that shows norm enforcement to lead to an increase in positive affect for the confederate portrayed in the video clip, the text analysis shows that enforcement leads to substantively large increases in the use of adjectives with positive valence, and concordant reductions in the use of negative valence terms. These effects are statistically significant at the 95% level, and remain robust to alternative codings of the outcome where we create a single positive versus negative valence score rather than the two separate dichotomous categories.

While these valence/sentiment results inspire confidence in our earlier analysis on generalized affect, we require evidence that supports the specific mechanisms associated with the decategorization and recategorization process. The results from the same analysis conducted on the topical outcomes, reported in figure 7.9, provide such corroboration.

The top two coefficients reported are estimated treatment effects of norm enforcement on the prevalence of adjective descriptors that invoke notions of religion or religious group membership and migration background. We find that in comparison to the control condition (no norm enforcement), norm enforcement leads respondents to describe our confederate in the video clip *less* frequently with terms that are associated with religion, especially among those exposed to norm enforcement by a hijab-wearing immigrant. The effect is a 1.7 percentage point reduction in topic prevalence, statistically significant at the 95% level. While the magnitude of this effect might look small at first glance, we argue that this is a substantively meaningful reduction when we account for the baseline prevalence of this topic—the topic prevalence in the no-enforcement condition is only 3.4%. This means that our estimated treatment effects account for almost a 50% reduction in the prevalence of

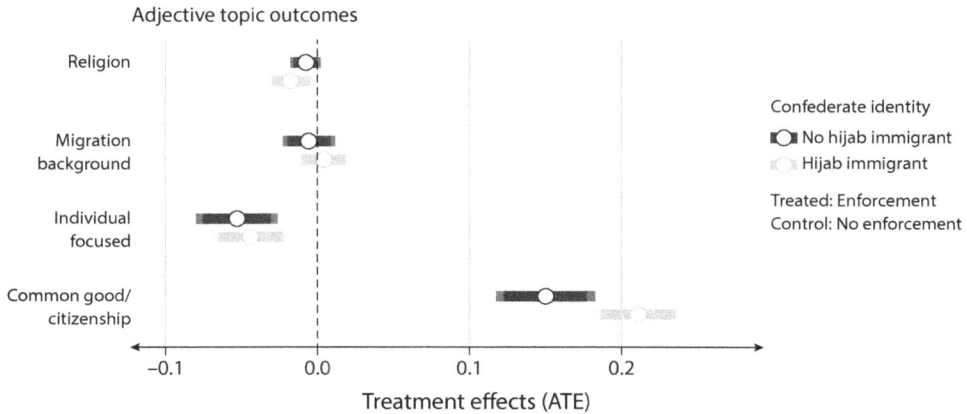

FIGURE 7.9. Text analysis: Adjective topics
Notes: Dots represent the estimated average treatment effects, with the darker and lighter bars denoting 90% and 95% confidence intervals, respectively.

religious adjectives in comparison to control. We detect no similar movement in the migration background topic; the estimated coefficient is statistically indistinguishable from zero.

The bottom two coefficients in figure 7.9 provide textual evidence for the recategorization mechanism that we stipulate to in figure 7.5. Our hypothesis was that, if treatment exposure induced the recategorization of immigrant confederates as citizens, we should expect to observe lower prevalence of individually focused adjectives, and simultaneously, higher prevalence of terms that invoke notions of the common good, civic-mindedness, and citizenship. Indeed, that is what we find. Norm enforcement leads to a 4–5 percentage point reduction in the use of individually focused adjectives for both the hijab and no-hijab immigrant conditions, statistically significant at the 95% level. We detect a concordant *increase* in the prevalence of adjectives that invoke ideas of common good and civic-mindedness of 21 percentage points and 10 percentage points in the hijab and no-hijab conditions, respectively, statistically significant at the 95% level. Taken together, we interpret these dual results to be indicative of a displacement of individually focused descriptors for adjectives that "recategorize" the minority confederates as a part of the German civic community.[19]

19. Suggestive evidence of this displacement can be found in the strong negative association between the individually focused topic and civic-mindedness topic that we observe in the data. The Pearson correlation coefficient is 0.37.

Discussion

The analysis presented in this chapter shows that German natives are more likely to view norm-enforcing Muslim immigrants as exceptions who are not typical of their group. The one-shot, brief interventions that we are able to capture on video and show respondents are not powerful enough to change natives' perceptions of Muslim immigrants in general. However, there is clear evidence that the norm-enforcement intervention resonates with our experimental subjects, who are significantly more likely to think of a norm-enforcing Muslim immigrant as similar to good, upstanding German citizens—*one of them*. Not only do survey subjects feel more warmly toward norm enforcing immigrants, but they also think that these immigrants become more similar to a typical member of the citizen ingroup. This evidence of recategorization is stronger among Germans who care more about norms. This group is more likely to see themselves in the videos of norm enforcement and is likely more concerned about the cultural differences that divide Germans and Muslim immigrants. However, as we have shown repeatedly in this book, the alignment of norms and ideas between natives and immigrants can help overcome the social distance that is created by differences in ascriptive characteristics. Importantly, for this effect to occur, it is not necessary to erase group boundaries and eliminate those ascriptive differences. This is an important lesson that can lead us to rethink the best way to integrate immigrants from different ethnoreligious groups. Our findings suggest that coercive assimilation designed to erase group differences is not necessary; bias can be overcome by the alignment of normative expectations and the sharing of ideas about group rights and responsibilities.

We have observed that this process of recategorization occurs in tandem with decategorization, which means that natives still feel distant from Muslims, most likely due to abstract ideas about the differences that separate them from Muslims as a group. We showed earlier in the book that these differences have actually narrowed significantly and, indeed, with respect to key questions regarding gender norms, there are no significant differences when we compare German natives and recent immigrants from Muslim-majority countries. Our survey results throughout this book confirm that Germans hold negative stereotypes about Muslims, but we have also shown that bias can be attenuated when this perception of belief dis-similarity changes—and these perceptions can in fact change. So the results from our survey experiments are particularly encouraging in that regard, even if they are limited to an analysis of one-shot interactions involving a small number of confederates and a single social norm. Imagine this type of positive interaction occurring multiple times a day, and occurring over a long period of time. Could this lead to broad-based, lasting changes in attitudes toward individual Muslims and Muslims as a group? Our hunch is that it would, though the persistence and generalizability of the effects we have identified in this chapter is a question left open for further research.

Importantly, our analysis shows that there does not need to be a direct relationship between recategorization and mutual differentiation. Group categories can remain salient and respondents' stereotypes could persist while their behavior toward specific members of the outgroup changes. This is encouraging for the short-term as it suggests that natives' behavior toward immigrants will improve as long as immigrants can effectively communicate their beliefs to others and they show that they share valued local norms. Perhaps a negative implication of the fact that our intervention has no mutual differentiation effects might be that native-immigrant conflict could more easily restart in a political or social context that makes intergroup differences more salient.

Although there is not necessarily a one-to-one relationship between perceived similarity of beliefs on the one hand and ingroup bias on the other hand (Mummendey and Schreiber, 1984), "inclusion within a common social boundary reduces social distance among group members, making it less likely that individuals will make sharp distinctions between their own and others' welfare" (Kramer and Brewer, 1984, p. 1045). This is consistent with the behavior we observed in the field. The implications of this experiment for multiculturalism are encouraging since it shows that the differences in ascriptive characteristics become secondary or even superficial when natives and immigrants discover how to build a foundation of shared citizenship based on *belief similarity*. We return to this idea in the concluding chapter, where we take stock of the implications of the entire range of empirical analyses presented in this book.

8

Overcoming Discrimination

THIS BOOK HAS shown that shared social norms can shape behavior and attitudes toward immigrants by reducing the perceived social distance separating natives from immigrants. The insights produced by our analysis revise much of the prevalent thinking regarding the challenge of integrating immigrant groups. Many believe that ethnic, racial, or religious differences cannot be overcome, and will produce a lasting rift between natives and immigrants. Yet we show that this rift can be bridged, in ways that neither group will find repressive. While it might not be possible to eliminate all bias, prejudice and discrimination can be reduced when it becomes clear that ascriptive differences need not imply ideational and normative differences between natives and immigrants. Moreover, we show that to overcome this perception of social distance, it is not necessary for immigrants to shed their identity. Immigrant assimilation that is based on erasing group differences has long been thought of as the only way to overcome anti-immigrant bias and to reduce discrimination. In contrast to such a perspective, we show that discrimination can be reduced simply by demonstrating that immigrants and natives share a common set of norms and ideas that define their identities as citizens.

Overall, this book presents a more optimistic view of multiculturalism than is usually articulated by European politicians and policymakers. We have defined multiculturalism simply as the acceptance of cultural difference rather than as support for specific policies of immigrant integration. As other studies have shown, there is growing pessimism regarding the future of multiculturalism in Europe, and the adoption of multiculturalism (i.e., pro-integration) policies has stalled in the past twenty years (Koopmans, 2013). This reassessment of policies designed to accommodate immigrants who are culturally different from native society reflects anxiety and prejudice in native publics and these fears can lead to the sort of discriminatory behavior that we have observed in our study.

Fears about the implications of multiculturalist policies in Europe have grown in the aftermath of the refugee crisis of 2015. The resurgence of sectarianism in regional wars in the Middle East, global terrorism motivated by *jihadi* ideology, a re-emerging Cold War among the great powers, and growing economic inequality in advanced democracies all combine to create intolerance around ethno-religious differences, and have been instrumentalized to raise suspicion toward politicians who promote multiculturalist agendas. As the resonance of populist messages increases, many politicians rush to declare that multiculturalism is dead. Many voters also increasingly seem to believe that cultural differences will inevitably produce social conflict. Yet our empirical evidence from a European country with a long and deep experience with multiculturalist policies suggests that these fears may be exaggerated. A key insight supported by our analysis is that natives are able to accommodate both cultural and ascriptive differences from immigrant groups, and will treat members of those groups almost as well as they do their co-ethnics, as long as doing so does not imperil core values of native society, and if immigrants do not challenge social norms that define the meaning of citizenship. This core insight defines the promise—but also potential limits—of multiculturalism in European societies. Our empirical results have implications for the design of policy interventions to reduce bias and our analysis suggests a number of new questions that could be addressed using the methods and theory developed in this book. Our contribution to the substantive debate on the challenges of immigrant integration is presented amidst a set of other contributions of this book to the literature on identity politics and immigration, to social science methods, and to extant theory.

Contributions to the Literature

A large literature on native-immigrant conflict has identified a broad range of motives for anti-immigrant bias and discrimination. These studies have highlighted both economic and cultural causes of conflict, and in many cases these motives are hard to separate from one another. Identity conflict often seems more consequential when economic concerns lurk in the background, and cultural factors similarly color the way individuals assess economic threat. By virtue of the fact that we follow an experimental approach, we can isolate the impact of cultural factors and speak to their importance while bracketing any confounding effects of economic competition, welfare state concerns, or other consequences of intergroup competition for resources.

Our book advances the literature on identity-based causes of anti-immigrant bias and discrimination by identifying specific cultural symbols and ethno-religious attributes that cause bias in everyday encounters between natives and immigrants. We focus mainly on explaining patterns of discrimination, but our empirical results also speak to sources of bias and prejudice, allowing us to compare how feasible it is to change behavior as compared to beliefs. We take a further step to compare the ethnic or religious attributes as causes of bias to civic behavior and adherence to a common set of beliefs and ideas. This allows us to separate ethno-religious attributes from the cultural meaning that is usually attributed to them and we can study whether ascriptive differences can be "defused" as causes of bias by behavior that affirms valued social norms in native society.

Contributions to Methods

While this book is not focused on social science methods per se, it does make some noteworthy contributions to experimental social science. Much of what we know about native-immigrant conflict comes from the analysis of observational data, often generated through public opinion surveys. Experimental "audit" studies have been used extensively to study discrimination in the labor market and in interactions with the state. Conjoint experiments similar to the one we presented in chapter 3 have also proliferated in recent years, and have improved our understanding of how different attributes influence natives' assessments of immigrants. We expand the scope of previous experimental work by designing field experiments that are based on social identity theory and allow us to test specific causal mechanisms in realistic settings of everyday life and on a large scale. While ours is of course not the only study to take such an approach, much experimental research in political science follows a more "opportunistic" approach, and relies on conducting randomized control trials of preexisting programs or testing policies which the researchers cannot control fully. Such studies can produce useful insights, but our approach allows for a particularly tight fit between the theory being tested and the experimental design.

The scope of our experimental studies is significantly larger than usual, especially by comparison to the psychology literature, which, from a thematic and theoretical standpoint, has offered the closest antecedents to our study.

Even though our field experiments on anti-immigrant bias are large and logistically complex, we replicate them to make sure that our conclusions are robust and we use experimental designs with a common core, while adding treatment arms to test new ideas and explore different mechanisms in each experiment. By virtue of the large scale and broad scope of our experiments, we can extrapolate to a larger population with greater confidence than is usually possible in other field or lab experiments. By integrating field and survey experiments in an iterative approach, we can identify key mechanisms underlying the behavior we observe in the field; and we can generate new theoretical intuitions that feed into the design of new field experiments.

Another distinctive feature of our analysis is that we use data from everyday interactions between natives and immigrants, and focus our attention on helping behavior—small acts of kindness toward strangers that are usually overlooked in studies of bias and discrimination. As such, our book pushes researchers to supplement the analysis of "big moments" such as wars, elections, or riots, or the usual focus on discrimination within different markets with an analysis of the day-to-day, seemingly mundane and routine interactions between citizens. The importance of exploring the subtleties of quotidian life is evident in the patterns of discrimination that we are able to uncover and our analysis suggests that there is much to be gained by analyzing "everyday" politics.[1]

Contributions to Theory

The approach taken in the experimental designs used in this book fits neatly within the tradition of Social Identity Theory (SIT) and Social Categorization Theory (SCT). These prominent theories of social psychology have been central to the burgeoning political science literature on native-immigrant conflict and other literatures on prejudice, discrimination, and various forms of intergroup conflict. Indeed, our empirical design was conceived as a way to test hypotheses derived from SIT and SCT and applied to the context of native-immigrant conflict. Our book also speaks to other literatures in social psychology and political behavior, including the highly

1. There is a growing sense that a focus on the "quotidian"—on everyday forms of interaction—should become a key concern of social science research. A recent example is Baker, Ames, and Rennó (2020), whose book demonstrates how everyday communication within social networks shapes political outcomes in some of Latin America's democracies.

influential literature on contact theory (Allport, 1954). That theory posits that more contact can improve intergroup relations under some conditions. The types and duration of contact that can produce positive outcomes are not fully established in that literature, and our study can be seen as providing relevant insights even though our research design is not directly inspired by Allport's classic theory.

We analyze the consequences of positive intergroup contact between members from culturally distant social groups and find that even brief encounters can shape behavior toward outgroups. Our analysis confirms key results in SIT as we demonstrate clear evidence of ingroup bias among native Germans. Prior research has demonstrated that individuals are sensitive to the "social distance" that divides social groups and differences in ascriptive characteristics such as race or ethnicity are thought to be the main determinants of that distance. We also know from previous literature that most individuals prefer to minimize the distance between themselves and groups they belong to, which makes them sensitive to cultural difference or differences in ascriptive traits. Thus, differences in skin color, language, religion, or other such "fixed" attributes of group membership have been the focus of most political science applications of SIT to study intergroup conflict. Inherited or "sticky" attributes that are hard to change can demarcate group boundaries and shape perceptions of similarity or difference between individuals who belong to different groups by virtue of the attributes they share with other members of the group. A vast literature on ethnicity and identity politics has explored this idea to study the importance of ethno-linguistic, racial, or religious characteristics for behavior with respect to a host of outcomes in politics. Our book fits centrally within the broad contours of such approaches, though we highlight the role of shared beliefs and ideas rather than differences in inherited and immutable attributes as key determinants of social distance. In the specific application that we study, we find that the importance of these ascriptive characteristics fades when we separate them from their normative and ideational content.

The closest theoretical antecedent to our argument is the Common Ingroup Identity Model (CIIM), which has been previously applied to study intergroup conflict in the political science literature. This model comes into play because it can explain how to overcome social distance between groups which might otherwise be in conflict as they compete for power or resources. Both violent and nonviolent conflict can be explained by the *social distance* mechanism put forth by SIT and SCT. The core insight of the CIIM is that such conflict can be reduced by invoking or creating a common ingroup identity among members of groups with different attributes, thereby reducing the perception of social distance separating those individuals. This shared identity becomes superordinate and can provide the basis for new affective ties among individuals without necessarily changing the boundaries of the subordinate groups they belong to. Multiple studies have invoked the CIIM to explain the emergence of cooperation among groups that were previously in conflict. Our book takes CIIM further by focusing on how shared norms can reduce bias and conflict by demonstrating that natives and immigrants share a common identity—that of *citizen*.

Many prior applications of the CIIM focus on demonstrating how invoking an already existing shared identity can dampen conflict along a subordinate set of social cleavages. A typical example is how inter-ethnic conflict can be reduced by making national identity more salient, which reduces the salience of ethnicity. Previous research on identity politics has assumed that ethnic, religious, or national identities are defined on the basis of shared attributes which are often visible and hard to change, and even identities that are clearly the result of deliberate choice (such as partisanship) are often treated as inherited or deeply embedded identities formed early in life. Our research juxtaposes the power of such identities to that of social norms and ideas, and makes clear that group identities are not really shared unless the ideas and norms that define the meaning of those identities are also shared. In other words, the conflict-reducing mechanism in the CIIM is premised on the idea that individuals share an understanding of what a given social identity implies. We thus go beyond the concept of social identities defined narrowly on the basis of shared attributes, and show that while individuals can be recognized as members of an ingroup or outgroup on the basis of such attributes, they need not identify as members of those groups unless they share core ideas and norms that define that group identity. This also means that ingroup-outgroup distinctions that are often thought to be insurmountable—such as the native-immigrant divide— are merely *nominal* distinctions that can be overcome by a shared citizen identity or by highlighting shared norms and ideas that define other superordinate identities.

In our empirical analysis, this insight becomes apparent in the analysis of discrimination due to the perception that immigrants are opposed to gender equality. We show that, while German women discriminate against Muslim immigrant women (with whom they share gender attributes) when they have no information about the immigrants' beliefs regarding gender roles, that discrimination is eliminated when immigrant women reveal that they hold views of women's rights and gender norms that are identical to those held by the majority of German women. This example of *belief similarity* unifies German and immigrant women by making their shared gender identity more salient than the native-immigrant distinction that still divides them. This transformation, and the activation of gender identity, however, only becomes possible when it becomes clear that they share common ideas about what gender identity means. Simply sharing ascriptive traits is not enough for individuals who nominally belong to the same group to identify with each other. This insight has broad implications for the study of identity politics beyond the specific example we develop in our book and our analysis suggests that ideological proximity forges a shared ingroup identity. This result is consistent with the idea that we should move beyond binary constructs of social identities such as race or ethnicity given the vital role of social context and political processes in defining the content of those social identities.

Contributions to Policy Design

The theoretical insights described above have clear implications for the design of policy with respect to immigrant integration. While most integration policies focus exclusively on immigrants and their behavior, our work implies that integration policies should also directly target natives whose stereotypes about ideational differences with immigrants lead to backlash and discrimination against immigrants. More specifically, a key implication of our findings is that discrimination can be reduced if natives get information that defies their stereotypes about immigrants or they experience that they actually share a set of norms or a common identity with immigrants.

In the introduction, we discussed the distinction between coercive assimilation and less coercive ways of reducing social distance based on norm-sharing. A key difference between our approach and previous studies of immigrant assimilation concerns the weight we place on more vs. less coercive mechanisms of assimilation. Our analysis suggests that coercive assimilation defined as a strategy or eliminating cultural difference by suppressing symbols of immigrants' identity are not necessary for intergroup conflict between natives and immigrants to subside. At the same time, our study brings up the question of how to achieve normative alignment between natives and immigrants and which types of norms can be shared and how can one communicate information that natives and immigrants actually share those norms?

Our experiments do not address all those questions, but they open the door for a research agenda that can explore non-coercive forms of immigrant integration. Recent research has found that integration policies that score high on an index of multiculturalism often fail to achieve positive integration (economic or political) outcomes for immigrant minorities as they remove incentives for immigrants to learn the native language and integrate in host society (Koopmans et al., 2005). A better approach might be to implement policies that induce normative alignment among natives and immigrants so as to encourage the formation of deeper social networks among them and facilitate immigrant integration. Cultural integration classes—which are mandatory for immigrants in some countries—could help achieve such normative alignment if they do not backfire; they might be less offensive and less likely to backfire if the ultimate aim of such classes is not to eliminate cultural difference and if they take into account immigrant communities' experiences and views rather than imagined differences.

However, for such policies to be successful, more reliable data on immigrant communities and their beliefs are needed. While public opinion research on natives and their *perceptions* of immigrants is abundant, representative survey data on different immigrant communities, their experiences, and beliefs are still rare. Such data, however, are crucial in order to identify common ground and inform more contextualized integration policies.

Not only are current integration policies often coercive, they are also routinely based on natives' generalized views about "immigrants" *en bloc* and perceived differences with such immigrants. Besides the fact that these assumed "differences" might be exaggerated or outdated, they ignore the immense diversity in views and backgrounds among immigrants (e.g., across different immigrant communities or different age cohorts). Integration policies (such as integration classes) that are grounded in better data about immigrants' beliefs and are responsive to the different immigrants' backgrounds have the potential to be less offensive to immigrants and be more effective.

Furthermore, such data that allows us to better understand normative overlap and disagreement between different groups of immigrants (and different groups of natives) is crucial in order to develop policies that can help change natives' stereotypes. If shared norms and ideas are a good way to reduce native-immigrant conflict, policies should aim to share information that normative conflict between natives and immigrants is not as severe as many believe. How can such information be communicated? Our study suggests that it can be communicated indirectly via casual observation of each other's behavior in everyday settings. In other words, repeated positive interactions may lead to bias-reduction, though this could take time. We found that even a single encounter might be enough to lead bystanders to update their priors vis-à-vis an immigrant. We saw in chapter 7 that this can occur even after watching a twenty-second video, though we also found that our experimental intervention does not change perceptions and biases toward an entire outgroup. Sustained, positive contact will be required to change attitudes, though our study does not tell us how much contact is enough to overturn deeply held biases.

Readers might wonder what are the long-term implications of exposure to norm-abiding behavior? Do our results last only seconds, or do they persist and for how long? The nature of the field experiments that we designed was such that it does not allow us to explore the durability of the effects that we have identified, though we recognize this as a vitally important question. In chapter 7, we found that immigrants who enforce the anti-littering norm become recategorized as citizens or seen as individuals rather than thought of as immigrants. It is perhaps unreasonable to think that the effect of a brief interaction (or a short video) could last forever and we could consider in future research the conditions under which these effects would last. As mentioned elsewhere in this chapter, we would expect the effects of these observations of norm adherence to work cumulatively over time, in ways that are consistent with the predictions of contact theory (whereby extensive positive contact reduces bias). Repeated observations of norm-abiding or stereotype-defying behavior over time could have a large enough cumulative effect as to reduce prejudice and improve attitudes toward immigrants as a group.

Our study does tell us that policy interventions aimed at immigrant integration should target natives so as to change biases that might be based on false beliefs about the extent of cultural difference between them and immigrant groups. Recent research on bias-reduction strategies has emphasized the use of techniques for the humanization of outgroups, either by providing information that counters negative public perceptions of the outgroup, or by highlighting commonalities (common experiences) between members of the ingroup and the outgroup. A common approach is to induce members of the ingroup to see the world from the perspective of the outgroup; these "perspective taking" and "personal story-sharing" mechanisms are thought to reduce bias by inducing empathy or greater understanding of others' actions, their habits, and their beliefs.

Our experiments share some of the features of a growing literature on "perspective taking," although our experimental treatments are more subtle and indirect than interventions that explicitly ask subjects to see the world through someone else's eyes. The common thread is that a natural consequence of establishing that immigrants share norms with natives is that natives can see themselves behaving the same way that immigrants would in analogous situations, which will make it harder for natives to dehumanize immigrants. This projection of the self on to immigrant others is more likely to occur among norm enforcers. In chapter 7, we showed clear evidence that natives who have observed immigrants enforce valued social norms have warmer feelings toward them relative to immigrants who do not enforce social norms. In the phone call experiment in chapter 6, we see something analogous, since the message conveyed via the phone call treatment is in a sense a type of intervention involving personal story-sharing. The confederate's telephone conversation is personal and reveals her views on topics about which natives will also have opinions, and which touch their personal lives. Depending on the degree of overlap between the immigrant confederate's and native bystanders' viewpoints, the message conveyed in the phone call can help establish a personal connection between them, which can humanize or dehumanize the other.

Are these insights drawn from our study directly translatable into policy? Much of the literature on perspective-taking and other experimental work based on informational interventions is premised on the idea that policies can be designed to reduce bias by sharing information about outgroups on a large scale. Our experiments suggest that this might be harder to do than previously thought given the complicated *intersectionality* of social identities. The types of stereotypes natives hold about immigrants are likely informed by the types of threats they perceive; and these threats are made salient by the identities that matter most to them. In other words, the threat is identity group-specific, which means that any intervention designed to overcome bias must also be targeted to the specific identity threat that matters to different groups. Thus, in chapter 6, we saw that German women's bias against Muslims is driven largely by beliefs that Muslims are regressive vis-à-vis issues of gender equality; and when those beliefs are countered, the bias disappears. However, the very intervention that produced this result did not affect men, who continued to discriminate against Muslims even when confronted with the same information about Muslims' views on gender equality issues.

A conclusion supported by this experimental result is that any single-topic information-based intervention to reduce bias can at best produce incomplete results since some groups of natives will be more receptive than others to the "message" conveyed by that intervention by virtue of their social identity being activated. Under some conditions, it is also possible for these interventions to backfire. This suggests that policy interventions must be attuned to the specific local context and to the implications of the intersectionality argument developed in our book. The design of policy interventions to forge a common identity must reflect such an understanding by highlighting a specific set of norms and ideas that have broad appeal (general civic norms) while leveraging the power of group-derived norms to reduce bias even further among specific groups of the native population without alienating others.

Next Steps

Taken as a whole, our analysis is encouraging about the potential to reduce intergroup conflict within a multicultural policy framework which accommodates group differences, while reducing their practical importance for everyday life. But while our book answers some important questions about mechanisms of bias-reduction toward immigrants, it also raises questions that are left open for further research. One of those questions concerns the way that natives and immigrants come to adhere to a common set of norms. Our empirical results suggest that bias is reduced when citizens have internalized lessons about appropriate civic behavior and when they share the same logic of appropriateness with respect to their civic duty. How does this ideational congruence come about in the first place? Is this something that can be taught in civic education classes—an initiative that several Western European countries have been implementing to teach immigrants the core values of the nation—and should such classes be mandatory for all immigrants? Or is it better to allow a process of mutual acculturation to unfold over time, recognizing that both the native and immigrant population will be influenced by sustained contact? How long does it take for natives and immigrants to come to share the same concept of citizenship? Is there a hierarchy of norms which define the meaning of citizenship and how can we identify the most important ones in different countries? How much do immigrants from different backgrounds have to adjust their beliefs and habits to align themselves to the native majority?

These questions can define an empirical research agenda that explores specific patterns of immigrant integration in different countries. We opened chapter 1 with a reference to mandatory classes in Danish culture and customs for all children of immigrant families who receive public assistance; this is a version of the "citizenship contract" idea put forth by Nicolas Sarkozy as Minister of the Interior in France in 2003. The idea is that immigrants commit to learning the national language and take classes on national values and, while such classes would be offered for free, they would be required before residential permits for immigrants are renewed. According to Chris Bowen, Australian Minister of Immigration, such an approach can balance the provision of liberal freedoms and rights to immigrants with the need for social cohesion and the inculcation of a sense of responsibility and the need to promote the national interest.[2] It is an open question whether this specific form of encouraging norm-sharing and belief-similarity is effective, or whether more indirect approaches must be taken to prevent backlash. Our empirical analysis does not provide any leverage over that question, but our intuition is that less coercive approaches are likely to be more effective. Indeed, the degree to which there is prior disagreement regarding norms and values between natives and immigrants cannot be taken for granted and may often be exaggerated, the result of stereotypes that can easily be corrected when natives observe immigrants behave in stereotype-defying ways.

Our results on shared norms naturally bring up the question of *whose norms* should be followed? In our analysis we have focused on deeply shared societal or group-derived norms that are prevalent in native society, which to some degree implies a directionality of convergence to a common superordinate identity that natives already share. In the short term, ideas of citizenship will be relatively inflexible, so the content of the superordinate identity (the identity of "citizen") will be defined by native society. In the longer term, ideas of citizenship change and can embrace "imported" ideas and habits as the national culture evolves. The imprint of immigrants on the national culture is felt over longer periods, yet our analysis does not allow us to explore such settings. More importantly, our analysis does not establish whether natives treat immigrants better only when immigrants have appeared to have *adapted to* locally salient norms or simply when immigrants show that they share those norms, which they may have internalized prior to immigrating. It would be

---

2. See https: // theconversation.com / why - chris - bowen - isnt - afraid-of-multiculturalism -but-others-are-703 (accessed 9/5/2021).

interesting to explore whether the perception of effort applied to assimilate to a norm that was previously foreign is appreciated more by natives than the realization that immigrants do not present a threat to natives' values.

Another obvious question is whether our results travel to other countries; and whether different countries have different hierarchies of norms that are core to the idea of citizenship which can produce cooperation and reduce bias. Although our book analyzes data from Germany alone, our hunch is that our conclusions are broadly applicable to other countries. In chapter 1 we argued that Germany is quite comparable to other Western European countries with large immigrant populations so we expect our book to speak to many of the debates regarding immigrant integration in other countries. Some of the data that we reviewed show that Germany is in the middle of the pack with regard to how immigrants are perceived and treated and with reference to indices of immigrant integration or the extent to which state policies respect multiculturalism. The data do not support the idea that anti-immigrant attitudes in Germany are so strong as to suggest that the social distance between natives and immigrants that must be overcome is much larger or smaller than it is in other European countries. Germany is not an outlier with respect to barriers of immigrant integration, but it is also not a best-case scenario.

Perhaps Germany is a "best case" for an empirical test of the power of norms to change behavior. After all, Germans have a reputation for being particularly norm-adhering and rule-bound. Yet Germany is certainly not the only well-functioning society in Europe where citizens share a sense of civic responsibility and every such society has a set of social norms that matter and which most citizens would recognize as vital for the common good. In that sense, our focus on the effect of shared norms on reducing social distance between native and immigrant groups should apply to countries beyond Germany, though perhaps the set of norms that can have the effects we identify in this book will be different across countries. We can only speculate about which norms will matter in other countries (perhaps welfare state norms will matter more in Scandinavian states), but the important point here is that our book is not just about a specific norm in a specific country. Although anti-littering norms were studied in chapter 5, we expect our analysis to apply to other deeply held societal norms such as paying taxes, voting in local/municipal elections, or participating in local/community activities. Norm-adhering behavior will be differentially observable depending on which norms one chooses to focus on, and it may be easier for immigrants to signal their pro-sociality via adhering to some norms versus others. These differences (e.g., with respect to "observability" of norm-adhering behavior) could be explored as a factor that might shape behavioral outcomes as natives and immigrants observe each other's behavior over longer periods. Additionally, for an adaptation of our analytical framework to a cross-country setting (where different norms can be analyzed), one would have to take into account the multiple ways in which countries might differ from each other, including with respect to their immigration history, any structural or legal barriers to integration of minority groups, and the *ex ante* social distance that defines relations between natives and those minorities. That distance, in turn, can be a function of past conflict or other unmeasured country- or group-level differences that could impact the specific way in which our ideas would apply to different contexts.

A premise of our analysis—a key scope condition for our theory—is that individuals must recognize and value good citizenship. This means that citizens will reward those who follow the rules; that they themselves will be likely to adhere to social norms; and that they will recognize the need to sanction non-cooperators. As long as a hierarchy of social norms exists and is shared among such citizens in any country, the conclusions of our empirical analysis should follow, regardless of the specific country context though the magnitude of the effects could be larger or smaller depending on that context. Where our argument might falter is in countries where rules are frequently broken, where there is uncertainty about which norms are important and which are not, where most citizens do not expect others to follow the rules, where they will not accept being sanctioned for breaking the rules, and where norm enforcement is rare. In such settings, we should observe low levels of social cooperation and low contribution to public goods across the board, and correspondingly large levels of anti-social behavior and anti-social punishment for those who attempt to enforce social norms. Such behavior is rare among Western democracies, where most citizens recognize the importance of contributing to the common good, but there are examples of such countries and it would be instructive to explore whether our thinking can gain any traction in these countries' contexts.[3]

A final question that one could ask and which we have not considered explicitly is what happens if the baseline level of social distance between natives

---

3. For a cross-country comparison that addresses the prevalence of pro-social behavior and anti-social punishment explicitly across twenty countries, see Herrmann, Thöni, and Gächter (2008).

and immigrants is just too large to overcome via norm convergence in a reasonable timeframe? How big of an effect can we expect norm adherence to have and is the size of that effect itself variable depending on who the immigrants are and how threatening or distant the natives find them? Part of our answer to that question is that prior perceptions of that social distance could depend entirely on beliefs about normative conflict and so when that conflict is resolved, that distance can be overcome. Indeed, given the depth of Christian-Muslim conflict in Europe combined with Germany's historical reluctance to open up to immigrants of any kind, we would argue that the bias-reducing effects of norm adherence that we have presented in this book look impressive. Yet in principle there could be other societies where the distance between natives and specific groups of immigrants is harder to overcome due to the particular significance of some immigrant attributes or symbols even when they no longer align with the natives' behavioral stereotypes of those immigrants. It would be interesting to explore the power of ideational factors in contexts with different *ex ante* social distance.

Returning to the debate on multiculturalism which frames much of the research in this book, we highlight the importance of exploring non-coercive forms of assimilation of immigrants though it is also important to understand that multiculturalism has limits and that it will be rejected if it threatens core values of native societies. The positive news is that immigration need not threaten those values and that it is possible to overcome most symbols of cultural difference. Even the hijab can be "overcome" and natives can learn that it does not need to represent irreconcilable value-conflict. The hijab is at the core of public debates regarding immigrant integration and symbolizes perennial conflict between Islam and Christianity, between East and West, modernity and tradition. Yet we have shown that a brief positive encounter that establishes an alignment of ideas between a hijab-wearing immigrant and a native is enough to erase the baggage carried by the hijab. This is particularly instructive in light of the theories of social identity that inform our analysis. Underlying social identity theory is the idea that humans have evolved with an innate tendency to form groups and recognize others as members of an ingroup—toward which they are favorably inclined—or outgroups—against which they are usually prejudiced. We have seen evidence of such innate tendencies for parochialism in our book, but we have also seen that those tendencies can be overcome as long as citizenship is promoted over ethnicity, civic-mindedness over religion.

Chapter 3

This section provides supplementary information on experiment logistics and other details as well as additional results referenced in the main text of chapter 3.

Experimental Sites: Train Stations

We present some additional details on the sites (train stations) where the experimental interventions were implemented. Because we were concerned about the possibility that (i) we would mistakenly expose bystanders to the experimental intervention multiple times, or (ii) bystanders who had already been exposed to the intervention would notice the intervention happening elsewhere at the train station, we deliberately chose medium-to-large train stations that had a sufficiently large number of train platforms. We list the train stations where we conducted the interventions below, with the number of train platforms listed in parentheses.

- **North Rhine-Westphalia**: Münster (9), Bielefeld (8), Minden (5), Rheine (6), Köln (11), Köln Messe/Deutz (12), Mönchengladbach (9), Neuss (8), Siegen (6), Bonn (5), Düsseldorf (20), Wuppertal (5), Dortmund (31), Duisburg (12), Bochum (8), Gelsenkirchen (6), Hagen (16), Essen (13), Wanne-Eickel (8)
- **Saxony**: Leipzig (21), Görlitz (6), Chemnitz (14), Dresden (16), Zwickau (8)
- **Lower Saxony**: Osnabrück (9), Hannover (12)
- **Brandenburg**: Potsdam (7), Forst (Lausitz) (5), Cottbus (10), Frankfurt-Oder (12), Brandenburg (6)

Training of Confederates and Enumerators

Training Before the beginning of the intervention in each state, the confederates and enumerators that would observe and code the behavior of the bystanders participated in day-long training workshops led by the authors to ensure a consistently high quality in the delivery of the intervention. These trainings focused on how to select the settings for the intervention, how to play the different roles, how to ensure consistent performances across actors and across teams, and how to code bystander behavior consistently. For the main outcome of the study—whether a bystander provided assistance—enumerators were instructed to code any attempt to offer help in picking up oranges/lemons that consisted of a clear physical movement toward the oranges in an effort to help as provision of help, i.e., a clear movement to signal willingness to provide help in picking up oranges/lemons was necessary. In order to ensure consistent coding across enumerators and teams, different scenarios were practiced and discussed through role-playing activities during the training sessions. These training workshops were followed by extensive test runs in actual train stations with the authors.

We took numerous precautions and trained the confederates and enumerators extensively in procedures to select the sites for the iterations in a way that minimizes the potential for bystanders to witness more than one iteration. First, the specific sites on each train platform were chosen such that it was hard to see the interaction from other platforms (e.g., by making use of walls and signs on the platform, timing the interaction such that stationary trains would block the sight). Second, platforms and the specific sites on those platforms were selected to minimize the chance of repeated participation by the same bystanders. After concluding one iteration on one platform, teams would switch to the platform farthest away from this one that had passengers waiting on it (only train stations with at least five tracks were used). Furthermore, the specific site on that new platform would be chosen to maximize the distance from the previous iteration (e.g., by going to the other end/side). Third, the enumerators tasked with observing the bystanders and coding their behavior were trained to make note of the bystanders for each iteration in order to avoid—despite the other precautions—bystanders witnessing more than one iteration (e.g., if passengers had stayed around after the departure of the train from that platform or had switched platforms). In the limited instances where the same team conducted interventions at the same train station on more than one day, we conducted field work on different days of the week, choosing a business day and a weekend day in order to minimize chances of commuters being exposed to more than one iteration. Furthermore, enumerators were instructed to begin on the opposite track/side of the train station than during the previous day.

A note on enumerator "blinding" as to the purpose of the project   It was not possible to blind confederates to the general purpose of the experiment. All the coders were intelligent students who were interested in learning about research, thus after a few iterations the coders would have figured out that we were collecting data on bystander behavior across the different treatment conditions. However, we took steps to reduce the risk that coding reflected demand effects and confederates who acted out parts of the scene were expressly told to follow the script and to avoid behaviors that might be designed to elicit specific responses from the bystanders. We did not share the PAP with the actors or coders so they did not know what our prior expectations were for this experiment. They were given a script to follow during the intervention, given detailed instructions on how to act, and monitored during the iterations. Finally, there was no normative content in the material we used for the training of confederates (e.g., we referred to measuring assistance to confederates, rather than measuring discrimination and did not use loaded terms such as "bias" or "racism").

Ethical considerations   We took great care to minimize the potential risk to study participants. For a full discussion of these measures, see the research protocol that was reviewed and approved by University of Pennsylvania's Institutional Review Board (IRB Protocols #829824 and #833206). Beyond our efforts to minimize potential risks to subjects participating in the study, we also took a number of steps to ensure the safety of our research assistants (confederates and enumerators) during the study. Prior to the onset of data collection, we consulted a number of German experts on how to minimize potential risks to our RAs. Furthermore, the other confederates and the enumerators within each team closely monitored the bystanders and stood by, ready to intervene, if necessary, though there was little cause for concern due to the innocuous nature of the phone call and the unobtrusive nature of the intervention. During the training sessions, we discussed potential risks and safety strategies extensively with the research assistants. RAs were instructed to stop the intervention if they felt unsafe at any point. The authors were in constant contact with all teams during the data collection, monitoring their progress and potential safety issues early on. Last, the German train company,

Deutsche Bahn, was instructed about research activities taking place at any given train station on any given day.

Manipulation Checks on Perception of Confederate Ethnicity

In this section of the appendix, we demonstrate that German native populations accurately recognize our minority confederates to be of immigrant minority background (in the control condition when they are *not* wearing a hijab). In order to do so, we conducted a follow-up survey on Clickworker.com, an online crowdsourcing work platform similar to Amazon's M-Turk to recruit adult German respondents to evaluate our confederates' photos and report their perceived country of origin. We conducted this survey on a sample of 208 German adults above nineteen years of age. Each evaluation question presented a photo of our confederate, and then asked, "In your best guess, where do you think this person is from?" Respondents were then asked to choose from "Germany" versus four other countries (Turkey, Egypt, Iraq, and Syria), which were the real countries of origin for our immigrant confederates. All respondents evaluated a total of fifteen immigrant confederate photographs, and roughly half of the total German native confederates that participated in the intervention of the experiment. This yields a total of 3,120 evaluations across all photos. Screen captures of a typical evaluation task for the manipulation checks are presented in figure A.1.

Was würden Sie vermuten, woher diese Person kommt? Wählen Sie bitte die Option aus, die Sie am ehesten vermuten.

| aus Syrien |
| aus dem Irak |
| aus Deutschland |
| aus Ägypten |
| aus der Türkei |

Was würden Sie vermuten, woher diese Person kommt? Wählen Sie bitte die Option aus, die Sie am ehesten vermuten.

| aus Syrien |
| aus der Türkei |
| aus Ägypten |
| aus Deutschland |
| aus dem Irak |

FIGURE A.1. Screen captures of "manipulation check" task

TABLE A1. Proportion of Respondents Identifying Confederate as a German Native

Native Confederates	Immigrant Confederates	Difference	p-Value
82.97%	15.38%	67.59%p	< 0.001

It is clear that respondents are able to draw stark distinctions in the country of origin of our German native confederates versus immigrant confederates. On average, respondents correctly identify German native confederates as Germans between 82–83% of the time. In stark contrast, only 15–16% of respondents mistakenly categorize our immigrant minority confederates' country of origin as Germany. The difference is consistently in excess of 65 percentage points, and is statistically distinguishable at p < 0.001. These manipulation checks provide strong evidence that our immigrant confederates were sufficiently different in terms of their ethnic attributes (phenotype, skin tone) to German native confederates, and bystanders in our main experiment are highly likely to have perceived our immigrant control confederates as immigrants or Germans with an immigrant background. As with every survey, it is possible to consider different ways of presenting the survey questions. For example, a longer list of countries could have been provided to respondents to choose from; other countries (beyond Germany) with majority Christian population could have been included; or responses could have been left open-ended. Nonetheless, the evidence in this survey is so stark as to suggest that these slight modifications would not impact our conclusions from the manipulation checks.

Balance Tests for the Field Experiments

We present in table A2 a balance test for each of the treatment conditions presented in figure 3.10. Balance statistics provide suggestive evidence that the random assignment process for the different treatment conditions was successful.

Additional Results

Results Disaggregated by Experiment   We present in figure A.2 our discrimination effects disaggregated by experiment (experiment conducted in summer 2018 vs. summer 2019). The disaggregated effects reveal strikingly similar

TABLE A2. Balance Across Experimental Conditions

	# Bystanders	Prop. Headphones	Prop. Women	Rush Hour
Columns (1) vs. (2)				
Mean Control	3.058	0.052	0.562	0.259
Mean Treated	2.900	0.055	0.546	0.275
CI Lower	−0.114	−0.017	−0.0177	−0.055
CI Upper	0.151	0.011	0.048	0.024
P Value	0.623	0.687	0.360	0.451
Columns (2) vs. (3)				
Mean Control	3.030	0.062	0.560	0.255
Mean Treated	3.058	0.052	0.562	0.259
CI Lower	−0.169	−0.004	−0.033	−0.041
CI Upper	0.112	0.022	0.028	0.033
P Value	0.689	0.174	0.885	0.815
Columns (1) vs. (3)				
Mean Control	3.030	0.062	0.560	0.255
Mean Treated	2.700	0.055	0.546	0.275
CI Lower	0.185	−0.009	−0.019	−0.060
CI Upper	0.473	0.022	0.045	0.020
P Value	0.001	0.434	0.426	0.328

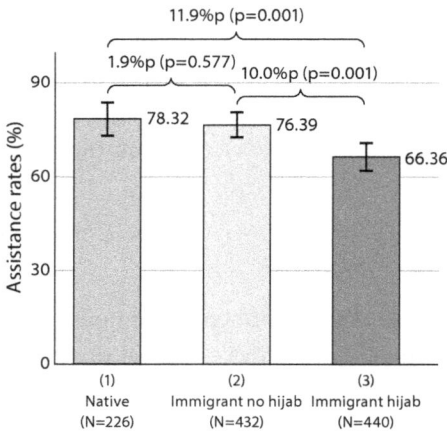

(a) Experiment 1: Summer 2018

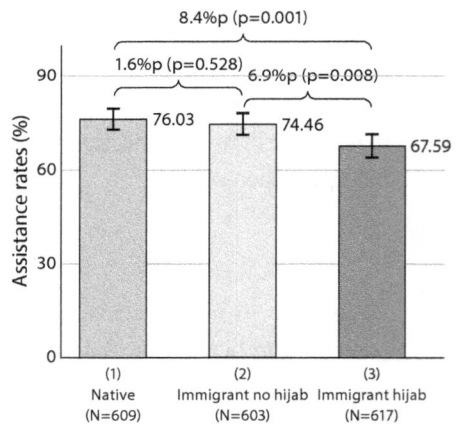

(b) Experiment 2: Summer 2019

FIGURE A.2. Discrimination against immigrants by experiment
Notes: The figure disaggregates the experimental results by experiment (summer 2018 vs. summer 2019). Bars represent the mean rates of assistance for the treatment conditions. The error bars present 95% confidence intervals for the means. The brackets and accompanying information report results of a standard two-tailed difference in means test of treatment conditions with p-values in parentheses.

patterns; we detect large and statistically significant discrimination among bystanders against hijab-wearing immigrant minorities. While the magnitude of the effect is somewhat smaller in the second experiment (11.9%p vs. 8.4%p), these differences do not reach conventional levels of significance. We observe similar lack of discrimination against immigrant minorities who do not wear religious attire; our minority confederates without the hijab are assisted only slightly less (less than 2%p) than native German confederates. These results show that the results reported in the main text are not driven by either of the two experiments.

Results Disaggregated by State   We present in figure A.3 our main discrimination results (native vs. immigrant with hijab) disaggregated by German federal state: North Rhine-Westphalia, Brandenburg, and Saxony. We pool observations from Lower Saxony into observations from NRW, because we did not implement a sufficient number of iterations in Lower Saxony to warrant separate analysis. We observe significant discrimination in the state of Saxony, where the difference in the assistance rates between our two experimental conditions expands to 15 percentage points ($p < 0.0001$). We see a smaller 6.5 percentage point difference in North Rhine-Westphalia that is also statistically distinguishable from zero at conventional levels ($p = 0.014$). While the

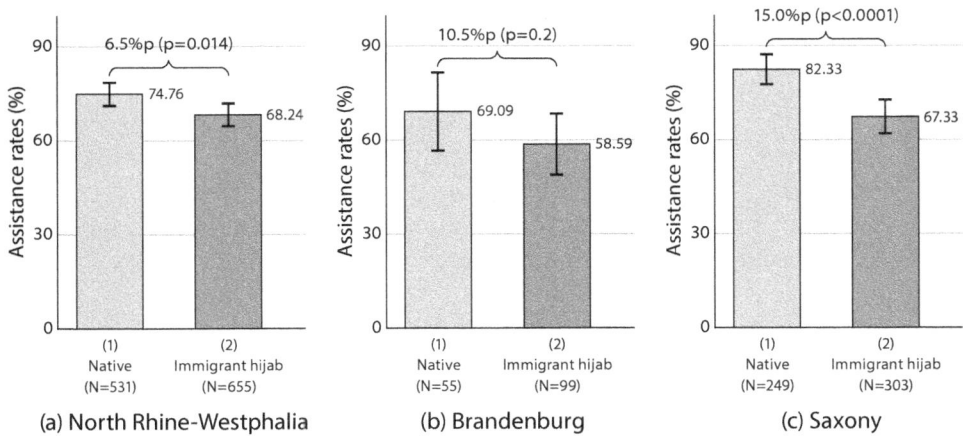

FIGURE A.3. Discrimination against immigrants by state
Notes: The figure is generated based on data that pools across the two experiments, but disaggregated by region (former West vs. East Germany). Bars represent the mean rates of assistance for the treatment conditions. The error bars present 95% confidence intervals for the means. The brackets and accompanying information report results of a standard two-tailed difference in means test of treatment conditions with p-values in parentheses.

size of the effect is large in magnitude in Brandenburg (10.5 percentage points, larger than NRW), we are underpowered to make claims about whether there is discrimination against hijab-wearing women in the state.

Results with Team Fixed Effects   In table A3 we present our hijab vs. native discrimination effects in a regression framework with team fixed effects. By including the team fixed effects, we restrict our inferences to discrimination effects observed within iterations run by the *same team*. The results are robust to the inclusion of team fixed effects.

TABLE A3. Analysis with Team Fixed Effects

	Hijab versus Native					
	Any help?					
	(1)	(2)	(3)	(4)	(5)	(6)
Hijab vs. Native	0.096***	0.096***	0.148***	0.133***	0.065**	0.074***
	(0.021)	(0.021)	(0.034)	(0.033)	(0.026)	(0.027)
Constant	0.671***		0.652***		0.682***	
	(0.014)		(0.022)		(0.018)	
Sample	Pooled	Pooled	East	East	West	West
Team FE	No	Yes	No	Yes	No	Yes
Observations	1,892	1,892	706	706	1,186	1,186
R^2	0.011	0.035	0.026	0.077	0.005	0.011

Note: $^*p < 0.1$; $^{**}p < 0.05$; $^{***}p < 0.01$.

Chapter 4

This section provides supplementary information on the experiment as well as additional results referenced in the main text of chapter 4.

Bystander Composition and Scene Characteristics

In Table A4 we present descriptive statistics and additional information on the composition of the bystanders and other iteration characteristics. As discussed above, treatment assignment was orthogonal to all bystander characteristics. Therefore, we should not expect these characteristics to affect the results. To further demonstrate empirically that, for example, the number of bystanders does not systemically affect the results, we also report specifications that have the number of bystander fixed effects, where the proportion outcome is used in the analysis. The estimates are virtually the

TABLE A4. Descriptive Statistics on Scene Characteristics

Statistic	N	Mean	St. Dev.	Min	Pctl(25)	Pctl(75)	Max
# of Bystanders	3,810	3.091	1.676	1	2	4	8
# of Bystanders with Earphones	3,807	0.185	0.452	0.000	0.000	0.000	4.000
Proportion of Female Bystanders	3,747	0.554	0.350	0.000	0.333	0.800	1
Temperature at Iteration	3,623	27.324	4.332	16.100	24.100	30.600	41.400
Rush Hour	3,810	0.253	0.435	0	0	1	1

same as without the fixed effects. We also include the full set of bystander composition and scene characteristics in our regression-based analyses. As expected, the inclusion of these additional covariates does not change our original findings.

Discrimination Against Immigrants

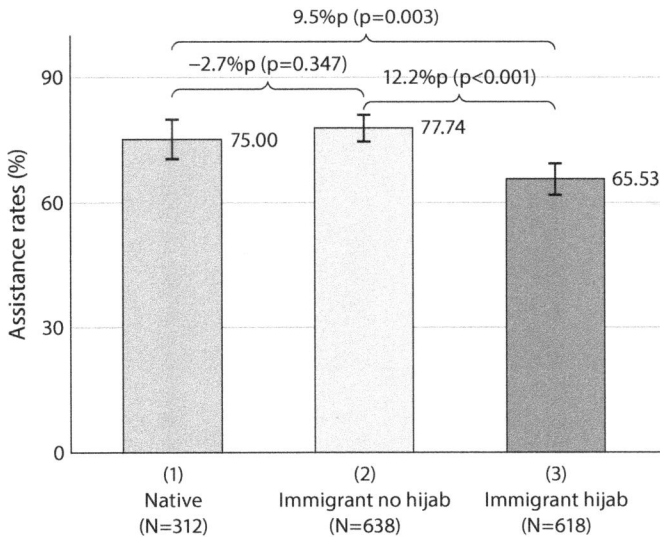

FIGURE A.4. Discrimination against immigrants: Merged (Experiment 1 & 2)
Notes: The bars reflect the mean rate of assistance for each of the treatment conditions, with 95% confidence intervals. The lines that connect the bars are from a two-tailed difference in means test of the conditions, with associated p-values. The figure pools data across experiments 1 (summer 2018) and 2 (summer 2019).

Effects Disaggregated by Region: Former West/East Germany

Next, we present results from the analysis disaggregated by region. Immigrant population density is lower in the East than the West and anti-immigrant sentiment is higher in the East. We test if perceived linguistic assimilation has different size effects in one of these regions, but find no such evidence.

Effects Disaggregated by Foreign Language Used by Confederate

In table A5 we assess whether there exist any heterogeneity in the effects of linguistic assimilation for hijab-wearing immigrant confederates. We specifically examine whether the type of foreign language used by the immigrant confederate drives any heterogeneity. In order to do so, we compare the language effects by whether the confederate spoke Arabic or Turkish during the phone

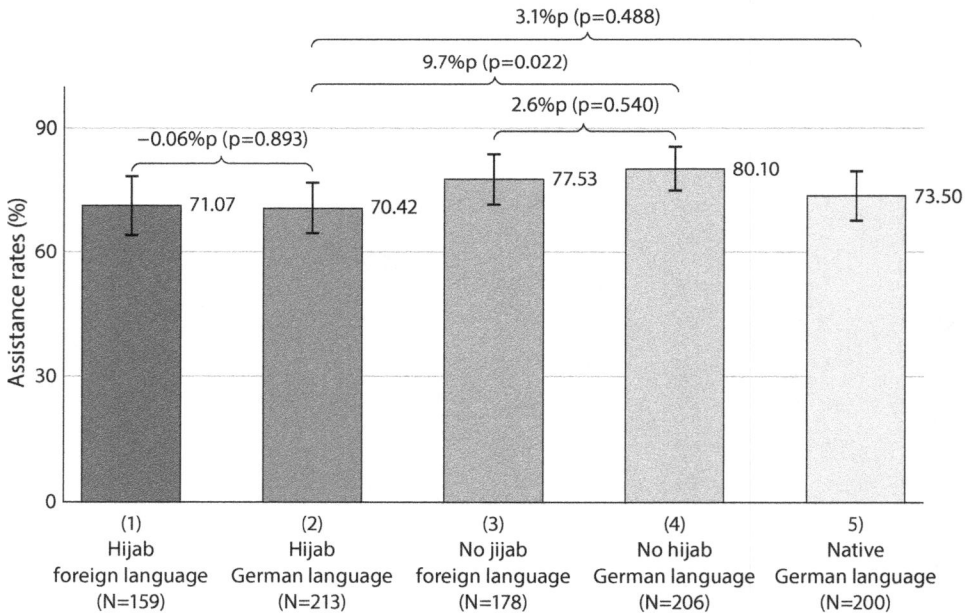

FIGURE A.5. Language effects: Former West Germany

Notes: The bars reflect the mean rate of assistance for each of the treatment conditions, with 95% confidence intervals. The lines that connect the bars are from a two-tailed difference in means test of the conditions, with associated p-values. The figure pools data across experiments 1 (summer 2018) and 2 (summer 2019), but subsets to data from German states that belonged to former West Germany (North Rhine-Westphalia and Lower Saxony).

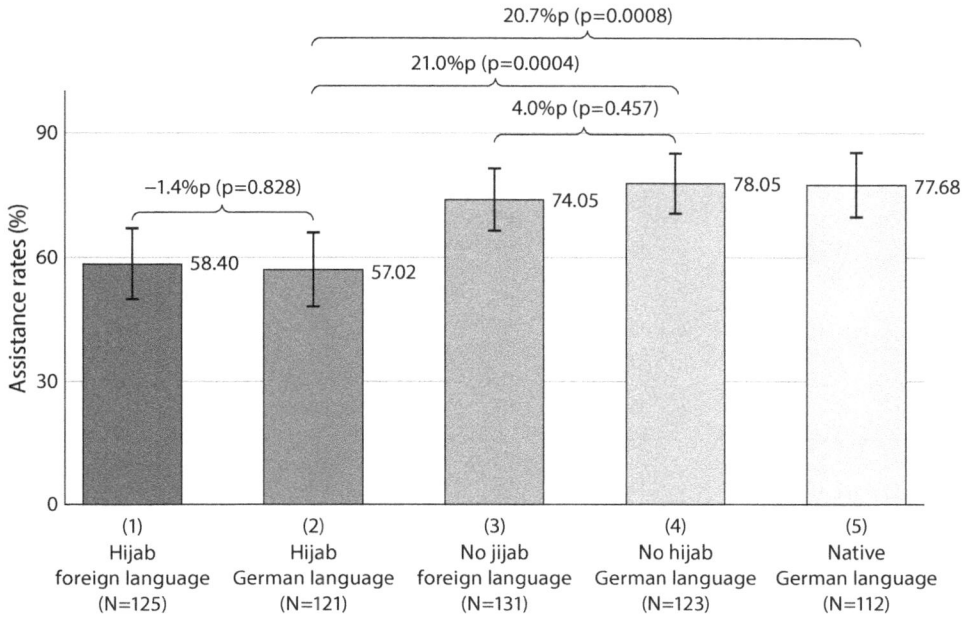

FIGURE A.6. Language effects: Former East Germany

Notes: The bars reflect the mean rate of assistance for each of the treatment conditions, with 95% confidence intervals. The lines that connect the bars are from a two-tailed difference in means test of the conditions, with associated p-values. The figure pools data across experiments 1 (summer 2018) and 2 (summer 2019), but subsets to data from German states that belonged to former East Germany (Brandenburg and Saxony).

call. Columns (1) and (2) subset the sample to find that there are no statistically significant linguistic assimilation effects (ATE = 0.8%p and −2.9%p, respectively). In column (3), we report the interaction term between our foreign vs. German language treatment with an indicator variable for Turkish language iterations. While the Turkish language iterations result in marginally higher assistance rates than Arabic language iterations, this difference falls far short of statistical significance.

Equivalence Tests

The analysis in the main paper has demonstrated that linguistic assimilation fails to reduce discrimination against Muslim immigrants; across a range of approaches, our analyses have shown that we are consistently unable to reject

TABLE A5. Effects by Foreign Language Used

| | Dependent Variable: | | |
| | Any help? | | |
	(1)	(2)	(3)
Foreign vs. German (Hijab)	0.008	−0.029	−0.029
	(0.043)	(0.084)	(0.082)
Turkish			0.034
			(0.064)
Foreign vs. German × Turkish			0.037
			(0.093)
Constant	0.663***	0.629***	0.629***
	(0.029)	(0.059)	(0.057)
Foreign Language	Turkish	Arabic	Merged
Observations	483	135	618
R^2	0.0001	0.001	0.002

Notes: Standard errors in parentheses. *p < 0.1; **p < 0.05; ***p < 0.01.

the null hypothesis that the true effect of linguistic assimilation on discrimination is zero at conventional levels. Skeptics might be concerned that our inability to reject the null hypothesis does not mean that the null hypothesis is statistically supported; it might potentially be the case that our failure to reject the null hypothesis is the result of a lack of statistical power to detect a true effect that exists and is positive, rather than the true effect being zero.

We note that our experiments are sufficiently well-powered to detect discrimination along a different dimension (religion) and, according to prior literature, linguistic differences should have had a *larger* effect than any other dimension of cultural difference. Moreover, the coefficient estimates for bias due to language differences are so small as to suggest that there is no substantively important effect. To further reinforce this argument, we provide additional evidence below that null effects on linguistic assimilation should be interpreted as an *absence* of a *substantively meaningful* effect using a series of equivalence tests (Berger, Hsu, et al., 1996; Seaman and Serlin, 1998; Wellek, 2010). We set equivalence bounds based on the size of the discrimination effect due to religious difference and present results using different bounds.

While demonstrating that the true effect of an experimental treatment is precisely zero is impossible, scholars in the frequentist paradigm of hypothesis testing have devised statistical tests that allow us to reject that the treatment effects are large enough to be of substantive import. In the so-called "equivalence testing" paradigm, scholars are able to statistically reject that the treatment effects are more extreme (larger in magnitude) than a *predetermined* upper and lower threshold at which the magnitude of the effect is deemed "large," and thus consider the true effect to be close enough to zero for practical purposes.

To find evidence *against* large treatment effects of linguistic assimilation, we adopt this equivalence testing approach, and the Two One-Sided Test (hereafter TOST) in particular. TOST has gained favor amongst scholars in the biomedical and psychological sciences for being a simple and intuitive approach to demonstrating equivalence. The logic of the TOSTs is as follows; first, the researcher must set an upper (B_U) and lower (B_L) equivalence bound, based on the smallest effect size of interest. Then, two null hypotheses—namely that (1) $B_T \leq -B_L$ and (2) $B_T \geq B_U$. By showing that these statistical tests can be rejected, we are able to claim that the observed effect falls within the equivalence bounds $B_L \leq B_T \leq B_U$, and thus is no longer meaningfully different from a negligible effect.

Since our outcomes are measured dichotomously, we apply the two one-sided test of *proportions* framework to our analyses. In order to do so, we need to specify equivalence bounds, or more intuitively, the threshold at which we would consider the effect to be no longer of substantive import. Setting these equivalence bounds is an inherently arbitrary practice, and the literature is divided as to what the most appropriate approach is. We make a deliberate choice to set equivalence bounds on the linguistic assimilation effects based on the magnitude of the discrimination observed in assistance rates between immigrant confederates and native confederates (12.0%p) that we documented in a peer-reviewed published study. For transparency's sake, we present results for equivalence tests that set equivalence bounds at 33% (1/3, 4%p), 50% (1/2, 6.0%p), 66% (2/3, 8%p) of the total discrimination effect. Given the extensive literature that predicts the importance of linguistic differences in driving discrimination, we find the parameters we use to be reasonable. It is also interesting to note that the 6%p bounds are roughly equivalent to the recommendation made by Simonsohn (2015) to set the equivalence bounds to the effect size that would have given a study 33% power.

We report the results of the TOSTs in table A6 and figure A.7. Whereas we are unable to claim equivalence when we set the equivalence bounds to one-third of the total discrimination effect (4 percentage points, Fisher's Exact Z test p value = 0.154), we are able to claim, based on the equivalence test and the original null hypothesis tests, that the observed effect for linguistic assimilation is statistically not different from zero, and statistically equivalent to

TABLE A6. Equivalence Tests for Linguistic Assimilation Effects

	Equivalence Bound	TOST Conf. Interval	Fisher's Exact Z Test
	Test 1: Immigrant Foreign vs. German Language (ATE: 1.4%p)		
Test 1 small (33%)	(−0.04, 0.04)	(−0.028, 0.056)	p = 0.154
Test 1 intermediate (50%)	(−0.06, 0.06)		p = 0.035
Test 1 large (66%)	(−0.08, 0.08)		p = 0.005
	Test 2: Hijab Foreign vs. German Language (ATE: 0.07%p)		
Test 2 small (33%)	(−0.04, 0.04)	(−0.062, 0.064)	p = 0.152
Test 2 intermediate (50%)	(−0.06, 0.06)		p = 0.061
Test 2 large (66%)	(−0.08, 0.08)		p = 0.019

zero; the confidence interval for the two one-sided tests falls within the equivalence bounds for intermediate and large bounds (6%, 8 percentage points) and the p-values for the Fisher's Exact Z test fall below conventional levels (p = 0.035, p = 0.004, respectively). When we conduct equivalence tests for linguistic assimilation effects for hijab-wearing immigrant confederates, we observe similar patterns (p = 0.061, p = 0.019, respectively).

We interpret these findings as statistical evidence against substantively large treatment effects of linguistic assimilation. Combined with the analyses presented in the main text of the paper, we are confident that linguistic assimilation is likely to have negligible influence on reducing discrimination against Muslim minority immigrants.

Chapter 5

This section provides supplementary information on the experiment as well as additional results referenced in the main text of chapter 5.

Experimental Setup

- **Step 1**: A German male confederate (the "violator") is instructed to violate a widely shared norm against littering in a train station platform in front of unknowing experimental subjects, as in the closely related experiment by Balafoutas et al. (2016).
- **Step 2**: A second female confederate sanctions the violator by politely, albeit firmly, asking the violator to pick up his trash. The violator picks up his trash and leaves the scene.

Equivalence bounds −0.06 and 0.06
Proportion difference = 0.014
TOST: 90% CI [−0.028; 0.056] significant
NHST: 95% CI [−0.036; 0.064] non-significant

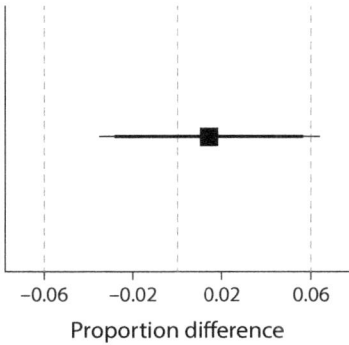

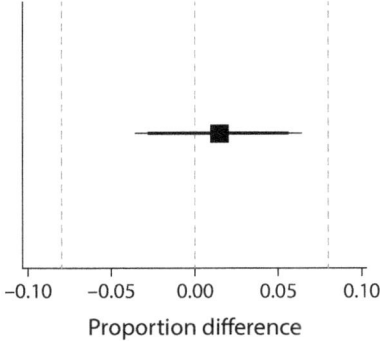

−0.06   −0.02   0.02   0.06
Proportion difference

(a) Test 1, equivalence bounds
(−0.06, 0.06)

Equivalence bounds −0.06 and 0.06
Proportion difference = 0.001
TOST: 90% CI [−0.062; 0.064] significant
NHST: 95% CI [−0.075; 0.076] non-significant

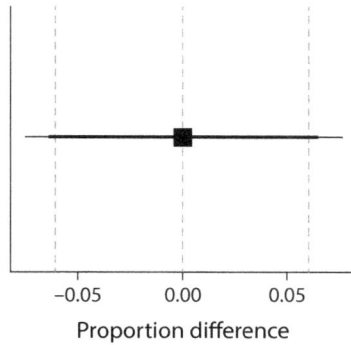

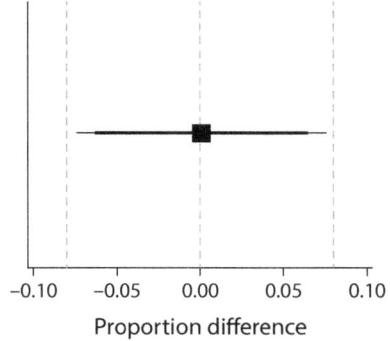

−0.05   0.00   0.05
Proportion difference

(b) Test 2, equivalence bounds
(−0.06, 0.06)

Equivalence bounds −0.08 and 0.08
Proportion difference = 0.014
TOST: 90% CI [−0.028; 0.056] significant
NHST: 95% CI [−0.036; 0.064] non-significant

−0.10   −0.05   0.00   0.05   0.10
Proportion difference

(c) Test 1, equivalence bounds
(−0.08, 0.08)

Equivalence bounds −0.08 and 0.08
Proportion difference = 0.001
TOST: 90% CI [−0.062; 0.064] significant
NHST: 95% CI [−0.075; 0.076] non-significant

−0.10   −0.05   0.00   0.05   0.10
Proportion difference

(d) Test 2, equivalence bounds
(−0.08, 0.08)

FIGURE A.7. Equivalence testing: Two one-sided test of proportions
Notes: The squares represent the point estimate for our effects, with the thick and thin lines
representing 90% confidence interval for the TOST and the 95% confidence interval for the
null hypothesis significance tests. The horizontal dotted lines represent the equivalence
bounds that we set for the TOSTs; ± 6 percentage points for subfigures (a) and (b) and
± 8 percentage points for subfigures (c) and (d).

- **Step 3**: The female confederate conducts an audible phone call within earshot of the experimental subject in either German or their mother tongue.
- **Step 4**: In the midst of the phone call, the female confederate drops her possessions (a large volume of groceries that disperse and are hard to pick up) and appears to be in need of assistance.
- **Step 5**: We observe in step 5 whether the punisher receives assistance from experimental subjects who have observed the sequence of events. The main behavioral outcomes of the study are (a) whether the female confederate receives *any* assistance from bystanders; and (b) the *proportion* of bystanders who offered assistance.

- **Dimension 1**: Ascriptive characteristics of female confederate (punisher).
  1. Immigrant confederate wearing a hijab
  2. Immigrant confederate wearing plain clothing without hijab
  3. Native confederate (German)
- **Dimension 2**: Enforcement of norm against littering.
  1. Norm is enforced by the female confederate (punisher) who is later in need of assistance.
  2. Norm is enforced by a different confederate (third party).

Bystander Composition and Scene Characteristics

In this subsection, we present descriptive statistics and additional information on the composition of the bystanders and other iteration characteristics. A minimum of three bystanders were required for each iteration. As discussed above, treatment assignment was orthogonal to all bystander characteristics. Therefore, we should not expect these characteristics to affect the results. To further demonstrate this empirically that, for example, the number of bystanders does not systemically affect the results, we also report specifications that have number of bystander fixed effects, where the proportion outcome is used in the analysis. The estimates are virtually the same as without the fixed effects. We also include the full set of bystander composition and scene characteristics in our regression-based analyses reported in table A11. As expected, the inclusion of these additional covariates also does not change our original findings.

TABLE A7. Bystander Composition and Scene Characteristics

Statistic	N	Mean	St. Dev.
Number of Bystanders	1,614	4.428	1.449
Proportion of Female Bystanders	1,614	0.542	0.258
Proportion with Headphones	1,614	0.071	0.130
Hour of Iteration	1,614	12.887	2.753
Iteration during Rush Hour (Binary)	1,614	0.170	0.376
Temperature During Iteration	1,614	29.053	3.708

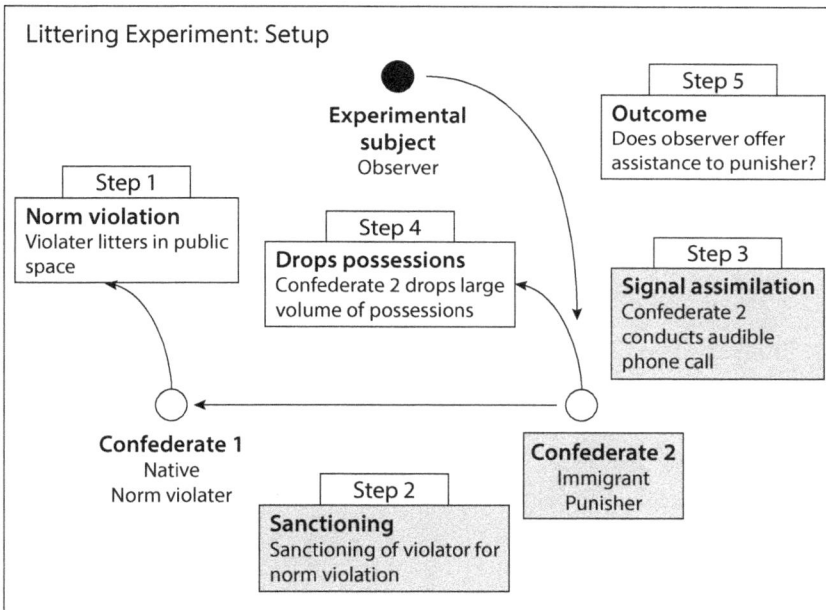

FIGURE A.8. Experimental setup

Covariate Balance

In this subsection, we present covariate balance statistics for our experimental treatment conditions. While covariate imbalance can arise due to chance, the randomization seems to have successfully obtained balance on each of the six pretreatment covariates we collected, both in the full sample as well as the samples disaggregated by state. Figures A8 and A9 present balance statistics for all statistical tests included in figures 5.5 and 5.6 of the main text.

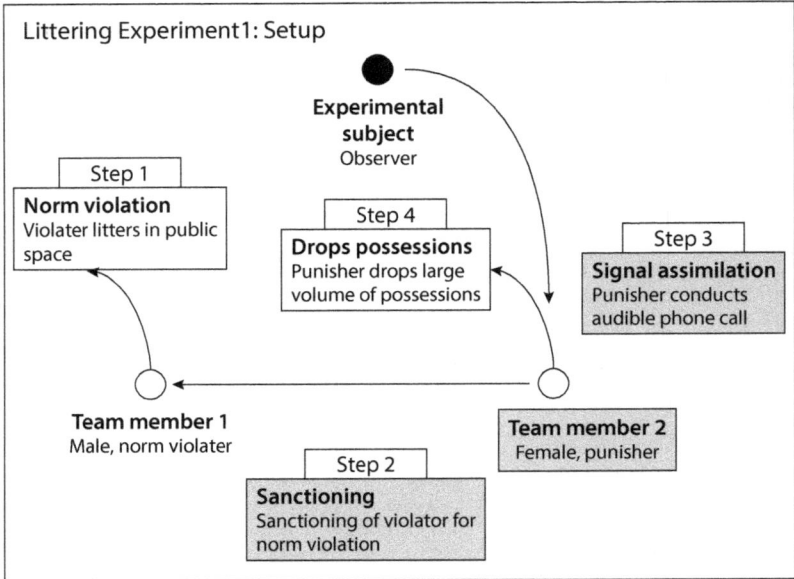

(a) Confederate enforces norm

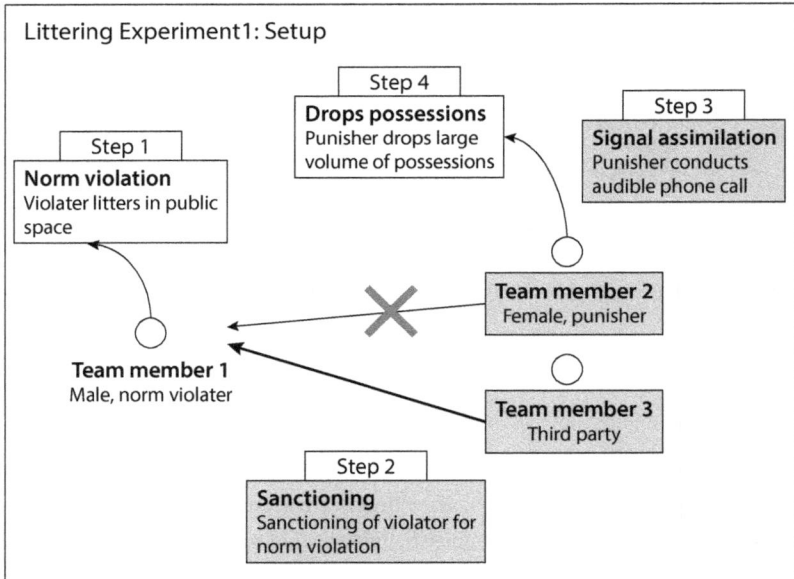

(b) Third party enforces norm

FIGURE A.9. Norm treatment dimensions

TABLE A8. Covariate Balance for Comparisons in Figure 3

	Mean Treated	Mean Control	T Test p-value	KS Test p-value
Column (1) vs. (2)				
Number of Bystanders	4.4301	4.4625	0.7807	0.7854
Proportion of Female Bystanders	0.5431	0.5293	0.4679	0.3018
Proportion with Headphones	0.0571	0.0736	0.0981	0.1814
Hour of Iteration	12.8064	12.9551	0.5227	0.1472
Iteration during Rush Hour (Binary)	0.1751	0.1571	0.5579	-
Temperature during Iteration	28.8234	28.9428	0.7041	0.3412
F-statistic: 0.6241 (p-value = 0.7111)				
Column (2) vs. (3)				
Number of Bystanders	4.3244	4.4243	0.3001	0.5102
Proportion of Female Bystanders	0.5600	0.5398	0.2872	0.8126
Proportion with Headphones	0.0698	0.0757	0.5115	0.8872
Hour of Iteration	12.9686	12.7075	0.1692	0.2560
Iteration during Rush Hour (Binary)	0.1855	0.1650	0.4368	-
Temperature during Iteration	28.9612	28.8490	0.6511	0.9642
F-statistic: 0.8374 (p-value = 0.5411)				
Column (1) vs. (3)				
Number of Bystanders	4.4301	4.4243	0.9597	0.6530
Proportion of Female Bystanders	0.5431	0.5398	0.8682	0.7282
Proportion with Headphones	0.0571	0.0757	0.0719	0.1730
Hour of Iteration	12.8064	12.7075	0.6789	0.4798
Iteration during Rush Hour (Binary)	0.1751	0.1650	0.7508	-
Temperature during Iteration	28.8234	28.8490	0.9365	0.4436
F-statistic: 0.5481 (p-value = 0.7716)				

TABLE A9. Covariate Balance for Comparisons in Figure 4

	Mean Treated	Mean Control	T Test p-value	KS Test p-value
Column (1) vs. (2)				
Number of Bystanders	4.4466	4.4159	0.8723	0.1078
Proportion of Female Bystanders	0.5343	0.5506	0.6030	0.2386
Proportion with Headphones	0.0472	0.0656	0.2346	0.4222
Hour of Iteration	12.7100	12.8888	0.6523	0.8228
Iteration during Rush Hour (Binary)	0.1500	0.1965	0.3664	-
Temperature during Iteration	29.1793	28.5192	0.2186	0.1334
F-statistic: 0.9079 (p-value = 0.4901)				
Column (2) vs. (3)				
Number of Bystanders	4.4159	4.4802	0.6446	0.5332
Proportion of Female Bystanders	0.5506	0.5633	0.6368	0.2036
Proportion with Headphones	0.0656	0.0860	0.1947	0.0446
Hour of Iteration	12.8888	12.7931	0.7667	0.3188
Iteration during Rush Hour (Binary)	0.1965	0.1477	0.2745	-
Temperature during Iteration	28.5192	28.8801	0.4276	0.2440
F-statistic: 0.7331 (p-value = 0.6232)				
Column (3) vs. (4)				
Number of Bystanders	4.4802	4.3729	0.4248	0.1332
Proportion of Female Bystanders	0.5633	0.5182	0.0642700	0.1822
Proportion with Headphones	0.0860	0.0663	0.1352	0.1144
Hour of Iteration	12.7931	12.6289	0.5427	0.4346
Iteration during Rush Hour (Binary)	0.1477	0.1809	0.3570	-
Temperature during Iteration	28.8801	28.8205	0.8674	0.9682
F-statistic: 1.325 (p-value = 0.2446)				

Additional Analyses

TABLE A10. Immigrant (Hijab + Control) versus Native Comparisons

	Immigrants (Hijab + Control) versus Native				
	Any help?		% of bystanders helped?		
	(1)	(2)	(3)	(4)	(5)
Immigrants (vs. Natives)	−0.070*	−0.070**	−0.050**	−0.051**	−0.053**
	(0.036)	(0.035)	(0.025)	(0.025)	(0.026)
Constant	0.783***		0.316***		
	(0.027)		(0.022)		
State FE	No	Yes	No	Yes	Yes
Bystander FE	No	No	No	No	Yes
Observations	1,098	1,098	1,098	1,098	1,098
R^2	0.004	0.018	0.008	0.019	0.092

Notes: Clustered standard errors in parentheses. $^*p < 0.1$; $^{**}p < 0.05$; $^{***}p < 0.01$.
Comparisons between immigrant hijab and immigrant control conditions versus native condition, pooling across norm enforcement dimension. Outcomes examined are (1) our dichotomous measure of whether any bystander helped (our main outcome), and (2) the percentage of bystanders who helped. Columns (1) and (2) report the average treatment effect (ATE) on our dichotomous main outcome, while columns (3)–(5) report the ATE using the percentage of bystanders who helped. Columns (1) and (3) report the average treatment effect (ATE) without state fixed effects, while columns (2) and (4) report the ATE with state fixed effects. Column (5) includes state fixed effects and number of bystander fixed effects. Constant terms for columns (1) and (3)—the baseline specifications—are the means for the control group (native category). Robust standard errors are reported in parentheses.

TABLE A11. Hijab versus Native comparisons

	Hijab versus Native									
	Any help?						% of bystanders helped?			
	(1)	(2)	(3)	(4)	(5)	(6)	(7)	(8)	(9)	(10)
Hijab (vs. Native)	-0.120***	-0.123***	-0.119***	-0.118***	-0.124***	-0.065**	-0.067**	-0.064**	-0.068**	-0.066**
	(0.043)	(0.043)	(0.042)	(0.043)	(0.045)	(0.030)	(0.029)	(0.027)	(0.030)	(0.031)
Constant	0.783***					0.316***				
	(0.027)					(0.022)				
State FE	No	Yes	No	Yes	Yes	No	Yes	No	Yes	Yes
Team FE	No	No	Yes	No	No	No	No	Yes	No	No
Bystander FE	No	No	No	Yes	Yes	No	No	No	Yes	Yes
Other Controls	No	No	No	No	Yes	No	No	No	No	Yes
Observations	666	666	666	666	641	666	666	666	666	641
R^2	0.015	0.029	0.072	0.058	0.066	0.016	0.027	0.084	0.110	0.115

Notes: Clustered standard errors in parentheses. * $p < 0.1$; ** $p < 0.05$; *** $p < 0.01$.

TABLE A12. Hijab versus Native Comparison, by Region, Clustered Standard Errors

	Hijab versus Native					
	Any help?		% of bystanders helped?			
	(1)	(2)	(3)	(4)	(5)	(6)
Hijab (vs. Native)	−0.162***	−0.087	−0.082***	−0.093***	−0.052	−0.045
	(0.049)	(0.070)	(0.030)	(0.033)	(0.050)	(0.050)
Constant	0.759***	0.807***	0.302***		0.330***	
	(0.030)	(0.045)	(0.022)		(0.038)	
Region	East	West	East	East	West	West
Bystander FE	No	No	No	Yes	No	Yes
Observations	313	353	313	313	353	353
R^2	0.027	0.009	0.026	0.109	0.010	0.106

Notes: *p < 0.1; **p < 0.05; ***p < 0.01.
Comparisons between immigrant hijab condition and native condition, pooling across norm enforcement dimension, but disaggregated by region (former East Germany and West Germany). Outcomes examined are (1) our dichotomous measure of whether any bystander helped and (2) the percentage of bystanders who helped. Columns (1) and (2) report the average treatment effect (ATE) on our dichotomous main outcome, while columns (3)–(6) report the ATE using the percentage of bystanders who helped. Columns (4) and (6) report specifications with number of bystander fixed effects. Constant terms for columns (1), (2), (3), and (5)—the baseline specifications—are the means for the control group (native category). Robust standard errors are reported in parentheses.

TABLE A13. Hijab versus Native Comparison, by state

| | Any help? | | | % of bystanders helped? | | | | | |
	(1)	(2)	(3)	(4)	(5)	(6)	(7)	(8)	(9)
Hijab (vs. Native)	-0.087	-0.217***	-0.105	-0.052	-0.045	-0.119***	-0.148***	-0.044	-0.049
	(0.070)	(0.054)	(0.070)	(0.050)	(0.050)	(0.039)	(0.042)	(0.034)	(0.035)
Constant	0.807***	0.825***	0.691***	0.330***		0.337***		0.266***	
	(0.045)	(0.031)	(0.034)	(0.038)		(0.028)		(0.017)	
State	NRW	Sachsen	Bburg	NRW	NRW	Sachsen	Sachsen	Bburg	Bburg
Bystander FE	No	No	No	No	Yes	No	Yes	No	Yes
Observations	353	159	154	353	353	159	159	154	154
R^2	0.009	0.050	0.011	0.010	0.106	0.054	0.174	0.008	0.084

Notes: Clustered standard errors in parentheses. $*p < 0.1$; $**p < 0.05$; $***p < 0.01$.

Comparisons between immigrant hijab condition and native condition, pooling across norm enforcement dimension, but disaggregated by federal state (North Rhine-Westphalia, Brandenburg, and Saxony). Outcomes examined are (1) our dichotomous measure of whether any bystander helped, and (2) the percentage of bystanders who helped. Columns (1)–(3) report the average treatment effect (ATE) on our dichotomous main outcome, while columns (4)–(9) report the ATE using the percentage of bystanders who helped. Constant terms for columns (1), (2), (3), (4), (6), and (8)—the baseline specifications—are the means for the control group (native category). Robust standard errors are reported in parentheses.

TABLE A14. Norm Enforcement Effects by Region

| | Dependent Variable | | | |
| | Any help? | | % of bystanders helped? | |
	(1)	(2)	(3)	(4)
Norm Enforcer	0.080**	0.028	0.049***	0.001
(vs. Non-enforcer)	(0.037)	(0.030)	(0.017)	(0.017)
Constant	0.643***	0.762***	0.220***	0.291***
	(0.026)	(0.022)	(0.011)	(0.012)
Region	East	West	East	West
Observations	639	749	639	749
R^2	0.007	0.001	0.012	0.00000

Notes: $p < 0.1$; **$p < 0.05$; ***$p < 0.01$.
Comparison of the level of assistance offered to immigrants who enforce the anti-littering norm and immigrants who do not enforce the norm, pooling across ascriptive differences dimension, disaggregated by region. Outcomes examined are (1) our dichotomous measure of whether any bystander helped (our main outcome), and (2) the percentage of bystanders who helped. Columns (1) and (2) report the average treatment effect (ATE) on our dichotomous main outcome, while columns (3) and (4) report the ATE using the percentage of bystanders who helped. Robust standard errors are reported in parentheses.

Chapter 6

This section provides supplementary information on the experiment as well as additional results referenced in the main text of chapter 6.

Site Selection

The list of cities and the number of train platforms (in parentheses) at each of the train stations where data collection was implemented is presented below.

- **North Rhine-Westphalia**: Münster (9), Bielefeld (8), Minden (5), Rheine (6), Köln (11), Köln Messe/Deutz (12), Mönchengladbach (9), Neuss (8), Siegen (6), Bonn (5), Düsseldorf (20), Wuppertal (5), Dortmund (31), Duisburg (12), Bochum (8), Gelsenkirchen (6), Hagen (16), Essen (13), Wanne-Eickel (8)
- **Saxony**: Leipzig (21), Görlitz (6), Chemnitz (14), Dresden (16), Zwickau (8)
- **Lower Saxony**: Osnabrück (9), Hannover (12)

Sampling Protocol for Post-intervention Survey

After each intervention, two enumerators approached the bystanders and conducted a putatively unrelated survey about social life in Germany. Enumerators randomly selected up to two bystanders to interview, following specific instructions regarding sampling. The selection of the interviewees was stratified by their help behavior in order to ensure adequate coverage of helpers and non-helpers in the sample: enumerators chose one bystander who helped and one who did not (or two who did not (two who did), if no one (both) helped).[1] Within each of these two categories, enumerators were instructed to choose the bystander who was closest to the "acting" confederate at the beginning of the iteration. Since the initial location of any given bystander (within each microenvironment) is by design orthogonal to the confederate's initial position and the randomly assigned treatment, this sampling strategy yields a stratified, random sample of bystanders.

Manipulation Checks

Although the findings presented in the main text of the paper and the appendix suggest that our experimental manipulation was successful, in this section, we provide additional evidence from manipulation checks conducted during our pilot and a partial replication of the intervention with various manipulation checks that the experimental manipulation worked as we had intended.

TABLE A15. Partial Replications with Manipulation Checks

Outcome	Rate	n
Noticed the Confederate	0.996	224
Noticed the Call	0.978	224
Recalled Treatment Direction Correctly	0.808	224

More specifically, for our intervention to have been successful, we require that the bystanders (1) noticed our female confederate, (2) noticed that she

1. Thereby, we deliberately over-sampled bystanders who helped so as to be able to conduct an exploratory analysis as to their characteristics vis-à-vis non-helpers. We collected survey data after each iteration, including iterations where no one helped, which means that there would be more individuals who did not help relative to helpers in our sample. We wanted to guard against the possibility that the number of helpers would be too small.

was engaged in a phone call, and (3) recalled the direction of our treatment in the phone call (progressive vs. regressive gender attitudes). The manipulation checks, which we conducted during a pilot in May 2019 and a follow-up study in January 2020, debriefed bystanders who had just been exposed to our experimental intervention, and asked them whether they had in fact noticed both our confederate and the phone call, and whether they could recall whether the phone conversation our confederate had revealed that she had progressive or regressive content with regard to gender (through open-ended questions). The results of this manipulation check exercise is presented in table A15.

Data Omitting Bystanders Perceived to Be Immigrants

TABLE A16. Effects of Ideas on Bias by Gender, Perceived Native German Bystanders

	Hijab vs. Native Comparison					
	Outcome: Did an individual bystander help?					
	(1)	(2)	(3)	(4)	(5)	(6)
Hijab vs. Native	−0.031	−0.164***	−0.132**	−0.144**	−0.102**	−0.083
	(0.050)	(0.054)	(0.050)	(0.056)	(0.050)	(0.055)
Gender Attitude Condition	Progressive	Progressive	Regressive	Regressive	Neutral	Neutral
Bystander Gender	Female	Male	Female	Male	Female	Male
Fixed Effects	✓	✓	✓	✓	✓	✓
Observations	449	320	407	315	418	316

Notes: Models are estimated with linear regression. Robust standard errors clustered at the iteration level in parentheses. *p < 0.1; **p < 0.05; ***p < 0.01. Fixed effects included number of bystanders at the iteration level, number of *female* bystanders at the iteration level, as well as individual-level attributes that enumerators coded; these included perceived age bracket and whether or not the bystander was wearing earphones. The number of female bystanders at the iteration level partially assuages concern that women are more susceptible to behavioral spillovers from other female bystanders.

Conditional Effects (Post-treatment Survey)

Drawing on data from the post-intervention survey, we can take a closer look at the effect of religious identity and education levels on shaping attitudes toward Muslim immigrants as a function of the gender-specific ideological message conveyed in the phone call experiment. Table A18 shows that the progressive message increases help to hijab-wearing Muslims (column 2, 16.0%p) while controlling for the number of bystanders as well as bystander

TABLE A17. Progressive versus Regressive Attitude Comparison by Confederate Type, Disaggregated by Gender: Individual-Level Analysis

	Progressive versus Regressive Phone Call Comparison					
	Did an individual bystander help?					
	(1)	(2)	(3)	(4)	(5)	(6)
Progressive	0.102**	0.067	−0.026	−0.013	−0.008	0.080
vs. Regressive Attitude	(0.047)	(0.058)	(0.048)	(0.052)	(0.052)	(0.053)
Confederate Identity Condition	Hijab	Hijab	No Hijab	No Hijab	Native	Native
Bystander Gender	Female	Male	Female	Male	Female	Male
Fixed Effects	✓	✓	✓	✓	✓	✓
Observations	426	311	434	328	430	324

Notes: Models are estimated with linear regression. Robust standard errors clustered at the iteration level in parentheses. *p < 0.1; **p < 0.05; ***p < 0.01. Fixed effects included number of bystanders at the iteration level, as well as all individual-level attributes that enumerators coded; these included perceived age bracket and whether or not the bystander was wearing earphones.

attribute fixed effects (e.g., wearing earphones). This effect is much larger for bystanders who declare no religion (column 6, 21.5%p) than for those who report that they are religious Christians (column 4, −0.9%p). Due to high attrition rates in the survey, we are limited in the analyses of conditional effects we can do. However, the results indicate that the progressive gender roles message resonates with secular bystanders, consistent with our theoretical expectations.

We also present results of the same analysis presented in table A18, weighted by the proportion of helpers and non-helpers in the experimental sample for H6A (progressive vs. regressive, hijab). The findings are reported in table A19. Although the treatment effects for the full sample are somewhat diminished, we still find strong effects among non-religious people in the sample, as reported in columns (5) and (6). We interpret these findings to be in line with the results reported in table A18.

We anticipated that the treatment effects of the progressive versus regressive message would likely be driven by female bystanders who themselves hold a progressive outlook with regard to women's role in society. We further expected that non-religious (atheist) women would be much more likely to hold progressive views, and thus respond to the progressive message more than other subgroups of the population. In table A20, we conduct

TABLE A18. Effect of the Progressive Gender Attitudes, Disaggregated by Bystander Religion: Post-intervention Survey Sample

| | Progressive versus Regressive Message | | | | | |
| | Did an individual offer help? | | | | | |
	(1)	(2)	(3)	(4)	(5)	(6)
Progressive vs.	0.178***	0.160**	−0.004	−0.009	0.240***	0.215**
Regressive, Hijab	(0.066)	(0.068)	(0.152)	(0.160)	(0.088)	(0.092)
Sample	Full	Full	Christian	Christian	Atheist	Atheist
# of Bystander FE	Yes	Yes	Yes	Yes	Yes	Yes
Bystander Attribute FE	No	Yes	No	Yes	No	Yes
Observations	230	220	53	49	109	105
R^2	0.176	0.191	0.170	0.207	0.247	0.245

Notes: Models are estimated with linear regression. Robust standard errors clustered at the iteration level in parentheses. *p < 0.1; **p < 0.05; ***p < 0.01. Columns (3) and (4) subset to individuals who self-identified as Christian in the post-intervention survey (Protestant and Catholic). Columns (5) and (6) subset to individuals who self-reported as having "no religion." Bystander attribute fixed effects includes all individual-level attributes that enumerators coded: perceived age bracket, perceived immigrant status, whether or not the bystander was wearing earphones.

TABLE A19. Effect of the Progressive Gender Attitudes, Disaggregated by Bystander Religion: Post-intervention Survey Sample, Weighted by Proportion of Helpers and Non-helpers in the Experimental Sample

| | Progressive versus Regressive Message | | | | | |
| | Did an individual offer help? | | | | | |
	(1)	(2)	(3)	(4)	(5)	(6)
Progressive vs. Regressive,	0.120*	0.102	−0.063	−0.066	0.192**	0.168*
Hijab (H6A)	(0.067)	(0.068)	(0.149)	(0.157)	(0.090)	(0.093)
Sample	Full	Full	Christian	Christian	Atheist	Atheist
# of Bystander FE	Yes	Yes	Yes	Yes	Yes	Yes
Bystander Attribute FE	No	Yes	No	Yes	No	Yes
Observations	230	220	53	49	109	105

Notes: Models are estimated with linear regression. Robust standard errors clustered at the iteration level in parentheses. *p < 0.1; **p < 0.05; ***p < 0.01. Columns (3) and (4) subset to individuals who self-identified as Christian in the post-intervention survey (Protestant and Catholic). Columns (5) and (6) subset to individuals who self-reported as having "no religion." Bystander attribute fixed effects includes all individual-level attributes that enumerators coded: perceived age bracket, perceived immigrant status, whether or not the bystander was wearing earphones.

TABLE A20. Effect of the Progressive Gender Attitudes, Disaggregated by Bystander Religion: Post-intervention Survey Sample

	Progressive versus Regressive Message					
	Did an individual offer help?					
	(1)	(2)	(3)	(4)	(5)	(6)
Progressive vs. Regressive, Hijab (H6A)	0.303	0.349*	−0.211	−0.237	0.303	0.338
	(0.220)	(0.204)	(0.185)	(0.184)	(0.220)	(0.213)
Atheist	0.081	−0.002	−0.254	−0.336**	0.081	−0.005
	(0.177)	(0.192)	(0.164)	(0.168)	(0.177)	(0.202)
Female	0.236	0.206				
	(0.180)	(0.192)				
H6A × Atheist	−0.161	−0.222	0.495**	0.528**	−0.161	−0.202
	(0.258)	(0.244)	(0.222)	(0.217)	(0.258)	(0.258)
H6A × Female	−0.514*	−0.583**				
	(0.264)	(0.249)				
Atheist × Female	−0.335	−0.328				
	(0.231)	(0.235)				
H6A × Atheist × Female	0.656**	0.741**				
	(0.324)	(0.308)				
Confederate Identity Condition	Hijab	Hijab	Hijab	Hijab	Hijab	Hijab
Sample	Full	Full	Female	Female	Male	Male
# of Bystander FE	Yes	Yes	Yes	Yes	Yes	Yes
Bystander Attribute FE	No	Yes	No	Yes	No	Yes
Observations	162	154	86	82	76	72

Notes: Models are estimated with linear regression. Robust standard errors clustered at the iteration level in parentheses. $^*p < 0.1$; $^{**}p < 0.05$; $^{***}p < 0.01$. Columns (3) and (4) subset to female bystanders. Columns (5) and (6) subset to male bystanders. Bystander attribute fixed effects includes all individual-level attributes that enumerators coded; perceived age bracket, perceived immigrant status, whether or not the bystander was wearing earphones.

regression analysis of individual-level treatment effects interacted by whether the bystander who completed the post-intervention survey self-identified as non-religious and was a female. Our results indicate that women who are non-religious are indeed more responsive to our progressive message treatment. The final row of columns (1) and (2), which utilizes the full survey response (male and female) data, shows a significant and positive interaction effect, suggesting that our posited mechanism is likely to be valid. These results are replicated in columns (3) and (4), where we just subset to female bystander survey respondents.

TABLE A21. Effect of the Progressive Gender Attitudes, Disaggregated by Bystander Religion: Post-intervention Survey Sample, Weighted by Proportion of Helpers and Non-helpers in the Experimental Sample

	Progressive versus regressive message					
	Did an individual offer help?					
	(1)	(2)	(3)	(4)	(5)	(6)
Progressive vs. Regressive, Hijab (H6A)	0.238	0.287	−0.274	−0.292	0.238	0.276
	(0.225)	(0.206)	(0.178)	(0.177)	(0.225)	(0.216)
Atheist	0.084	−0.009	−0.253	−0.343**	0.084	−0.011
	(0.185)	(0.195)	(0.160)	(0.159)	(0.185)	(0.204)
Female	0.234	0.198				
	(0.182)	(0.186)				
H6A × Atheist	−0.164	−0.214	0.493**	0.534**	−0.164	−0.195
	(0.263)	(0.245)	(0.219)	(0.212)	(0.263)	(0.260)
H6A × Female	−0.512*	−0.577**				
	(0.265)	(0.245)				
Atheist × Female	−0.336	−0.330				
	(0.234)	(0.229)				
H6A × Atheist × Female	0.657**	0.742**				
	(0.325)	(0.303)				
Sample	Full	Full	Female	Female	Male	Male
# of Bystander FE	Yes	Yes	Yes	Yes	Yes	Yes
Bystander Attribute FE	No	Yes	No	Yes	No	Yes
Observations	162	154	86	82	76	72

Notes: Models are estimated with linear regression. Robust standard errors clustered at the iteration level in parentheses. *p < 0.1; **p < 0.05; ***p < 0.01. Columns (3) and (4) subset to female bystanders. Columns (5) and (6) subset to male bystanders. Bystander attribute fixed effects includes all individual-level attributes that enumerators coded; perceived age bracket, perceived immigrant status, whether or not the bystander was wearing earphones.

We also present results of the same analysis presented in table A20, weighted by the proportion of helpers and non-helpers in the experimental sample for H6A (progressive vs. regressive, hijab). The findings are reported in table A21. They do not substantively change the results reported in table A20.

In order to further validate our intuition regarding the treatment effect being driven by *female* bystanders who hold a progressive outlook with regard to women's role in society, we look at heterogeneity in the treatment effect for the progressive versus regressive message based on the level of education, a strong correlate of gender attitudes in the German context. The results are presented in table A22. For observations in the post-intervention survey, we

TABLE A22. Effect of the Progressive Gender Attitudes, Disaggregated by Bystander Education: Post-intervention Survey Sample

| | Progressive versus Regressive Message | | |
| | Did an individual offer help? | | |
	(1)	(2)	(3)
Progressive versus Regressive, Hijab (H6A)	−0.022	−0.022	0.265**
	(0.131)	(0.131)	(0.113)
High Education	0.029		
	(0.131)		
H6A × High Education	0.287*		
	(0.169)		
Constant	0.429***	0.429***	0.457***
	(0.098)	(0.098)	(0.086)
Sample Gender	Female	Female	Female
Sample Education	Full	Low	High
Observations	131	60	71
R^2	0.069	0.001	0.073

Note: *p < 0.1; **p < 0.05; ***p < 0.01.

collected information on the level of education for the bystanders, and created a dummy variable "high education" to denote individuals who passed the university entrance qualification exam (Abitur) or obtained bachelor's, master's, or doctoral degrees. We interacted (and also subsetted) this dummy with the treatment indicator for the progressive vs. regressive message for hijab confederates (column 1). We find that, as expected, women who are highly educated (and thus more likely to hold progressive views on gender) are significantly more likely to be responsive to the progressive vs. regressive message treatment than those who are not.

We also present results of the same analysis presented in table A22, weighted by the proportion of helpers and non-helpers in the experimental sample for H6A (progressive vs. regressive, hijab). The findings are reported in table A23. They do not substantively change the results reported in table A22.

Although we adjust the regression analysis in table A20 with the number of bystander fixed effects as well as bystander attribute fixed effects, some might still be concerned that the post-intervention survey is susceptible to differential attrition in responses across treatment conditions. If this were the case, any findings that utilize data collected through the post-intervention survey might be driven by differences in the characteristics of individuals by

TABLE A23. Effect of the Progressive Gender Attitudes, Disaggregated by Bystander Education: Post-intervention Survey Sample, Weighted by Proportion of Helpers and Non-helpers in the Experimental Sample

	Progressive versus Regressive Message		
	Did an individual offer help?		
	(1)	(2)	(3)
Progressive versus Regressive, Hijab (H6A)	−0.090	−0.090	0.196*
	(0.133)	(0.133)	(0.113)
High Education	0.029		
	(0.132)		
H6A × High Education	0.286*		
	(0.170)		
Constant	0.501***	0.501***	0.530***
	(0.100)	(0.100)	(0.086)
Sample Gender	Female	Female	Female
Sample Education	Full	Low	High
Observations	131	60	71

Note: *p < 0.1; **p < 0.05; ***p < 0.01.

treatment condition. In order to assuage this concern, we present results from a simple difference in means test on the survey respondents' characteristics across the progressive and regressive gender attitude conditions presented in table A20. The results are presented in table A24. Across all covariates that can likely be considered pretreatment, we have very strong balance across the progressive message vs. regressive message conditions; the t-test for each of the five covariates fail to reach statistical significance at conventional levels, and the magnitude of the differences are small. The joint F-statistic is also insigifnicant, with a p-value of 0.822. These results should alleviate much of the concern that the findings in table A20 are merely reflective of systematic differences in bystander characteristics among people who answered the post-intervention survey.

Effects Disaggregated by Former East vs West Germany

It is instructive to examine whether political context conditions the treatment effects in our field experiment, so we disaggregate the two main findings—(a) discrimination against hijab-wearing immigrants, and (b) the offsetting effect of the progressive gender attitude—by whether the iterations were conducted in states that fell in either former West or East Germany. Our intuition behind

TABLE A24. Lack of Evidence on Differential Response/Attrition in the Post-treatment Survey

	Treated Mean	Control Mean	Diff. in Means	T-Test p-Value
Progressive vs. Regressive Gender Attitude Comparison, Hijab Confederates Only				
Female	0.5609756	0.5263158	0.0346598	0.6645659
Self-reported Atheist	0.6951220	0.6710526	0.0240693	0.7472783
Self-reported Christian	0.3048780	0.3289474	−0.0240693	0.7472783
Wore Earphone/Headphone	0.0487805	0.0526316	−0.0038511	0.9129750
Perceived as Native	1.0000000	0.9868421	0.0131579	0.3205260

Joint F-Statistic: 0.3813   p-Value = 0.8217

why we expect that there might be some heterogeneity across the former West and East are discussed in some detail in other parts of the book. We expected that given the electoral support for the AfD in state and local elections in the former East, the discrimination effects against immigrant minorities would be significantly larger in the East than in the West.

We present the tests for the hijab vs. native comparison reported in the main text in tabular form in table A25. As predicted, we observe that the ATE estimate for the hijab vs. native comparison is larger in the iterations run in the former East (11.6%p) than those run in the former West (7%p), although the differences between the treatment effects are not statistically distinguishable. Some interesting patterns emerge when we disaggregate by the content of the message—progressive, neutral, regressive. The native hijab comparisons in which confederates signaled progressive gender attitudes are statistically indistinguishable from zero, meaning that once the hijab immigrant signaled their progressive outlook with regard to women, discrimination against them decreased in both the East and West. Differences between native and hijab conditions persist in most of the message conditions.

Although our intuition regarding the treatment effects for the progressive vs. regressive gender attitudes is less clear, we nonetheless disaggregate the effect of gender attitudes by whether iterations were run in the former West versus the East. Results are reported in table A26. Note that the offsetting effect of the progressive vs. regressive gender attitude we report in the main text was for the iterations with immigrant confederates wearing a hijab. We find that when we disaggregate the effects by former West vs. East, the effects are larger in the West by around 5 percentage points (12.5%p vs. 7.0%p).

TABLE A25. Discrimination Against Hijab Immigrants, Former West/East Germany

| | Hijab versus Native | | | | | | | |
| | Any help? | | | | | | | |
	(1)	(2)	(3)	(4)	(5)	(6)	(7)	(8)
Hijab vs. Native (H2), Pooled	−0.070** (0.032)	−0.116*** (0.043)						
H2, Progressive Message			−0.044 (0.052)	0.009 (0.074)				
H2, Neutral Message					−0.121** (0.059)	−0.142** (0.068)		
H2, Regressive Message							−0.043 (0.054)	−0.198** (0.081)
Constant	0.731*** (0.022)	0.823*** (0.030)	0.750*** (0.036)	0.781*** (0.052)	0.702*** (0.043)	0.863*** (0.047)	0.737*** (0.039)	0.818*** (0.060)
Region	West	East	West	East	West	East	West	East
Observations	833	393	292	126	260	141	281	126
R^2	0.006	0.019	0.002	0.0001	0.016	0.031	0.002	0.047

Note: *$p < 0.1$; **$p < 0.05$; ***$p < 0.01$.

TABLE A26. Progressive vs. Regressive Message Effects, Former West/East Germany

| | Progressive vs. Regressive Message | | | | | | | |
| | Any help? | | | | | | | |
	(1)	(2)	(3)	(4)	(5)	(6)	(7)	(8)
Prog vs. Reg (H6), Pooled	0.057* (0.032)	−0.001 (0.044)						
H6, Hijab			0.125** (0.058)	0.070 (0.076)				
H6, No Hijab					−0.003 (0.054)	0.010 (0.087)		
H6, Native							0.048 (0.054)	−0.082 (0.065)
Constant	0.667*** (0.023)	0.768*** (0.030)	0.581*** (0.041)	0.721*** (0.052)	0.716*** (0.036)	0.710*** (0.058)	0.702*** (0.040)	0.863*** (0.045)
Region	West	East	West	East	West	East	West	East
Observations	836	379	272	130	284	112	280	137
R^2	0.004	0.00000	0.017	0.007	0.00001	0.0001	0.003	0.012

Note: * $p < 0.1$; ** $p < 0.05$; *** $p < 0.01$.

Overall, we find suggestive evidence that political/geographic context may condition the treatment effects. Exploring regional differences can be helpful in adjudicating among rival mechanisms underlying our results. For example, one might conjecture that the progressive treatment exposes bystanders not only to ideas about gender norms, but also about the confederate's work ethic. A "work ethic" interpretation of our treatment would be inconsistent with the gender differences in outcomes we have observed (we would have expected equally strong effects among men under such an interpretation of the treatment), and we believe that women who choose to work at home could also have a strong work ethic. Nonetheless, we can explore regional differences in outcomes to think more about this question. To the extent that female labor market participation was historically larger in the East due to legacies of the Communist system, these results also suggest that differences in work ethic or participation in the formal economy cannot drive the results that we report in the paper (since such differences would have suggested larger effects in the East vs the West). There are other differences between East and West, including significant differences in the density of immigrant populations, which results in more frequent and more varied forms of intergroup contact between natives and immigrants in the West. These differences could be relevant to our findings. While we cannot make definitive causal claims regarding the East vs. West differences, we believe that these analyses open up the opportunity for future work to probe precisely why these differences may be observed.

Potential Behavioral Spillovers

When conducting individual-level analyses of helping behavior, it may be of concern to some that bystanders might adjust their behavior in accordance with the behavior of others. However, in table A27, we present the mean individual-level assistance rate by the size and gender composition of the bystander pool at the iteration level. In general, we observe that as the number of bystanders (or size of the bystander pool) at the iteration level increases, the mean rate of assistance decreases; this is consistent with the notion that a sole bystander might feel highly pressured to help our confederate in collecting her possessions since there is no one else near by who is offering assistance. The decrease in the assistance rates seems to be relatively monotonic, as seen in the *cross-row* comparisons. Second, we also observe that there are no clear patterns of heterogeneity in individual assistance rates based on the gender composition of the bystander pool, as seen in the *cross-column* comparisons.

TABLE A27. Help Rates by Bystander Gender Composition

	Help Rates					
	Number of Women Bystanders in Iteration					
	n(women) = 5	n(women) = 4	n(women) = 3	n(women) = 2	n(women) = 1	n(women) = 0
Help Rate n(bystander) = 5	0.400 (0.216)	0.367 (0.069)	0.178 (0.070)	0.167 (0.061)	0.100 (0.100)	0.300 (0.300)
Observations	20	60	45	30	10	10
Help Rate n(bystander) = 4		0.429 (0.100)	0.271 (0.037)	0.372 (0.040)	0.321 (0.130)	0.333 (0.083)
Observations		56	140	180	28	12
Help Rate n(bystander) = 3			0.440 (0.046)	0.384 (0.028)	0.430 (0.032)	0.432 (0.061)
Observations			159	375	270	81
Help Rate n(bystander) = 2				0.497 (0.027)	0.551 (0.020)	0.629 (0.035)
Observations				394	742	194
Help Rate n(bystander) = 1					0.691 (0.024)	0.725 (0.024)
Observations					369	342

TABLE A28. Gender Spillovers (Iteration Level)

	Help Rates	
	Male Bystander Help	Female Bystander Help
	(1)	(2)
Hijab vs. Native (H2A)	−0.064	0.006
	(0.089)	(0.074)
Female Bystander Present	−0.404***	
	(0.070)	
H2A × Female Present	0.019	
	(0.103)	
Male Bystander Present		−0.424***
		(0.064)
H2A × Male Present		0.080
		(0.094)
Constant	0.738***	0.706***
	(0.059)	(0.050)
Observations	418	418

Note: *p < 0.1; **p < 0.05; ***p < 0.01.

In table A28, we address the concern that differential help rates to hijabed (Muslim) women might be driven by male bystanders who are unsure if their helpful intervention would be welcomed by Muslim women. If this logic were to hold, we would expect that male bystanders would hold off on helping a Muslim woman in the presence of female bystanders, as they feel that women would be less threatening.

In order to probe this intuition, we created a set of alternative outcomes that codes (at the iteration level) whether any male bystander offered assistance and whether any female bystander offered assistance. We also created a dummy variable that takes on a value of "1" when there is a woman bystander present at the scene. We ran a regression in which we interact this dummy variable with the treatment indicator for hijab vs. native comparisons. In column (1) we examine whether the presence of a female bystander affects the helping behavior of male bystanders with respect to treatment. Although we observe that men are less likely to assist both hijabed and native women when there is a female bystander present *overall*—already made clear in table A27—there is no evidence of heterogeneous effects; the presence of the female bystander does not moderate the differential help rates between hijabed (Muslim) vs. native confederates. The same applies for female bystander behavior in the presence of male bystanders, presented in column (2).

Chapter 7

This section provides additional results referenced in the main text of chapter 7.

Feeling thermometer
On a scale from 0–100, how negative/unfriendly (0) or positive/friendly (100) do you feel toward this woman?

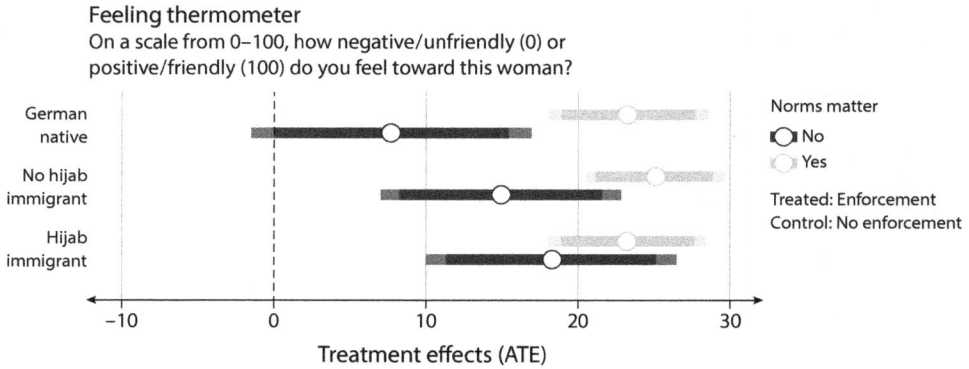

FIGURE A.10. Heterogeneous effects: Norm enforcement effects on generalized affect

How similar do you think the confederate is to upstanding citizens?

No hijab immigrant

Hijab immigrant

I would sanction jaywalkers

No
Yes

Treated: Enforcement
Control: No enforcement

−1.0 Less similar   0.0   1.0 More similar

Treatment effects (ATE)

(a) Recategorization

How typical do you think the confederate is of Muslims in Germany?

No hijab immigrant

Hijab immigrant

I would sanction jaywalkers

No
Yes

Treated: Enforcement
Control: No enforcement

−1.0 Less similar   0.0   1.0 More similar

Treatment effects (ATE)

(b) Decategorization

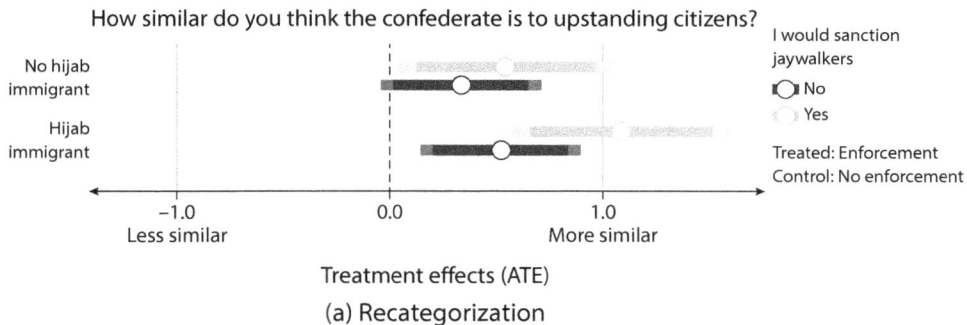

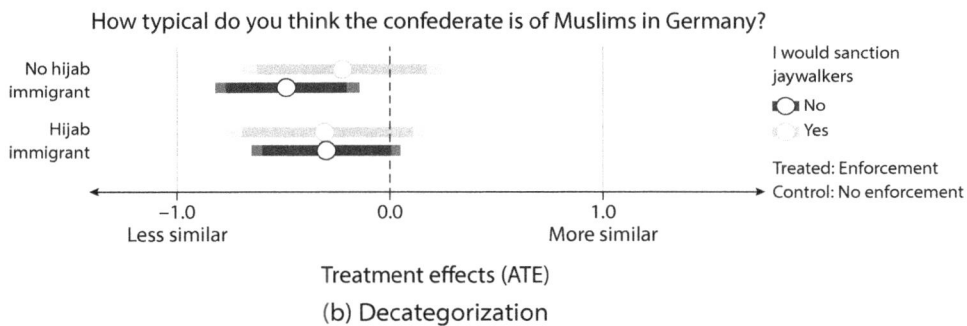

FIGURE A.11. Heterogeneous effects: Norm importance 3

Notes: Heterogeneity in treatment effects disaggregated based on survey item that asks respondents whether they agree with the statement: "I would do something if I saw someone jaywalking in front of a child."

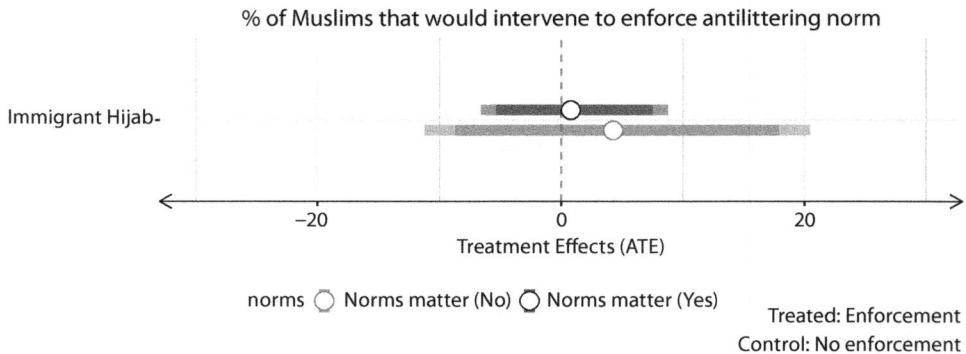

(a)

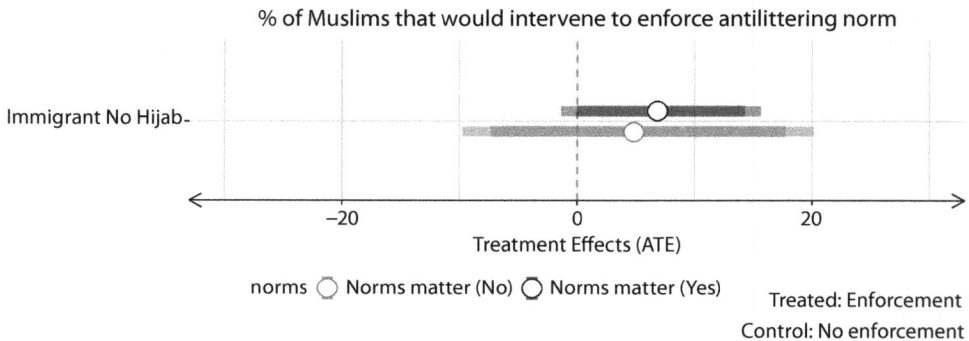

(b)

FIGURE A.12. Perceptions on the likelihood that Muslim will intervence to stop
norm violation

Notes: Heterogeneity in treatment effects disaggregated based on survey item that asks
respondents whether they agree with the statement: "I believe rules, norms, and customs are
necessary for social coexistence." Dots represent the estimated average treatment effects, with
the darker and lighter bars denoting 90% and 95% confidence intervals, respectively.

BIBLIOGRAPHY

[1]   L. Aarøe, M. B. Petersen, and K. Arceneaux. "The Behavioral Immune System Shapes Political Intuitions: Why and How Individual Differences in Disgust Sensitivity Underlie Opposition to Immigration." In: *American Political Science Review* 111.2 (2017), pp. 277–294.

[2]   Aala Abdelgadir and Vasiliki Fouka. "Secular Policies and Muslim Integration in the West: The Effects of the French Headscarf Ban." In: *American Political Science Review* 114.3 (2020), pp. 707–723.

[3]   Arash Abizadeh. "Was Fichte an Ethnic Nationalist? On Cultural Nationalism and Its Double." In: *History of Political Thought* XXVI.2 (2005), pp. 334–359.

[4]   F. E. Aboud, R. Clement, and D. M. Taylor. "Evaluational Reactions to Discrepancies Between Social Class and Language." In: *Sociometry* 37 (1974), pp. 239–250.

[5]   Marisa Abrajano and Zoltan L. Hajnal. *White Backlash: Immigration, Race, and American Politics*. Princeton University Press, 2015.

[6]   D. Abrams et al. "Knowing What to Think by Knowing Who You Are: Self-categorization and the Nature of Norm Formation, Conformity and Group Polarization." In: *British Journal of Social Psychology* 29 (1990), pp. 97–119.

[7]   Claire L. Adida, David D. Laitin, and Marie-Anne Valfort. "Identifying Barriers to Muslim Integration in France." In: *Proceedings of the National Academy of Sciences* 107.52 (2010), pp. 22384–22390.

[8]   Claire L. Adida, David D. Laitin, and Marie-Anne Valfort. *Why Muslim Integration Fails in Christian-heritage Societies*. Harvard University Press, 2016.

[9]   Claire L. Adida, Adelina Lo, and Melina R. Platas. "Americans Preferred Syrian Refugees Who Are Female, English-speaking, and Christian on the Eve of Donald Trump's Election." In: *PLOS ONE* 14.10 (2019), e0222504.

[10]   Akbar Ahmed. *Journey into Europe: Islam, Immigration, and Identity*. Brookings Press, 2018.

[11]   Dennis J. Aigner and Glen G. Cain. "Statistical Theories of Discrimination in Labor Markets." In: *Industrial and Labor Relations Review* 30.2 (1977), pp. 175–187.

[12]   George A. Akerlof and Rachel E. Kranton. "Economics and Identity." In: *Quarterly Journal of Economics* 115.3 (2000), pp. 715–753.

[13]   Alia Al-Saji. "The Racialization of Muslim Veils: A Philosophical Analysis." In: *Philosophy and Social Criticism* 36.8 (2010), pp. 875–902.

[14]   Alexis Alabastro et al. "Intergroup Bias and Perceived Similarity: Effects of Successes and Failures on Support for In- and Outgroup Political Leaders." In: *Group Processes and Intergroup Relations* 16.1 (2013), pp. 58–67.

[15]   A. Alesina, R. Baqir, and W. Easterly. "Public Goods and Ethnic Divisions." In: *Quarterly Journal of Economics* 114.4 (1999), pp. 1243–1284.

[16]   A. Alesina and Eliana LaFerra. "Who Trusts Others?" In: *Journal of Public Economics* 85.2 (2002), pp. 207–234.

[17]   Alberto Alesina and Enrico Spolaore. *The Size of Nations*. Cambridge, MA: MIT Press, 2005.

[18]   V. L. Allen and D. A. Wilder. "Categorization, Belief-similarity and Intergroup Discrimination." In: *Journal of Personality and Social Psychology* 32 (1975), pp. 971–977.

[19]   G. W. Allport and H. Cantril. "Judging Personality from Voice." In: *Journal of Social Psychology* 5 (1934), pp. 37–55.

[20]   Gordon Willard Allport. *The Nature of Prejudice*. Cambridge, MA: Addison-Wesley, 1954.

[21]   Gordon Willard Allport. *The Nature of Prejudice*. Basic Books, 1979.

[22]   Ala' Alrababa'h et al. "Attitudes Toward Migrants in a Highly Impacted Economy: Evidence from the Syrian Refugee Crisis in Jordan." In: *Comparative Political Studies* 54.1 (2021), pp. 33–76.

[23]   Benedict Anderson. *Imagined Communities: Reflections on the Origin and Spread of Nationalism*. Verso, 1983.

[24]   Kate Antonovics and Brian G. Knight. "A New Look at Racial Profiling: Evidence from the Boston Police Department." In: *Review of Economics and Statistics* 91.1 (2009), pp. 163–177.

[25]   R. L. Archer et al. "The Role of Dispositional Empathy and Social Evaluation in the Empathic Mediation of Helping." In: *Journal of Personality and Social Psychology* 46 (1981), pp. 786–796.

[26]   Scott Atran and Jeremy Ginges. "Religious and Sacred Imperatives in Human Conflict." In: *Science* 336.6083 (2012), pp. 855–857.

[27]   Peter Auer. "Türkenslang: Ein jugendsprachlicher Ethnolekt des Deutschen und seine Transformationen." In: *Spracherwerb und Lebensalter*. Ed. by Annelies Häcki Buhofer. Tübingen/Basel: Francke, 2003, pp. 255–264.

[28]   Andy Baker, Barry Ames, and Lúcio Rennó. *Persuasive Peers: Social Communication and Voting in Latin America*. Princeton, NJ: Princeton University Press, 2020.

[29]   Loukas Balafoutas, Nikos Nikiforakis, and Bettina Rockenbach. "Altruistic Punishment Does Not Increase with the Severity of Norm Violations in the Field." In: *Nature Communications* (2016), pp. 1–6.

[30]   Loukas Balafoutas, Nikos Nikiforakis, and Bettina Rockenbach. "Direct and Indirect Punishment among Strangers in the Field." In: *PNAS* 111.45 (2014), pp. 15924–15927.

[31]   Katherine Baldwin and John D. Huber. "Economic versus Cultural Differences: Forms of Ethnic Diversity and Public Goods Provision." In: *American Political Science Review* 104.4 (2010), pp. 644–662.

[32]   Kirk Bansak, Jens Hainmueller, and Dominik Hangartner. "How Economic, Humanitarian, and Religious Concerns Shape European Attitudes Toward Asylum Seekers." In: *Science* (2016), aag2147.

[33] Gary S. Becker. *The Economics of Discrimination*. Chicago, IL: University of Chicago Press, 1957.

[34] Seyla Benhabib. *The Claims of Culture: Equality and Difference in the Global Era*. Princeton University Press, 2002.

[35] Seyla Benhabib. "The Return of Political Theology: The Scarf Affair in Comparative Constitutional Perspective in France, Germany and Turkey." In: *Philosophy and Social Criticism* 36.3-4 (2010), pp. 451–471.

[36] P. L. Benson, S. A. Karabenick, and R. M. Lerner. "Pretty Pleases: The Effects of Physical Attractiveness, Race, and Sex on Receiving Help." In: *Journal of Experimental Social Psychology* 12 (1976), pp. 409–415.

[37] Roger L. Berger, Jason C. Hsu, et al. "Bioequivalence Trials, Intersection-union Tests and Equivalence Confidence Sets." In: *Statistical Science* 11.4 (1996), pp. 283–319.

[38] Adam J. Berinsky, Gregory A. Huber, and Gabriel S. Lenz. "Evaluating Online Labor Markets for Experimental Research: Amazon.com's Mechanical Turk." In: *Political Analysis* 20.3 (2012), pp. 351–368.

[39] Helen Bernhard, Urs Fischbacher, and Ernst Fehr. "Parochial Altruism in Humans." In: *Nature* 442.7105 (2006), p. 912.

[40] Marianne Bertrand, Dolly Chugh, and Sendhil Mullainathan. "Implicit Discrimination." In: *American Economic Review Papers and Proceedings* 95.2 (2005), pp. 94–98.

[41] Marianne Bertrand and Esther Duflo. "Field Experiments on Discrimination." NBER Working Paper 22014. February 2016. http://www.nber.org/papers/w22014.

[42] Marianne Bertrand and Sendhil Mullainathan. "Are Emily and Greg More Employable than Lakisha and Jamal? A Field Experiment on Labor Market Discrimination." In: *American Economic Review* 94.4 (2004), pp. 991–1013.

[43] Cristina Bicchieri. *Norms in the Wild: How to Diagnose, Measure, and Change Social Norms*. Oxford: Oxford University Press, 2017.

[44] Cristina Bicchieri. *The Grammar of Society: The Nature and Dynamics of Social Norms*. Cambridge: Cambridge University Press, 2006.

[45] L. Bickman and M. Kamzan. "The Effect of Race and Need on Helping Behavior." In: *Journal of Social Psychology* 89 (1973), pp. 73–77.

[46] Michael G. Billig and Henri Tajfel. "Social Categorization and Similarity in Intergroup Behaviour." In: *European Journal of Social Psychology* 3 (1973), pp. 27–52.

[47] Graeme Blair, Winston Chou, and Kosuke Imai. "List Experiments with Measurement Error." In: *Political Analysis* 27.4 (2019), pp. 455–480.

[48] Emory Stephen Bogardus. "A Social Distance Scale." In: *Sociology & Social Research* (1933).

[49] Robert Böhm. "Intuitive Participation in Aggressive Intergroup Conflict: Evidence of Weak versus Strong Parochial Altruism." In: *Frontiers of Psychology* 7.1535 (2016), p. 1525.

[50] C. M. Bonam, H. B. Bergsieker, and J. L. Eberhardt. "Polluting Black Space." In: *Journal of Experimental Psychology: General* 145.11 (2016), pp. 1561–1582.

[51] Gary Bornstein. "Intergroup Conflict: Individual, Group, and Collective Interests." In: *Personality and Social Psychology Review* 7.2 (2003), pp. 129–145.

[52]   R. Y. Bourhis, H. Giles, and H. Tajfel. "Language as a Determinant of Welsh Identity."
       In: *European Journal of Social Psychology* 3 (1973), pp. 447–460.

[53]   Richard Y. Bourhis. "Quebecois Francophone Attitudes Toward the Hihab and
       Niqab: Implications for the 'Chartes des valeurs Quebequioses.'" In: *Canadian Di-
       versity* 10.3 (2013).

[54]   Richard Y. Bourhis and Andre Gagnon. "Social Orientations in the Minimal Group
       Paradigm." In: *Intergroup Processes: Blackwell Handbook in Social Psychology*. Ed. by R.
       Brown and S. Gaertner. Oxford: Blackwell, 2001, pp. 89–111.

[55]   Samuel Bowles. "Did Warfare among Ancestral Hunter-gatherers Affect the Evolution
       of Human Social Behaviors?" In: *Science* 324.5932 (2009), pp. 1293–1298.

[56]   Samuel Bowles. "Group Competition, Reproductive Leveling, and the Evolution of
       Human Altruism." In: *Science* 314.8 (December 2006), pp. 1569–1572.

[57]   Samuel Bowles. "Warriors, Levelers, and the Role of Conflict in Human Social Evo-
       lution." In: *Science* 336.8 (December 2012), pp. 876–879.

[58]   Samuel Bowles and Jung-Kyoo Choi. "The Coevolution of Parochial Altruism and
       War." In: *Science* 318.26 (October 2007), pp. 636–640.

[59]   Ted Brader, Nicholas A. Valentino, and Elizabeth Suhay. "What Triggers Public
       Opposition to Immigration? Anxiety, Group Cues, and Immigration Threat." In:
       American Journal of Political Science 52.4 (2008), pp. 959–978.

[60]   Suzanne Brenner. "Private Moralities in the Public Sphere: Democratization, Islam,
       and Gender in Indonesia." In: *American Anthropologist* 113.3 (2011), pp. 478–490.

[61]   M. B. Brewer and M. Silver. "Ingroup Bias as a Function of Task Characteristics." In:
       European Journal of Social Psychology 8 (1973), pp. 393–400.

[62]   Marilynn Brewer. "A Dual Process Model of Impression Formation." In: *Advances
       in Social Cognition*. Ed. by K. T. Srull and R. S. Wyer. Hillsdale, NJ: Erlbaum, 1988,
       pp. 1–36.

[63]   Marilynn Brewer and Roderick Kramer. "The Psychology of Intergroup Attitudes and
       Behavior." In: *Annual Review of Psychology* 36 (1985), pp. 219–43.

[64]   Marilynn B. Brewer. "In-Group Bias in the Minimal Group Situation: A Cognitive-
       Motivational Analysis." In: *Psychological Bulletin* 86 (1979), pp. 307–324.

[65]   Marilynn B. Brewer. "The Psychology of Prejudice: Ingroup Love and Outgroup
       Hate?" In: *Journal of Social Issues* 55.3 (1999), pp. 429–444.

[66]   Marilynn B. Brewer. "When Contact Is Not Enough: Social Identity and Intergroup
       Cooperation." In: *International Journal of Intercultural Relations* 20.3/4 (1996), pp. 291–
       303.

[67]   M. B. Brewer. "The Social Self: On Being the Same and Different at the Same Time."
       In: *Personality and Social Psychology Bulletin* 17 (1991), pp. 475–482.

[68]   Rupert J. Brown and Gillian Wade. "Superordinate Goals and Intergroup
       Behavior: The Effect of Role Ambiguity and Status on Intergroup Attitudes
       and Task Performance." In: *European Journal of Social Psychology* 17.2 (1987), pp. 131–
       142.

[69]   Statistisches Bundesamt. *Bevölkerung und Erwerbstätigkeit: Bevölkerung mit Migration-
       shintergrund—Ergebnisse des Mikrozensus 2017*. Statistisches Bundesamt: Fachserie 1,
       Reihe 2.2, 2018, pp. 34–58.

[70]   Nancy Burns et al. "The Politics of Gender." In: *New Directions in Public Opinion*. Ed. by Adam Berinsky. New York: Taylor and Francis, 2015, pp. 124–45.

[71]   Leonardo Bursztyn, Alessandra L. González, and David Yanagizawa-Drott. "Misperceived Social Norms: Women Working Outside the Home in Saudi Arabia." In: *American Economic Review* 110.10 (2020), pp. 2997–3029.

[72]   Christopher Caldwell. *Reflections on the Revolution in Europe: Immigration, Islam, and the West*. Anchor Books, 2009.

[73]   Lars-Erik Cederman and Luc Girardin. "Beyond Fractionalization: Mapping Ethnicity onto Nationalist Insurgencies." In: *American Political Science Review* 101.1 (2007), pp. 173–185.

[74]   Michel de Certau. *The Practice of Everyday Life*. University of California Press, 1984.

[75]   Kanchan Chandra. "What is Ethnicity and Does It Matter?" In: *Annual Review of Political Science* 9 (2006), pp. 397–424.

[76]   Kanchan Chandra and Steven Wilkinson. "Measuring the Effect of Ethnicity." In: *Comparative Political Studies* 41.4–5 (2008), pp. 515–563.

[77]   Volha Charnysh, Christopher Lucas, and Prerna Singh. "The Ties that Bind: National Identity Salience and Pro-Social Behavior Toward the Ethnic Other." In: *Comparative Political Studies* 48.3 (2015), pp. 267–300.

[78]   Yan Chen and Sherry Xin Li. "Group Identity and Social Preferences." In: *American Economic Review* 99.1 (2009), pp. 431–457.

[79]   Donghyun Danny Choi, Mathias Poertner, and Nicholas Sambanis. "Linguistic Assimilation Does Not Reduce Discrimination Against Immigrants." In: *Journal of Experimental Political Science* 8.3 (2021), pp. 235–246.

[80]   Donghyun Danny Choi, Mathias Poertner, and Nicholas Sambanis. "Parochialism, Social Norms, and Discrimination Against Immigrants." In: *Proceedings of the National Academy of Science* 116.33 (2019), pp. 16274–16279.

[81]   Donghyun Danny Choi, Mathias Poertner, and Nicholas Sambanis. "Temperature and Outgroup Discrimination." In: *Political Science Research and Methods* (forthcoming a).

[82]   Donghyun Danny Choi, Mathias Poertner, and Nicholas Sambanis. "The Hijab Penalty: Feminist Backlash to Muslim Immigrants." In: *American Journal of Political Science* (forthcoming b).

[83]   R. B. Cialdini and D. J. Baumann. "Littering: A New Unobtrusive Measure of Attitude." In: *Social Psychology Quarterly* 44 (1981), pp. 254–259.

[84]   R. B. Cialdini, R. R. Reno, and C. A. Kallgren. "A Focus Theory of Normative Conduct: Recycling the Concept of Norms to Reduce Littering in Public Places." In: *Journal of Personality and Social Psychology* 58.6 (1990), pp. 1015–1026.

[85]   R. B. Cialdini et al. "Empathy-based Helping: Is It Selflessly or Selfishly Motivated?" In: *Journal of Personality and Social Psychology* 52 (1987), pp. 749–758.

[86]   Mina Cikara and Jay van Bavel. "The Neuroscience of Intergroup Relations: An Integrative Review." In: *Perspectives on Psychological Science* 9.3 (2014), pp. 245–274.

[87]   Jack Citrin et al. "Testing Huntington." In: *Perspectives on Politics* 5.1 (2007), pp. 31–48.

[88]   R. D. Clark. "Effects of Sex and Race on Helping Behavior in a Nonreactive Setting." In: *Representative Research in Social Psychology* 5 (1974), pp. 1–6.

[89]   Marcel Coenders and Peer Scheepers. "The Effect of Education on Nationalism and Ethnic Exclusionism: An International Comparison." In: *Political Psychology* 24.2 (2003), pp. 313–343.

[90]   Elizabeth Adell Cook and Clyde Wilcox. "Feminism and the Gender Gap—Second Look." In: *Journal of Politics* 3.4 (1991), pp. 111–122.

[91]   Lewis A. Coser. *The Functions of Social Conflict.* New York: Free Press, 1956.

[92]   Mathew J. Creighton and Amaney Jamal. "Does Islam Play a Role in Anti-immigrant Sentiment? An Experimental Approach." In: *Social Science Research* 53 (2015), pp. 89–103.

[93]   I. Cuellar et al. "Ethnic Identity and Acculturation in a Young Adult Mexican-origin Population." In: *Journal of Community Psychology* 25.6 (1997), pp. 535–549.

[94]   Ralf Dahrendorf. *Class and Class Conflict in Industrial Society.* Stanford, CA: Stanford University Press, 1959.

[95]   Rafaela M. Dancygier. *Dilemmas of Inclusion: Muslims in European Politics.* Princeton University Press, 2017.

[96]   R. M. Dancygier and M. J. Donnelly. "Sectoral Economies, Economic Contexts, and Attitudes Toward Immigration." In: *Journal of Politics* 75 (2013), pp. 17–35.

[97]   Keith A. Darden. *Economic Liberalism and Its Rivals: The Formation of International Institutions Among the Post-Soviet States.* Cambridge University Press, 2009.

[98]   Carsten K. W. De Dreu, D. Berno Dussel, and Femke S. Ten Velden. "In Intergroup Conflict, Self-sacrifice Is Stronger Among Pro-social Individuals, and Parochial Altruism Emerges Especially Among Cognitively Taxed Individuals." In: *Frontiers of Psychology* 6.572 (2015), pp. 1–9.

[99]   Carsten K. W. De Dreu et al. "The Neuropeptide Oxytocin Regulates Parochial Altruism in Intergroup Conflict Among Humans." In: *Science* 328.5984 (2010), pp. 1408–1411.

[100]   Karl W. Deutsch. *Nationalism and Social Communication, An Inquiry into the Foundations of Nationality.* MIT Press, 1953.

[101]   Karl W. Deutsch. "Social Mobilization and Political Development." In: *American Political Science Review* 55.3 (1961), pp. 493–514.

[102]   Thierry Devos and Mahzarin R. Banaji. "American = White?" In: *Journal of Personality and Social Psychology* 88.3 (2005), pp. 447–466.

[103]   Peter T. Dinesen and Kim Sønderskov. "Ethnic Diversity and Social Trust: Evidence from the Micro-Context." In: *American Sociological Review* 80.3 (2015), pp. 550–573.

[104]   Peter T. Dinesen and Kim M. Sønderskov. "Ethnic Diversity and Social Trust: A Critical Review of the Literature and Suggestions for a Research Agenda." In: *The Oxford Handbook on Social and Political Trust.* Ed. by Eric Uslaner. New York: Oxford University Press, 2018, pp. 175–204.

[105]   William Dodd. "Under Pressure? The Anglicisms Debate in Contemporary Germany as a Barometer of German National Identity Today." In: *German Politics and Society* 114.33 (2015), pp. 58–68.

[106]   J. F. Dovidio et al. *The Social Psychology of Prosocial Behavior.* Marwah, NJ: Erlbaum, 2006.

[107] John F. Dovidio et al. "Recategorization and Prosocial Behavior." In: *The Psychology of Prosocial Behavior: Group Processes, Intergroup Relations, and Helping.* Ed. by Stefan Stürmer and Mark Snyder. Hoboken, NJ: Wiley-Blackwell, 2010, pp. 289–309.

[108] James R. Dow. "Germany." In: *Handbook of Language and Ethnic Identity.* Ed. by Joshua A. Fishman. New York: Oxford University Press, 1999, pp. 286–299.

[109] Julie A. Dowling, Christopher G. Ellison, and David L. Leal. "Who Doesn't Value English? Debunking Myths about Mexican Immigrants' Attitudes toward the English Language." In: *Social Science Quarterly* 93.2 (2012), pp. 356–378.

[110] Emma E. Dresler-Hawke and James H. Liu. "Collective Shame and the Positioning of German National Identity." In: *Psicología Política* 32 (2006), pp. 131–153.

[111] Thad Dunning et al. "Voter Information Campaigns and Political Accountability: Cumulative Findings from a Preregistered Meta-analysis of Coordinated Trials." In: *Science Advances* 5.7 (2019), eaaw2612.

[112] Charles Efferson, Rafael Lalive, and Ernst Fehr. "The Coevolution of Cultural Groups and Ingroup Favoritism." In: *Science* 321.5897 (2008), pp. 1844–1849.

[113] Patricia Ehrkamp. "'We Turks Are No Germans': Assimilation Discourses and the Dialectical Construction of Identities in Germany." In: *Environment and Planning* A.38 (2006), pp. 1673–1692.

[114] Ben Eifert, Edward Miguel, and Daniel N. Posner. "Political Competition and Ethnic Identification in Africa." In: *American Journal of Political Science* 54.2 (2010), pp. 494–510.

[115] C. M. Elwell, R. J. Brown, and D. R. Rutter. "Effects of Accent and Visual Information on Impression Formation." In: *Journal of Language and Social Psychology* 3 (1984), pp. 297–299.

[116] Ryan D. Enos. "Causal Effect of Intergroup Contact on Exclusionary Attitudes." In: *Proceedings of the National Academy of Sciences* 111.10 (2014), pp. 3699–3704.

[117] ESS. *ESS Round 1: European Social Survey Round 1 Data. Data file edition 6.6. NSD— Norwegian Centre for Research Data, Norway—Data Archive and distributor of ESS data for ESS ERIC. doi:10.21338/NSD-ESS1-2002, retrieved: 06/08/2020.* doi:10.21338/NSD-ESS1-2002. Bergen, 2002. DOI: doi:10.21338/NSD-ESS1-2002.

[118] ESS. *ESS Round 2: European Social Survey Round 2 Data. Data file edition 3.6. NSD— Norwegian Centre for Research Data, Norway—Data Archive and distributor of ESS data for ESS ERIC. doi:10.21338/NSD-ESS2-2004, retrieved: 06/08/2020.* doi:10.21338/NSD-ESS2-2004. Bergen, 2004. DOI: doi:10.21338/NSD-ESS2-2004.

[119] ESS. *ESS Round 3: European Social Survey Round 3 Data. Data file edition 3.7. NSD— Norwegian Centre for Research Data, Norway—Data Archive and distributor of ESS data for ESS ERIC. doi:10.21338/NSD-ESS3-2006, retrieved: 06/08/2020.* doi:10.21338/NSD-ESS3-2006. Bergen, 2006. DOI: doi:10.21338/NSD-ESS3-2006.

[120] ESS. *ESS Round 4: European Social Survey Round 4 Data. Data file edition 4.5. NSD— Norwegian Centre for Research Data, Norway—Data Archive and distributor of ESS data for ESS ERIC. doi:10.21338/NSD-ESS4-2008, retrieved: 06/08/2020.* doi:10.21338/NSD-ESS4-2008. Bergen, 2008. DOI: doi:10.21338/NSD-ESS4-2008.

[121] ESS. *ESS Round 5: European Social Survey Round 5 Data. Data file edition 3.4. NSD— Norwegian Centre for Research Data, Norway—Data Archive and distributor of ESS data*

for ESS ERIC. doi:10.21338/NSD-ESS5-2010, retrieved: 06/08/2020. doi:10.21338/NSD-ESS5-2010. Bergen, 2010. DOI: doi:10.21338/NSD-ESS5-2010.

[122]   ESS. *ESS Round 6: European Social Survey Round 6 Data. Data file edition 2.4. NSD— Norwegian Centre for Research Data, Norway—Data Archive and distributor of ESS data for ESS ERIC. doi:10.21338/NSD-ESS6-2012, retrieved: 06/08/2020.* doi:10.21338/NSD-ESS6-2012. Bergen, 2012. DOI: doi:10.21338/NSD-ESS6-2012.

[123]   ESS. *ESS Round 7: European Social Survey Round 7 Data. Data file edition 2.2. NSD— Norwegian Centre for Research Data, Norway—Data Archive and distributor of ESS data for ESS ERIC. doi:10.21338/NSD-ESS7-2014, retrieved: 06/08/2020.* doi:10.21338/NSD-ESS7-2014. Bergen, 2014. DOI: doi:10.21338/NSD-ESS7-2014.

[124]   ESS. *ESS Round 8: European Social Survey Round 8 Data. Data file edition 2.1. NSD— Norwegian Centre for Research Data, Norway—Data Archive and distributor of ESS data for ESS ERIC. doi:10.21338/NSD-ESS8-2016, retrieved: 06/08/2020.* doi:10.21338/NSD-ESS8-2016. Bergen, 2016. DOI: doi:10.21338/NSD-ESS8-2016.

[125]   ESS. *ESS Round 9: European Social Survey Round 9 Data. Data file edition 2.0. NSD— Norwegian Centre for Research Data, Norway—Data Archive and distributor of ESS data for ESS ERIC. doi:10.21338/NSD-ESS9-2018, retrieved: 06/08/2020.* doi:10.21338/NSD-ESS9-2018. Bergen, 2018. DOI: doi:10.21338/NSD-ESS9-2018.

[126]   Joan Esteban and Debraj Ray. "Linking Conflict to Inequality and Polarization." In: *American Economic Review* 101.4 (2011), pp. 1345–1374.

[127]   Jim A. C. Everett, Nadira S. Faber, and Molly Crockett. "Preferences and Beliefs in Ingroup Favoritism." In: *Frontiers in Behavioral Neuroscience* 9 (2015), p. 15.

[128]   Thomas Faist. "How to Define a Foreigner? The Symbolic Politics of Immigration in German Partisan Discourse, 1978–1992." In: *West European Politics* 17.2 (1994), pp. 50–71.

[129]   Frantz Fanon. *Black Skin, White Masks.* New York: Grove Press, 2008[1952].

[130]   James Fearon and David Laitin. "Violence and the Social Construction of Ethnic Identity." In: *International Organization* 54.4 (2000), pp. 845–877.

[131]   James D. Fearon. "Ethnic and Cultural Diversity by Country." In: *Journal of Economic Growth* 8.2 (2003), pp. 195–222.

[132]   Martha Finnemore. *National Interests in International Society.* Cornell University Press, 1996.

[133]   Martha Finnemore and Kathryn Sikkink. "International Norm Dynamics and Political Change." In: *International Organization* 52.4 (1998), pp. 887–918.

[134]   Susan T. Fiske. "Stereotyping, Prejudice, and Discrimination." In: *The Handbook of Social Psychology* 2 (1998), pp. 357–411.

[135]   Michael Fix and Raymond J. Struyk editors. *Clear and Convincing Evidence: Measurement of Discrimination in America.* Washington, DC: Urban Institute Press, 1993.

[136]   John H. Fleming et al. "Migrant Acceptance Index: A Global Examination of the Relationship Between Interpersonal Contact and Attitudes Toward Migrants." In: *Border Crossing* 8.1 (2018), pp. 103–132.

[137]   Christina M. Fong and Erzo F. P. Luttmer. "What Determines Giving to Hurricane Katrina Victims? Experimental Evidence on Racial Group Loyalty." In: *American Economic Journal: Applied Economics* 1.2 (2009), pp. 64–87.

[138] Ulrike Freywald et al. "Kiezdeutsch as a Multiethnolect." In: *Panethnic Styles of Speaking in European Metropolitan Cities*. Ed. by Frederike Kern and Margret Selting. Amsterdam/Philadelphia: John Benjamins Publishing, 2011, pp. 45–74.

[139] S. L. Gaertner and L. Bickman. "Effects of Race on the Elicitation of Helping Behavior: The Wrong Number Technique." In: *Journal of Personality and Social Psychology* 20 (1971), pp. 218–222.

[140] S. L. Gaertner and J. F. Dovidio. "The Aversive Form of Racism." In: *Prejudice, Discrimination, and Racism*. Ed. by S. L. Gaertner and J. F. Dovidio. Orlando, FL: Academic Press, 1986, pp. 61–90.

[141] S. L. Gaertner et al. "The Contact Hypothesis: The Role of a Common Ingroup Identity on Reducing Intergroup Bias Among Majority and Minority Group Members." In: *What's Social about Social Cognition: Research on Socially Shared Cognition in Small Groups*. Ed. by J. L. Nye and A. M. Bower. Thousand Oaks, CA: Sage, 1996, pp. 230–260.

[142] Samuel L. Gaertner and John F. Dovidio. *Reducing Intergroup Bias: The Common Ingroup Identity Model*. Psychology Press, 2000.

[143] Adam D. Galinsky and Gordon B. Moskowitz. "Perspective-taking: Decreasing Stereotype Expression, Stereotype Accessibility, and In-Group Favoritism." In: *Journal of Personality and Social Psychology* 78.4 (2000), pp. 708–724.

[144] Andreas Gardt. "Das Fremde und das Eigene. Versuch einer Systematik des Fremdwortbegriffs in der deutschen Sprachgeschichte." In: *Neues und Fremdes im deutschen Wortschatz. Aktueller lexikalischer Wandel*. Ed. by Gerhard Stickel. Berlin: de Gruyter, 2001, pp. 30–58.

[145] Ernest Gellner. *Nations and Nationalism*. Ithaca, NY: Cornell University Press, 1983.

[146] Johanna Gereke, Max Schaub, and Delia Baldassarri. "Gendered Discrimination Against Immigrants: Experimental Evidence." In: *Frontiers in Sociology* 5 (2020), p. 59.

[147] GESIS. *ALLBUS 1980-2016 - Allgemeine Bevölkerungsumfrage der Sozialwissenschaften*. Leibniz-Institut für Sozialwissenschaften. GESIS Datenarchiv, Köln. ZA4586 Datenfile Version 1.0.0, doi:10.4232/1.13029, retrieved: 04/03/2020., https://doi.org/10.4232/1.13395. Köln, 2018. DOI: 10.4232/1.13029.

[148] H. Giles, R. Bourhis, and D. M. Taylor. "Towards a Theory of Language in Ethnic Group Relations." In: *Language, Ethnicity and Intergroup Relations*. Ed. by H. Giles. London, England: Academic Press, 1977, pp. 307–348.

[149] H. Giles and P. Johnson. "Ethnolinguistic Identity Theory: A Social Psychological Approach to Language Maintenance." In: *International Journal of the Sociology of Language* 68 (1987), pp. 69–100.

[150] M. M. Gill. "Accent and Stereotypes: Their Effect on Perceptions of Teachers and Lecture Comprehension." In: *Journal of Applied Communication Research* 22.4 (1994), pp. 348–361.

[151] Paul Gilroy. *After Empire: Melancholia or Convivial Culture?* Routledge Press, 2004a.

[152] Paul Gilroy. *Postcolonial Melancholia*. Columbia University Press, 2004b.

[153] Agata Gluszek and John F. Dovidio. "The Way They Speak: A Social Psychological Perspective on the Stigma of Nonnative Accents in Communication." In: *Personality and Social Psychology Review* 14.2 (2010), pp. 214–237.

[154]   Theo Goldberg. "Racial Europeanization." In: *Ethnic and Racial Studies* 29.2 (2005), pp. 331–364.

[155]   Judith L. Goldstein and Margaret E. Peters. "Nativism or Economic Threat: Attitudes Toward Immigrants During the Great Recession." In: *International Interactions* 40.3 (2014), pp. 376–401.

[156]   Sara Wallace Goodman. "Fortifying Citizenship: Policy Strategies for Civic Integration in Western Europe." In: *World Politics* 64.4 (2012), pp. 659–698.

[157]   E. G. Green et al. "Keeping the Vermin Out: Perceived Disease Threat and Ideological Orientations as Predictors of Exclusionary Immigration Attitudes." In: *Journal of Community and Applied Social Psychology* 20.4 (2010), pp. 299–316.

[158]   Anthony G. Greenwald, Debbie E. McGhee, and Jordan L. K. Schwartz. "Measuring Individual Differences in Implicit Cognition: The Implicit Association Test." In: *Journal of Personality and Social Psychology* 74.6 (1998), pp. 1464–1480.

[159]   Anthony G. Greenwald, Brian A. Nosek, and Nene Sriram. "Consequential Validity of the Implicit Association Test." In: *American Psychologist* 61.1 (2006), pp. 56–61.

[160]   Anthony G. Greenwald et al. "Understanding and Using the Implicit Association Test: III. Meta-analysis of Predictive Validity." In: *Journal of Personality and Social Psychology* 97.1 (2009), p. 17.

[161]   John J. Gumperz. *Language and Social Identity*. Vol. 2. Cambridge University Press, 1982.

[162]   C. Gustavo et al. "The Altruistic Personality: In What Contexts Is It Apparent?" In: *Journal of Personality and Social Psychology* 61 (1991), pp. 450–458.

[163]   Jürgen Habermas. "Citizenship and National Identity: Some Reflections on the Future of Europe." In: *Praxis International* 12.1 (1993), pp. 1–19.

[164]   Jürgen Habermas. "Struggles for Recognition in the Democratic Constitutional State." In: *Multiculturalism*. Ed. by Amy Gutmann. Princeton, NJ: Princeton University Press, 1994, pp. 107–148.

[165]   James Habyarimana et al. "Why does Ethnic Diversity Undermine Public Goods Provision?" In: *American Political Science Review* 101.4 (2007), pp. 709–725.

[166]   L. Hagendoorn and Paul Sniderman. "Experimenting with a National Sample: A Dutch Survey of Prejudice." In: *Patterns of Prejudice* 35.4 (2001), pp. 19–31.

[167]   Jens Hainmueller and Dominik Hangartner. "Who Gets a Swiss Passport? A Natural Experiment in Immigrant Discrimination." In: *American Political Science Review* 107.01 (2013), pp. 159–187.

[168]   Jens Hainmueller and Michael J. Hiscox. "Attitudes Toward Highly Skilled and Low-skilled Immigration: Evidence from a Survey Experiment." In: *American Political Science Review* 104.01 (2010), pp. 61–84.

[169]   Jens Hainmueller and Daniel J. Hopkins. "Public Attitudes Toward Immigration." In: *Annual Review of Political Science* 17 (2014), pp. 225–249.

[170]   Jens Hainmueller and Daniel J. Hopkins. "The Hidden American Immigration Consensus: A Conjoint Analysis of Attitudes Toward Immigrants." In: *American Journal of Political Science* 59.3 (2015), pp. 529–548.

[171]   Jens Hainmueller, Daniel J. Hopkins, and Teppei Yamamoto. "Causal Inference in Conjoint Analysis: Understanding Multidimensional Choices via Stated Preference Experiments." In: *Political Analysis* 22.1 (2013), pp. 1–30.

[172] Gordon H. Hanson, Kenneth Scheve, and Matthew J. Slaughter. "Public Finance and Individual Preferences Over Globalization Strategies." In: *Economics & Politics* 19.1 (2007), pp. 1–33.

[173] Reid Hastie and Purohit A. Kumar. "Person Memory: Personality Traits as Organizing Principles in Memory for Behaviors." In: *Journal of Personality and Social Psychology* 37.1 (1979), p. 25.

[174] Michael Hechter. *Containing Nationalism.* Oxford: Oxford University Press, 2001.

[175] James J. Heckman and Peter Siegelman. "The Urban Institute Audit Studies: Their Methods and Findings." In: *Clear and Convincing Evidence: Measurement of Discrimination in America.* Ed. by Michael Fix and Raymond Struyk. Urban Institute Press, 1993, pp. 187–258.

[176] Havard Hegre and Nicholas Sambanis. "Sensitivity Analysis of Empirical Results on Civil War Onset." In: *Journal of Conflict Resolution* 50.4 (2006), 508–535.

[177] Wilhelm Heitmeyer et al. *Group-oriented Animosity Against People (GMF-Survey 2003).* GESIS Datenarchiv, Köln. *ZA5568 Datenfile Version 2.0.0, https://doi.org/10.4232 /1.11809, retrieved: 16/07/2020.,* https://doi.org/10.4232/1.11809. Köln, 2013a. DOI: 10.4232/1.11809.

[178] Wilhelm Heitmeyer et al. *Group-oriented Animosity Against People (GMF-Survey 2005).* GESIS Datenarchiv, Köln. *ZA5570 Datenfile Version 2.0.0, https://doi.org/10.4232 /1.11811, retrieved: 16/07/2020.,* https://doi.org/10.4232/1.11811. Köln, 2013b. DOI: 10.4232/1.11811.

[179] Marc Helbling and Richard Traunmüller. "What Is Islamophobia? Disentangling Citizens' Feelings Toward Ethnicity, Religion and Religiosity Using a Survey Experiment." In: *British Journal of Political Science* (2018), pp. 1–18.

[180] Benedikt Herrmann, Christian Thöni, and Simon Gächter. "Antisocial Punishment Across Societies." In: *Science* 319.7 March (2008), pp. 1362–1367.

[181] Melville J. Herskovits. *Acculturation: The Study of Culture Contact.* Gloucester, MA: Peter Smith, 1958.

[182] M. Hewstone. "Contact and Categorization: Social Psychological Interventions to Change Intergroup Relations." In: *Stereotypes and Stereotyping.* Ed. by C. N. Macrae, C. Stangor, and M. Hewstone. London: Guilford, 1996, pp. 323–368.

[183] M. Hewstone and R. Brown. "Contact Is Not Enough: An Intergroup Perspective on the 'Contact Hypothesis.'" In: *Social Psychology and Society. Contact and Conflict in Intergroup Encounters.* Ed. by M. Hewstone and R. Brown. Cambridge, MA: Basil Blackwell, 1986, pp. 1–44.

[184] Seth Hill, Daniel J. Hopkins, and Gregory Huber. "Demographic Change, Threat, and Presidential Voting: Evidence from U.S. Electoral Precincts, 2012–2016." In: *Proceedings of the National Academy of Sciences* 116.50 (2019), pp. 25023–25028.

[185] James L. Hilton and William Von Hippel. "Stereotypes." In: *Annual Review of Psychology* 47.1 (1996), pp. 237–271.

[186] Eric Hobsbawm and Terrence Ranger. *The Invention of Tradition.* Cambridge: Cambridge University Press, 1983.

[187] Ted Hopf. *Social Construction of International Politics: Identities and Foreign Policies, Moscow 1955 and 1999.* Cornell University Press, 2002.

[188]   Daniel J. Hopkins. "The Upside of Accents: Language, Inter-group Difference, and Attitudes toward Immigration." In: *British Journal of Political Science* 45 (2014a), pp. 531–557.

[189]   Daniel J. Hopkins, Van C. Tran, and Abigail Fisher Williamson. *See No Spanish: Language, Local Context, and Attitudes toward Immigration*. 2011.

[190]   Daniel L. Hopkins. "One Language, Two Meanings: Partisanship and Responses to Spanish." In: *Political Communication* 31.3 (2014b), pp. 421–455.

[191]   Matthew J. Hornsey and Michael A. Hogg. "Subgroup Relations: A Comparison of Mutual Intergroup Differentiation and Common Ingroup Identity Models of Prejudice Reduction." In: *Personality and Social Psychology* 26.2 (2000), pp. 242–256.

[192]   Donald Horowitz. *Ethnic Groups in Conflict*. Los Angeles: University of California Press, 1985.

[193]   Leonie Huddy and Nayda Terkildsen. "Gender Stereotypes and the Perception of Male and Female Candidates." In: *American Journal of Political Science* 37.1 (1993), pp. 119–147.

[194]   Samuel P. Huntington. *The Clash of Civilizations and the Remaking of World Order*. Simon & Schuster, 1996.

[195]   R. Inglehart et al. *World Values Surveys and European Values Surveys, 1981–1984, 1990–1993 and 1995–1997. ICPSR Version*. Ann Arbor, MI: Institute for Social Research, 2000.

[196]   ISSP. *International Social Survey Program (ISSP): National Identity. 1995. ICPSR release*. Köln, Germany: Zentralarchiv fuer Empirische Sozialforschung [producer]/Ann Arbor, MI: Inter-university Consortium for Political and Social Research, 1998.

[197]   Christian Jansen. "The Formation of German Nationalism, 1740–1850." In: *The Oxford Handbook of Modern German History*. Ed. by Helmut Walser Smith. Oxford: Oxford University Press, 2011, pp. 234–259.

[198]   Hélène Joffe and Christian Staerklé. "The Centrality of the Self-control Ethos in Western Aspersions Regarding Outgroups: A Social Representational Approach to Stereotype Content." In: *Culture & Psychology* 13.4 (2007), pp. 395–418.

[199]   Joshua L. Kalla and David E. Broockman. "Reducing Exclusionary Attitudes through Interpersonal Conversation: Evidence from Three Field Experiments." In: *American Political Science Review* (2020), pp. 1–16.

[200]   Tomasz D. I. Kamusella. "Language as an Instrument of Nationalism in Central Europe." In: *Nations and Nationalism* 7.2 (2001), pp. 235–251.

[201]   Sonia K. Kang and Galen V. Bodenhausen. "Multiple Identities in Social Perception and Interaction: Challenges and Opportunities." In: *Annual Review of Psychology* 66 (2015), pp. 547–574.

[202]   Sonia K. Kang and A. L. Chasteen. "Beyond the Double-jeopardy Hypothesis: Assessing Emotion on the Faces of Multiply-categorizable Targets of Prejudice." In: *Journal of Experimental Social Psychology* 45 (2009), pp. 1281–1285.

[203]   Annika K. Karinen et al. "Disgust Sensitivity and Opposition to Immigration: Does Contact Avoidance or Resistance to Foreign Norms Explain the Relationship?" In: *Journal of Experimental Social Psychology* 84 (2019), pp. 1–11.

[204]   I. Katz, S. Cohen, and D. Glass. "Some Determinants of Cross-racial Helping Behavior." In: *Journal of Personality and Social Psychology* 32 (1975), pp. 964–970.

[205] Mathias Kauff et al. "When Immigrant Groups 'misbehave': The Influence of Perceived Deviant Behavior on Increased Threat and Discriminatory Intentions and the Moderating Role of Right-wing Authoritarianism." In: *European Journal of Social Psychology* 45.5 (2015), pp. 641–652.

[206] Marc Keuschnigg and Tobias Wolbring. "Disorder, Social Capital, and Norm Violation: Three Field Experiments on the Broken Windows Thesis." In: *Rationality and Society* 27.1 (2015), pp. 96–126.

[207] Donald R. Kinder and Cindy D. Kam. *Us Against Them: Ethnocentric Foundations of American Opinion.* University of Chicago Press, 2010.

[208] Katherine D. Kinzler et al. "Accent Trumps Race in Guiding Children's Social Preferences." In: *Social Cognition* 27.4 (2009), pp. 623–634.

[209] Samantha Klar. "When Common Identities Decrease Trust: An Experimental Study of Partisan Women." In: *American Journal of Political Science* 62.3 (2018), pp. 610–622.

[210] Ulrich Kober and Orkan Kösemen. *Willkommenskultur zwischen Skepsis und Pragmatik: Deutschland nach der "Fluchtkrise," Survey Data.*, https://www.bertelsmann-stiftung.de/de/publikationen/publikation/did/willkommenskultur-zwischen-skepsis-und-pragmatik/. Gütersloh, 2019.

[211] R. Koopmans et al. *Contested Citizenship: Immigration and Cultural Diversity in Europe.* Minneapolis: University of Minnesota Press, 2005.

[212] Ruud Koopmans. "Multiculturalism and Immigration: A Contested Field in Cross-national Comparison." In: *Annual Review of Sociology* 39 (2013), pp. 147–169.

[213] Roderick M. Kramer and Marilynn B. Brewer. "Effects of Group Identity on Resource Use in a Simulated Commons Dilemma." In: *Journal of Personality and Social Psychology* 46.5 (1984), pp. 1044–1057.

[214] James H. Kuklinski, Michael D. Cobb, and Martin Gilens. "Racial Attitudes and the 'New South'." In: *Journal of Politics* 59.2 (1997), pp. 323–349.

[215] W. Kymlicka. *Multicultural Citizenship: A Liberal Theory of Minority Rights.* Oxford University Press, 1995.

[216] R. M. Lerner and P. Frank. "Relation of Race and Sex to Supermarket Helping Behavior." In: *Journal of Social Psychology* 94 (1974), pp. 201–203.

[217] Matthew Levendusky. "Americans, Not Partisans: Can Priming American National Identity Reduce Affective Polarization?" In: *Journal of Politics* 80.1 (2018), pp. 59–70.

[218] Robert A. LeVine and Donald T. Campbell. *Ethnocentrism: Theories of Conflict, Ethnic Attitudes, and Group Behavior.* New York: John Wiley and Sons, 1972.

[219] Uli Linke. " 'There Is a Land where Everything Is Pure.' Linguistic Nationalism and Identity Politics in Germany." In: *Race, Nature, and the Politics of Difference.* Ed. by Donald S. Moore, Jake Kosak, and Anand Pandian. Durham: Duke University Press, 2003, pp. 149–174.

[220] Seymour Martin Lipset and Stein Rokkan. *Party Systems and Voter Alignments.* New York: Free Press, 1967.

[221] A. J. Lott and B. E. Lott. "Group Cohesiveness as Interpersonal Attraction: A Review of Relationships with Antecedent and Consequent Variables." In: *Psychological Bulletin* 64 (1965), pp. 259–309.

[222]   Vally Lytra. "Language and Ethnic Identity." In: *The Routledge Handbook of Language and Identity*. Ed. by Siân Preece. New Jersey: Routledge, 2016, pp. 131–145.

[223]   Julianne Maher. "A Crosslinguistic Study of Language Contact and Language Attrition." In: *First Language Attrition*. Ed. by Herbert W. Seliger and Robert M. Vago. Cambridge: Cambridge University Press, 1991, pp. 67–86.

[224]   N. Malhotra, Y. Margalit, and C. H. Mo. "Economic Explanations for Opposition to Immigration: Distinguishing between Prevalence and Conditional Impact." In: *American Journal of Political Science* 57.2 (2013), pp. 391–410.

[225]   J. K. Maner et al. "The Effects of Perspective-taking on Motivations for Helping: Still No Evidence for Altruism." In: *Personality and Social Psychology Bulletin* 28 (2002), pp. 1601–1610.

[226]   J. March. *A Primer on Decision-making: How Decisions Happen*. New York: Free Press, 1994.

[227]   J. G. March and J. P. Olsen. *Democratic Governance*. New York: Free Press, 1995.

[228]   Offenbach Marplan. *Ausländer in Deutschland 1988. GESIS Datenarchiv, Köln. ZA1678 Datenfile Version 1.0.0, https://doi.org/10.4232/1.1678, retrieved: 16/04/2020.* https://doi.org/10.4232/1.1678. Köln, 1988. DOI: 10.4232/1.1678.

[229]   Offenbach Marplan. *Ausländer in Deutschland 1989. GESIS Datenarchiv, Köln. ZA1787 Datenfile Version 1.0.0, https://doi.org/10.4232/1.1787, retrieved: 16/04/2020.* https://doi.org/10.4232/1.1787. Köln, 1989. DOI: 10.4232/1.1787.

[230]   Offenbach Marplan. *Ausländer in Deutschland 1991. GESIS Datenarchiv, Köln. ZA2291 Datenfile Version 1.0.0, https://doi.org/10.4232/1.2291, retrieved: 16/04/2020.* https://doi.org/10.4232/1.2291. Köln, 1992. DOI: 10.4232/1.2291.

[231]   Offenbach Marplan. *Ausländer in Deutschland 1993. GESIS Datenarchiv, Köln. ZA2423 Datenfile Version 1.0.0, https://doi.org/10.4232/1.2423, retrieved: 16/04/2020.* https://doi.org/10.4232/1.2423. Köln, 1994. DOI: 10.4232/1.2423.

[232]   Offenbach Marplan. *Ausländer in Deutschland 1994. GESIS Datenarchiv, Köln. ZA2847 Datenfile Version 1.0.0, https://doi.org/10.4232/1.2847, retrieved: 16/04/2020.* https://doi.org/10.4232/1.2847. Köln, 1996. DOI: 10.4232/1.2847.

[233]   Offenbach Marplan. *Ausländer in Deutschland 1995. GESIS Datenarchiv, Köln. ZA2848 Datenfile Version 1.0.0, https://doi.org/10.4232/1.2848, retrieved: 16/04/2020.* https://doi.org/10.4232/1.2848. Köln, 1996. DOI: 10.4232/1.2848.

[234]   Offenbach Marplan. *Ausländer in Deutschland 1996. GESIS Datenarchiv, Köln. ZA2849 Datenfile Version 1.0.0, https://doi.org/10.4232/1.2849, retrieved: 16/04/2020.* https://doi.org/10.4232/1.2849. Köln, 1996. DOI: 10.4232/1.2849.

[235]   Offenbach Marplan. *Ausländer in Deutschland 1997. GESIS Datenarchiv, Köln. ZA3523 Datenfile Version 2.0.0, https://doi.org/10.4232/1.11079, retrieved: 16/04/2020.* https://doi.org/10.4232/1.11079. Köln, 2012. DOI: 10.4232/1.11079.

[236]   Offenbach Marplan. *Ausländer in Deutschland 1998. GESIS Datenarchiv, Köln. ZA3524 Datenfile Version 2.0.0, https://doi.org/10.4232/1.11080, retrieved: 16/04/2020.* https://doi.org/10.4232/1.11080. Köln, 2012. DOI: 10.4232/1.11080.

[237]   Offenbach Marplan. *Ausländer in Deutschland 1999 - 1. Welle. GESIS Datenarchiv, Köln. ZA3366 Datenfile Version 2.0.0, https://doi.org/10.4232/1.11081, retrieved: 16/04/2020.* https://doi.org/10.4232/1.11081. Köln, 2012. DOI: 10.4232/1.11081.

[238]   Offenbach Marplan. *Ausländer in Deutschland 1999 - 2. Welle. GESIS Datenarchiv, Köln. ZA3367 Datenfile Version 2.0.0, https://doi.org/10.4232/1.11082, retrieved: 16/04/2020.* https://doi.org/10.4232/1.11082. Köln, 2012. DOI: 10.4232/1.11082.

[239]   Offenbach Marplan. *Ausländer in Deutschland 2000 - 1. Welle. GESIS Datenarchiv, Köln. ZA3649 Datenfile Version 2.0.0, https://doi.org/10.4232/1.11084, retrieved: 16/04/2020.* https://doi.org/10.4232/1.11084. Köln, 2012. DOI: 10.4232/1.11084.

[240]   Offenbach Marplan. *Ausländer in Deutschland 2000 - 2. Welle. GESIS Datenarchiv, Köln. ZA3650 Datenfile Version 2.0.0, https://doi.org/10.4232/1.11085, retrieved: 16/04/2020.* https://doi.org/10.4232/1.11085. Köln, 2012. DOI: 10.4232/1.11085.

[241]   Offenbach Marplan. *Ausländer in Deutschland 2001 - 1. Welle. GESIS Datenarchiv, Köln. ZA4059 Datenfile Version 2.0.0, https://doi.org/10.4232/1.11086, retrieved: 16/04/2020.* https://doi.org/10.4232/1.11086. Köln, 2012. DOI: 10.4232/1.11086.

[242]   Offenbach Marplan. *Ausländer in Deutschland 2001 - 2. Welle. GESIS Datenarchiv, Köln. ZA4060 Datenfile Version 2.0.0, https://doi.org/10.4232/1.11087, retrieved: 16/04/2020.* https://doi.org/10.4232/1.11087. Köln, 2012. DOI: 10.4232/1.11087.

[243]   Offenbach Marplan. *Ausländer in Deutschland 2002 - 1. Welle. GESIS Datenarchiv, Köln. ZA4061 Datenfile Version 2.0.0, https://doi.org/10.4232/1.11088, retrieved: 16/04/2020.* https://doi.org/10.4232/1.11088. Köln, 2012. DOI: 10.4232/1.11088.

[244]   Offenbach Marplan. *Ausländer in Deutschland 2002 - 2. Welle. GESIS Datenarchiv, Köln. ZA4062 Datenfile Version 2.0.0, https://doi.org/10.4232/1.11089, retrieved: 16/04/2020.* https://doi.org/10.4232/1.11089. Köln, 2012. DOI: 10.4232/1.11089.

[245]   Offenbach Marplan. *Ausländer in Deutschland 2003. GESIS Datenarchiv, Köln. ZA4458 Datenfile Version 1.0.0, https://doi.org/10.4232/1.4458, retrieved: 16/04/2020.* https://doi.org/10.4232/1.4458. Köln, 2006. DOI: 10.4232/1.4458.

[246]   Offenbach Marplan. *Ausländer in Deutschland 2004. GESIS Datenarchiv, Köln. ZA4459 Datenfile Version 1.0.0, https://doi.org/10.4232/1.4459, retrieved: 16/04/2020.* https://doi.org/10.4232/1.4459. Köln, 2006. DOI: 10.4232/1.4459.

[247]   Offenbach Marplan. *Ausländische Arbeitnehmer in der Bundesrepublik (Datenpool 1970-1982). GESIS Datenarchiv, Köln. ZA1358 Datenfile Version 1.0.0, https://doi.org/10.4232/1.1358, retrieved: 16/04/2020.* https://doi.org/10.4232/1.1358. Köln, 1982. DOI: 10.4232/1.1358.

[248]   Klaus J. Mattheier. "German." In: *Germanic Standardizations. Past to Present*. Ed. by Ana Demuert and Wim Vandenbussche. Amsterdam/Philadelphia: John Benjamins Publishing, 2003, pp. 211–245.

[249]   Rahsaan Maxwell. "Occupations, National Identity, and Immigrant Integration." In: *Comparative Political Studies* (2017), p. 0010414016655535.

[250]   A. M. Mayda. "Who Is Against Immigration? A Cross-country Investigation of Individual Attitudes Toward Immigrants." In: *Review of Economics and Statistics* 88 (2006), pp. 510–530.

[251]   Craig McGarty and R.E.C. Penny. "Categorization, Accentuation and Social Judgement." In: *British Journal of Social Psychology* 27.2 (1988), pp. 147–157.

[252]   W. J. McGuire et al. "Salience of Ethnicity in the Spontaneous Self-concept as a Function of One's Ethnic Distinctiveness in the Social Environment." In: *Journal of Personality and Social Psychology* 36.5 (1978), pp. 511–520.

[253]   Kristin Michelitch. "Does Electoral Competition Exacerbate Interethnic or Interpartisan Economic Discrimination? Evidence from a Field Experiment in Market Price Bargaining." In: *American Political Science Review* 109.1 (2015), pp. 43–61.

[254]   D. Miller. "Multiculturalism and the Welfare State: Theoretical Reflections." In: *Multiculturalism and the Welfare State: Recognition and Redistribution in Contemporary Democracies*. Ed. by K. Banting and W. Kymlicka. Oxford: Oxford University Press, 2006, pp. 323–338.

[255]   Cynthia Miller-Idriss and Bess Rothenberg. "Ambivalence, Pride and Shame: Conceptualisations of German Nationhood." In: *Nations and Nationalism* 18.1 (2012), pp. 132–155.

[256]   Jose G. Montalvo and Marta Reynal-Querol. "Ethnic Polarization, Potential Conflict, and Civil Wars." In: *American Economic Review* 95.3 (2005), pp. 796–816.

[257]   M. K. Moss and R. A. Page. "Reinforcement and Helping Behavior." In: *Journal of Applied Social Psychology* 2 (1972), pp. 360–371.

[258]   Jan Werner Mueller. *Constitutional Patriotism*. Princeton University Press, 2007.

[259]   A. Mummendey and H.-J. Schreiber. "Social Comparison, Similarity and Ingroup Favouritism: A Replication." In: *European Journal of Social Psychology* 14.2 (1984), pp. 231–233.

[260]   Amelie Mummendey and Michael Wenzel. "Social Discrimination and Tolerance in Intergroup Relations: Reactions to Intergroup Difference." In: *Personality and Social Psychology Review* 3.2 (1999), pp. 158–174.

[261]   Diana C. Mutz. "The Consequences of Cross-Cutting Networks for Political Participation." In: *American Journal of Political Science* 46.4 (2002), pp. 838–855.

[262]   Harris Mylonas. *The Politics of Nation-building*. Cambridge University Press, 2013.

[263]   Harris Mylonas. *The Politics of Nation-building: Making Co-nationals, Refugees, and Minorities*. Cambridge: Cambridge University Press, 2012.

[264]   C. D. Navarette et al. "Prejudice at the Nexus of Race and Gender: An Outgroup Male Target Hypothesis." In: *Journal of Personality and Social Psychology* 98 (2010), pp. 933–945.

[265]   Thomas E. Nelson and Donald R. Kinder. "Issue Frames and Group-Centrism in American Public Opinion." In: *Journal of Politics* 58.4 (1996), pp. 1055–1078.

[266]   Benjamin J. Newman, Todd K. Hartman, and Charles S. Taber. "Foreign Language Exposure, Cultural Threat, and Opposition to Immigration." In: *Political Psychology* 33.5 (2012), pp. 635–657.

[267]   Anne Norton. "A Discussion of Claire L. Adida, David D. Laitin, and Marie-Anne Valfort's *Why Muslim Integration Fails in Christian-Heritage Societies*." In: *Perspectives on Politics* 16.3 (2018), pp. 765–766.

[268]   Anne Norton. *On the Muslim Question*. Princeton, NJ: Princeton University Press, 2013.

[269]   Brian A. Nosek et al. "Pervasiveness and Correlates of Implicit Attitudes and Stereotypes." In: *European Review of Social Psychology* 18.1 (2007), pp. 36–88.

[270]   L. Nunziata. "Immigration and Crime: Evidence from Victimization Data." In: *Journal of Population Economics* 28.3 (2015), pp. 697–736.

[271]   Susan Olzak. *The Dynamics of Ethnic Competition and Conflict*. Stanford University Press, 1992.

[272] Simone Paci, Nicholas Sambanis, and William Wolforth. "Status-Seeking and Nation-Building: The 'Piedmont Principle' Revisited." In: *Journal of Inter-disciplinary History* 51.1 (2020), pp. 65–95.

[273] Devah Pager and Hana Shepherd. "The Sociology of Discrimination: Racial Discrimination in Employment, Housing, Credit, and Consumer Markets." In: *Annual Review of Sociology* 34 (2008), pp. 181–209.

[274] Elizabeth Levy Paluck, Seth A. Green, and Donald P. Green. "The Contact Hypothesis Re-evaluated." In: *Behavioral Public Policy* 3.2 (2019), pp. 129–158.

[275] Elizabeth Levy Paluck. "How to Overcome Prejudice." In: *Science* 352.6282 (2016), p. 147.

[276] Elizabeth Levy Paluck and Donald P. Green. "Prejudice Reduction: What Works? A Review and Assessment of Research and Practice." In: *Annual Review of Psychology* 60 (2009), pp. 339–367.

[277] Robert E. Park and Ernest W. Burgess. "Assimilation." In: *Introduction to the Science of Sociology*. Ed. by Robert E. Park and Ernest W. Burgess. Chicago: University of Chicago Press, 1924, pp. 734–783.

[278] Pamela Paxton. "What's to Fear from Immigrants? Creating an Assimilationist Threat Scale." In: *Political Psychology* 27.4 (2006), pp. 549–568.

[279] Margaret E. Peters. "Trade, Foreign Direct Investment, and Immigration Policy Making in the United States." In: *International Organization* 68.4 (2014), pp. 811–844.

[280] Thomas F. Pettigrew. "Intergroup Contact Theory." In: *Annual Review of Psychology* 49 (1998), pp. 65–85.

[281] PEW Forum on Religion & Public Life. *The World's Muslims: Religion, Politics, and Society*. 2013.

[282] Falco Pfalzgraf. "Linguistic Purism in the History of the German Language." In: *Landmarks in the History of the German Language*. Ed. by Geraldine Horan, Nils Langer, and Sheila Watts. Bern: Peter Lang, 2009, pp. 137–168.

[283] Falco Pfalzgraf. "Recent Developments Concerning Language Protection Organisations and Right-Wing Extremism in Germany." In: *German Life and Letters* 56.4 (2003).

[284] Edmund S. Phelps. "The Statistical Theory of Racism and Sexism." In: *American Economic Review* 62.4 (1972), pp. 659–661.

[285] Jean S. Phinney et al. "The Role of Language, Parents, and Peers in Ethnic Identity among Adolescents in Immigrant Families." In: *Journal of Youth and Adolescence* 30.2 (2001), pp. 135–153.

[286] I. M. Piliavin, J. Rodin, and J. A. Piliavin. "Good Samaritanism: An Underground Phenomenon?" In: *Journal of Personality and Social Psychology* 13 (1969), pp. 289–299.

[287] Daniel N. Posner. "Measuring Ethnic Fractionalization in Africa." In: *American Journal of Political Science* 48.4 (2004), pp. 849–863.

[288] Tamara Rakic, Melanie C. Steffens, and Amelie Mummendey. "Blinded by the Accent! The Minor Role of Looks in Ethnic Categorization." In: *Journal of Personality and Social Psychology* 100.1 (2011), pp. 16–29.

[289] D. T. Regan. "Effect of a Favor on Liking and Compliance." In: *Journal of Experimental Social Psychology* 7 (1971), pp. 627–639.

[290]   P. Riach and J. Rich. "Field Experiments of Discrimination in the Marketplace." In: *Economic Journal* 112 (2002), pp. 480–518.

[291]   Blake M. Ricke et al. "Does a Common Ingroup Identity Reduce Intergroup Threat?" In: *Group Processes and Intergroup Relations* 13.4 (2010), pp. 403–423.

[292]   S. Roccas et al. "Toward a Unifying Model of Identification with Groups: Integrating Theoretical Perspectives." In: *Personality and Social Psychology Review* 12 (2008), pp. 280–306.

[293]   Krystyna Rojahn and Thomas F. Pettigrew. "Memory for Schema-relevant Information: A Meta-analytic Resolution." In: *British Journal of Social Psychology* 31.2 (1992), pp. 81–109.

[294]   Milton Rokeach and Louis Mezei. "Race and Shared Belief as Factors in Social Choice." In: *Science* 151.3707 (1966), pp. 167–172.

[295]   Hannes Rusch. "The Evolutionary Interplay of Intergroup Conflict and Altruism in Humans: A Review of Parochial Altruism Theory and Prospects for Its Extension." In: *Proceedings of the Royal Society B* 281.20141539 (2014), pp. 1–9.

[296]   Kevin Russell and Nicholas Sambanis. "Stopping the Violence But Blocking the Peace: Dilemmas of Foreign-Imposed Nation-building after Civil War." In: *International Organization* (forthcoming), pp. 1–38.

[297]   Abraham M. Rutchick and Collette P. Eccleston. "Ironic Effects of Invoking Common Ingroup Identity." In: *Basic and Applied Psychology* 32.2 (2010), pp. 109–117.

[298]   E. B. Ryan, M. A. Carranza, and R. W. Moffie. "Reactions Toward Varying Degrees of Accentedness in the Speech of Spanish-English Bilinguals." In: *Language and Speech* 20 (1977), pp. 267–273.

[299]   Ayse Safak-Ayvazoglu, Filiz Kunuroglu, and Kutlay Yagmur. "Psychological and Socio-cultural Adaptation of Syrian Refugees in Turkey." In: *International Journal of Intercultural Relations* 80 (2020), pp. 99–111.

[300]   Nicholas Sambanis and Moses Shayo. "Social Identification and Ethnic Conflict." In: *American Political Science Review* 107.2 (2013), pp. 294–325.

[301]   Nicholas Sambanis, Stergios Skaperdas, and William Wolforth. "Nation-Building Through War." In: *American Political Science Review* 109.2 (2015), pp. 279–296.

[302]   Melissa L Sands. "Exposure to Inequality Affects Support for Redistribution." In: *Proceedings of the National Academy of Sciences* 114.4 (2017), pp. 663–668.

[303]   D. A. Saucier, S. J. Smith, and J. L. McManus. "The Possible Role of Discrimination in the Rescue Response after Hurricane Katrina." In: *Journal of Race and Policy* 3 (2007), pp. 113–121.

[304]   D. A. Saucier, C. T. Miller, and N. Doucet. "Differences in Helping Whites and Blacks: A Meta-analysis." In: *Personality and Social Psychology Review* 9 (2005), pp. 2–16.

[305]   Donald A. Saucier, Jessica L. McManus, and Sara J. Smith. "Discrimination Against Out-Group Members in Helping Situations." In: *The Psychology of Prosocial Behavior*. Ed. by Stefan Sturmer and Mark Snyder. Cambridge, MA: Wiley-Blackwell, 2010, pp. 103–120.

[306]   Alexandra Scacco and Shana S. Warren. "Can Social Contact Reduce Prejudice and Discrimination? Evidence from a Field Experiment in Nigeria." In: *American Political Science Review* 112.3 (2018), pp. 654–677.

[307]   Kenneth F. Scheve and Matthew J. Slaughter. "Labor Market Competition and Individual Preferences over Immigration Policy." In: *Review of Economics and Statistics* 83.1 (2001), pp. 133–145.

[308]   Eric Schickler and Donald Green. "The Stability of Party Identification in Western Democracies: Results from Eight Panel Surveys." In: *Comparative Political Studies* 30.4 (1997), pp. 450–483.

[309]   Deborah J. Schildkraut. *Americanism in the Twenty-first Century: Public Opinion in the Age of Immigration.* Cambridge University Press, 2010.

[310]   Deborah J. Schildkraut. *Press One for English: Language Policy, Public Opinion, and American Identity.* Princeton, NJ: Princeton University Press, 2005.

[311]   Silke L. Schneider. "Anti-immigrant Attitudes in Europe: Outgroup Size and Perceived Ethnic Threat." In: *European Sociological Review* 24.1 (2008), pp. 53–67.

[312]   Joan Wallach Scott. *The Politics of the Veil.* Princeton, NJ: Princeton University Press, 2007.

[313]   Michael A. Seaman and Ronald C. Serlin. "Equivalence Confidence Intervals for Two-group Comparisons of Means." In: *Psychological Methods* 3.4 (1998), p. 403.

[314]   Moses Shayo and Asaf Zussman. "Judicial Ingroup Bias in the Shadow of Terrorism." In: *Quarterly Journal of Economics* 126.3 (2011), pp. 1447–1484.

[315]   C. A. Shepard, H. Giles, and B. A. Le Poire. "Communication Accommodation Theory." In: *The New Handbook of Language and Social Psychology.* Ed. by W. P. Robinson and H. Giles. Wiley: New York, NY, 2001, pp. 33–56.

[316]   Muzafer Sherif et al. *The Robbers' Cave Experiment.* Norman OK: Institute of Group Relations, University of Oklahoma, 1961.

[317]   J. Sidanius and R. C. Veniegas. "Gender and Race Discrimination: The Interactive Nature of Disadvantage." In: *Reducing Prejudice and Discrimination: The Claremont Symposium on Applied Social Psychology.* Ed. by S. Oskamp. Hillsdale, NJ: Erlbaum, 2000, pp. 47–69.

[318]   J. Sides and J. Citrin. "European Opinion about Immigration: The Role of Identities, Interests, and Information." In: *British Journal of Political Science* 37 (2007), pp. 477–504.

[319]   Uri Simonsohn. "Small Telescopes: Detectability and the Evaluation of Replication Results." In: *Psychological Science* 26.5 (2015), pp. 559–569.

[320]   Paul M. Sniderman and Louk Hagendoorn. *When Ways of Life Collide: Multiculturalism and Its Discontents in the Netherlands.* Princeton University Press, 2007.

[321]   Paul M. Sniderman, Louk Hagendoorn, and Markus Prior. "Predisposing Factors and Situational Triggers: Exclusionary Reactions to Immigrant Minorities." In: *American Political Science Review* 98.1 (2004), pp. 35–49.

[322]   Paul M. Sniderman et al. "Racial Prejudice and Attitudes toward Affirmative Action." In: *American Journal of Political Science* 41.2 (1997), pp. 402–419.

[323]   Paul M. Sniderman et al. *The Outsider: Prejudice and Politics in Italy.* Princeton University Press, 2002.

[324]   K. Sole, J. Marton, and H. A. Hornstein. "Opinion Similarity and Helping: Three Field Experiments Investigating the Bases of Promotive Tension." In: *Journal of Experimental Social Psychology* 11 (1975), pp. 1–13.

[325]   Enrico Spolaore. "Civil Conflict and Secessions." In: *Economics of Governance* 9.1 (2008), pp. 45–63.

[326]   Thomas K. Srull. "Person Memory: Some Tests of Associative Storage and Retrieval Models." In: *Journal of Experimental Psychology: Human Learning and Memory* 7.6 (1981), p. 440.

[327]   Thomas K. Srull, Meryl Lichtenstein, and Myron Rothbart. "Associative Storage and Retrieval Processes in Person Memory." In: *Journal of Experimental Psychology: Learning, Memory, and Cognition* 11.2 (1985), p. 316.

[328]   Walter G. Stephan and C. W. Stephan. "An Integrated Theory of Prejudice." In: *Reducing Prejudice and Discrimination*. Ed. by S. Oskamp. Mahwah, NJ: Lawrence Erlbaum, 2000, pp. 23–45.

[329]   Walter G. Stephan, Oscar Ybarra, and Guy Bachman. "Prejudice Toward Immigrants." In: *Journal of Applied Social Psychology* 29.11 (1999), pp. 2221–2237.

[330]   Patrick Stevenson. "The Language Question in Contemporary Germany: The Challenges of Multilingualism." In: *German Politics and Society* 114.33 (2015), pp. 69–83.

[331]   Henri Tajfel. *Human Groups and Social Categories: Studies in Social Psychology*. CUP Archive, 1981.

[332]   Henri Tajfel et al. "Social Categorization and Intergroup Behaviour." In: *European Journal of Social Psychology* 1.2 (1971), pp. 149–178.

[333]   Charles Taylor. "The Politics of Recognition." In: *Multiculturalism*. Ed. by Amy Gutmann. Princeton, NJ: Princeton University Press, 1994, pp. 25–73.

[334]   Aysecan Terzioglu. "The Banality of Evil and the Normalization of the Discriminatory Discourses Against Syrians in Turkey." In: *Anthropology of the Contemporary Middle East and Central Eurasia* 4 (2017), pp. 34–47.

[335]   Raymond H. C. Teske Jr. and Bardin H. Nelson. "Acculturation and Assimilation: A Clarification." In: *American Ethnologist* 1.2 (1974), pp. 351–367.

[336]   Elizabeth Theiss-Morse. *Who Counts as an American? The Boundaries of National Identity*. New York: Cambridge University Press, 2009.

[337]   Kathrin Thomas. *Women's Rights in the Middle East and North Africa*. Arab Barometer, 2019.

[338]   Triadafilos Triadafilopoulos and Karen Schönwälder. "How the Federal Republic Became an Immigration Country: Norms, Politics and the Failure of West Germany's Guest Worker System." In: *German Politics & Society* 24.3 (2006), pp. 1–19.

[339]   John Turner. "Toward a Cognitive Redefinition of the Social Group." In: *Social Identity and Intergroup Relations*. Ed. by Henri Tajfel. Cambridge: Cambridge University Press, 1982, pp. 15–36.

[340]   John C. Turner et al. *Rediscovering the Social Group: A Self-categorization Theory*. Basil Blackwell, 1987.

[341]   D. Urada, D. M. Stenstrom, and N. Miller. "Crossed Categorization Beyond the Two-group Model." In: *Journal of Personality and Social Psychology* 74 (2007), pp. 649–664.

[342]   Kare Vernby and R. M. Dancygier. "Can Immigrants Counteract Employer Discrimination? A Factorial Field Experiment Reveals the Immutability of Ethnic Hierarchies." In: *PLOS One* (July 24 2019), pp. 1–19.

[343] Wilma Vollebergh, Justus Veenman, and Louk Hagendoorn. *Integrating Immigrants in the Netherlands: Cultural versus Socio-Economic Integration.* Routledge, 2017.

[344] Michael Walzer. "What Does It Mean to Be an 'American'?" In: *Social Research* 71.3 (2004), pp. 633–654.

[345] X. Wang. "Undocumented Immigrants as Perceived Criminal Threat: A Test of the Minority Threat Perspective." In: *Criminology* 50.3 (2012), pp. 743–776.

[346] Dalston G. Ward. "Public Attitudes Toward Young Immigrant Men." In: *American Political Science Review* 113.1 (2019), pp. 264–269.

[347] J. Mark Weber, Shirli Kopelman, and David M. Messick. "A Conceptual Review of Decision Making in Social Dilemmas: Applying a Logic of Appropriateness." In: *Personality and Social Psychology Review* 8.3 (2004), pp. 281–307.

[348] Stefan Wellek. *Testing Statistical Hypotheses of Equivalence and Noninferiority.* Chapman and Hall/CRC, 2010.

[349] Alexander Wendt. *A Social Theory of International Politics.* Cambridge University Press, 1999.

[350] S. G. West, G. Whitney, and R. Schnedler. "Helping of a Motorist in Distress: The Effects of Sex, Race, and Neighborhood." In: *Journal of Personality and Social Psychology* 13 (1975), pp. 289–299.

[351] M. A. Whatley et al. "The Effect of a Favor on Public and Private Compliance: How Internalized is the Norm of Reciprocity?" In: *Basic and Applied Social Psychology* 21 (1999), pp. 251–259.

[352] Andreas Wimmer. *Nation Building: Why Some Countries Come Together While Others Fall Apart.* Princeton, NJ: Princeton University Press, 2018.

[353] Matthew Wright, Jack Citrin, and Jonathan Wand. "Alternative Measures of American National Identity: Implications for the Civic-Ethnic Distinction." In: *Political Psychology* 33.4 (2012), pp. 469–482.

[354] Aristide Zolberg and Long Litt Woon. "Why Islam Is Like Spanish: Cultural Incorporation in Europe and the United States." In: *Politics and Society* 27.1 (1999), pp. 5–38.

accents, 50n18, 94n4, 108–9, 149

acceptance: assimilation and, 194; average treatment effects (ATE) and, 180, *181*, *187–88*, *192–93*; belief similarity and, 181–82, 186, 194–95; categorization and, 171, *181*, 189; citizenship and, 178–80, 186–95; Common Ingroup Identity Model (CIIM) and, 172; control conditions and, 175, 192; decategorization and, 171–72, 176–84; ethnicity and, 174, 186, 187n16; experiment logistics and, *250–53*; gender and, 170, 175, 182, 194; helping behavior and, 172, 182; hijabs and, 170, 174–75, 179–82, 186–93; ideologies and, 170; ingroup identity and, 171–72, 181–84, 194–95; integration and, 170; multiculturalism and, 195; Muslims and, 170–84, *187*, 188, 190, 194–95; mutual differentiation and, 171–72, 176–84, 195; norm adherence and, 171–72; outgroup identity and, 170–72, 181–89, 195; partisanship and, 177; prejudice and, 171; psychology and, 171; public opinion and, 170; recategorization and, 171–72, 176–95; religion and, 170, 174–75, 177, *178*, 190–94; rules and, 185, *187*; social identity theory (SIT) and, 181; social norms and, 171, 185, 195; stereotypes and, 170, 183, 184n12, 194–95; women and, 170, 175

acculturation: civic norms and, 112, 114, 131; concept of, 38, 40–41; gender and, 138; intergroup conflict and, 9, 13; language and, 110–11; overcoming

discrimination and, 206; social distance and, 38, 40–41, 47

Afghanistan, xv, 35, 45n12

ALLBUS surveys, 21n10, 22–23, *139*, *151*, *161*

Alliance 90/The Greens, 100

Allport, G. W., 5, 26, 44, 200

Alternative für Deutschland (AfD), 82, 88, 100, 120, *178*, 244

Ames, Barry, 199n1

anxiety, 2, 5, 38, 60, 196

appearance, 8–9, 94n4. *See also* hijabs

assimilation: acceptance and, 194; civic norms and, 112, 114, 131–32; concept of, 40–41; experiment logistics and, 220–25, 227–28; forced, 1, 166; gender and, 138, 166; intergroup conflict and, 1–9, 13–16, 29; language and, 50, 91–111; measuring discrimination and, 57, 85n21, 90; overcoming discrimination and, 196, 202, 208, 210; religious, 51, 57; social distance and, 39n9, 40–41, 47–53

asylum, 20–21, 23, 82, 87, 91, 101n13, 120

atheists: acceptance and, *178*; experiment logistics and, 238, *239–41*, 244; gender equality and, 139–40, *151*, *159*, *160*

audit studies, 7, 76, 198

average marginal component effects (AMCEs), 64, 69

average treatment effects (ATE): acceptance and, 180, *181*, *187–88*, *192–93*; experiment logistics and, 221, *222*, *231–35*, 244, *250–52*; language and, 105–6;

average treatment effects (ATE) (cont.)
measuring discrimination and, 83, 105,
180–81, *187–88*, *192–93*, *231–35*, *252*

Baker, Andy, 199n1
Balafoutas, Loukas, xvii
balance tests, 215
Bansak, Kirk, 101n13
Basic Law, 98, 100
belief similarity: acceptance and, 181–82,
186, 194–95; overcoming discrimination and, 202, 207; social norms and,
46, 54–55, 181–82, 186, 194–95, 202, 207;
social distance and, 46, 54–55
Bertrand, Marianne, 73n11, 74n14
Black people, 70–71, 74–75, 115
blinding, 213
Bogardus, Emory S., 40, 62
burqas, 133
Buschkowsky, Heinz, 115–16

categorization: acceptance and, 171, *181*,
189; decategorization, 30, 53–54, 171–72,
176–84, *251*; intergroup conflict and, 5, 11;
language and, 94n4, 109; littering and,
171, *181*, 189; measuring discrimination
and, 70n9, 71; overcoming discrimination and, 199; recategorization and, 10–11,
26, 30, 46–47, 53, 132, 145, 168–69, 171–
72, 176–95, 204, *251*; self-categorization
theory (SCT), 11, 44, 199–200; social
distance and, 32n2, 44–46, 49
CDU, 98n9, *178*
children: civic norms and, 49, 116; Danish
values and, 1, 207; ghetto, 1; maternal care
of, 139, 149n22, 150n23, *151*, 161; overcoming discrimination and, 207; paternal
care of, 140; school and, 6, 49, 63–68, 95,
99, 116; setting example for, 186n14; social
distance and, 49; working mothers and,
149n22, 160, *161*
Christians: civic norms and, 124n17; experiment logistics and, 215, 238, 239, *244*, 249;
gender and, 134–35, 139–40, *151*, *159*, 160,

164n38, 166, 168; intergroup conflict and,
1–2, 6, 17; language and, 111; measuring
discrimination and, *63–68*, 70, 85n21, 88;
Muslims and, 2, 6, 17, 51, *64*, 70, 85n21, 88,
111, 134–35, 140, 166, 168, 210; overcoming
discrimination and, 210; social distance
and, 51
Chugh, Dolly, 73n11
citizenship: acceptance and, 178–80, 186–95;
civic norms and, 127–30; gender and, 136;
identity of citizen and, 8, 47–48, 54, 168,
201, 207; intergroup conflict and, 2, 4, 6,
10, 13; language and, 99n10; littering experiment and, 176–80, 186–95; next steps
for, 206–10; overcoming discrimination
and, 197, 206–10; Sarkozy contract for,
207; shared, 13, 47, 195; social distance
and, 37n7, 39, 47, 54
civic norms: acculturation and, 112, 114, 131;
assimilation and, 112, 114, 131–32; children
and, 49, 116; Christians and, 124n17;
citizenship and, 127–30; Common Ingroup Identity Model (CIIM) and, 114,
132; competition and, 130; conservatism
and, 115, 125; control conditions and, 124,
128; ethics and, 125n20; ethnicity and,
114–15, 128–31; everyday interactions and,
127–28; experiment logistics for, 224–27,
229–35; fear and, 115; fixed effects and,
125–26; gender and, 122–26; globalization and, 130; group-derived norms and,
132; helping behavior and, 131; hijabs
and, 124–28, *129*, 131n24; host country
and, 115–16, 121–22; identity threat and,
130; ideologies and, 116; ingroup identity and, 114, 123–24, 130–32; integration
and, 128, 130; internalization of, 112–14,
125–26; legal issues and, 116; littering and,
15, 29, 48–49, 114–32, 170–76, 179–85,
204, 208, 224–27, 235, *252*; multiculturalism and, 130, 133; Muslims and, 112,
127–28, 130, 131n24; nationalism and,
129–30; norm adherence and, 113–14, 122,
131; norm enforcement and, *124*, 125–31,

171, 175–94, 205, *228*, *231–35*, *250*; norm-sharing and, 12, 112, 114, 129, 131, 141, 169; outgroup identity and, 123, 126, 143–45, 167; parochialism and, *127*, 128, 130; partisanship and, 130n23; prejudice and, 130, 160, 167; psychology and, 130n23, 131–32; race issues and, 115, 124, 128; recategorization and, 132; refugees and, 118–20; religion and, 114, 124–32; respect, 118–22, 170, 208; rules and, 6, 9, 14, 19–20, 113, 116, 120–21; shared identity and, 113, 116n8, 121n15; similarity and, 114, 176–77, 181–84, 187, 194–95; social norms and, 112, 121n15, 125–26, 130, 132; stereotypes and, 115; Turks and, 119

Common Ingroup Identity Model (CIIM): acceptance and, 172; civic norms and, 114, 132; expansion of, 13–15, 25; forging a new, 44–47; gender and, 13–14, 144–45, 167–69; intergroup conflict and, 11–15, 25–26; overcoming discrimination and, 200–201; overcoming identity threat and, 12–13; social distance and, 44–47, 52–55; superordinate identity and, 11–12

competition: civic norms and, 130; gender and, 134, 136, 143–45, 163–66; intergroup conflict and, 12, 18; for jobs, 18, 60, 75, 87, 143, 161–64; language and, 111; measuring discrimination and, 66, 87; overcoming discrimination and, 198, 200; over resources, 35–36; self-interest and, 17, 35–36, 44, 144; social distance and, 32, 34–35

conformity, 16, 48n16, 49, 130, 156

Connemann, Gitta, 98n9

conservatism: civic norms and, 115, 125; gender and, 133n3, 136–37, 145n14; language and, 98

control conditions: acceptance and, 175, 192; civic norms and, 124, 128; experiment logistics and, *214*, *231*; gender and, 148–50, 156; helping behavior and, 79, 85; language and, 104, 109

coordination problems, 32

correspondence studies, 76

covariate balance, 227, *229–30*

Cremer, Claus, 120

crime, 5n4, 80, 115

cultural threat: gender and, 136n5, 169; intergroup conflict and, 4, 25; language and, 97, 100, 111; measuring discrimination and, 73; perceived, 4, 25, 35, 39, 43, 100, 136n5, 169; religion and, 73; social distance and, 35, 39, 43; symbolic, 111; Turks and, 136n5

Dancygier, Rafaela, 38

decategorization: acceptance and, 171–72, 176–84; experiment logistics and, *251*; intergroup conflict and, 30; littering and, 171–72, 176–84; social distance and, 53–54

democracies, 199n1; growing inequality in, 197; liberal, 2, 19, 36–38, 51, 56, 133, 136, 145, 166; measuring discrimination and, 56; multiculturalism and, 17, 19; postwar pride and, 97; social cooperation and, 209; surge of anti-immigrant bias in, 56; women's suffrage and, 136, 138

Denmark, 1, 7, 59, 207

Deutsche Sprachwelt (German language world), 98

Deutschtümelei, 96

differential discrimination, 52

Dilemmas of Inclusion (Dancygier), 38

discrete-choice experiment: analysis and, 64–69; attribute list and, 62–63; average marginal component effects (AMCEs) and, 64, 69; evaluation task and, 61–62, 64, 67; gender and, *63–68*; implementation and, 63–64; language and, 66–68; market research background of, 61; measuring discrimination and, 61–69, 88; Muslims and, *63–67*, 68–69; random profiles and, 61–66

diversity: gender and, 156; intergroup conflict and, 3, 25; language and, 92, 99n11, 100; multiculturalism and, 3

diversity (cont.)
   (*see also* multiculturalism); overcoming
   discrimination and, 203; social distance
   and, 37

egalitarianism, 38, 133, 145n14
Egypt, 137, 142, 214
equality: atheists and, 30; gender, 15, 19,
   30, 38, 48–49 (*see also* gender); group-
   derived norms and, 15; intergroup
   conflict and, 15, 19, 23, 30; measuring
   discrimination and, 61; overcoming discrimination and, 197, 201, 205; social
   distance and, 38, 48–49
equivalence tests, 53, 108n22, 221–25
ethics: civic norms and, 125n20; experiment
   logistics and, 213–14, 225, 247; gender
   and, 133, 150n25; Institutional Review
   Board (IRB) and, 105, 105n20, 125n20,
   154n29, 174, 213; social distance and, 39
Ethiopians, *63–68*
ethnicity: acceptance and, 174, 186, 187n16;
   civic norms and, 114–15, 128–31; confederate, 214–15; experiment logistics
   and, 214–15; gender and, 134, 143–44,
   149, 152n28, 156, 169; intergroup conflict
   and, 2–6, 11–13, 20; language and, 93–96,
   99n11, 101, 103–4, 109–10; littering and,
   174–75, 186, 187n16; measuring discrimination and, 56–57, 61, 62n6, 66, 77–82, 89;
   overcoming discrimination and, 196–202,
   210; social distance and, 33–40, 45–54
ethnocentrism, 5, 42–43, 93
European Social Survey (ESS), 25, 101n12
European Union (EU), 20, 21n10, 97
everyday interactions: civic norms and,
   127–28; experimental intervention and,
   78–82; gender and, 166; helping behavior
   and, 75–78, 89, 199; intergroup conflict
   and, 8, 10, 16; language and, 93, 100, 102;
   measuring discrimination and, 68, 77, 85,
   88–89; micro-environment to observe,
   78; overcoming discrimination and,
   199; social distance and, 55; treatment
   dimensions and, 78–79

experiment: acceptance and, *250–53*;
   ALLBUS surveys, 21n10, 22–23, *139*, *151*,
   161; assimilation and, 220–25, 227–28;
   average treatment effects (ATE) and,
   221, 222, 231–35, 244, 250–52; balance tests
   and, 215; bystander composition and,
   218–19; Christians and, 215, 238, 239, 244,
   249; civic norms and, 224–27, 229–35;
   concepts for, 39–42; conditional effects
   and, 160, 237–43; covariate balance and,
   227, 229–30; decategorization and, 251;
   disaggregated results and, 215–18, 220–21,
   243–47; equivalence tests and, 53, 108n22,
   221–25; ethics and, 213–14, 225, 247; ethnicity and, 214–15; evidence for, 15–19;
   fixed effects and, 218–19, 226, 231, 233,
   237–41, 242; Gallup polls, 21n11, 24; gender and, 235–49; helping behavior and,
   247, 249; hijabs and, 214–18, *219–22*, 224–
   26, *231–34*, 237–46, 249–50; hypotheses,
   51–52; ideologies and, 237; labor and,
   214; language and, 220–25; manipulation
   checks and, 103n17, 119, 156n31, 180n7,
   214–15, 236–37; measuring discrimination
   and, 211–17; mechanisms for, 51–55; Muslims and, 221, 224, 237, 249, 251–52; norm
   enforcement and, 228, 231–35, 250; null
   effects, 29, 95, 107–9, 183n10, 184, 222–25;
   progressive vs. regressive message effects
   and, 237–42, 244, 246; psychology and,
   223; race issues and, 213; recategorization and, 251; religion and, 217, 222–23,
   237–40, *241*; rules and, 252; scene characteristics and, 85n20, 218–19, 226; site
   selection and, 81–82, 235; spillovers and,
   157n32, 237, 247–49; subgroups and, 238;
   training of confederates and enumerators, 211–14; train stations and, 8, 78,
   81, 82n18, 102, 104, 125, 147, 152, *153*, 163,
   211–14, 224, 235; women and, *216*, 218, 237,
   238–44, 247–49

FDP, 120
fear: anxiety and, 2, 5, 38, 60, 196; civic
   norms and, 115; gender and, 133–34, 163,

164n37; intergroup conflict and, 1–2, 5n4, 7, 11, 16; language and, 92–93, 111; measuring discrimination and, 58–59, 73–74, 87–88; multiculturalism and, 197; overcoming discrimination and, 197; public opinion and, 35, 58; social distance and, 33–35

fractionalization, 92–93

France: hijabs and, 1, 6n5, 7, 166; intergroup conflict and, 1, 6n5, 7, 21, 24n14; language and, 101n12; measuring discrimination and, 59; overcoming discrimination and, 207; Sarkozy, 1, 207; secularism of, 166

Franco-Prussian War, 20, 45n12, 95

Freywald, Ulrike, 99n11

Galinsky, Adam D., 184n12

Gallup polls, 21n11, 24

Gardt, Andreas, 96n5

Gasterbeiter (guest workers), 21, 87

gender: acceptance and, 170, 175, 182, 194; acculturation and, 138; assimilation and, 138, 166; attitudinal differences in, 160–62; Christians and, 134–35, 139–40, *151*, *159*, 160, 164n38, 166, 168; citizenship and, 136; civic norms and, 116, 122–26, *125*; Common Ingroup Identity Model (CIIM) and, 13–14, 144–45, 167–69; competition and, 134, 136, 143–45, 163–66; conservatism and, 133n3, 136–37, 145n14; control conditions and, 148–50, 156; cultural threat and, 136n5, 169; democracies and, 133, 136, 138, 145, 166; discrete-choice experiment and, *63–68*; diversity and, 156; ethics and, 133, 150n25; ethnicity and, 134, 143–44, *149*, 152n28, 156, 169; everyday interactions and, 166; experimental field evidence on, 146–54; experiment logistics and, 235–49; fear and, 133–34, 163, 164n37; fixed effects and, 151n26, 157nn32–33, *158*, *159*; globalization and, 134, 136; group-derived norms and, 142–46; group-specific norms and, 145–46, 169; helping behavior and, 75–80, 85, 146–47, 152, 160n34, 166–67; hijabs

and, 69 (*see also* hijabs); identity threat and, 143–46; ideologies and, 135, 156, 159, 165–66; ingroup identity and, 144–46, 167–69; inheritance and, 137; integration and, 138, *141*, 144, 149, 169; intergroup conflict and, 15, 18–19, 26, 30; iteration-level analysis on, 154–57; labor and, 138n8, 143, 150n25, 161, 163, 247; Labour Party and, 38; language and, 105; LGBT groups, 71; liberalism and, 133, 136, 140, 145, 166, 169; littering and, 122–26; maternal care and, 149n22, 150n23, *151*, 161; measuring discrimination and, 57, 59n4, *63–68*, 73; multiculturalism and, 166, 169; Muslims and, 133–47, *151*, 152–59, 162–69; overcoming discrimination and, 201–2, 205; parochialism and, 144, *154*; partisanship and, 143n11, 168n42; progressive vs. regressive message effects and, 157–58, *159*; psychology and, 147n17, 167; public opinion and, 134, 136–38, 142; race issues and, 143–44, 169; recategorization and, 145, 168–69; refugees and, 134, 138; religion and, 133–40, 146, 149, 154, 159–60, 164–69; respect and, 135; rules and, 162; security and, 134, 142, 163–64; shared identity and, 167; social distance and, 38, 48–49, 51; social identity theory (SIT) and, 143; stereotypes and, 134, 140, 144, 155–56, 165–66; study results on, 154–60; subgroups and, 144, 166–67, 169; superordinate identity and, 145, 167n41, 168; treatment dimensions and, 78–79; Turks and, 133, 136–37, 140; working mothers, 149n22, 160, *161*

Germany: Basic Law and, 98, 100; Bundestag, 98, 100; cleanliness of, 29, 114–22, 170, 184; cross-country analysis and, 208–9; cultural issues and, 3, 10, 16–17, 20–25, 28, 73, 89, 95–101, 104, 111–16, 120, 128–31, 137–38, 142–43, 160n34, 165, 170, 194, 200, 208; East (GDR), 78, *81*, *82*, 86–87, 94, 98, 127, 152n28, 217, 220, 221, 233, 243, 245–46; Federal Republic of (FDR), 21, 82, 87; Franco-Prussian War

Germany (cont.)
 and, 20, 45n12, 95; importance of language in, 95–97; Nazi, 20, 96–97; postwar pride and, 97; purity and, 20, 96–102; research context of, 15–25, 208–9; respect for rules in, 14, 20; reunification and, 82, 87, 97, 152n28; World War II and, 20, 96–97, 101
globalization: civic norms and, 130; gender and, 134, 136; intergroup conflict and, 2; language and, 97; measuring discrimination and, 56, 58, 77; social distance and, 38
Greeks, xv-xvi, 21, 58, 63, 65–68, 87, 115
Green Party, 100, 119, 178
group-derived norms: civic norms and, 132; gender equality and, 142–46; intergroup conflict and, 14–18, 29; overcoming discrimination and, 206; role of ideas in forging, 144–46; social distance and, 42, 48, 55
group-specific norms: gender and, 145–46, 169; intergroup conflict and, 13–19; overcoming discrimination and, 205–7, 210; social distance and, 39, 46–47
guest workers, 3, 21, 87, 99

Hagendoorn, L., 58, 73n12
Hainmueller, Jens, 101n13
Hämmerling, Claudia, 119
Hangartner, Dominik, 101n13
helping behavior: acceptance and, 172, 182; audit studies and, 76; civic norms and, 131; common courtesy and, 76; control conditions and, 79, 85; correspondence studies and, 76; everyday interactions and, 75–78, 89, 199; examples of, 76; experimental intervention and, 78–82; experiment logistics and, 247, 249; gender and, 75–80, 85, 146–47, 152, 160n34, 166–67; language and, 95, 103n16; measuring discrimination and, 75–80, 85, 89; motivation for using, 75–76; overcoming discrimination and, 199; social distance and, 52; treatment dimensions and, 78–79

hijabs: acceptance and, 170, 174–75, 179–82, 186–93; civic norms and, 124–28, 129, 131n24; experiment logistics and, 214–18, 219–22, 224–26, 231–34, 237–46, 249–50; France and, 166; gender equality and, 133–36, 140–46, 149, 154, 155–59, 162–69; individual-level analysis on, 157–60; iteration-level analysis on, 154–57; language and, 103–6, 107–8; measuring discrimination and, 69–73, 78–80, 83–90; overcoming discrimination and, 210; public perceptions of, 139–41, 162–65; significance of, 162–65; treatment dimensions and, 103–6, 107–8
host country: civic norms and, 115–16, 121–22; learning language of, 6, 91–92, 101n12; respect for, 5–6, 29, 121–22
hostility: intergroup conflict and, 6, 8, 12, 16, 28, 68, 77, 80, 85, 93; language and, 93; measuring discrimination and, 68, 77, 80, 85
Hungary, 58, 101n12

identity threat: civic norms and, 130; gender and, 143–46; intergroup conflict and, 2, 5, 12–13, 15; language and, 93, 109–10; measuring discrimination and, 58, 73n12, 88; overcoming, 12–13, 205; realistic, 5; social distance and, 36–37, 51; stereotypes and, 2–5, 12, 50, 58, 88, 205; symbolic, 5
ideologies: acceptance and, 170; civic norms and, 116; experiment logistics and, 237; gender and, 135, 156, 159, 165–66; intergroup conflict and, 2–4, 15; language and, 96, 101, 110; overcoming discrimination and, 197, 202; social distance and, 31, 38, 51
Immigration Law, 99n10, 100
implicit association test (IAT), 69–73
inclusion, 20, 36–39, 41, 89, 195

ingroup identity: acceptance and, 171–72, 181–84, 194–95; CIIM and, 11 (*see also* Common Ingroup Identity Model (CIIM)); civic norms and, 114, 123–24, 130–32; ethnocentrism and, 5, 42–43, 93; gender and, 144–46, 167–69; identity of citizen and, 8, 47–48, 54, 168, 201, 207; inclusion and, 20, 36–39, 41, 89, 195; intergroup conflict and, 5, 8–13, 18, 25–26; language and, 93, 110; measuring discrimination and, 75–78, 86n23, 90; overcoming discrimination and, 200–204, 210; parochialism and, 26, 31–37, 130, 210; recategorization and, 10–11, 26, 45–47, 53, 132, 145, 169–72, 182–83, 194; role of ideas in forging, 144–46; security and, 33; social distance and, 31–34, 37, 39, 42–47, 51–55; solidarity and, 32–33, 77, 89, 146, 167

Institutional Review Board (IRB), 105n20, 125n20, 154n29, 174, 213

integration: acceptance and, 170; civic norms and, 128, 130; concept of, 39–42; conformity and, 16, 48n16, 49, 130, 156; gender and, 138, *141*, 144, 149, 169; intergroup conflict and, 1–8, 13, 15, 17, 19–21, 24n14; language and, 91, 97, 100–101, 110; measuring discrimination and, 77; overcoming discrimination and, 196–97, 202–4, 207–10; social distance and, 36–51, 50

intergroup conflict: acculturation and, 9, 13; appearance and, 8–9, 94n4; assimilation and, 1–9, 13–16, 29; atrocities and, 20, 32; broader impacts of, 25–28; categorization and, 5, 11; Christians and, 1–2, 6, 17; citizenship and, 2, 4, 6, 10, 13; Common Ingroup Identity Model (CIIM) and, 11–15, 25–26; competition and, 12, 18; concepts for, 39–42; cultural threat and, 4, 25; decategorization and, 30; diversity and, 3, 25; equality and, 15, 19, 23, 30; ethnicity and, 2–6, 11–13, 20; everyday interactions and, 8, 10, 16;

evidence on, 15–19; fear and, 1–2, 5n4, 7, 11, 16; France and, 1, 6n5, 7, 21, 24n14; gender and, 15, 18–19, 26, 30; German context and, 19–25; globalization and, 2; group-derived norms and, 14–18, 29; group-specific norms and, 13–19; hostility and, 6, 8, 12, 16, 28, 68, 77, 80, 85, 93; identity threat and, 2, 5, 12–13, 15; ideologies and, 2–4, 15; ingroup identity and, 5, 8–13, 18, 25–26; integration policies and, 1–8, 13, 15, 17, 19–21, 24n14; labor and, 21; legal issues and, 4, 7; liberalism and, 1–2, 19; literature on, 197–98; multiculturalism and, 1–10, 17–20, 24, 30; Muslims and, 1–7, 10, 15–19, 22–25, 28–29; mutual differentiation and, 30; national identity and, 2–3, 5, 11–12, 20, 26; next steps for, 206–10; norm adherence and, 20, 30, 49–51, 204, 208–10; norm-sharing and, 7, 10, 13, 26–27, 30; outgroup identity and, 12, 26; parochialism and, 12, 18, 26; partisanship and, 18; perceptions of differences and, 5; prejudice and, 5, 8, 17, 24, 28, 30; psychology and, 5, 11, 26–30; public opinion and, 7, 20, 25; race issues and, 4–5, 10, 16–17, 20; recategorization and, 10–11, 26, 30; refugees and, 20, 21n10, 23, 28; religion and, 2n3, 3–13, 16–17, 24n14, 28–30; research approach to, 8–15, 28–30; respect and, 2–9, 13–15, 20, 29; rules and, 6, 9, 14, 19–20; self-categorization theory (SCT) and, 11; shared identity and, 9, 12, 26; social cohesion theory and, 45–47, 207; social identity theory (SIT) and, 10–11; social norms and, 4–10, 14–17, 20, 29; stereotypes and, 2–5, 10, 12, 24, 28–30; subgroups and, 9, 13, 17–19, 29; superordinate identity and, 11–14, 26; veils and, 6–7; women and, 1, 14, 18–19, 30

intermarriage, 22, 47

intersectionality, 13, 19, 25, 145, 167–68, 205–6

Iraq, 35, 45n12, 137, 142, 214
Islamophobia, 88, 134–35
Italians, 21–22, 23, 28, 45n12, 58, 59, 87

kinship groups, 33

labor, xv; blue-collar, 18; competition
for jobs, 18, 60, 75, 87, 143, 161–64;
discrimination and, 7, 21, 24n14; experiment logistics and, 214; *Gastarbeiter*, 21,
87; gender and, 138n8, 143, 150n25, 161,
163, 247; guest workers, 3, 21, 87, 99; intergroup conflict and, 21; language and,
97–99, 111; measuring discrimination
and, 63n7, 66, 74n14, 78, 87; mobility and,
97; overcoming discrimination and, 198;
security and, 60, 163–64; social distance
and, 32, 35; wives and, 138n8
language: accents and, 50n18, 94n4, 108–9,
149; acculturation and, 110–11; assimilation and, 50, 91–111; average treatment
effects (ATE) and, 105–6; Basic Law
and, 98, 100; categorization and, 94n4,
109; Christians and, 111; citizenship and,
99n10; competition and, 111; conservatism and, 98; control conditions and,
104, 109; cultural threat and, 97, 100, 111;
Denglisch, 97–102; discrete-choice experiment and, 66–68; diversity and, 92,
99n11, 100; ethnicity and, 93–96, 99n11,
101, 103–4, 109–10; everyday interactions
and, 93, 100, 102; experimental intervention on, 101–5; experiment logistics and,
220–25; fear and, 92–93, 111; fractionalization and, 92–93; France and, 101n12;
gender and, 105; globalization and, 97;
helping behavior and, 95, 103n16; hijabs
and, 103–6, *107–8*; host country and, 6,
91–92, 101n12; hostility and, 16–17, 93;
identity threat and, 93, 109–10; ideologies
and, 96, 101, 110; Immigration Law and,
99n10, 100; importance of in German
identity, 95–97; ingroup identity and,
93, 110; integration and, 91, 97, 100–101,

110; labor and, 97–99, 111; legal issues
and, 98–100; main findings on, 105–9;
multiculturalism and, 94–95, 98, 100–
101, 111; Muslims and, 91, 95, 103, 105–6,
110–11; names and, 6, 9; national identity
and, 95–97, 101, 103n17, 110; nationalism
and, 95–98, 110; native assimilation preference and, 91–95; norm-sharing and,
111; null effects and, 95, 107–9; outgroup
identity and, 93, 94n4, 99, 109–10; partisanship and, 93; prejudice and, 93;
psychology and, 108; purity and, 96–102;
race issues and, 94n4, 96; refugees and,
91, 100, 101n13; religion and, 91, 94–95,
100–108, 111; respect and, 111; rules and, 6;
social hierarchy from, 96; social identity
theory (SIT) and, 93; Turks and, 99–103,
106–7; women and, 106, 109n23
legal issues, 209; civic norms and, 116;
gender and, 137; inheritance, 137; intergroup conflict and, 4, 7; language and,
98–100; measuring discrimination and,
58; Tajfel's law and, 182n8
LGBT groups, 71
liberalism: Cameron on, 1; democracies
and, 2, 19, 36–38, 51, 56, 133, 136, 145, 166;
gender and, 133, 136, 140, 145, 166, 169; intergroup conflict and, 1–2, 19; measuring
discrimination and, 56; social distance
and, 36–38, 51
Libya, 35, 45n12
littering: categorization and, 171, *181*, 189;
civic norms and, 15, 29, 48–49, 114–32,
170–76, 179–85, 204, 208, 224–27, 235, 252;
decategorization and, 171–72, 176–84; as
disrespect, 19, 118, 120–22, 170, 184; experiment design for, 122–25, 172–75; as
foreign practice, 15, 29, 48–49, 114, 115–22,
125–28, 131, 170–84, 204, 208, 235; gender
and, 122–26; generalized affect of, 176;
intuitive interpretation of, 116; norms
against, 29, 114–22, 170, 184; recategorization and, 171–72, 176–95; religion and,
114, 170–84, *187*, 188, 190, 194–95; results

of experiment, 126–32, 179–95; strong views on, 117–18; survey on, 116–22; text analysis of, 189–93; video survey of, 172–77, 180, 183–86, 189, 192, 194, 204

manipulation checks, 103n17, 119, 156n31, 180n7, 214–15, 236–37

marriage, 22, 23, 47, 51, 62, 134, 136n5

measuring discrimination: assimilation and, 57, 85n21, 90; attitudes and, 58–73; capturing anti-immigrant behavior in the field, 73–88; categorization and, 70n9, 71; Christians and, 63–68, 70, 85n21, 88; competition and, 66, 87; cultural threat and, 73; democracies and, 56; discrete-choice experiment and, 61–69, 88; equality and, 61; ethnicity and, 56–57, 61, 62n6, 66, 77–82, 89; everyday interactions and, 68, 77–82, 85, 88–89; experiment logistics and, 211–17; fear and, 58–59, 73–74, 87–88; France and, 59; gender and, 57, 59n4, 63–68, 73; globalization and, 56, 58, 77; helping behavior and, 75–82, 85, 89; hijabs and, 69–73, 78–80, 83–90; hostility and, 68, 77, 80, 85; identity threat and, 58, 73n12, 88; implicit association test and, 69–73; ingroup identity and, 75–78, 86n23, 90; integration and, 77; labor and, 63n7, 66, 74n14, 78, 87; legal issues and, 58; liberalism and, 56; multiculturalism and, 58, 77, 85, 89–90; Muslims and, 56–58, 63–67, 68–74, 78–80, 83–90; national identity and, 56–59; native/immigrant distinction and, 56–57; norm adherence and, 57; outgroup identity and, 76, 90; Polish and, 59, 63, 65–68; prejudice and, 57–58, 66, 89; psychology and, 70–71, 74, 76; public opinion and, 58, 60n5, 69; Qualtrics Panels and, 59n4, 71–72, 163; race issues and, 57, 59, 71–79, 82, 85; refugees and, 58, 60, 82, 87–88; religion and, 57–59, 61–75, 78, 80, 83–90; results of, 88–90; security and, 59–60, 65, 73, 88–89; site selection and, 81–82, 235; social

norms and, 76, 80; statistical vs. taste-based, 75, 89; stereotypes and, 58, 88; subgroups and, 86n22; Turks, 63, 65–68, 87; women and, 65, 69, 71–75, 80, 89–90

Minimal Group Paradigm, 32, 132

Moskowitz, Gordon B., 184n12

Mullainathan, Sendhil, 73n11, 74n14

multiculturalism: acceptance and, 195; Cameron on, 1; civic norms and, 130, 133; democracies and, 17, 19; as failure, 1, 3, 89; fear of, 197; gender and, 166, 169; Immigration law and, 99n10, 100; intergroup conflict and, 1–10, 17–20, 24, 30; language and, 94–95, 98, 100–101, 111; limits of, 4; measuring discrimination and, 58, 77, 85, 89–90; optimistic view of, 196–97; overcoming discrimination and, 196–97, 203, 206–10; policy index for, 24n14; social distance and, 31, 35, 38, 53–55

Muslims: acceptance and, 170–84, 187, 188, 190, 194–95; as backward, 23–24; burkas and, 133; Christians and, 2, 6, 17, 51, 64, 70, 85n21, 88, 111, 134–35, 140, 166, 168, 210; civic norms and, 112, 127–28, 130, 131n24; discrete-choice experiment and, 63–67, 68–69; experiment logistics and, 221, 224, 237, 249, 251–52; gender and, 133–47, 151, 152–59, 162–69; hijabs and, 69 (see also hijabs); implicit association test and, 68–73; intergroup conflict and, 1–7, 10, 15–19, 22–25, 28–29; invasion of, 1–2, 58; Islamophobia, 88, 134–35; language and, 91, 95, 103, 105–6, 110–11; littering experiment and, 170–84, 187, 188, 190, 194–95; measuring discrimination and, 56–58, 63–67, 68–74, 78–80, 83–90; niqab and, 133; overcoming discrimination and, 201, 205, 210; PEW Forum on Religion & Public Life, 137; social distance and, 35, 38, 51, 55; terrorism and, 88, 197; Turks and, 22, 24, 103, 106, 133, 136–37, 140; value conflicts in, 135–42; women and, 1, 19, 38, 69, 71–74, 80, 106, 133–47, 155–57, 162–70, 201, 205, 249 mutual differentiation: acceptance and, 171–72, 176–84, 195; intergroup conflict and, 30; social distance and, 53–54

Mutual Ingroup Differentiation Model (MIDM), 54

names, 6, 9

national identity: civic norms and, 130; intergroup conflict and, 2–3, 5, 11–12, 20, 26; language and, 95–97, 101, 103n17, 110; measuring discrimination and, 56–59; overcoming discrimination and, 201; social distance and, 35–39, 50

nationalism: civic norms and, 129–30; intergroup conflict and, 2, 12, 20; language and, 95–98, 110; patriotism and, 38, 97; social distance and, 45n12; superordinate identity and, 11–14, 26, 44–45, 53–54, 145, 167n41, 168, 201, 207

Nazis, 20, 96–97

Netherlands, 21, 58, 59, 101n12, 133

Niebel, Matthias, 120

Nigeria, 63–68

Nikiforakis, Nikos, xvii

niqab, 133

norm adherence: acceptance and, 171–72; civic norms and, 113–14, 122, 131; intergroup conflict and, 20, 30, 49–51, 204, 208–10; measuring discrimination and, 57; as moderator of intergroup difference, 49–51; overcoming discrimination and, 204, 208–10; social distance and, 49–52, 54

norm enforcement: civic norms and, 124, 125–31, 171, 175–94, 205, 228, 231–35, 250; experiment logistics and, 228, 231–35, 250; heterogeneous effects and, 184–89; intergroup conflict and, 29; internalization and, 125; overcoming discrimination and, 205; social distance and, 48–49

norm-sharing: civic norms and, 12, 112, 114, 129, 131, 141, 169; intergroup conflict and, 7, 10, 13, 26–27, 30; language and, 111; moderating effects of, 52; overcoming

discrimination and, 201, 202–3, 207–8; social distance and, 39, 41, 51–52, 54

Orthodox religion, 166

outgroup discrimination, 44, 52

outgroup identity: acceptance and, 170–72, 181–89, 195; civic norms and, 123, 126, 143–45, 167; intergroup conflict and, 12, 26; language and, 93, 94n4, 99, 109–10; measuring discrimination and, 76, 90; overcoming discrimination and, 201, 204; social distance and, 31–34, 39–41, 44–54

overcoming discrimination: acculturation and, 206; assimilation and, 196, 202, 208, 210; belief similarity and, 202, 207; Christians and, 210; citizenship and, 197, 206–10; Common Ingroup Identity Model (CIIM) and, 200–201; competition and, 198, 200; diversity and, 203; equality and, 197, 201, 205; ethnicity and, 196–202, 210; everyday interactions and, 199; fear and, 197; France and, 207; gender and, 201–2, 205; group-derived norms and, 206; group-specific norms and, 205–7, 210; helping behavior and, 199; hijabs and, 210; identity threat and, 205; ideologies and, 197, 202; ingroup identity and, 200–204, 210; integration and, 196–97, 202–4, 207–10; labor and, 198; multiculturalism and, 196–97, 203, 206–10; Muslims and, 201, 205, 210, 221, 224, 237–38, 249, 251–52; national identity and, 201; norm adherence and, 204, 208–10; norm enforcement and, 205; norm-sharing and, 201–3, 207–8; outgroup identity and, 201, 204; parochialism and, 210; partisanship and, 201; prejudice and, 196–99, 204; psychology and, 198–99; public opinion and, 198, 203; race issues and, 196, 200, 202; recategorization and, 204; refugees and, 197; religion and, 196–201, 210; rules and, 209; self-categorization theory (SCT) and, 199–200; shared identity and, 201;

similarity and, 200, 202, 207; social distance and, 200; social identity theory (SIT) and, 198–200, 210; social norms and, 196–98, 201, 205, 208–9; stereotypes and, 202–7, 210; superordinate identity and, 201, 207; women and, 201–2, 205

parochialism: civic norms and, 127, 128, 130; confronting, 31–36; gender and, 144, 154; ingroup identity and, 26, 31–37, 130, 210; intergroup conflict and, 12, 18, 26; Minimal Group Paradigm and, 32; native-immigrant interactions and, 34–36; overcoming discrimination and, 210; social distance and, 31–37, 40, 48–49

partisanship: acceptance and, 177; civic norms and, 130n23; gender and, 143n11, 168n42; intergroup conflict and, 18; language and, 93; overcoming discrimination and, 201; social distance and, 43

patriotism, 38–39, 97

peer pressure, 76

Penn Identity & Conflict (PIC) Lab, xvii–xviii

perspective taking, 184, 204–5

PEW Forum on Religion & Public Life, 137

pluralism, 3, 37

police, 118

Polish, xv, 59, 63, 65–68

prejudice: acceptance and, 171; civic norms and, 130, 160, 167; intergroup conflict and, 5, 8, 17, 24, 28, 30; language and, 93; measuring discrimination and, 57–58, 66, 89; overcoming discrimination and, 196–99, 204; social distance and, 31–32, 36, 42–43, 50, 52

progressive vs. regressive message effects: experiment logistics and, 237–42, 244, 246; gender and, 157–58, 159

Prussia, 20, 45n12, 95

psychology: acceptance and, 171; civic norms and, 130n23, 131–32; experiment logistics and, 223; gender and, 147n17,

167; helping behavior and, 52 (see also helping behavior); intergroup conflict and, 5, 11, 26–30; language and, 108; measuring discrimination and, 70–71, 74, 76; overcoming discrimination and, 198–99; social distance and, 34, 39–40, 41n10, 45, 49, 53

public goods, 33, 93, 209

public opinion: acceptance and, 170; ALL-BUS surveys, 21n10, 22–23, 139, 151, 161; anxiety and, 60nn5; fear and, 35, 58; Gallup polls, 21n11, 24; gender and, 134, 136–38, 142; intergroup conflict and, 7, 20, 25; measuring discrimination and, 58, 60n5, 69; overcoming discrimination and, 198, 203; social distance and, 35

Qualtrics Panels, 59n4, 71–72, 163

race issues: civic norms and, 115, 124, 128; gender and, 143–44, 169; homogeneity, 20, 96; ingroup identity and, 10, 32, 34, 144, 200; intergroup conflict and, 4–5, 10, 16–17, 20; language and, 94n4, 96; measuring discrimination and, 57, 59, 71–79, 82, 85; Muslims and, 4 (see also Muslims); overcoming discrimination and, 196, 200, 202; social distance and, 32, 34, 39–40, 43, 49, 51, 52; social identity and, 200, 202

recategorization: acceptance and, 171–72, 176–95; civic norms and, 132; experiment logistics and, 251; gender and, 145, 168–69; ingroup identity and, 10–11, 26, 45–47, 53, 132, 145, 169–72, 182–83, 194; intergroup conflict and, 10–11, 26, 30; littering and, 171–72, 176–95; overcoming discrimination and, 204; social distance and, 45–47, 53

refugees: asylum and, 20–21, 23, 82, 87, 91, 101n13, 120; civic norms and, 118–20; gender and, 134, 138; intergroup conflict and, 20, 21n10, 23, 28; language and, 91, 100, 101n13; measuring discrimination

refugees (cont.)
and, 58, 60, 82, 87–88; overcoming
discrimination and, 197; social distance
and, 35
religion: acceptance and, 170, 174–75, 177,
178, 190–94; atheists and, 139–40, 151, 159,
160, 178, 238, 239–41, 244; civic norms
and, 114, 124–32; experiment logistics
and, 217, 222–23, 237–40, 241; gender and,
133–40, 146, 149, 154, 159–60, 164–69;
intergroup conflict and, 2n3, 3–13, 16–17,
24n14, 28–30; language and, 91, 94–95,
100–108, 111; littering and, 170–84, 187,
188, 190, 194–95; measuring discrimination and, 57–59, 61–75, 78, 80, 83–90;
overcoming discrimination and, 196–201,
210; PEW Forum on Religion & Public
Life, 137; secularism and, 134, 136, 166;
social distance and, 33, 35, 37, 40, 43, 45,
47, 49, 51–54; veils and, xvii, 6–7, 72, 136
(see also hijabs). See also specific faith
Rennó, Lúcio, 199n1
respect: civic norms and, 118–22, 170, 208;
gender and, 135; intergroup conflict and,
2–9, 13–15, 20, 29; language and, 111; littering and, 19, 118, 120–22, 170, 184; social
distance and, 53
reunification, 82, 87, 97, 152n28
Rockenbach, Bettina, xvii
rules: acceptance and, 185, 187; civic norms
and, 6, 9, 14, 19–20, 113, 116, 120–21;
experiment logistics and, 252; gender
and, 162; German respect for, 14, 20;
intergroup conflict and, 6, 9, 14, 19–20;
language and, 6; overcoming discrimination and, 209; repressive, 9; social
distance and, 42

Sarkozy, Nicolas, 1, 207
Sarrazin, Thilo, 119
scene characteristics, 85n20, 218–19,
226
Schily, Otto, 100
school, 6, 49, 63–68, 95, 99, 116

secularism, 134, 136, 166
security: economic, 59–60, 134, 163–
64; gender and, 134, 142, 163–64;
ingroup identity and, 33; measuring discrimination and, 59–60, 65, 73,
88–89
self-categorization theory (SCT), 11, 44,
199–200
self-interest, 17, 35–36, 44, 144
shared identity: civic norms and, 113, 116n8,
121n15; Common Ingroup Identity Model
(CIIM) and, 12; gender and, 167; intergroup conflict and, 9, 12, 26; overcoming
discrimination and, 201; social distance
and, 45, 49
similarity: belief, 46, 54–55, 181–82, 186,
194–95, 202, 207; categorization and,
45 (see also categorization); citizenship
and, 13 (see also citizenship); civic norms
and, 114, 176–77, 181–84, 187, 194–95;
ideational, 11; kinship groups, 33; overcoming discrimination and, 200, 202,
207; parochialism and, 33; social distance
and, 45–46, 48, 54–55
site selection, 81–82, 235
Sniderman, Paul, 58, 73n12
social cohesion theory, 45–47, 207
social distance: acculturation and, 38, 40–
41, 47; assimilation and, 39n9, 40–41,
47–53; belief similarity and, 45–46, 48,
54–55; Bogardus on, 40; categorization
and, 32n2, 44–46, 49; children and, 49;
Christians and, 51; citizenship and, 37n7,
39, 47, 54; Common Ingroup Identity
Model (CIIM) and, 44–47, 52–55; competition and, 32, 34–35; concepts for,
39–42; cultural threat and, 35, 39, 43; decategorization and, 53–54; diversity and,
37; equality and, 38, 48–49; ethics and,
39; ethnicity and, 33–40, 45–54; everyday interactions and, 55; fear and, 33–35;
gender and, 38, 48–49, 51; globalization
and, 38; group-derived norms and, 42,
48, 55; group-specific norms and, 39,

46–47; helping behavior and, 52; identity of citizen and, 8, 47–48, 54, 168, 201, 207; identity threat and, 36–37, 51; ideologies and, 31, 38, 51; inclusion and, 20, 36–39, 41, 89, 195; ingroup identity and, 31–34, 37, 39, 42–47, 51–55; integration and, 36–51, 50; labor and, 32, 35; Minimal Group Paradigm and, 32; multiculturalism and, 31, 35, 38, 53–55; Muslims and, 35, 38, 51, 55; mutual differentiation and, 53–54; national identity and, 35–39, 50; nationalism and, 45n12; norm adherence and, 49–52, 54; norm enforcement and, 48–49; norm-sharing and, 39, 41, 51–52, 54; outgroup identity and, 31–34, 39–41, 44–54; overcoming discrimination and, 200; overcoming native-immigrant divide and, 42–47; parochialism and, 31–37, 40, 48–49; partisanship and, 43; prejudice and, 31–32, 36, 42–43, 50, 52; psychology and, 34, 39–40, 41n10, 45, 49, 53; public opinion and, 35; race issues and, 32, 34, 39–40, 43, 49, 51–52; recategorization and, 45–47, 53; refugees and, 35; religion and, 33, 35, 37, 40, 43, 45, 47, 49, 51–54; respect and, 53; rules and, 42; self-categorization theory (SCT) and, 44; shared identity and, 45, 49; similarity and, 45–46, 48, 54–55; social identity theory (SIT) and, 44–46; social norms and, 35, 42n11, 48–55; stereotypes and, 36, 46n14, 49–51; subgroups and, 39, 48; superordinate identity and, 44–45, 53–54; women and, 38, 48–49
social identity theory (SIT): acceptance and, 181; fundamental insights of, 10–11; gender and, 143; intergroup conflict and, 10–11; language and, 93; overcoming discrimination and, 198–99, 200, 210; social distance and, 44–46
social norms: acceptance and, 171, 185, 195; belief similarity and, 46, 54–55, 181–82, 186, 194–95, 202, 207; civic norms and, 112, 121n15, 125–26, 130, 132; conformity and, 16, 48n16, 49, 130, 156; descriptive, 48; gender, 134–35 (*see also* gender); intergroup conflict and, 4–10, 14–17, 20, 29; measuring discrimination and, 76, 80; norm enforcement and, 10, 13 (*see also* norm enforcement); overcoming discrimination and, 196–98, 201, 205, 208–9; peer pressure and, 76; social distance and, 35, 42n11, 48–55
solidarity, 32–33, 77, 89, 146, 167
SPD, 100, *178*
spillovers, 157n32, 237, 247–49
statistical discrimination, 75
stereotypes: acceptance and, 170, 183, 184n12, 194–95; appearance and, 8–9, 94n4; civic norms and, 115; gender and, 134, 140, 144, 155–56, 165–66; identity threats and, 2–5, 12, 50, 58, 88, 205; intergroup conflict and, 2–5, 10, 12, 24, 28–30; measuring discrimination and, 58, 88; negative, 2, 5, 12, 28, 51, 58, 140, 144, 155, 194; overcoming discrimination and, 202–7, 210; role of ideas in forging, 144–46; social distance and, 36, 46n14, 49–51; stereotype-conforming (SC) behavior and, 49–50; stereotype-defying (SD) behavior and, 49–50
subgroups: experiment logistics and, 238; gender and, 144, 166–67, 169; intergroup conflict and, 9, 13, 17–19, 29; measuring discrimination and, 86n22; social distance and, 39, 48
superordinate identity: gender and, 145, 167n41, 168; intergroup conflict and, 11–14, 26; nationalism and, 11–14, 26, 44–45, 53–54, 145, 167n41, 168, 201, 207; overcoming discrimination and, 201, 207; social distance and, 44–45, 53–54
suspicion, xvi, 18, 33, 197
Syria, 24, 35, 63–68, 135n5, 138, 214

taste-based discrimination, 75, 89
terrorism, 88, 197

text analysis, 189–93

Tunisia, 21, 137, 140

Turks, 222; civic norms and, 119; gender and, 133, 136–37, 140; intergroup conflict and, 22–24; intermarriage and, 22; labor and, 21; language and, 99–103, 106–7, 220–21; manipulation checks and, 214; measuring discrimination and, 63, 65–68, 87; rights of, 22

Turner, John, 46n14

unemployment, 5n4, 87

United Kingdom, 1, 21, 38, 59, 101n12

valence, 70–72, 150, 189–92

veils: France and, 1, 6n5, 7, 166; gender and, xvii, 6–7, 72, 116, 125, 136, 140, 141, 156n31, 157, 160n34, 163, 164n38, 166; intergroup conflict and, 6–7; measuring discrimination and, 72. See also hijabs

Verein DeutscherSprachee.V., 98

violence, xv, 20, 34n6, 93, 127, 134, 200

Volksgenossen, 101

welfare system, 36, 73, 163–64, 198, 208

women: acceptance and, 170, 175; burqas and, 133; experiment logistics and, 216, 218, 237, 238–44, 247–49; gender equality and, 133–69 (see also gender); hijabs and, 124–28 (see also hijabs); intergroup conflict and, 1, 14, 18–19, 30; Islamic value conflicts and, 135–42; language and, 106, 109n23; marriage and, 22, 23, 47, 51, 62, 134, 136n5; maternal care and, 149n22, 150n23, 151, 161; measuring discrimination and, 65, 69, 71–75, 80, 89–90; Muslim, 1, 19, 38, 69, 71–74, 80, 106, 133–47, 155–57, 162–70, 201, 205, 249; niqab and, 133; overcoming discrimination and, 201–2, 205; rights of, 38, 134–37, 142–47, 150, 156, 160, 162, 168nn42–43, 169, 202; social distance and, 38, 48–49; symbolism of bodies of, 133; working mothers, 149n22, 160, 161

World War II, 20, 35, 96–97, 101

Yugoslavia, 21

A NOTE ON THE TYPE

<small>THIS BOOK</small> has been composed in Arno, an Old-style serif typeface in the classic Venetian tradition, designed by Robert Slimbach at Adobe.

GPSR Authorized Representative: Easy Access System Europe - Mustamäe tee 50, 10621 Tallinn, Estonia, gpsr.requests@easproject.com